Morgan's Raid Across Ohio
The Civil War Guidebook of the John Hunt Morgan Heritage Trail

Lora Schmidt Cahill
and
David L. Mowery

Edited by Edd Sharp and Michele Collins
Graphics Design by Jason Cannon

Published by the Ohio Historical Society
Columbus, OH 43211
www.ohiohistory.org

Copyright © 2014 by the Ohio Historical Society
All rights reserved

First published August 2013
Second edition published November 2014

Manufactured in the United States

ISBN 978-0-9898054-3-8

Library of Congress CIP data applied for.

Notice: The information in this book is true and complete to the best of our knowledge. It is offered without guarantee on the part of the authors or the Ohio Historical Society. The authors and the Ohio Historical Society disclaim all liability in connection with the use of this book.

All rights reserved. No part of this book may be reproduced or transmitted in any form whatsoever without prior written permission from the publisher except in the case of brief quotations embodied in critical articles and reviews.

The Ohio Civil War Trail Commission

Welcome to Ohio and to the *John Hunt Morgan Heritage Trail*. The Trail was a joint project between the Ohio Department of Transportation, the Ohio Historical Society, and the Ohio Civil War Trail Commission. The Ohio Civil War Trail Commission is an all-volunteer organization which thoroughly researched all the history along the Trail's 557 mile path. The research lasted 17 years right up the printing of this guidebook. There are many people to thank for their dedication to this project. Our organization depended on volunteers from each County to coordinate research and implementation of the Trail. Here is a short listing of those County Coordinators.

David Mowery	David Brown	Richard Crawford
Jeff Yoest	Ned Lodwick	Brian McKee
Stephen Kelley	Tom Snyder	Edd Sharp
Bob Wirkner	Leland Schuler	Tim Brookes
Harold Paddock	Tom Cross	Michael Stroth

I must thank George Kane, Ly Foor, Jason Cannon, Michele Collins, and Bill Mahon of the Ohio Historical Society, who helped to bring it all together and make it the best it can be. I need to thank Bev Kirk who made all the illustrations for the Trail signage and helped to bring the stories alive. I want to thank Dr. Lorle Porter, who inspired us all along the way.

I also need to thank my right hand in this project, David Mowery, who checked on us all to make sure it was the best history we could find. I also need to thank all the wives and families who sacrificed many days with loved ones to allow us to investigate all the research and get it right the first time. And I especially need to thank my wife Carrie, whom was always there to help, and to inspire. And we must not forget the County Highway agencies that help to install the signs that will inform and guide you along your way.

And let us also remember the men of the men who first traveled this Trail back in 1863, both Blue and Gray, may their efforts never be forgotten. And remember all the Civilians along the Trail and all their stories.

As you travel the Trail, always remember those trying days in our State's history, read the stories in this guidebook, and watch history come alive.

Edd Sharp

The Ohio Civil War Trail Commission

Table of Contents

This Guidebook and the *John Hunt Morgan Heritage Trail of Ohio*		1
How To Use This Guide		9
List of Interpretive Signs of the *John Hunt Morgan Heritage Trail of Ohio*		13
Guidebook Route Map Overview		19
Introduction		39
Chapter One	Harrison to Camp Dennison	49
Chapter Two	Camp Dennison to Williamsburg	75
Chapter Three	Williamsburg to Locust Grove	91
Chapter Four	Locust Grove to Jackson	109
Chapter Five	Jackson to Buffington Island	125
Chapter Six	Battle of Buffington Island	141
Chapter Seven	Buffington Island to Nelsonville	153
Chapter Eight	Nelsonville to Old Washington	185
Chapter Nine	Old Washington to West Point	209
Appendix A	Alternate: Miamitown Feint Toward Cincinnati	241
Appendix B	Alternate: Miamitown to New Haven Road	245
Appendix C	Alternate: New Haven Area	249
Appendix D	Alternate: Greenhills Route	253
Appendix E	Alternate: Duke's Column Moved Through Northeastern Suburbs	257
Appendix F	Alternate: Flankers Through Reading	265
Appendix G	Alternate: Company to Goshen	269
Appendix H	Alternate: Union Forces from Mulberry to Batavia	275
Appendix I	Side Trip to Withamsville, Amelia, and New Richmond	281
Appendix J	Alternate: Dick Morgan's Column to Ripley	289
Appendix K	Alternate: Over Yankee Hill to Jasper	303
Appendix L	Alternate: Johnson's Column Passed Through Vinton en Route to Middleport	307
Bibliography		315
About the Authors		327

This Guidebook and
the *John Hunt Morgan Heritage Trail of Ohio*

This book serves as the official guide to the *John Hunt Morgan Heritage Trail of Ohio*, a self-guided driving tour utilizing 557 miles of Ohio's roadways and connecting nineteen counties. The *John Hunt Morgan Heritage Trail* is a system of roads linked by nonstandard directional signs. This heritage trail generally follows the path of Confederate Brigadier General John Hunt Morgan's 1863 Indiana-Ohio Raid (also known as the Great Raid or Ohio Raid), an American Civil War military operation considered by some modern historians to be among the world's top land-based raids since Sir Francis Drake's raid on Cadiz, Spain, in 1587 (source: Samuel A. Southworth, *Great Raids in History: From Drake to Desert One*, Edison, NJ, 1997).

The concept of the *John Hunt Morgan Heritage Trail* originated in 1999 when a group of volunteers from Tennessee, Kentucky, Indiana, and Ohio met to discuss the possibility of marking the route of the Indiana-Ohio Raid through their respective states. In Ohio, the volunteer historians of the Ohio Civil War Trail Commission garnered donations from public and private sources to fund the trail. The Trail Commission also performed the historical research and community planning legwork required to produce an accurate, sustainable driving route. After a dozen years of exhaustive research and tireless effort, a first-class driving tour has emerged for all people to travel, to study, and to enjoy. With the outstanding cooperation of the Ohio Historical Society and the Ohio Department of Transportation, without whom none of this would have been possible, the *John Hunt Morgan Heritage Trail of Ohio*, the Buckeye State's longest marked heritage trail, became a reality in 2012.

The 557-mile *John Hunt Morgan Heritage Trail of Ohio* consists of fifty-six interpretive signs and more than 600 specialized directional signs. The **interpretive signs** present the historical information and stories about Morgan's Indiana-Ohio Raid as it pertains to the location of each sign. The interpretive signs found on the Morgan Trail are erected on two poles, sit low to the ground, and look like this:

An interpretive sign contains text and drawings describing the scene as it would have appeared in 1863 to a person watching Morgan's men ride by.

A **directional sign** is a standard aluminum road sign about the size of a "No U-Turn" sign and attached to a single pole. However, the image imprinted on the sign is unique to the *John Hunt Morgan Heritage Trail of Ohio*. It looks like this:

The directional signs lead the traveler from one interpretive sign to the next without the need for a map.

This Guidebook and the *John Hunt Morgan Heritage Trail of Ohio*

The primary objective of the *John Hunt Morgan Heritage Trail* is to commemorate Morgan's Indiana-Ohio Raid by incorporating not only the perspectives of the Confederate and the Union soldiers involved in the raid, but also the experiences of the civilians who were unwilling participants in the event. The authors of this guide have sifted through a large number of sources, both primary and secondary, to distinguish facts from myth. The Great Raid was a dramatic event to many soldiers and civilians who afterward shared their fascinating experiences with their friends, children, and grandchildren at family gatherings. Unfortunately, much too often these accounts were passed down to future generations through oral tradition and were never written down by the persons who experienced the raid firsthand. As a result, the stories lost their factual integrity over time. Therefore, whenever possible, this book's authors have strived to use primary sources to validate every story they have gleaned from the secondary sources. The reader may find that some Morgan Raid accounts presented in previously published secondary sources are missing from this guidebook. More than likely, the stories are missing here because they were found to be false or unverifiable.

It is important to distinguish for the traveler the difference between the route described in this guidebook and the route marked by the directional signs of the *John Hunt Morgan Heritage Trail of Ohio*. Although both routes attempt to follow Morgan's raid path through Ohio, they do not use the same roads.

When Morgan's Confederates passed through a region, their tactic was to split into smaller groups riding on parallel roads. This practice allowed the soldiers to forage for supplies and horses from a larger selection of residences. Splitting the main group also prevented the cavalry column from being strung out on one road, thus exposing fewer men to enemy attack.

Given the many roads that Morgan's men used during their raid, it would take months for a person to drive them all. When the raiding force split up, the largest cavalry group, normally led by General Morgan or by one of his brigade commanders, was often referred to as the "main column." The smaller groups, ranging in size from two men to several hundred men, were frequently called the "flanking columns" or "flankers." The flankers were in charge of gathering provisions for the men in the main column while screening the main column's flanks. The route of the *John Hunt Morgan Heritage Trail of Ohio* attempts to follow the roads that General Morgan himself used (the "main column" route). On the other hand, the route of this guidebook also explores some of the flanking paths (termed "side trips" and "alternate routes"), if sites located along those paths seemed worthwhile to visit.

David Mowery, one of the authors of this guidebook, found from his research that Morgan's main column traveled a total of 586 miles within the State of Ohio. Mowery determined this figure by sketching the main column's path onto Civil War era road maps, which were then overlaid on top of Google Earth's USGS satellite-imagery maps. After matching the scales of the old maps with the images on Google Earth, Mowery tallied the distance of Morgan's 1863 path using Google Earth's measurement tools. It is very likely that the raiders who reached the surrender site near West Point rode more than 586 miles, since each man was assigned to foraging or scouting duty at one time or another during the course of the raid.

Another major difference between the *John Hunt Morgan Heritage Trail of Ohio* and the guidebook route concerns safety and convenience for the traveler. The *John Hunt Morgan Heritage Trail of Ohio* is designed with the casual traveler in mind. Casual travelers may not have access to a vehicle suitable for dirt roads, and they may not want to travel far from modern amenities such as gas stations, convenience stores, restaurants, or lodging. Also, casual travelers may not be able to afford to spend the whole day in the car, perhaps because they have children traveling with them who are impatient to get to their destination ("Daddy, are we there yet?"). With these factors taken into account, the route of the *John Hunt Morgan Heritage Trail of Ohio* tends to follow modern highways and the most direct paths between interpretive signs, even though these highways and paths may not fall in line with

Morgan's actual route. Whenever possible, the *John Hunt Morgan Heritage Trail of Ohio* tries to stay close to towns and cities with businesses that serve travelers. After all, one of the main benefits of a heritage trail is to increase tourist exposure to local businesses.

Unlike the Heritage Trail, this guidebook is designed to follow the *exact* path of Morgan's main column and some of its flanking columns, if the roads that they used exist today. Particularly in rural areas where strip mining, clear-cutting, and modern farming have changed Ohio's landscape since 1863, the Civil War era roads many times have been moved or have been completely obliterated. However, a large number of the roads that Morgan's raiders rode on still exist today, although the roads most likely have been widened, grated, straightened, and paved. In some cases, the roads have not changed their Civil War appearance, except for the addition of gravel to make them negotiable for motor vehicles. It is therefore highly recommended that travelers who want to follow the roads in this guidebook carefully consider this fact. If one's vehicle is not suitable for driving on dirt and gravel roads, many of which are steep, narrow, and prone to washouts, then do not follow the guidebook route; instead, follow the *John Hunt Morgan Heritage Trail of Ohio*, whose roads are good for almost all motor vehicles, including buses and motorcycles.

Both the *John Hunt Morgan Heritage Trail of Ohio* and the guidebook route visit all fifty-six of the heritage trail interpretive signs, which serve as the common anchors for the guidebook and the heritage trail. The interpretive signs allow travelers to get off of, and back on to, their Morgan Raid driving tours, no matter which route they choose. Following the *John Hunt Morgan Heritage Trail of Ohio* from Harrison to West Point will take several days to complete (one week minimum is recommended), while the guidebook route may take twice as much time. A Morgan Trail interpretive sign serves as a portal where visitors can temporarily leave the trail to find food, gas, or lodging, or to simply take a break from the rigors of travel. Later, the visitors can return to that interpretive sign to restart their journey where they left off. This practice also provides travelers the chance to explore places in Ohio besides those related to Morgan's Raid.

No matter which route one chooses, both tours will offer the visitor a unique view into what it was like for John Hunt Morgan and his raiders as they marched through a rugged territory, chased by veteran enemy soldiers and surrounded by a citizenry determined to defend their homes. Travelers should allocate time to leisurely follow the paths of Morgan's men and their Union adversaries. Stop at a site and let one's mind drift back to one of the most dramatic events in America's history. The Morgan Raid tours present a facet of Ohio's history not normally studied, through parts of the Buckeye State less frequently visited — a combination that makes for a unique, fun, and fulfilling vacation.

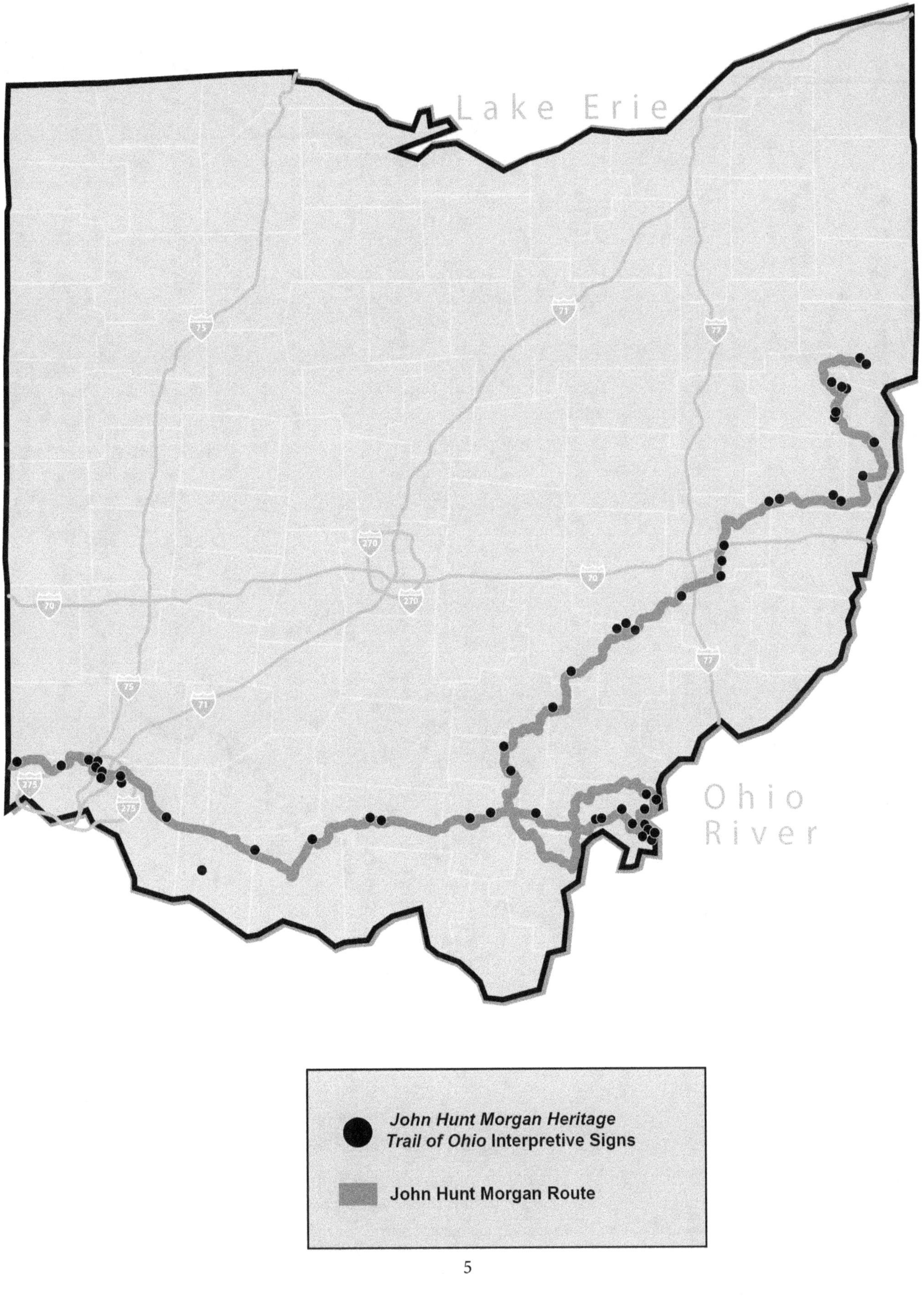

Lake Erie
Ohio River
75
71
77
270
70
275
John Hunt Morgan Heritage Trail of Ohio Interpretive Signs
John Hunt Morgan Route

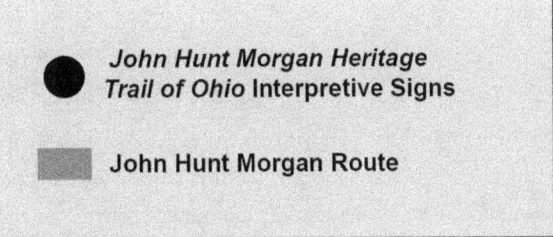

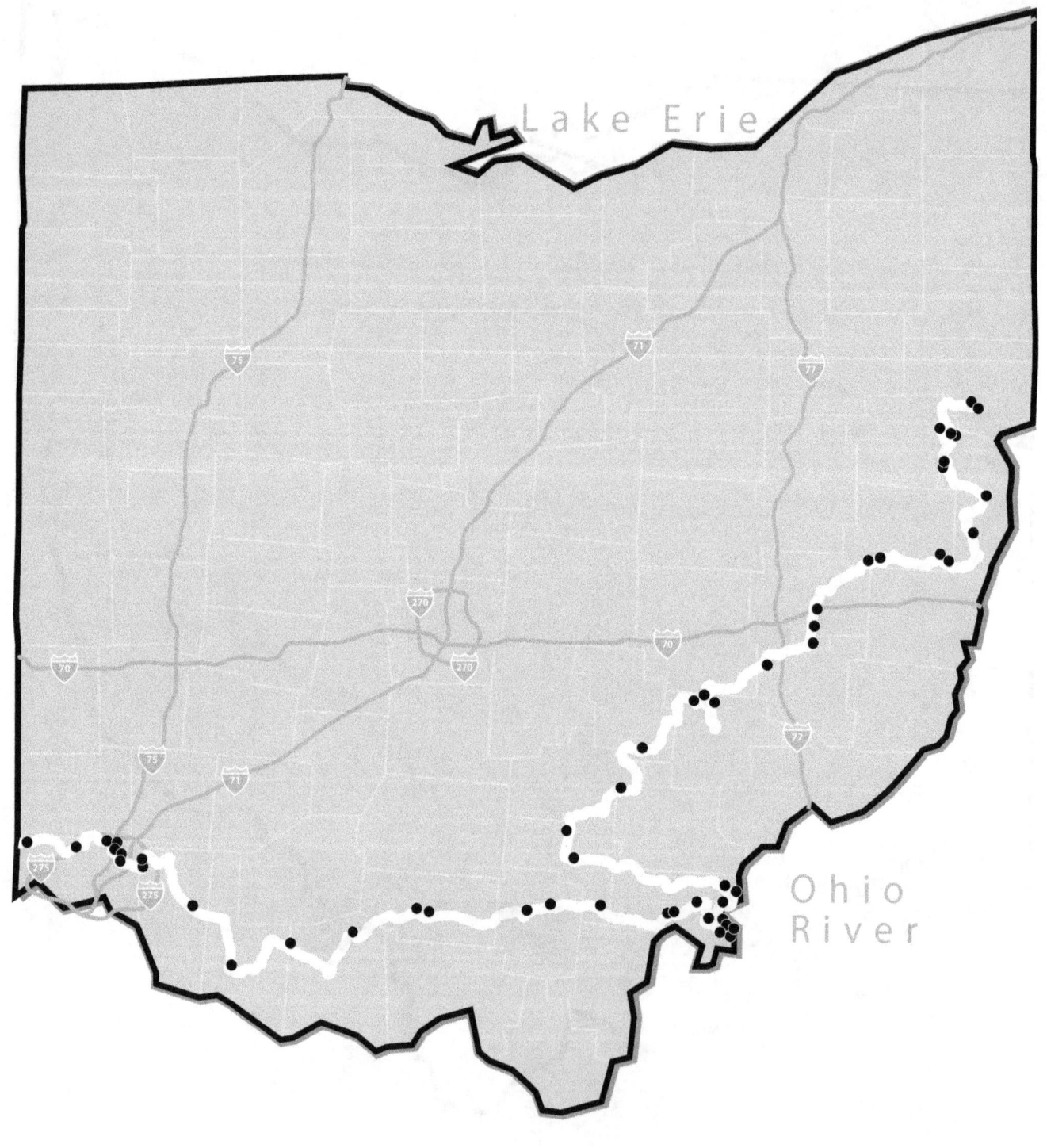

This Guidebook and the *John Hunt Morgan Heritage Trail of Ohio*

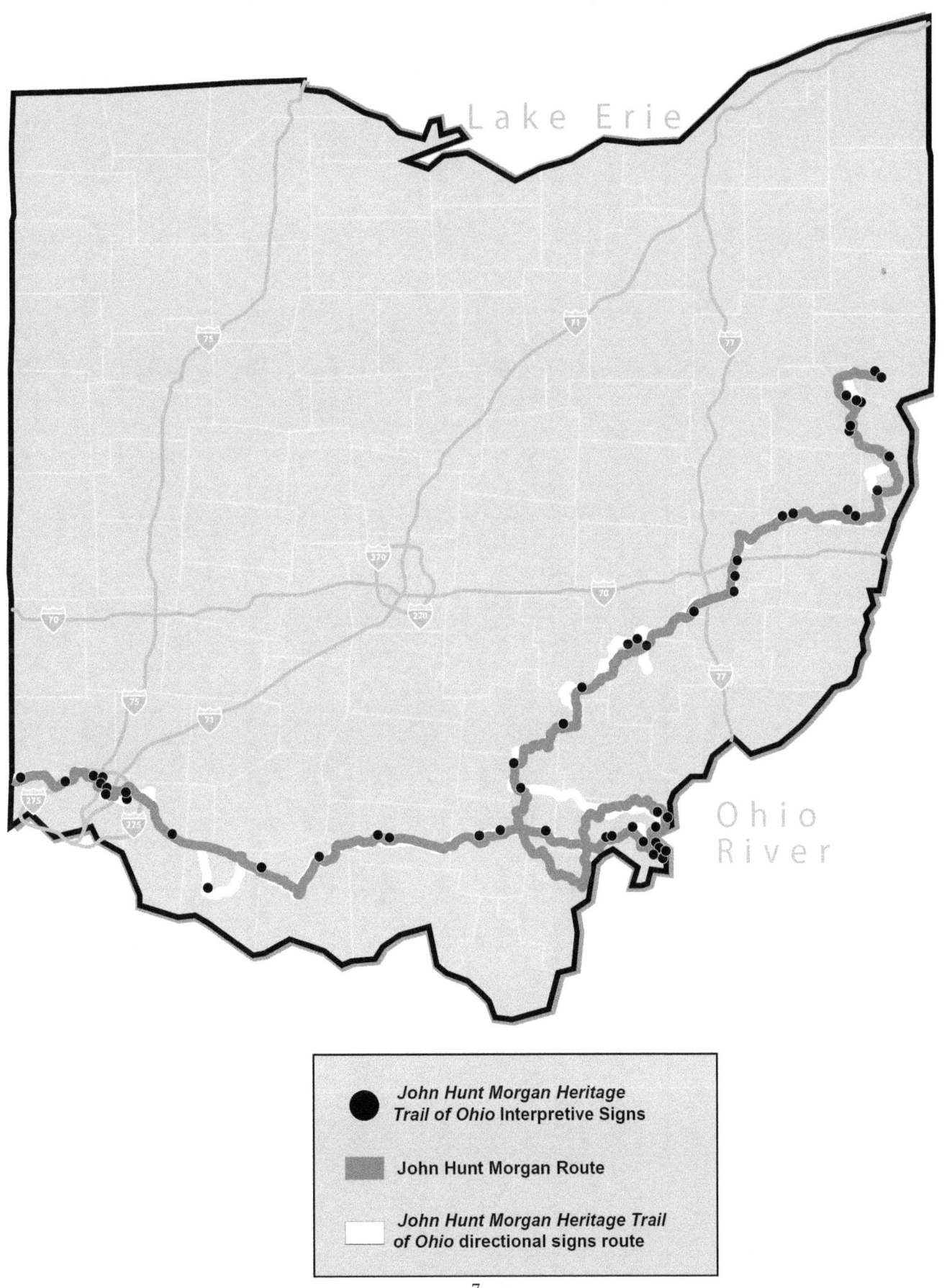

How to Use This Guide

Before starting a trip on the Morgan Trail, it is suggested that the traveler read this guidebook's **Introduction**. After reading it, the visitor will have a basic understanding of the Civil War events immediately preceding the raid and the reasons behind the operation. In addition, the Introduction summarizes the Indiana-Ohio Raid up to the time General John Hunt Morgan entered Ohio. One may also want to bolster one's knowledge of the Great Raid by reading David L. Mowery's book *Morgan's Great Raid: The Remarkable Expedition from Kentucky to Ohio* (2013) or Lester Horwitz's book *The Longest Raid of the Civil War* (1999), which are considered to be the most comprehensive works on the subject to date. Below is a list of other recommended books written about the Great Raid or John Hunt Morgan, most of which may be found at public libraries:

- Brown, Dee Alexander. *Morgan's Raiders*. New York, 1959.
- Duke, Basil W. *A History of Morgan's Cavalry*. Cincinnati, 1867. (Available for free online reading at *www.archive.org*.)
- Gorin, Betty J. *"Morgan Is Coming!" Confederate Raiders in the Heartland of Kentucky*. Louisville, KY, 2006.
- Holland, Cecil Fletcher. *Morgan and His Raiders: A Biography of the Confederate General*. New York, 1942.
- Keller, Alan. *Morgan's Raid*. New York, 1961.
- Longacre, Edward G. *Mounted Raids of the Civil War*. New York, 1975.
- Metzler, William E. *Morgan and His Dixie Cavaliers: An Account of the Confederate Cavalryman's Most Famous Exploits*. Manchester, TN, 1978.
- Ramage, James A. *Rebel Raider: The Life of John Hunt Morgan*. Lexington, KY, 1986.

Next, travelers should begin their tours using the main body of the guidebook. The main body describes the trail of General Morgan and his main column, which is referred to here as the **Main Column Route**. The first chapter of the Main Column tour, titled "Harrison to Camp Dennison," begins at the corner of North Dearborn Road and South State Street, one mile south of downtown Harrison, Ohio. One can reach downtown Harrison by taking Interstate 74 to Exit 1 (New Haven Road) and following New Haven Road southward for two blocks to Harrison Avenue. At this intersection, turn right (west) and drive exactly one mile on Harrison Avenue to the stoplight at State Street. Turn left to reach the starting point of the guidebook route as well as the beginning of the *John Hunt Morgan Heritage Trail of Ohio*. There, also, one will find the last interpretive signs of Indiana's John Hunt Morgan Heritage Trail.

Throughout this guide, one can see the driving directions highlighted from the rest of the surrounding text. Follow these directions carefully to get from one site to the next. Obey all traffic laws, observe road signs, and watch for pedestrians, especially in the urban areas such as Cincinnati, Batavia, Georgetown, Jackson, and Nelsonville. When one reaches each new site, it is highly recommended that one stop the motor vehicle in a safe place. This will permit one to safely read the history of the site and the stories associated to it. **Please do not trespass on private property**. Most of the sites and many of the interpretive signs are located on private property. Adhere to warnings on all posted signs.

The interpretive signs are highlighted in the Main Column text as follows: **JOHN HUNT MORGAN HERITAGE TRAIL INTERPRETIVE SIGN #XX**. The "XX" is a number from 1 to 56 in the order that the signs appear on the *John Hunt Morgan Heritage Trail of Ohio* as one drives east from Harrison. Please understand that the guidebook's driving directions will very often take the traveler off the marked roadways of the *John Hunt Morgan Heritage Trail of Ohio* (as explained in the chapter titled "This Guidebook and the *John Hunt Morgan Heritage Trail of Ohio*"). Therefore, do not follow the Morgan Heritage Trail directional signs when the guidebook is being used. The guidebook directs the visitor along the route most closely followed by General Morgan and his main column, whereas the *John Hunt Morgan Heritage Trail of Ohio* follows the safer and more convenient route to the next interpretive sign.

If the weather turns severe, or if darkness approaches, it might be preferable for the traveler to

How to Use This Guide

discontinue the guidebook route and change to the *John Hunt Morgan Heritage Trail of Ohio* route until one can find a safer time to return to the guidebook trail. **WARNING!** Always keep in mind that many of the roads used by the guidebook, especially roads in the southeast and northeast quarters of Ohio, can be dangerous to drive on during severe weather or at night. These parts of Ohio are some of the most beautiful and most remote portions of the state, offering a rewarding experience to the traveler; however, the roads in these regions are harder for road crews to maintain. Therefore, the driver is warned to use caution and common sense to negotiate the roads in these areas and in the twenty counties visited by the guidebook.

Additionally, this guidebook gives visitors the option to follow some of the paths used by Morgan's flankers. Two types of tour options exist. The first type is the **Side Trip**. This type of route will take the visitor on a complete driving loop that will end at the same point where the Side Trip began. Side Trips are a great way of seeing out-of-the-way Morgan Raid sites if one has extra time built into one's travel day. The second type of tour option is the **Alternate Route**, several of which are found in the Appendices of this guidebook. The Alternates are designed to retrace Morgan's large flanking columns, which covered multiple sites, some of which still exist today. The Alternate Routes travel much longer distances and contain more sites to visit than the Side Trips. Most importantly, Alternate Routes do not start and end at the same point. An Alternate Route begins at one place on the Main Column Route, but it finishes at a different place, farther along on the Main Column Route. The start point for each Alternate Route is indicated within the Main Column Route text *by italicized text surrounded by stars* to make it easier for the traveler to know where to leave the Main Column tour. However, the Alternate Route will always return to the Main Column Route, just as the flankers returned to Morgan's main column in 1863.

Travelers always should plan ahead to build in enough time to adequately visit the many Morgan Raid sites that Ohio has to offer. However, many persons enjoy traveling on a whim, which can be quite exciting and fun, too. Whichever way the visitor wants to travel, the guidebook and the *John Hunt Morgan Heritage Trail of Ohio* are flexible. Use the interpretive signs and the GPS coordinates to one's advantage. A complete list of Ohio's fifty-six John Hunt Morgan Heritage Trail interpretive signs is given in the next chapter.

Some history buffs may even want to follow Morgan's 1,000-mile path from start to finish. If one wishes to travel the present-day roads associated to Morgan's Great Raid from Tennessee through Kentucky and Indiana, one should purchase the official guidebooks or acquire the free brochures and maps that resulted from the John Hunt Morgan Heritage Trail project.

Tennessee:

Free *Tennessee Civil War Trails* brochures showing the markers related to Morgan's 1863 Ohio Raid are obtainable from:

http://www.civilwartraveler.com/WEST/TN/M-MoreSites.html

One may also pick up these brochures from Tennessee Welcome Centers or by calling (615) 532-7520.

Kentucky:

A free guide to the John Hunt Morgan Heritage Trail of Kentucky is available online at:

Trails-R-Us — John Hunt Morgan, "The Great Raid, Summer 1863"

http://www.trailsrus.com/morgan/greatraid.html

One may also call WMHT Corporation at (270) 792-5300 for more information about the *Trails-R-Us* tour.

Indiana:

Free brochures, tour maps, and other items associated with the John Hunt Morgan Heritage Trail of Indiana are available from the following Web site:

Historic Hoosier Hills RC&D — John Hunt Morgan Heritage Trail *http://www.hhhills.org/John-Hunt-Morgan.html*

One can purchase from Historic Hoosier Hills the official guidebook to the Indiana portion of Morgan's Indiana-Ohio Raid, either by calling (812) 689-4107, or by visiting the above Web site. The guidebook information is as follows:

Cahill, Lora Schmidt. *The John Hunt Morgan Heritage Trail in Indiana: A Tour Guide to the Indiana Portion of Morgan's Great Raid July 8–13, 1863*. Attica, Ohio: K-Hill Publications, 1997.

Have a safe and enjoyable trip through the beautiful, historic State of Ohio!

List of Interpretive Signs of the
John Hunt Morgan Heritage Trail of Ohio

County
Location, Interpretive Sign Number
GPS Coordinates (Decimal Format)
Longitudinal (W)
Latitudinal (N)
Nearest Road Intersection

Hamilton
Harrison, 1
84°49.0960'
39°15.7168'
Harrison Ave. & S. Walnut St. (in front of fire station)

Hamilton
Bevis, 2
84°35.7630'
39°14.9352'
Springdale Rd. & Colerain Ave. (next to sitting bench & telephone adjacent to Arby's Restaurant)

Hamilton
Glendale, 3
84°27.5607'
39°16.2773'
Glendale Village Square (on north end of the center island of the square)

Hamilton
Sharonville, 4
84°24.7740'
39°16.1077'
Sharon Rd. & Reading Rd. (NE corner)

Hamilton
Evendale, 5
84°25.5027'
39°14.7108'
Gorman Heritage Farm Ln. & Reading Rd. (US 42) (parking lot of Gorman Heritage Farm Museum)

Hamilton
Blue Ash, 6
84°23.4477'
39°13.7737'
Hunt Rd. & Victor Ave. (in front of Hunt House Museum)

Hamilton
Deer Park, 7
84°23.7765'
39°12.3617'
Schenck Ave. & Lake Ave. (on sidewalk in front of Schenck house at 4208 Schenck Ave)

Hamilton
Camp Dennison, 8
84°17.5252'
39°11.3647'
Kugler Mill Rd. & State Route (SR) 126 (on W corner of Secrest Monument Park)

Clermont
Miamiville, 9
84°17.7607'
39°12.7762'
Little Miami Scenic Bike Trail & SR 126 (SE corner)

Clermont
Miamiville, 10
84°17.7607'
39°12.7762'
Little Miami Scenic Bike Trail & SR 126 (SE corner)

Clermont
Williamsburg, 11
84°3.8377'
39°3.6102'
W. Main St. (SR 133/276) & Toll Gate Rd. (SR 133) between Dollar General Store and Williamsburg Church of Christ, next to sidewalk and ditch

Brown
Georgetown, 12
83°54.2490'
38°51.9450'
Grant Ave. & N. Main St. (at NW corner of Courthouse Square)

Adams
Winchester, 13
83°39.0323'
38°56.5492'
Washington St. & SR 136 (NE corner next to gazebo and monument)

List of Interpretive Signs

Adams
Locust Grove, 14
83°22.6662'
38°59.2920'
SR 41 & SR 73 (NE corner at firehouse)

Pike
Stoney Ridge, 15
83°6.4927'
39°3.7092'
Jasper Rd. (Co. Rd. [CR] 43) & Waldren Hill Rd. (at pullover under high-voltage power lines)

Pike
Jasper, 16
83°3.3000'
39°2.9210'
Jasper Rd. (CR 43) & Hill St. (across Jasper Rd. from a church)

Jackson
Jackson, 17
82°38.2497'
39°3.1528'
Main St. & Portsmouth St. (along sidewalk on north side of Main St. about halfway between Portsmouth St. and Broadway St.)

Jackson
Berlin Crossroads, 18
82°32.2930'
39°4.8480'
SR 327 & CR 78 (0.04 mile north of the intersection, at church parking lot)

Vinton
Wilkesville, 19
82°19.5882'
39°4.4633'
SR 160 (S. Mill St.) & SR 124 (Rutland St) (SE corner of intersection, along east side of SR 160)

Meigs
Salisbury Township, 20
82°2.2903'
39°3.1270'
Burdette Rd. (Twp. Rd. 205) & Laurel Cliff Rd. (NE corner of intersection, near Laurel Cliff Free Methodist Church)

Meigs
Rock Springs, 21
82°0.9333'
39°3.5323'
Rocksprings Rd. & CR 51A (SE corner of intersection, in Meigs County Fairgrounds)

Meigs
Chester, 22
81°55.3182'
39°5.2688'
SR 248 & Twp. Hwy. 1037 (at town square next to historic sign and war memorial)

Meigs
Bashan, 23
81°51.9132'
39°2.5915'
Bashan Rd. & Eagle Ridge Rd. (at SW corner of firehouse, which stands at SE corner of intersection)

Meigs
Portland, 24
81°46.6235'
39°0.7945'
Bald Knob-Stiversville Rd. & SR 124 (0.22 mile west of intersection, at SE corner of Bald Knob-Stiversville Rd. with a farm lane)

Meigs
Buffington Island Battlefield State Memorial Park, 25
81°46.4467'
39°0.1355'
SR 124 & Twp. Hwy. 153 (in Buffington Island Battlefield St. Mem. Pk., at the informational kiosk)

Meigs
Old Portland Road, 26
81°46.1000'
39°0.0667'
Old Portland Rd. & Twp. Hwy. 153 (about 0.14 mile south of the intersection, near the lane that leads to the former river ford)

Meigs
Dry Run, 27
81°46.4878'
38°59.6843'
SR 124 & south end of Old Portland Rd. (about 0.34 mile south of Old Portland Rd., next to Daniel McCook monument)

Meigs
North End Valley, 28
81°46.5157'
39°1.3133'
SR 124 & north end of Old Portland Rd. (NE corner of intersection)

Meigs
Long Bottom, 29
81°48.2445'
39°5.1448'
SR 124 & SR 248 (0.02 mile south of intersection)

Meigs
Reedsville, 30
81°44.8283'
39°7.7473'
SR 124 & Barr Hollow Rd. (SW corner)

Meigs
Tuppers Plains, 31
81°47.3548'
39°8.8032'
SR 681 & Barton Rd. (in Flatwoods (Joppa) Cemetery)

Vinton
Vinton Station, 32
82°26.2163'
39°14.0875'
SR 677 & US 50 (NW corner of intersection)

Vinton
Creola, 33
82°27.8770'
39°18.9135'
SR 93 & Dunkle Creek Rd. (in front of building at 28225 SR 93)

Athens
Nelsonville, 34
82°14.3573'
39°27.5522'
SR 278 & US 33 Business (between Hocking River bridge on SR 278 and railroad tracks)

Perry
Hemlock, 35
82°8.8470'
39°35.4750'
SR 155 & Main St. (0.43 mile E of intersection at bus lot)

Morgan
Deerfield Township, 36
81°57.3958'
39°44.6545'
SR 669 & east end of Eppley Rd. (at parking lot of Soloman Lutheran Church on SR 669)

Morgan
Eagleport, 37
81°54.8780'
39°44.1510'
SR 669 & Eagleport Ln. (at parking lot of St. Saviour By The River Anglican Church)

Morgan
Rokeby Lock, 38
81°54.5017'
39°44.0230'
SR 60 & N. Greer Rd. (in cul-de-sac at Muskingum River Lock No. 8 Park)

Guernsey
Cumberland, 39
81°39.4182'
39°51.2487'
SR 146 (N. Cambridge St.) & Walnut St. (in yard of old school)

Guernsey
Senecaville, 40
81°27.7445'
39°55.9057'
SR 313 & SR 285 (NE corner)

List of Interpretive Signs

Guernsey
Lore City, 41
81°27.5712'
39°59.1228'
SR 285 & B&O railroad tracks bike path (NW corner)

Guernsey
Old Washington, 42
81°26.7090'
40°2.2460'
SR 285 (Morgans Way) & Old Mill Rd. (NE corner)

Harrison
Piedmont, 43
81°13.1220'
40°11.5360'
US 22 (Cadiz-Piedmont Rd.) & Twp. Hwy. 125 (Campbell Rd.) (at Piedmont Lake State Rest Area)

Harrison
Moorefield, 44
81°10.4452'
40°11.8003'
US 22 & Ramsey Rd. (next to Moorefield Historical Society Morgan Raid plaque)

Harrison
Georgetown, 45
80°55.2410'
40°12.4520'
US 250 & Branson Rd. (next to Township building)

Harrison
Harrisville, 46
80°53.2420'
40°10.8940'
US 250 (E. Main St.) & Twp. Hwy. 82 (SE corner, across the street from post office, along church sidewalk)

Jefferson
Deyamonville, 47
80°45.5455'
40°12.6460'
Co. Hwy 8 (Dry Fork Rd.) & SR 150 (NE corner of intersection next to Morgan Raid Monument)

Jefferson
Smithfield, 48
80°46.8760'
40°16.2440'
SR 152 & Tanner St. (in front of post office parking lot at 1303 Main St.)

Jefferson
Wintersville, 49
80°43.7523'
40°23.6677'
Two Ridges Presbyterian Church driveway & Two Ridge Rd. (at Two Ridges Presbyterian Church building, next to Morgan Raid Monument)

Jefferson
The Eastern, 50
80°53.6590'
40°29.6947'
CR 75 (Wolf Run Rd.) & CR 75A (0.2 mile SE of intersection, in front of County Maintenance building)

Jefferson
Bergholz, 51
80°53.2780'
40°30.8890'
SR 164 & Twp. Hwy. 263 (at SW corner of Yellow Creek Bridge next to "Welcome to Bergholz" sign and Morgan Raid Monument)

Jefferson
Monroeville, 52
80°50.4940'
40°35.8760'
SR 164 & Monroeville-Irondale Rd. (Co. Hwy. 55) (on east side of Monroeville Cemetery entrance, located 0.2 mile W of intersection on SR 164)

Jefferson
West Grove Cemetery, 53
80°51.7150'
40°35.9142'
Twp. Rd. 294 (Opal Rd.) & Twp. Rd. 295 (McGavern Rd.) (along cemetery lane in West Grove Cemetery, located 0.35 mile W of intersection)

Carroll
Salineville (Vicinity), 54
80°54.0910'
40°37.2325'
Salineville Rd. NE (SR 39) & Ocean Rd. NE (next to Northernmost Raid Monument)

Columbiana
Gavers, 55
80°45.0873'
40°41.9350'
SR 518 & Black Rd. (Twp. Hwy. 784) (0.25 mile west of intersection along SR 518, in the island of driveway)

Columbiana
West Point (Vicinity), 56
80°44.6302'
40°41.8338'
SR 518 & Black Rd. (Twp. Hwy. 784) (0.17 mile east of intersection, next to Morgan Surrender Boulder)

Guidebook Route Map Overview

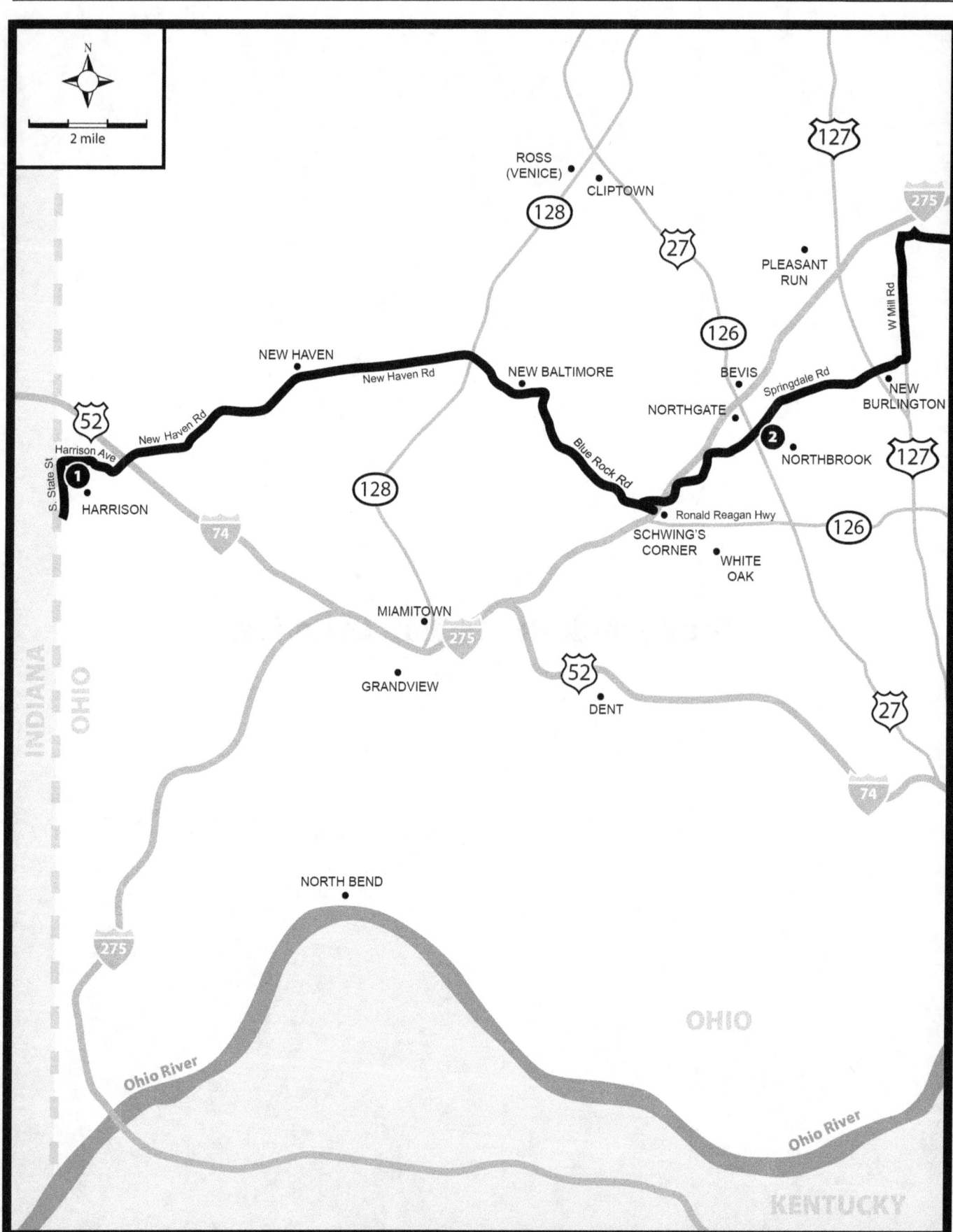

Guidebook Route Map Overview

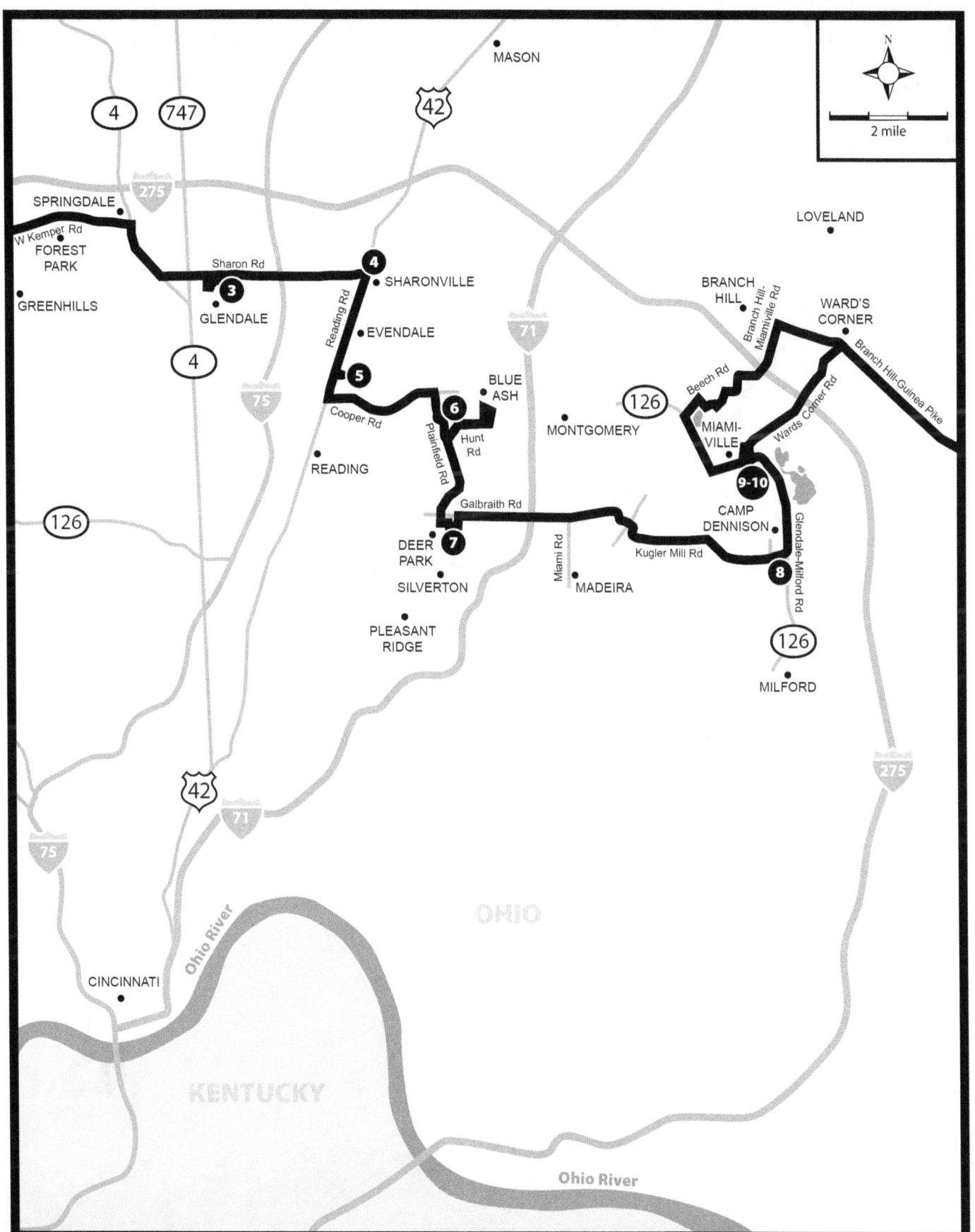

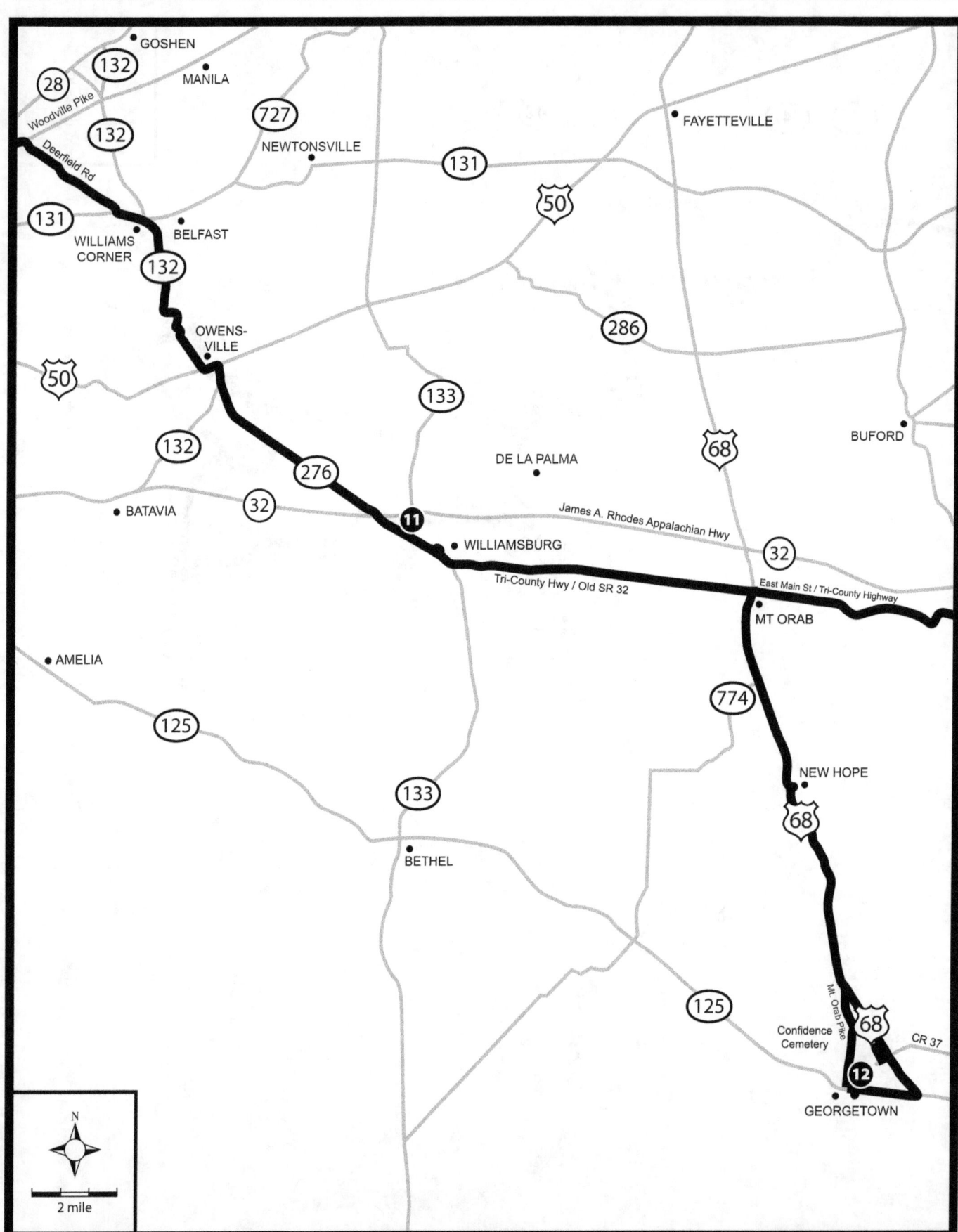

Guidebook Route Map Overview

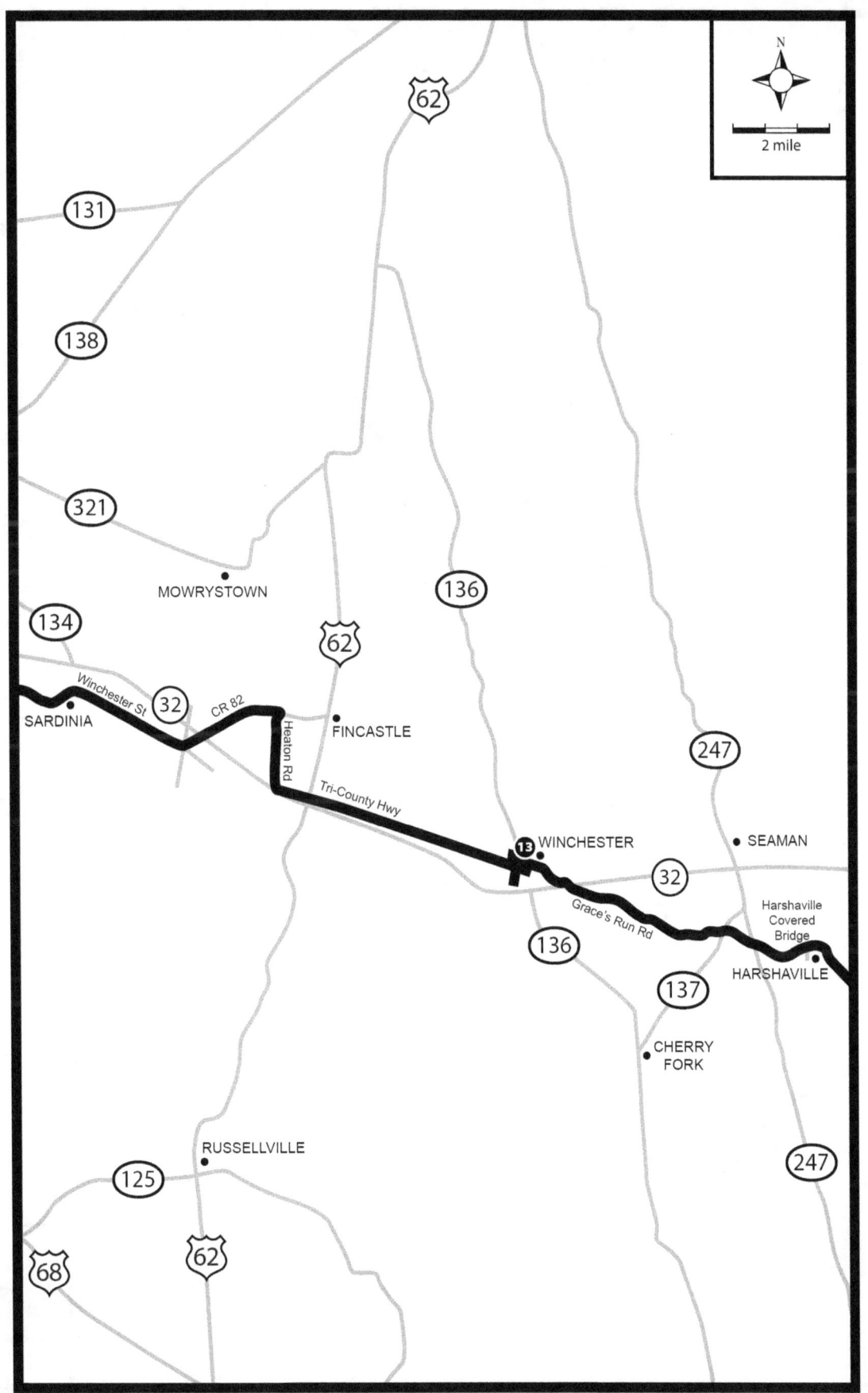

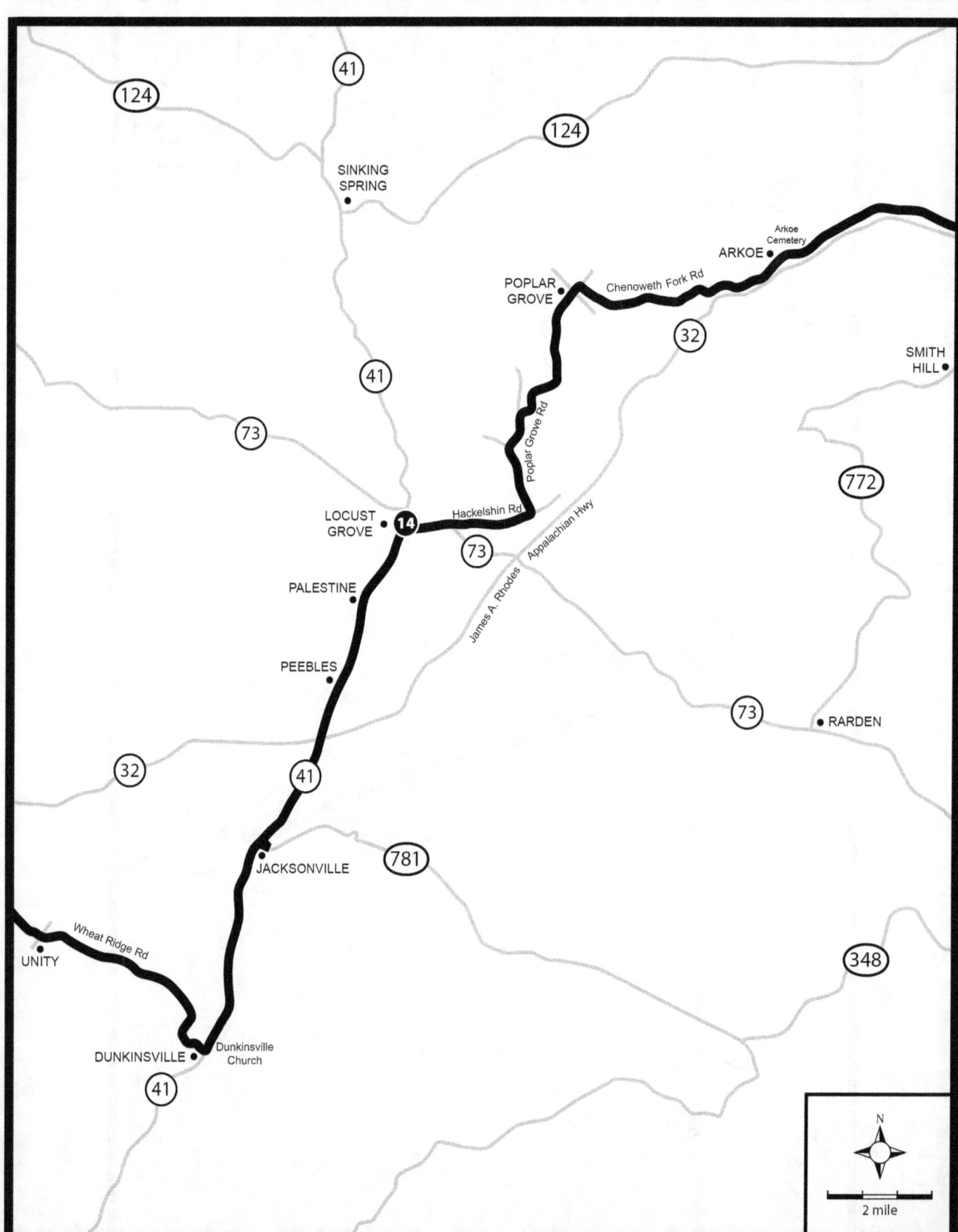

Guidebook Route Map Overview

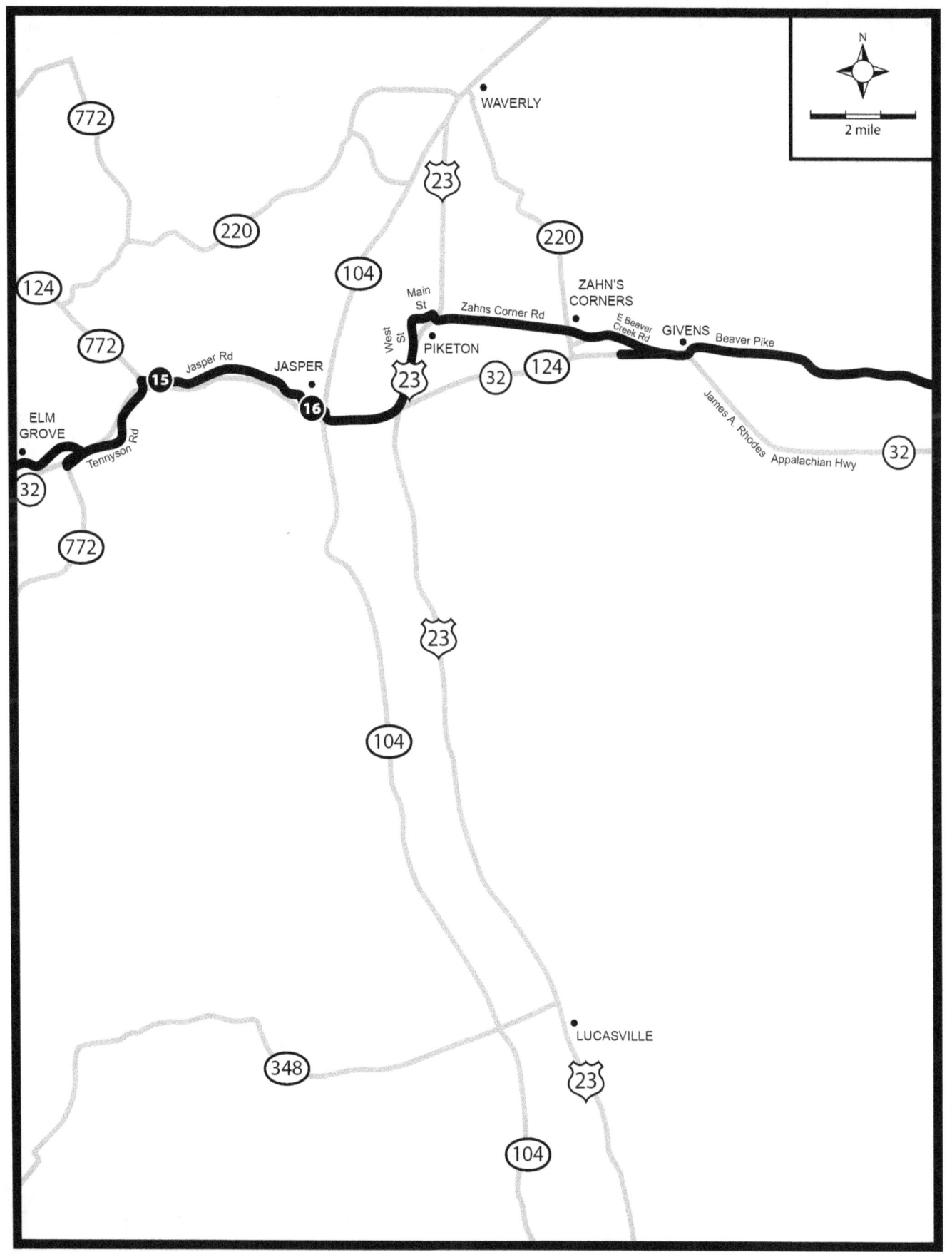

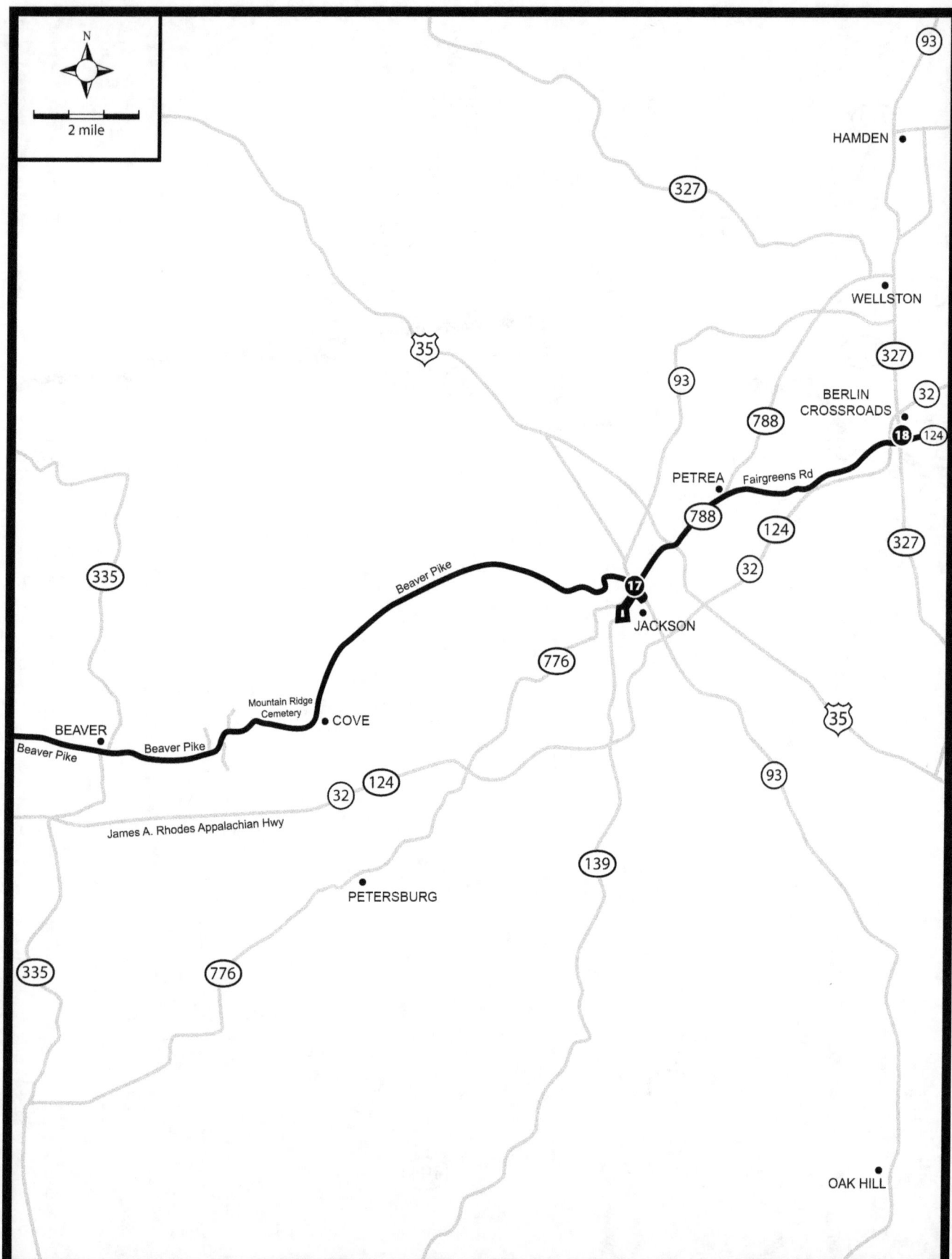

Guidebook Route Map Overview

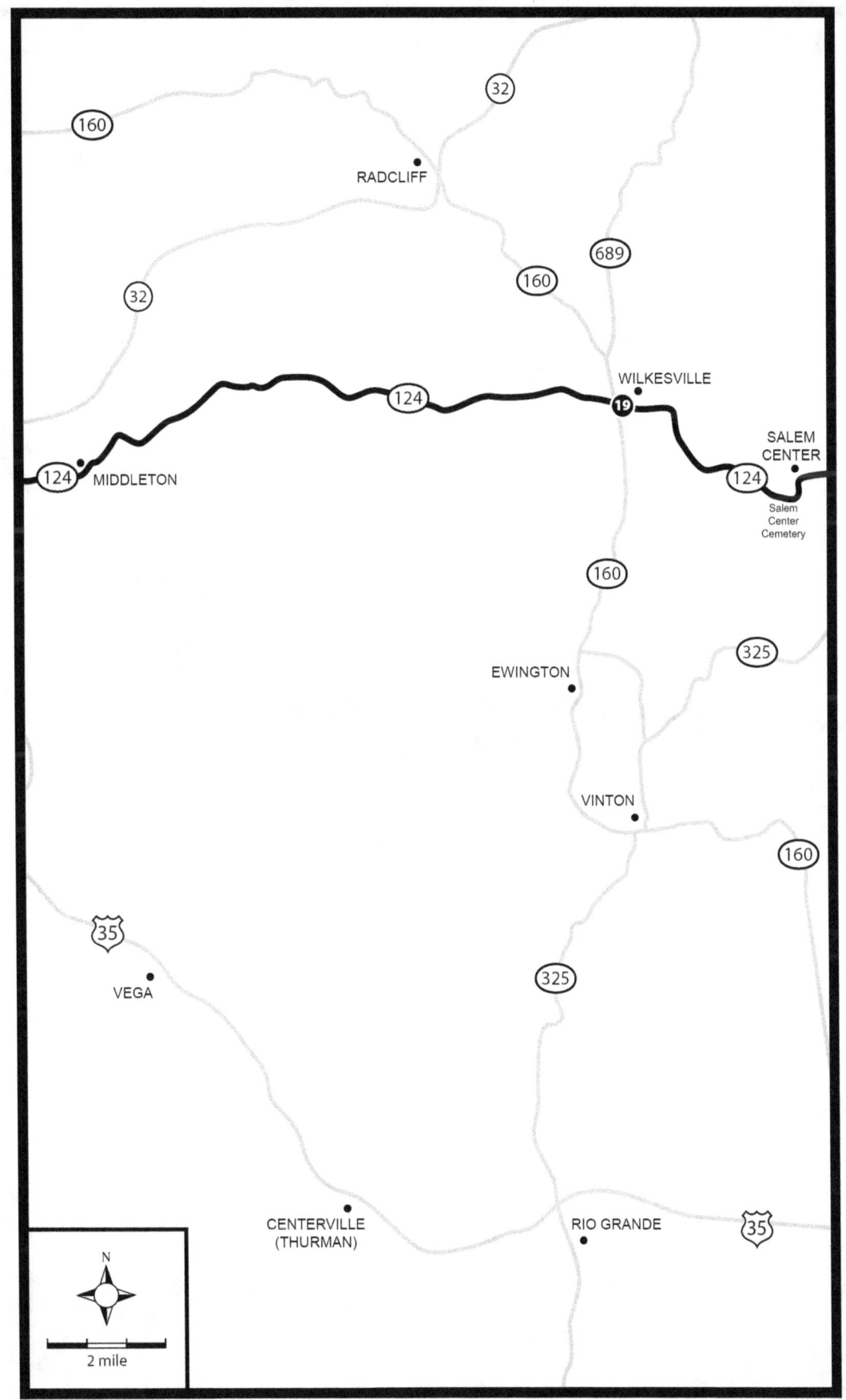

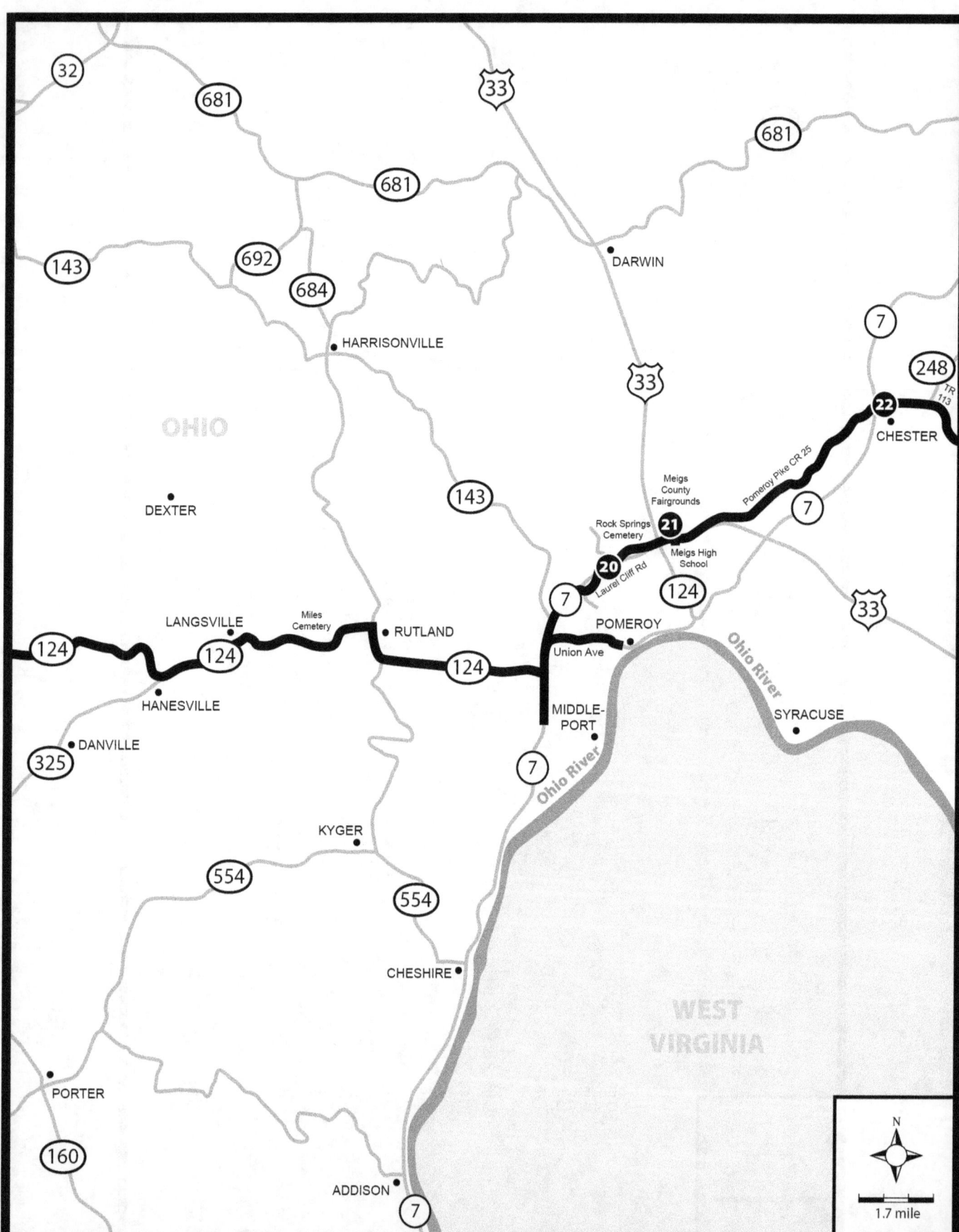

Guidebook Route Map Overview

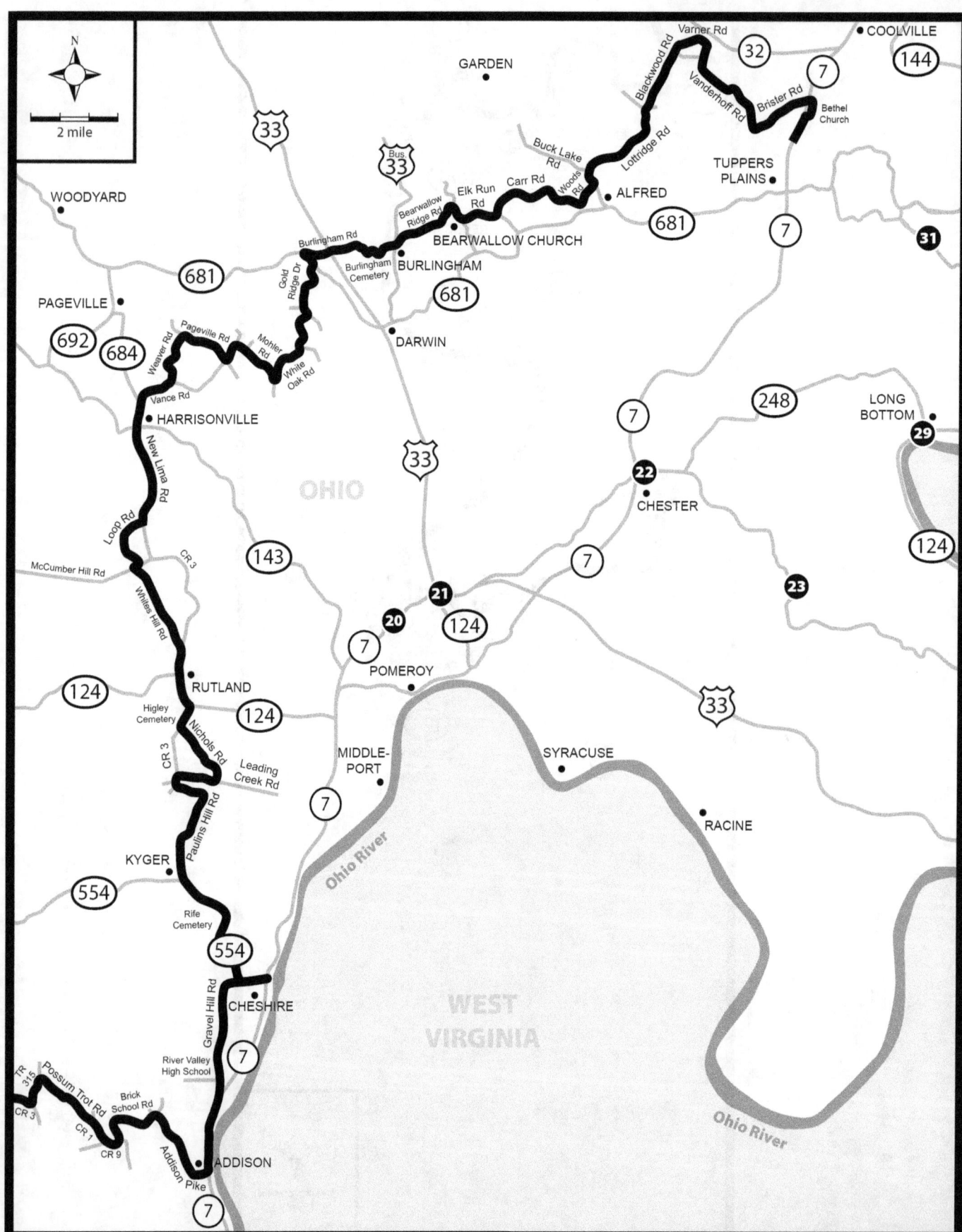

Guidebook Route Map Overview

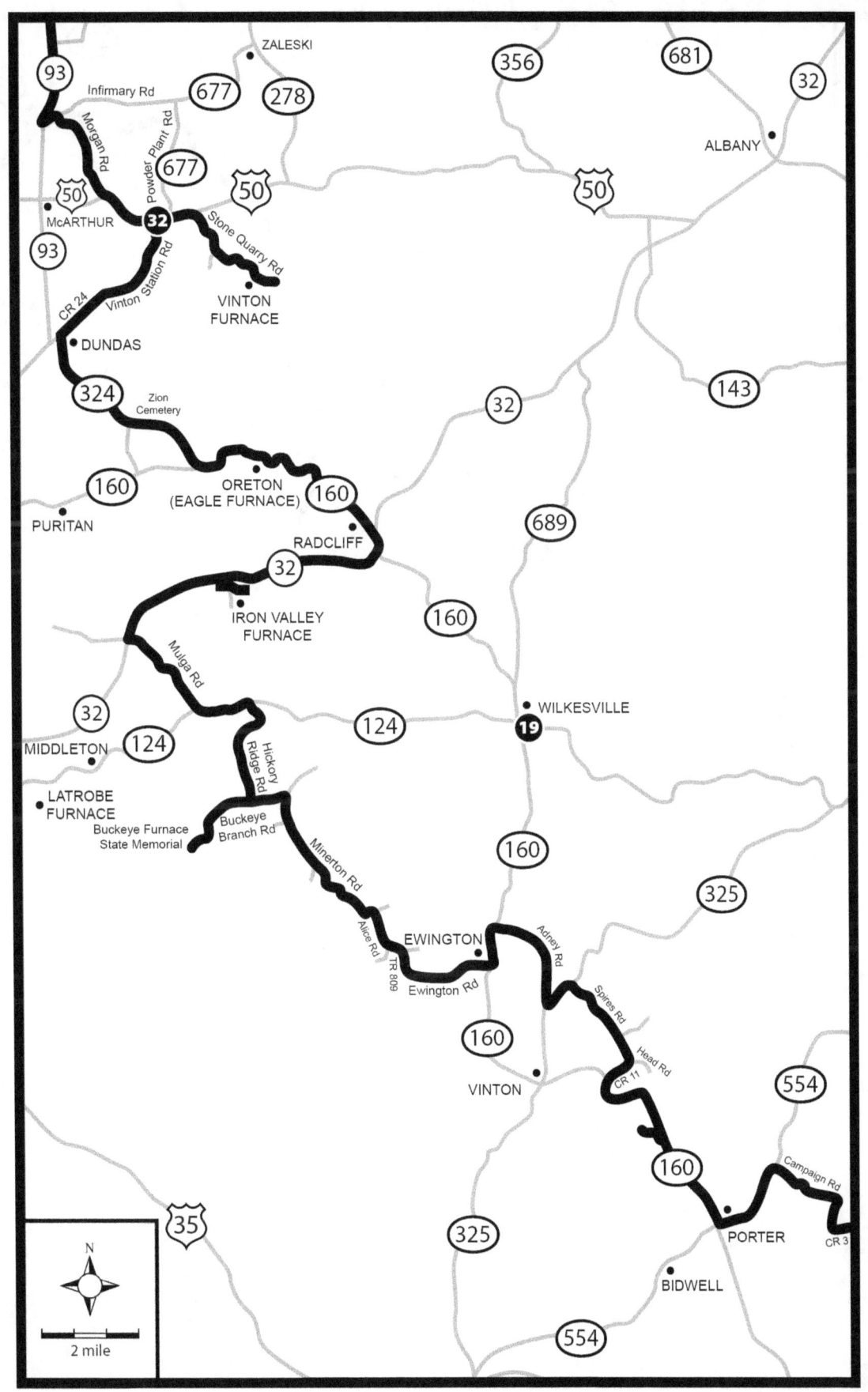

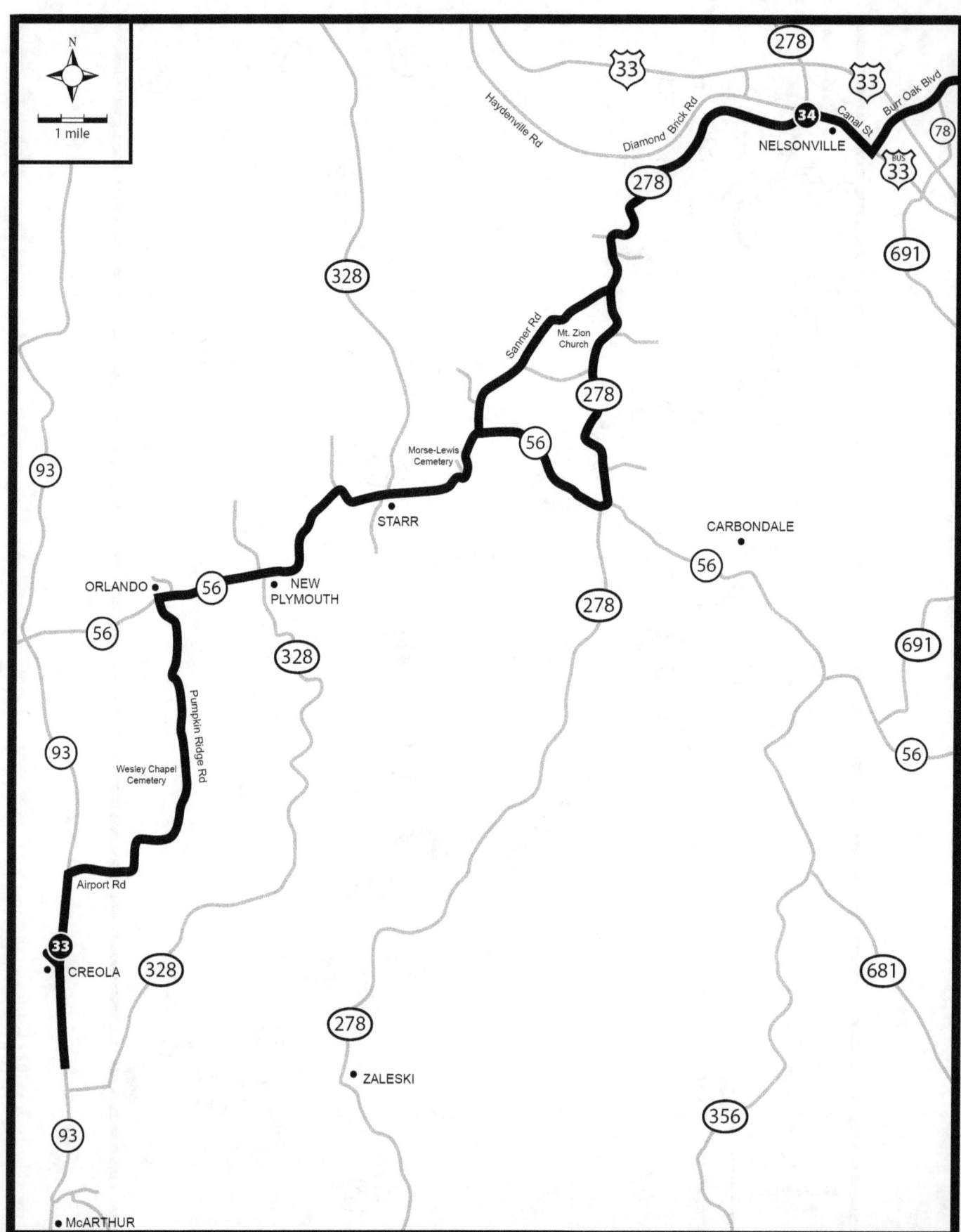

Guidebook Route Map Overview

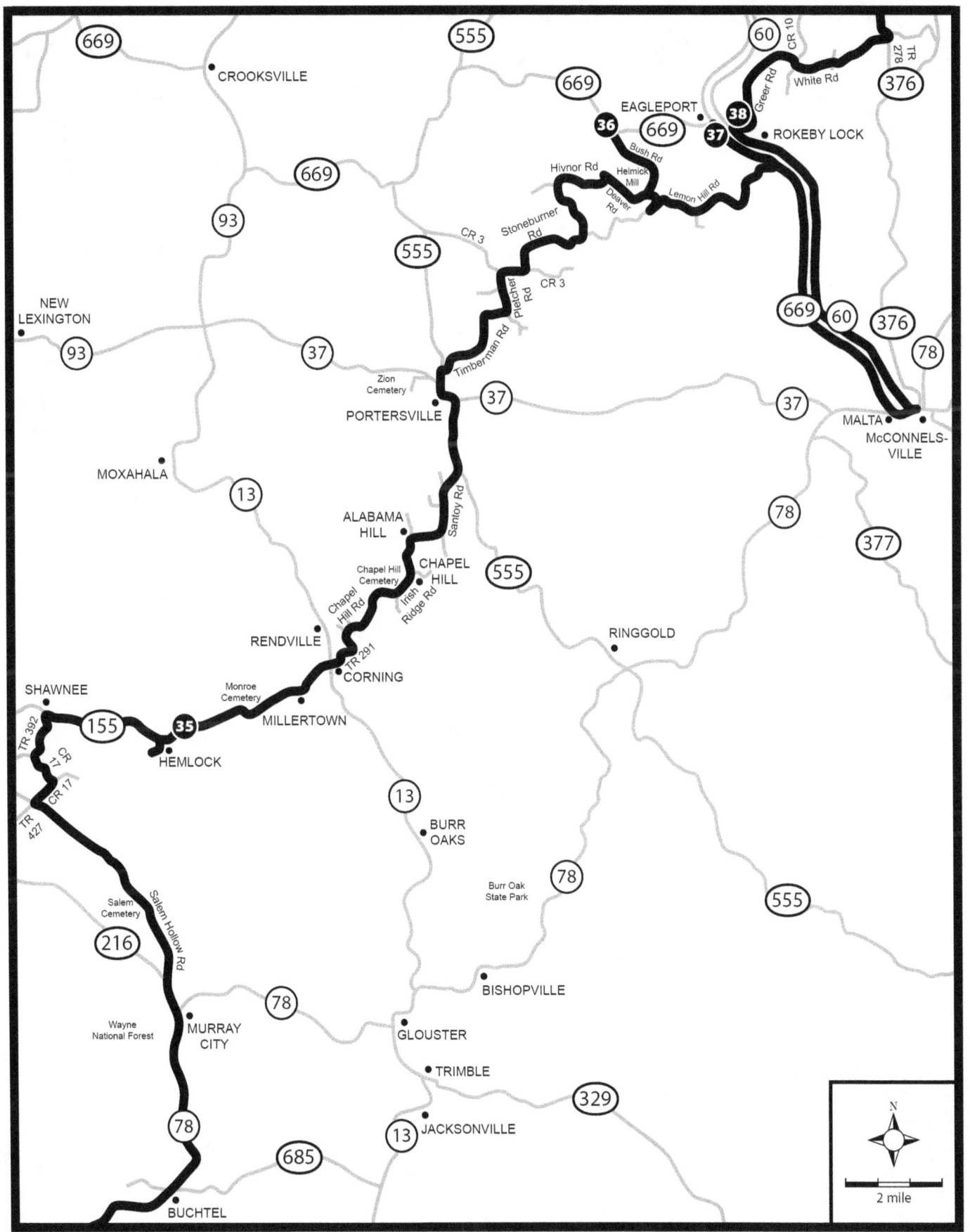

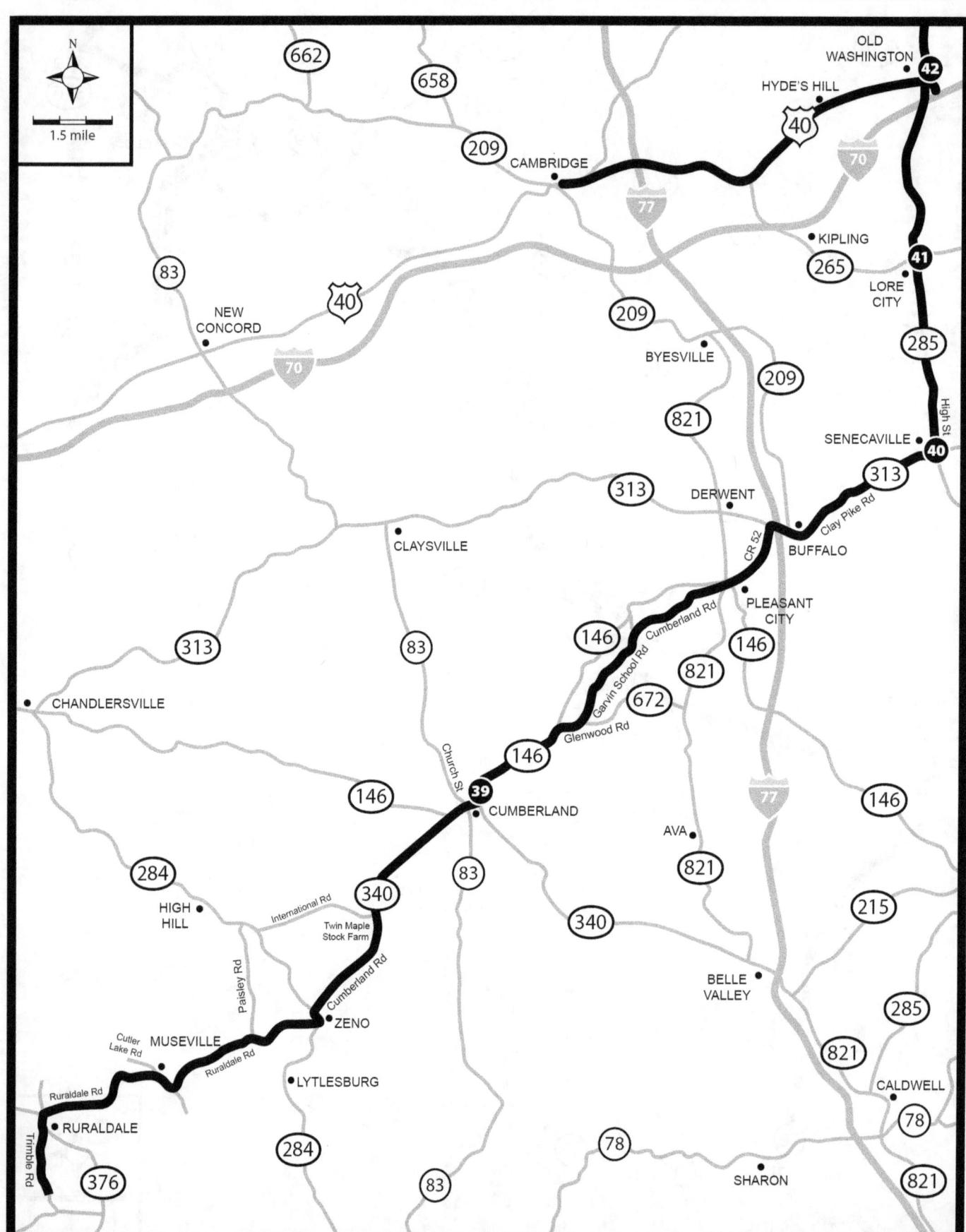

Guidebook Route Map Overview

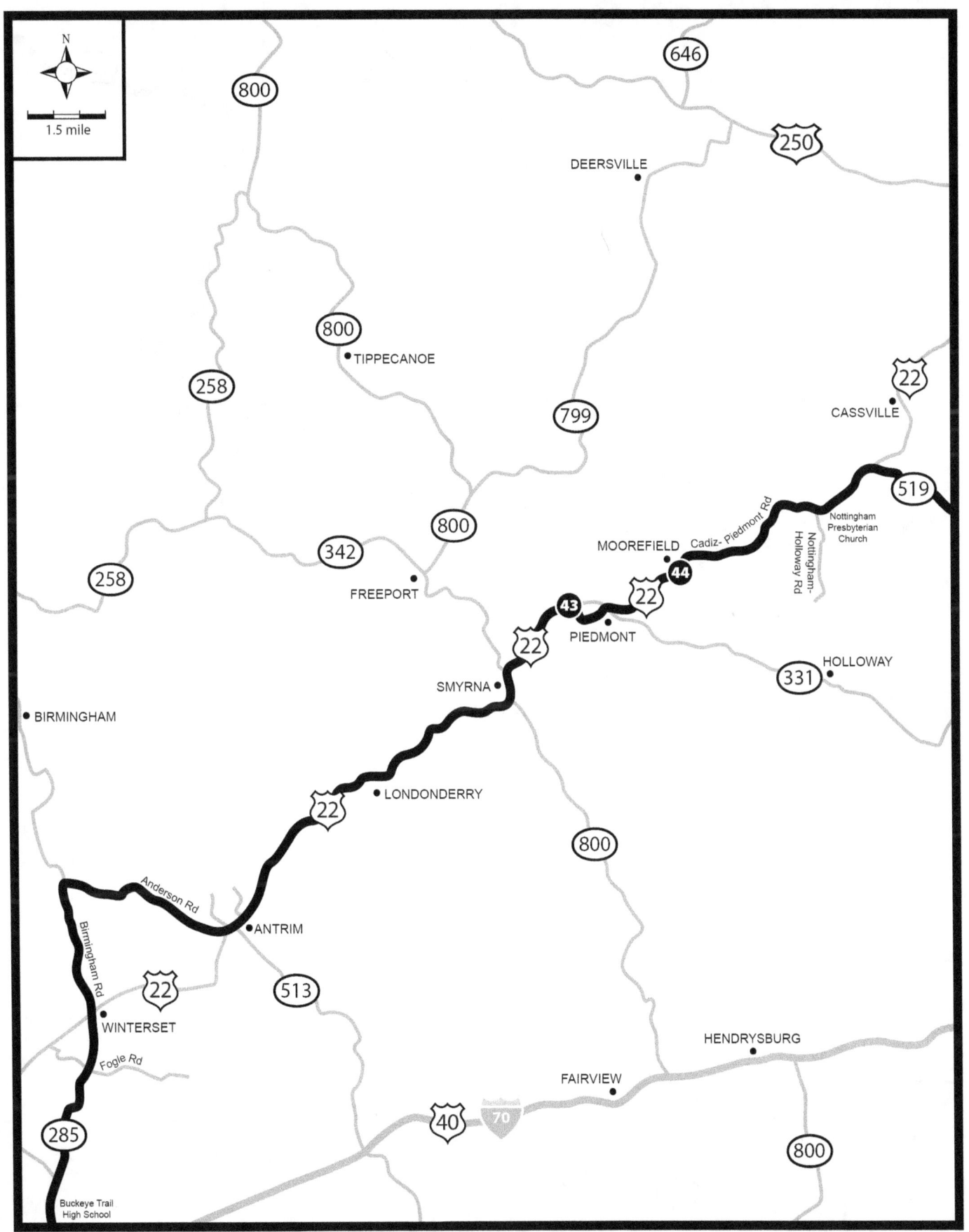

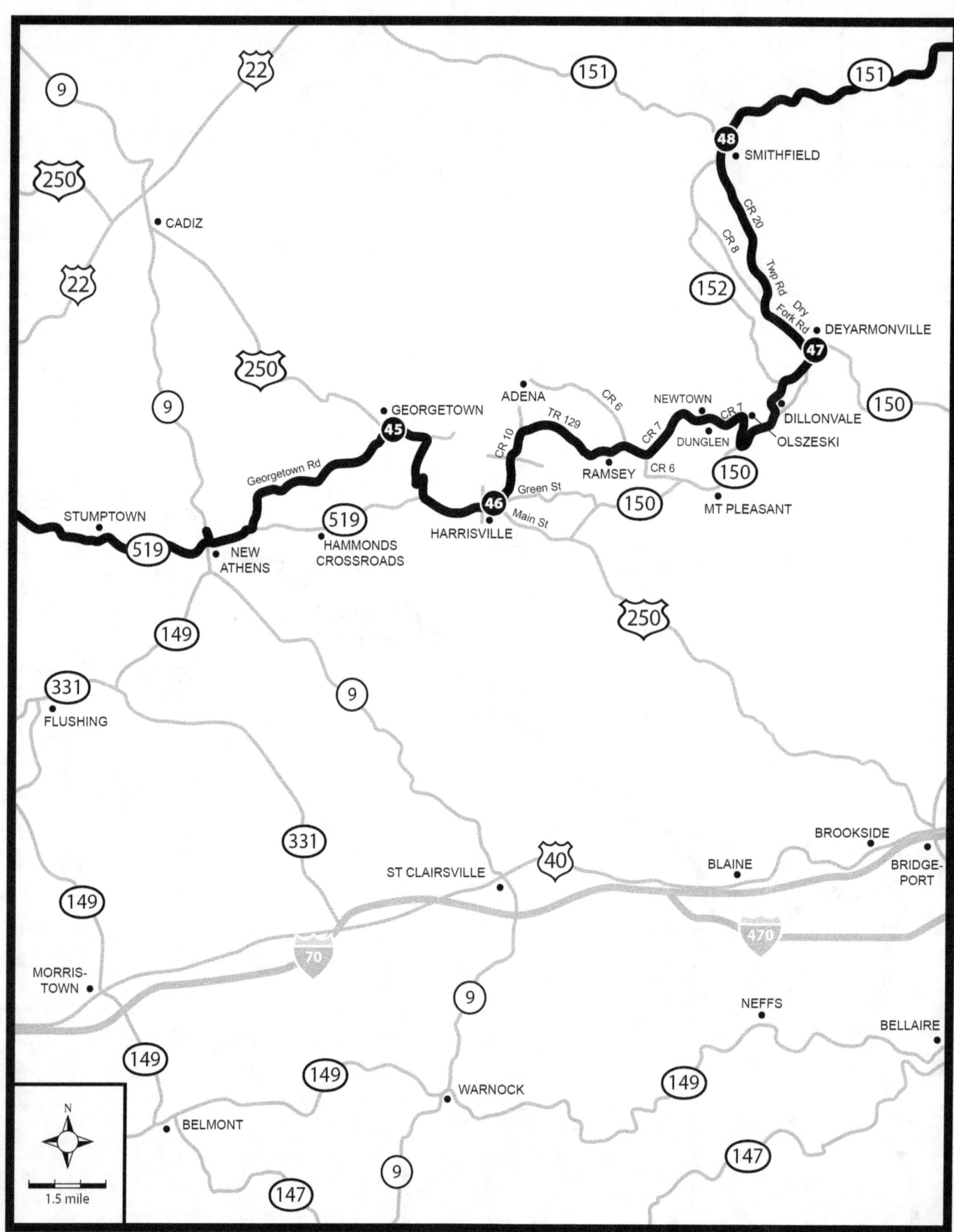

Guidebook Route Map Overview

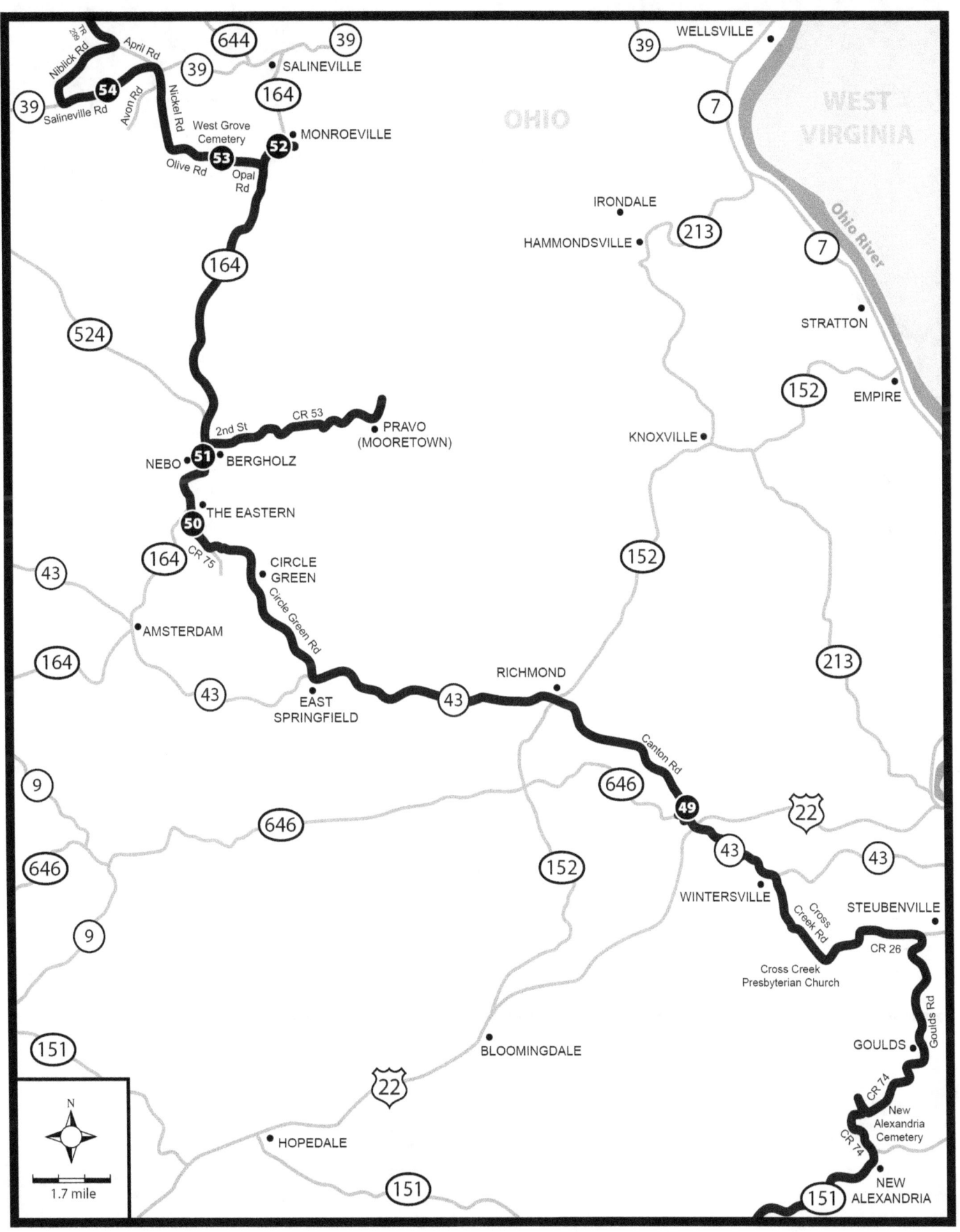

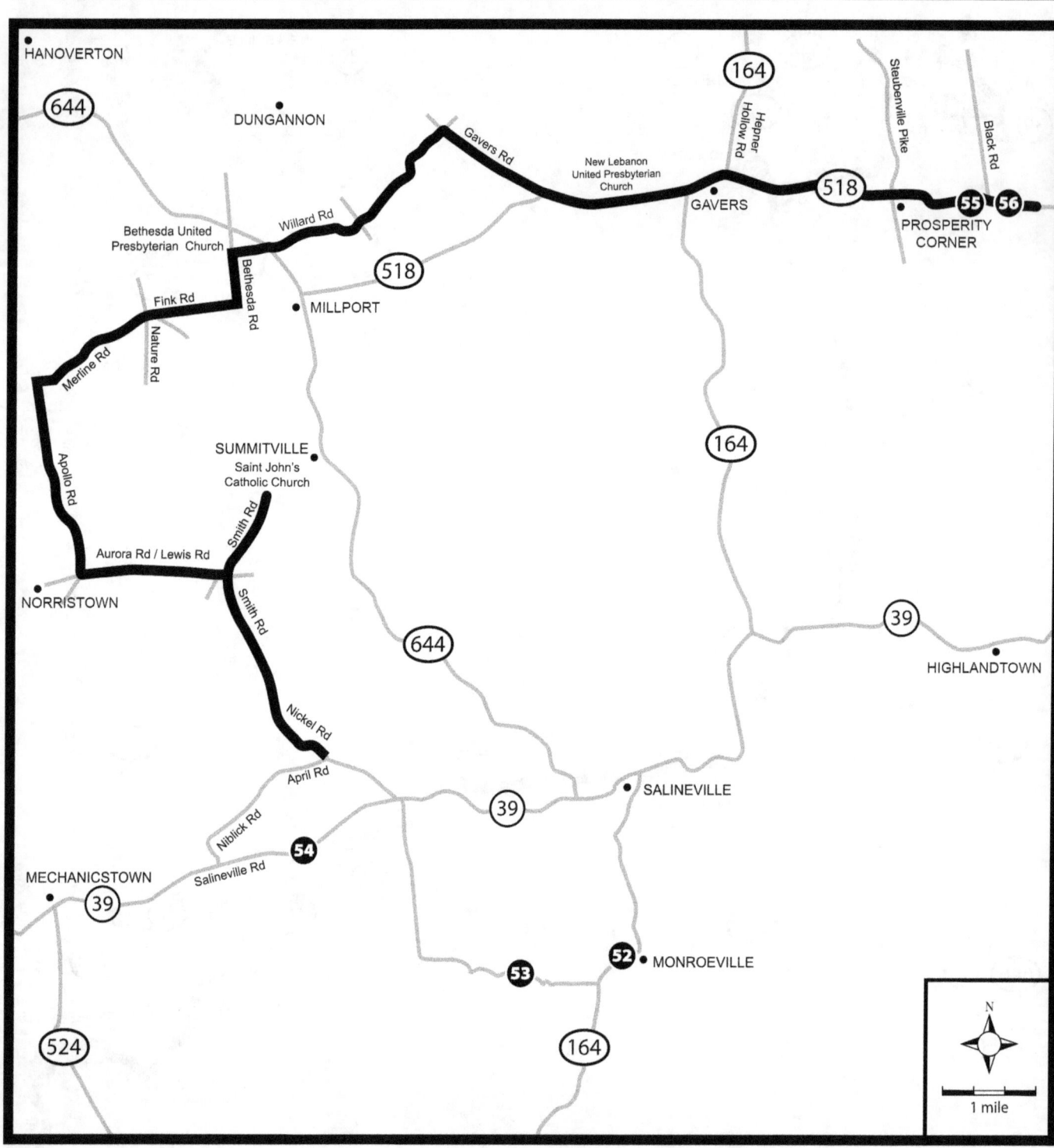

Introduction

The year 1863 of the American Civil War marked a sharp decline in the fortunes of the Confederate States of America, even though the first few months had shown vestiges of great hope. General Robert E. Lee's back-to-back victories at Fredericksburg (December 1862) and Chancellorsville (May 1863) in Virginia had given the Confederate people renewed confidence that it could win its independence from the United States. However, the loss of Confederate territory and manufacturing capabilities in Tennessee and Louisiana the previous year had opened a fatal wound from which the fledgling nation would never recover.

Two major armies defended the western states of the Confederacy in 1863. Lieutenant General John C. Pemberton's Army of Mississippi held the river port at Vicksburg, Mississippi, considered so vital to the Confederacy's survival that the city was known as the "Gibraltar of the West." Farther to the east, General Braxton Bragg's Army of Tennessee stood along the Duck River, north of Manchester and Shelbyville in Tennessee. Together, these armies were tasked to hold a territory stretching from the Appalachian Mountains to the Mississippi River. In between them lurked smaller Confederate forces, such as Major General Simon B. Buckner's infantry and cavalry stationed at Knoxville and Cumberland Gap in eastern Tennessee, and Brigadier General Nathan Bedford Forrest's cavalry posted in the western part of the state. Working cooperatively, these disjointed forces would converge on one another based on the movements of the Federal armies.

Facing Pemberton at Vicksburg was the Union Army of the Tennessee, commanded by the determined Major General Ulysses S. Grant. Grant's brilliant campaign against Fort Henry and Fort Donelson in February 1862 had caused the surrender of one of the South's most important industrial cities, Nashville, Tennessee. In May 1863, Grant conducted another ingenious campaign that allowed his army to surround Pemberton's force and besiege the city of Vicksburg. Meanwhile, Major General William S. Rosecrans's Army of the Cumberland stared down Bragg from its base at Murfreesboro, Tennessee. Farther north, Major General Ambrose Burnside formed a large Union force in central Kentucky, with the goal of confronting Buckner's men in East Tennessee.

The deteriorating military situation in the western Confederacy in May 1863 placed Bragg into a bind. If Grant would be successful in capturing Pemberton's army and opening the Mississippi River at Vicksburg, Bragg's left flank would be left vulnerable to attack from Grant. Similarly, if Burnside's forces in Kentucky would be able to push Buckner out of East Tennessee, Bragg's right flank would be in jeopardy. Bragg would not only be compelled to abandon all of Tennessee to the Union, but he also would be in danger of being attacked simultaneously by three Union armies. Even though General Lee's success in the east had stoked the people's dreams of defeating the Union, it seemed the Confederacy was about to crumble.

The Confederates desperately needed help. A diversion to prevent Burnside from invading East Tennessee would certainly act as one valuable form of aid. Keeping Burnside off Buckner's back would at least allow Bragg to focus on Rosecrans and Grant. When a thirty-eight-year-old factory owner and Mexican War veteran, Brigadier General John Hunt Morgan, approached General Bragg with a solution, the usually overly conservative Bragg was open to suggestions.

John Hunt Morgan, a veteran leader of cavalry, was a man harboring new ideas on how the cavalry branch of the army could be used to break the enemy's ability to wage war at the front. Like his colleague Nathan Bedford Forrest, General Morgan was a firm believer that cavalry could do more than just scout enemies and protect flanks. He felt that horses could be employed to move infantry from one place to another rather than follow the conventional method of marching infantrymen by foot. When the mobility of the cavalryman was combined with the firepower of the infantryman, the resulting mobile infantryman (formally termed the "mounted infantryman") could perform duties neither branch of the army could accomplish on its own. The mounted infantryman's speed allowed him to penetrate deep behind the enemy's front without fear of being caught, while his weaponry, which included rifles and artillery, was sufficient to defeat small enemy infantry groups in a long-range fight.

Introduction

Introduction

Morgan understood the Federal armies had the upper hand in manpower and supplies. If his mounted infantry could be used to deplete both, it would help make the playing field even between the Union and the Confederate armies facing each other. During the first two years of the Civil War, Morgan had proven his theory could work. His highly successful raids on enemy outposts, supply depots, and railroads in Kentucky and Tennessee had caused such disruption to the Union war effort that Federal authorities had specifically earmarked troops to defend against Morgan's actions and those of other "raiders" like him. These rear-guard troops were extracted from the armies of Grant, Rosecrans, and Burnside, which naturally made the Federals weaker at the front. The Confederate raiders' destruction of supplies and railroads stopped some Union campaigns in their tracks, including Grant's December 1862 Mississippi Campaign, which had been forced to turn back after Confederate Major General Earl Van Dorn's cavalry had destroyed Grant's supply base at Holly Springs, Mississippi.

Morgan proposed to take his crack cavalry division behind the Union lines defending the Cumberland River. From there, he would lead his men into Kentucky and threaten Louisville, one of Rosecrans's main supply bases. However, Morgan had no intention of destroying the Louisville warehouses and returning to Confederate lines. Instead, he would use his movement against Louisville as a decoy to allow him to cross the Ohio River into Indiana. His plan took his division northeast through southern Indiana, around the Federal bastion at Cincinnati, across southern Ohio, and back over the Ohio River into Kentucky and to the safety of Confederate lines in Tennessee.

Morgan was confident that an incursion into the Northern states would cause the Northerners such great anxiety over having a Confederate force on their soil that they would insist on the maximum protection of their military. The result would be that Rosecrans and Burnside would have no choice but to send large contingents of their armies to chase Morgan's division across Indiana and Ohio rather than send them against Bragg. Morgan provided a case study in the form of Union Colonel Benjamin Grierson's Mississippi Raid of April 1863. Grierson's raid, one of the greatest in American military history, had diverted General Pemberton's attention long enough to permit Grant's army to slip across the Mississippi River unmolested. Morgan believed that if the Union cavalry could divert an army's attention, then his cavalry could do better.

Bragg liked Morgan's proposal except for one major point: He did not want Morgan to cross the Ohio River. With Rosecrans showing signs of moving against the Army of Tennessee, Bragg wanted assurance that he could recall Morgan's division at a moment's notice and bring it back to Tennessee to protect his flank. On June 10, 1863, Bragg gave Morgan his oral approval to immediately conduct a raid into Kentucky, with Louisville as the primary target. The raiders would not— under any circumstances — enter the Northern states.

Morgan, like most of his colleagues in the Army of Tennessee, thought Bragg was an inept and timid leader. Morgan resolved from the start to disobey Bragg's order to stay within Kentucky. He knew of no other way to effectively divert the attention of Rosecrans or Burnside. On the night of June 10, Morgan gathered his brigade and regimental officers and briefed them on his plan, including the crossing of the Ohio River into Indiana and Ohio. The plan was sound, and all approved it, albeit with some reservations. Morgan informed only Colonel Basil Duke, the 1st Brigade commander and Morgan's brother-in-law, that they would be violating General Bragg's orders by entering Indiana. Nevertheless, Duke knew there was no point in dissuading Morgan from this aim; it had been the General's idea since early 1862 to raid the North. With the western Confederacy on the verge of collapse, Morgan had already made up his mind that a raid into the North was a necessity.

The raiders started north from their camps around Alexandria, Tennessee, on June 11 and trotted toward the Union-held garrison at Carthage. Many thought the anticipated raid had begun. Three days later, Morgan received a telegram from Major General Joseph Wheeler, commander of the Army of Tennessee's Cavalry Corps, giving Morgan permission from Bragg to start the special operation into Kentucky. Unfortunately, Bragg had allocated only 1,500 cavalrymen with artillery for the raid; the rest would need to be left behind to guard the army's flank. Morgan was disgusted. His division numbered 2,743 effective soldiers, the minimum amount he felt he needed to be successful. He complained to Wheeler, asking for more men. Four days later, Bragg compromised with an allowance of 2,000 men with artillery. Morgan quietly accepted Bragg's order by leaving 280 men of his 9th Kentucky Cavalry regiment in Tennessee, but he took the remaining 2,460 men of his division with him.

Morgan's veteran soldiers were armed mostly with Colt revolvers and short-barreled or medium-length Enfield rifles. Many of the men also carried sabers, shotguns, breech-loading carbines, and various muskets from the pre-Civil War days. Because the cavalry was the worst-supplied branch of the Confederate army, Morgan's men scavenged anything they could find. Confederate uniforms were in short supply for the cavalry; thus, Morgan's men often confiscated blue uniforms from Union cavalrymen or wore civilian clothes. The Confederate cavalrymen even had to find their own horses. Morgan's men had no choice but to requisition horses from civilians if suitable mounts could not be taken from enemy soldiers. The Confederate high command sanctioned all these foraging actions. It was war, after all.

Accompanying the division was a four-gun battery of artillery. Its guns, two 3-inch Parrott rifles and two 12-pounder field howitzers, were the types typically found to support infantry as well as cavalry. The Parrotts had the ability to accurately hit a target from a mile away. Artillery of this nature provided Morgan the firepower he needed to reduce a Union blockhouse or a small fort.

Morgan's cavalry division was organized into two brigades. Both of his brigade commanders were seasoned leaders of guerrilla warfare, known today as Special Operations. Colonel Basil W. Duke, Morgan's most trusted officer and second-in-command, had accompanied the fearless cavalry leader on his first raids in 1861. Duke had tried to raid Ohio with his own command in August 1862, but the operation had failed at the river port of Augusta, Kentucky. On the other hand, Colonel Adam Rankin Johnson, Morgan's 2nd Brigade leader, had commanded an independent force for nearly a year. Johnson's highly touted raid on Newburgh, Indiana, in July 1862 served as a model for Morgan's upcoming Indiana-Ohio Raid. Morgan could not have asked for any better leaders to serve under him on this occasion.

Morgan's Cavalry Division Brig. Gen. John Hunt Morgan	
First Brigade Col. Basil W. Duke	Second Brigade Col. Adam R. Johnson
2nd Kentucky Cavalry, Maj. Thomas B. Webber	7th Kentucky Cavalry, Lt. Col. John M. Huffman
5th Kentucky Cavalry, Col. D. Howard Smith	8th Kentucky Cavalry, Col. Roy S. Cluke
6th Kentucky Cavalry, Col. J. Warren Grigsby	10th Kentucky Cavalry, Maj. George W. Owen
9th Tennessee Cavalry, Col. William W. Ward	11th Kentucky Cavalry, Col. David W. Chenault (Lt. Col. Joseph T. Tucker, beginning July 4, 1863)
9th Kentucky Cavalry (Co. A), Capt. Thomas H. Hines	14th Kentucky Cavalry, Col. Richard C. Morgan
Kentucky Battery (two 3-inch Parrott rifles; two 12-pounder field howitzers) Capt. Edward P. Byrne	

General Bragg delayed Morgan's raid for another week to counter Union Colonel William P. Sanders's daring cavalry raid into East Tennessee. Before Morgan could cut off Sanders's retreat, the Union raider had returned to Union lines. Morgan and Sanders would contend with each other again soon enough.

Morgan marched Duke's men out of Albany, Kentucky, on June 23 and positioned them on the south side of the Cumberland River several miles from Burkesville. Johnson's brigade joined them from Celina, Tennessee. After a week of resupplying them and recouping their strength, Morgan ordered his men to move toward the river on the night of June 30. There would be no turning back from here. Their destiny was at hand.

Introduction

Throughout the day of July 1, 1863, and into the following afternoon, Morgan's division crossed the rain-swollen Cumberland River. Using multiple fords located several miles above and below Burkesville, the raiders ferried their wagons, artillery, and equipment on hastily improvised canoes and rafts. With the aid of these crafts, the men swam their horses to the opposite side. Union resistance was feeble; the crossing was completed mostly unmolested. Morgan's Indiana-Ohio Raid, alternatively called the Great Raid or the Ohio Raid, had officially begun.

Generals Rosecrans and Burnside were caught napping. They never thought anyone, not even Morgan, would attempt to swim the river when it was flooded. On July 2, when the generals received reports that Morgan's troopers were on the north bank of the Cumberland River, they immediately felt a sense of dread. Panic would soon follow. Rosecrans had already initiated his famed Tullahoma Campaign against Bragg's army, and therefore he could not afford to send troops after Morgan. Besides, Kentucky was Burnside's jurisdiction. Burnside called on his field commander in the area, Brigadier General Henry M. Judah, to find Morgan and cut him off before he could cross the Green River. Judah, known for his overcautious nature, was too slow to respond to Morgan's swift incursion into the Bluegrass State. Judah's inability to close the gap north of Burkesville with three nearby brigades of veteran Union cavalrymen left an avenue wide open for Morgan's column to reach the Green River. The Union cavalry's inaction left Morgan's division with only a few scattered enemy detachments and outposts to sweep out of its path.

Morgan's men entered Columbia, Kentucky, on July 3, after defeating small Union cavalry detachments there and at Marrowbone Creek. Unfortunately, Morgan lost Tom Quirk, the leader of his famed scouts, who was badly wounded at Marrowbone and left behind to recover. On the morning of July 4, the division reached the Green River at Tebbs Bend. There, Morgan's poor decision to assault the enemy fortifications held by Colonel Orlando H. Moore and two hundred men of the 25th Michigan Infantry resulted in the death of David W. Chenault, colonel of the 11th Kentucky Cavalry, along with eighty other dead and wounded. Later it was concluded that the rash attack had been unnecessary. Morgan's scouts had discovered several undefended fords of the Green River that allowed the raiders to completely avoid the enemy's works.

The next day, the Confederates rode north to Lebanon, Kentucky, where they found Lieutenant Colonel Charles Hanson's 380 Federal troops defending the town. When Morgan attacked the garrison, the Union soldiers fell back into the fortified Louisville & Nashville Railroad depot. During the ensuing melee, Lieutenant Thomas Morgan, the general's younger brother, was instantly killed by a sniper. Forty other raiders fell in the fight. Hanson surrendered his troops when the Confederates threatened to burn them out of the depot, but his defense had stalled Morgan for several hours. With the losses of Tom Quirk and the much beloved Tom Morgan, coupled with the many soldiers killed or wounded over the past two days, a sense of impending doom seemed to prevail among the men.

After confiscating much-needed equipment, the raiders continued on their northbound journey. They rode through Springfield, where Morgan's column turned northwest. They reached Bardstown before dawn on July 6, at which point Morgan sent large detachments in multiple directions, including one toward Louisville, to deceive Federal authorities as to his next destination. Later that day, at Bardstown Junction, Morgan's telegrapher, George "Lightning" Ellsworth, used his unique skills to listen to messages from Union authorities. He learned that Burnside's subordinates were convinced Morgan was heading to Louisville. Of course, they were wrong.

Besides listening to enemy telegrams, Ellsworth was also masterful at sending deceptive messages to Union headquarters. Throughout the raid, Ellsworth would often emulate a telegraph operator's tapping style to send believable messages containing incorrect information about Morgan's whereabouts, his intended destination, or his force's strength. These false telegrams confused Burnside's officers even more than they were, resulting in indecision and turmoil among the Federal leadership.

Meanwhile, Burnside's headquarters in Cincinnati was frenetic. Reports that Morgan was advancing on Louisville, one of the North's most valuable supply depots, put Burnside into a panic. Judah's mounted troops had not yet started a concerted chase after their foe, and Burnside had done nothing to rectify the debacle. On the morning of July 6, one of Judah's subordinates, Brigadier General Edward H. Hobson, decided to take matters into his own hands. He led his brigade from Greensburg to Campbellsville, Kentucky, where he and Brigadier General James M. Shackelford joined forces. Together they rode to Lebanon, where they met with Colonel Frank Wolford, Colonel August Kautz, and their brigades. Wolford and Kautz followed Hobson and Shackelford as they turned north in pursuit of the elusive Confederate raider.

After hearing of Hobson's actions, and completely frustrated by Judah's ineptitude, Burnside sent Hobson an order, at 4:30 p.m. on July 6, to take command of all mounted troops in the immediate vicinity and go after Morgan. This order gave Hobson seniority over the other brigade commanders as well as Judah, even though Judah was Hobson's superior officer. Hobson's command, called the Provisional Cavalry Division, contained about 2,500 men with artillery when the brigades of Shackelford, Wolford, and Kautz were combined with his own. Hobson awarded temporary command of his brigade to Shackelford.

Edward Hobson was a former lawyer and a decorated Mexican War veteran. He was a man known for his bulldog determination and independent nature. Hobson was well acquainted with Morgan's tactics and trickery. Most of his soldiers had experienced guerrilla warfare first hand, having fought Morgan's men over the past two years. From this point forward, Hobson would not let up on Morgan. Hobson's relentless pursuit created the greatest fear for his antagonist in gray.

Morgan's troopers continued their night march westward, eventually reaching Garnettsville, Kentucky, on the afternoon of July 7. While Morgan's

Provisional Cavalry Division (July 6–21, 1863)* Brig. Gen. Edward H. Hobson		
Kautz's Brigade Col. August V. Kautz	Wolford's Brigade Col. Frank L. Wolford	Shackelford's Brigade Brig. Gen. James M. Shackelford
2nd Ohio Cavalry, Lt. Col. George A. Purington	1st Kentucky (U.S.) Cavalry, Lt. Col. Silas Adams	3rd Kentucky (U.S.) Cavalry (1 bttn.), Maj. Lewis W. Wolfley
7th Ohio Cavalry, Col. Israel Garrard	2nd East Tennessee (Mounted) Infantry, Lt. Col. James M. Melton	8th Kentucky (U.S.) Cavalry, Col. Benjamin H. Bristow (Lt. Col. James H. Holloway, beginning July 15, 1863)
	45th Ohio (Mounted) Infantry, Lt. Col. George E. Ross	9th Kentucky (U.S.) Cavalry, Col. Richard T. Jacob
		12th Kentucky (U.S.) Cavalry, Col. Eugene W. Crittenden
Hammond's Battery, attached to 65th Indiana (Mounted) Infantry (Co. K) (two guns) Capt. John W. Hammond Law's Mountain Howitzer Battery (four 12-pounder mountain howitzers) Lt. Jesse S. Law		
*Col. William P. Sanders's brigade would join Hobson's division on July 15, 1863. Sanders's brigade consisted of the 8th Michigan Cavalry (10 companies), Lt. Col. Grover S. Wormer; 9th Michigan Cavalry (Companies A, B, F, and L), Lt. Col. George S. Acker; and two rifled guns of Battery L, 1st Michigan Light Artillery [11th Michigan Battery], Lt. Cyrus D. Roys.		

division rested at Garnettsville until midnight, a small group of scouts under Captains Sam Taylor and Clay Meriwether rode ahead and casually entered Brandenburg, a small town on the Ohio River west of Louisville. There they rendezvoused with Captain Thomas Hines of the 9th Kentucky Cavalry, whose handpicked company had made a secret raid into Indiana over the prior three weeks. Hines reached Brandenburg with only two men remaining of the original sixty-two who had left with him, but the intelligence he had gathered from his month-long sojourn in the North would prove invaluable for the rest of the division.

Morgan's feints had worked; no Union troops, and most importantly, no U.S. Navy gunboats awaited them at Brandenburg to prevent a river crossing. Only privately owned steamboats plied the waters that morning, and they were unaware of Morgan's presence. Through trickery, the scouts boarded two steamboats, the *John T. McCombs* and the *Alice Dean*, and convinced the captains that it was prudent to surrender their vessels rather than make a run for it. From General Morgan's perspective, the two captured boats were like a miracle from heaven; now he could ferry his men, horses, wagons, and artillery across the river safely and quickly. The timing could not have been any better. Hobson's division lagged behind by only a day's ride.

With 175 miles already put behind them, the rest of Morgan's division rode quietly into Brandenburg. From the early morning of July 8 until after midnight, Morgan's division crossed the Ohio River through repeated roundtrips of the *John T. McCombs* and the *Alice Dean*. After this undertaking had begun in earnest, Union resistance appeared — but too little and too late. The raiders with their long-range artillery easily dispersed the Indiana militiamen who peppered them with shots from the Indiana bank of the river. Later in the day, Morgan's Parrott and howitzer guns turned back the U.S. Navy gunboat, USS *Springfield*, which attempted to stop the ferrying activity. After completing the crossing, Morgan ordered the *Alice Dean* burned, while the *John T. McCombs* was sent upstream, escaping the flames because its skipper was an old friend of Basil Duke. Before dawn on July 9, as the rear guard of Morgan's column disappeared into the Indiana countryside, General Hobson and his advance troopers reached the shore at Brandenburg. Hobson could not believe his eyes. Morgan's rebels were loose in the North!

The raiders must have felt they had entered the Land of Milk and Honey. Unlike Kentucky, Indiana had been mostly untouched by the hard hand of war. Beautiful farm fields grew rich with corn, wheat, and oats. Barns were well stocked with hay and fodder. Cupboards were filled with pies, cakes, fruits, vegetables, jams, breads, cheeses, and milk. Most importantly, the Hoosier farmers owned many horses. However, as the raiders would soon discover, horse breeding in Indiana and Ohio fell well below the standards of breeding in Kentucky. Most of the mounts in the North were meant for performing laborious tasks, such as plowing and hauling; the horses were not bred for long-distance rides at swift speeds. This would prove to be a problem for Morgan's Raiders, because they depended on replenishing their horses from the stock of the residents.

At dawn on July 9, Morgan's men left their camp north of Brandenburg, bypassed Mauckport, and headed toward Corydon. Awaiting them on the southern outskirts of Corydon was a hodgepodge group of 450 Sixth Indiana Legion militiamen and citizens armed with various muskets and rifles. Their commander, Colonel Lewis Jordon, had instructed them to build a barricade of fence rails behind which they would hold their line. When Morgan's advance guards charged the enemy barricade, the raiders were repulsed.

General Morgan would not repeat the mistake he had made at Tebbs Bend. He ordered Captain Byrne's artillery to bombard the barricade while he deployed his cavalry regiments to attack both flanks of the Union line. The ensuing barrage, combined with the coordinated assault of Morgan's dismounted cavalrymen, proved too much for the untrained Hoosier defenders. The militiamen broke and ran after a fight that lasted less than thirty minutes. Colonel Jordan surrendered the town. Morgan's men rode into Corydon victorious and eager to replenish their horses and provisions. Confederate casualties at the Battle of Corydon amounted to 8 killed and 33 wounded, while the Hoosiers lost 5 killed and wounded along with 345 captured. Following his normal procedure, Morgan paroled the prisoners and sent them home.

At Corydon, General Morgan heard the disturbing news from around the country. Confederate General Pemberton had surrendered his army to General Grant on July 4, making Vicksburg a Union-occupied city, opening the Mississippi River to the U.S. Navy, and splitting the Confederacy in two. In the east, Robert E. Lee's Confederate Army of Northern Virginia had been defeated at the Battle of Gettysburg in Pennsylvania, and Lee was retreating back into Maryland. Any distant hopes that Morgan might meet up with Lee in Pennsylvania were gone. However, Morgan was determined to continue his raid as planned. The raiders camped for the night near Palmyra, Indiana.

General Hobson and his subordinates unanimously chose to pursue the Rebels into Indiana, despite the fact that Burnside's orders did not explicitly permit them to do so. Hobson and his officers understood that waiting for confirmation from Burnside would waste valuable time. Instead, they spent the morning of July 9 in Brandenburg commandeering boats to ferry themselves across the Ohio River. Hobson's division used the better part of the day to cross their men, horses, and material to the Indiana side of the river. They encamped that evening near Mauckport.

Governor Oliver P. Morton, appalled by Morgan's invasion of Indiana, declared a state of emergency. The presence of the enemy on Northern soil greatly alarmed not only the Hoosiers, specifically, but also the citizens of the lower Midwest, generally. Ellsworth's flurry of misleading telegrams made things worse; he tapped out messages indicating that Morgan carried with him 4,000 to 12,000 troopers. Before long, Ellsworth had some people thinking that a full-scale invasion of Indiana was underway.

Burnside was equally flabbergasted by the turn of events. He immediately contacted the Indianapolis-based headquarters of Brigadier General Orlando B. Willcox. Burnside placed General Willcox in charge of defending the capitol city from a possible attack by the Confederate cavalrymen. Willcox would also coordinate the Indiana troops to stop Morgan's advance or drive him out of the state. The task of intercepting the raiders before they could escape to Kentucky or, even worse, enter into Ohio would ultimately result in a fruitless effort from the Union general.

On the morning of July 10, Morgan's division marched north to Salem, Indiana, where it captured the town and its home guard without firing a shot. After the raiders cleaned out Salem's stores and burned the Louisville, New Albany & Chicago Railroad depot and bridges, they moved out in the direction of Vienna around 2 p.m. Morgan sent a large detachment toward Seymour to destroy tracks and bridges along the Ohio & Mississippi Railroad, while the main column continued due east. The Confederates arrived late that afternoon in Vienna, where the same fate that had befallen Salem awaited this railroad town. Morgan continued his push eastward through the Hoosier State and encamped at Lexington. Although General Willcox could not pinpoint Morgan's whereabouts, Hobson's men made good progress that day; the bluecoats from Kentucky reached Salem in the evening, only seven hours after the raiders had departed.

At dawn the next day, the Rebel raiders rode north to Paris, Indiana, and then to Vernon. Morgan also sent a squad south toward Madison to make a feint. This maneuver caused the desired effect of raising an alarm such that Madison's militia stayed to protect the city. On the way to Vernon, the raiders foraged for food and drink from the farmhouses, pilfered supplies from the stores and taverns, and traded broken horses for new ones. The men were averaging twenty-one hours a day in the saddle and forty miles between camps, all under a blazing July sun. The best horses normally broke down after about twenty miles of continuous riding, but the clumsy workhorses often went lame quicker. Consequently, Morgan's men were leaving a trail of half-dead or lame horses in their wake, which placed Hobson's men at a disadvantage. The Union cavalrymen also had to forage horses from the citizens in order to keep up with Morgan's incredible pace. In the end, the Hoosiers living along the raid path were pleased with neither their enemy in gray nor their saviors in blue.

Introduction

When Morgan's scouts arrived at Vernon, they discovered more than 1,000 militiamen and regular troops positioned along the Muscatatuck River, south of the town. Under a flag of truce, Morgan called for the Union commander, Brigadier General John Love, to surrender his force and the town, or face annihilation from Morgan's division. Love refused the offer. Knowing that Hobson was gaining on him, Morgan decided to back away from this potential fight. He turned his men southeast toward Dupont, where they arrived around 11 p.m. This withdrawal cost Morgan valuable time. Hobson's division encamped the same evening at Lexington, located only seventeen miles southwest of Dupont. Morgan did not realize that by retreating to Dupont he had shortened the gap between himself and his Union adversary.

At 3 a.m. on Sunday, July 12, 1863, Morgan's men left their camp at Dupont and traveled northeast through Bryantsburg toward Versailles. At Versailles, the general convinced Colonel James Cravens and his 300 home guards to surrender without a shot. Morgan's men did not stay long. After confiscating the horses and provisions they needed, the men rode northeast through Pierceville, Milan, and Clinton. They ended their long day in the saddle at the Ferris Schoolhouse, two miles south of Sunman, just as Hobson's division stopped for the night near Versailles. A train loaded with 2,500 Union soldiers under the overall command of Major General Lew Wallace, the future author of *Ben Hur* and the destined captor of Billy the Kid, unwittingly sat idle all night on a side track at Sunman.

Burnside received confirmation on July 12 that the raiders had passed through Versailles. He realized then that Morgan was heading toward Ohio. Around 1 p.m., Burnside telegraphed Ohio Governor David Tod to request militia to defend Cincinnati, and soon afterward, the general declared martial law to be imposed on the seventh largest city in the United States. Tod followed up Burnside's order with a call out to the Ohio militia.

Before dawn on a relatively cool July 13, Morgan ordered boots and saddles to be sounded. The exhausted men pulled themselves up onto their horses and urged them forward. Little did these men know that they had started on the longest continuous march of a cavalry division within enemy territory in American military history. The raiders trotted eastward through Hubbell's Corner, New Alsace, Dover, and Logan's Crossroads before reaching West Harrison, Indiana, which sits astride the Indiana-Ohio border eighteen miles east of the Ferris Schoolhouse. Along the way, the raiders destroyed some tracks, trestles, and bridges of the Indianapolis, Lawrenceburg & Cincinnati Railroad. Looking over his shoulder, General Morgan could plainly see the dust cloud churned up by Hobson's column several miles to the rear. The Union cavalry were only five hours behind the Confederates.

Morgan's scouts galloped over the Whitewater River Bridge south of Harrison, Ohio, just before noon. Morgan's division, now reduced to about 2,000 men, had covered 186 miles since the crossing of the Ohio River. The people of Indiana breathed a sigh of relief when they learned of Morgan's departure from their borders. The raiders returned the sentiment. They were happy to be leaving the Hoosier State, whose citizens had shown more resistance than the Rebels had expected. The raiders did not realize how much worse it would be for them in the Buckeye State.

Chapter One
HARRISON TO CAMP DENNISON

Major General Ambrose Burnside

Ohio Governor David Tod

Sunday, July 12, 1863

Over the course of the prior week, frightening rumors and stories spread across Ohio about Morgan's Raiders' rampage through Indiana. During Brigadier General John Hunt Morgan's last day in Indiana, the Department of the Ohio commander, Major General Ambrose E. Burnside, declared martial law in Cincinnati. Governor David Tod called out the Ohio militia. Ohio was preparing to welcome her uninvited visitors from Dixie.

If Morgan thought he had received a cool reception in Indiana, he would find Ohio even less receptive to the raiders. During their drive across Ohio, his soldiers were dodging militiamen in front of them while racing to escape the Union cavalry close at their heels.

Monday, July 13, 1863

With the enemy at their doorstep, the citizens of Harrison prepared for the worst. They hid their valuables in clever places, such as in gardens or under floorboards. Some led their horses deep into the woods in hopes that the raiders would not search for them there. The townsfolk closed up their shops, drew the shutters on their windows, locked their doors, and waited.

We will begin the Ohio raid in Indiana. Leave Harrison, going south on South State Street. Cross the Whitewater River Bridge; turn right on North Dearborn Road and stop. As the raiders followed North Dearborn Road down the hill on the left, Ohio lay before them. The scene was described by Private Curtis Burke, of Company B, 14th Kentucky Cavalry:

> We were on a high range of hills still in Indiana. The road led to the right down the side of the hill. At the foot of the hills run the Whitewater River and a canal. Beyond was the city of Harrison and a large rich valley-like strip of bottom land, which was cultivated mostly in corn. The finest of the season that I had seen. The scenery would make a splendid picture for an artist. As we wound our way to the bottom of the hill I looked up and back at our long string of horsemen displayed against the face of the hill and felt

proud of them. We crossed the river and canal bridge and quietly entered the city.

Turn around. There is an **Indiana Morgan Trail Marker** on the right. Reset your odometer; turn left on South State Street toward Harrison.

The wooden covered bridge burned by Colonel Roy S. Cluke's rear guard was located upstream, 360 yards from the center pier of today's State Street Bridge over the Whitewater River.

In 1863, the water level would have been higher. Approximately 100 yards downstream of the present-day bridge, the river was dammed to form a pool in which the Whitewater Canal boats crossed the river.

At the time of the raid, the Whitewater Canal ran along the south side of the river, and the Cincinnati-Whitewater Canal followed the north side. The covered bridge acted as a towpath connecting both canals. Because the advent of railroad transportation had made canal usage around Cincinnati unprofitable, both canals were in disuse by the Civil War.

The canal on the south riverbank was washed away by floods in the late 1800s, leaving no trace of it in this immediate area. On the north bank, the towpath of the canal was converted into a railroad embankment, while the rest of the canal was leveled. Remnants of both canals still exist at various spots upstream and downstream of Harrison.

As the first of the pursuing Union cavalry started down the hill, they could see the steam rising from the burning bridge that had fallen into the river. It would be hours before Union Brigadier General Edward H. Hobson's troops were able to complete the crossing using nearby fords. Consequently, Hobson and his exhausted men were forced to spend the night in Harrison. Many soldiers found rooms at the hotels in town or in the homes of generous citizens, but most simply fell asleep in the streets.

Drive across the bridge and the railroad. The Cincinnati-Whitewater Canal channel was located just beyond the railroad. There is a **Whitewater Canal Historical Marker** on the left.

Continue into West Harrison on South State Street. The original road lay off to the left; it followed the present-day railroad bed, which formerly served as the towpath for the canal. Morgan's men came out onto South State Street at Clinker Run Lane, having crossed the area that is now a soccer field.

At 0.5 mile, there is an old two-story, red brick school building on the left side of South State Street. There are two **Indiana Morgan Trail Markers** in front of the former school.

Continue to Mill Street, the next road on the left. The two-story brick house at 102 Mill Street was the Barney Simonson home. Simonson's corncrib provided food for more than 1,500 rebel horses. The corncrib was located a few yards behind the house.

View from the present bridge looking upstream towards the covered bridge site, located at the river bend on the right. Stone abutment on the left is from a post-Civil War span.

Barney Simonson house (c. 1830)

Continue 0.3 mile. The last **Indiana Morgan Stone Marker** is on the southwest corner of State Street and Harrison Avenue.

Turn right onto Harrison Avenue (Market Street in 1863) and park. In the next several blocks, there are a number of raid-related buildings and the first of the Ohio Morgan Trail markers.

Shortly before noon, Morgan's troops, led by Colonel Basil W. Duke's 2nd Kentucky Cavalry, entered Ohio. Duke's memoirs claim that Morgan entered Ohio with approximately 2,000 men. This number did not include the slaves who were acting as personal servants and teamsters.

Note: A recently published book by Drs. Elizabeth and Dwight G. Watkins suggests Morgan's Division contained more than 3,000 men when they entered the state. Other researchers reviewing this work feel that number is inflated because some of the men's names were listed twice or, in some cases, even three times.

William C. Vincent's bakery was located at 112 Harrison Avenue. The raiders offered to pay for their purchase of $64.80 in baked goods with worthless Confederate scrip. Vincent later filed a claim for his losses.

The Fischer Block, located at 118–122 Harrison Avenue, was erected in 1888. In 1863, Frederick Fischer's clothing and leather goods store occupied the same site. Fischer, a German immigrant, founded his leather business in 1848. He lost $86 worth of shoes, boots, leather, and tools to the raiders.

Following the Civil War, Frederick Fischer gave the business to his son, John. Frederick was severely burned in an 1878 explosion at the town hall.

While in Harrison, Morgan used the American House Hotel as his headquarters (third floor, third and fourth windows from the left). The American House attendants cooked 312 meals for Morgan's men. The building still stands at 130–134 Harrison Avenue. The bricks of the original section are lighter colored.

General John Morgan marched east along this road on Monday, July 13, 1863, in his raid across southern Indiana.

William C. Vincent's bakery

Fischer's post-war store (c. 1888)

HARRISON TO CAMP DENNISON

An 1889 addition can be seen to the right of and above the older portion of the building.

American House Hotel (c. 1820)

When General Hobson arrived, he established his headquarters in the same building. The hotel cook served an even larger number of meals to the Union troopers. The American House also provided many bushels of feed to the horses of both armies.

The raiders appropriated horses from stables, carriages, omnibuses, and hitching posts, while they left their jaded mounts roaming the streets of Harrison.

Continue one block to Walnut Street. The Harrison Fire Department is on the southeast corner.

JOHN HUNT MORGAN HERITAGE TRAIL INTERPRETIVE SIGN #1

The present-day firehouse occupies the site of the 1863 Market House. The building housed Abram Clark's post office and Robert A. Keen's store. The raiders stole Clark's postage stamps and went through the mail, taking an undetermined amount of money. During the Civil War, it was common practice to include cash in letters. Keen lost boots and shoes to the raiders.

While in Harrison, George A. "Lightning" Ellsworth, Morgan's wizard of the telegraph, tapped out misleading messages on the telegraph in Abram Clark's post office. Ellsworth reported that Morgan was headed to Hamilton. He also sent wires that Morgan was attacking Cincinnati.

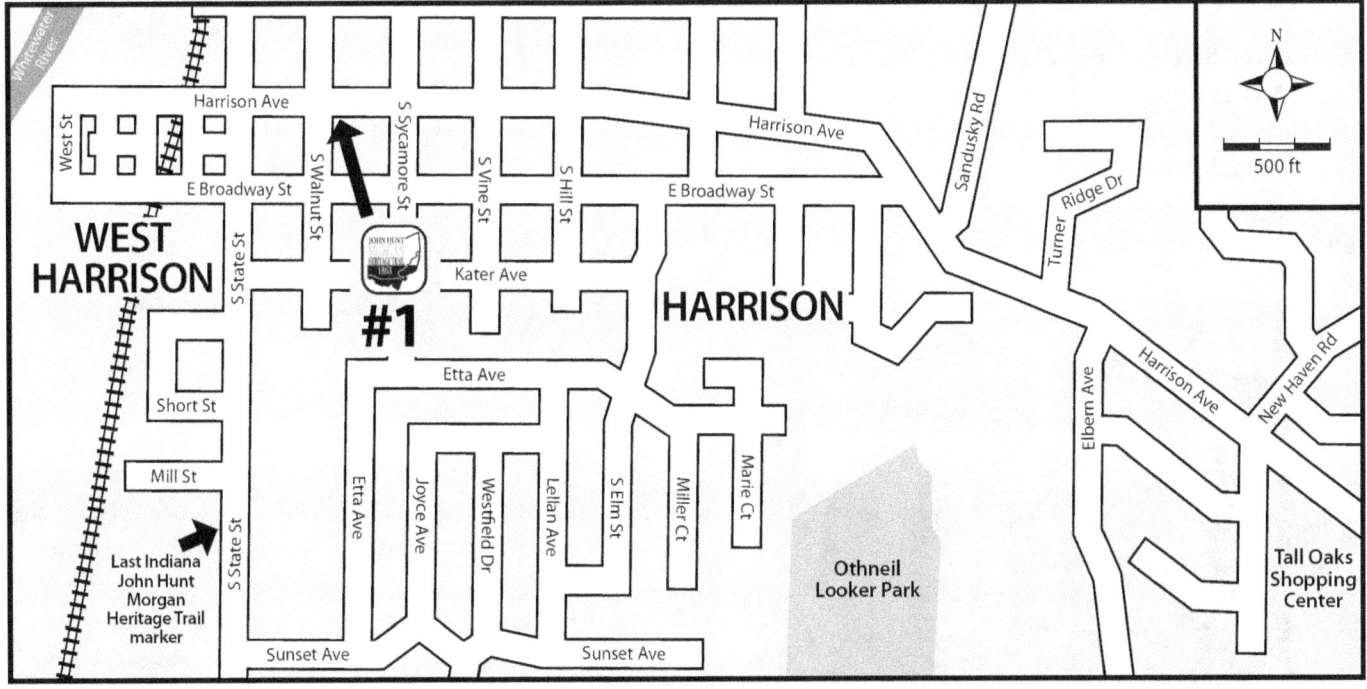
John Hunt Morgan Heritage Trail Interpretive sign #1 map

"Lightning" Ellsworth

Harrison citizens being held as prisoners were allowed to overhear that Morgan intended to attack Cincinnati. They spread the word upon their release. As a result, General Ambrose Burnside's downtown Cincinnati headquarters was in a state of total confusion.

George Becker's grocery store occupied the building at 230-236 Harrison Avenue. Becker was not in the store when the raiders arrived. They broke into the business and stole $91 in merchandise. Meanwhile, another group of Morgan's soldiers met Becker on the road and stole his watch and cash.

George Becker's grocery store.

Benedict Hetterick operated a tavern in the building on the northeast corner of Harrison Avenue and Sycamore Street, at 301 Harrison Avenue. He claimed to have lost $42 worth of liquor and $14 worth of food to the raiders. He was reimbursed for the food but not for the liquor. Claims commissions in both Indiana and Ohio failed to award liquor claims. He also received compensation for the fifty bushels of corn confiscated by the Union cavalry.

Benedict Hetterick's tavern

Turn right on Sycamore Street and walk one block to Broadway. Frederick Weilemann's dry goods store occupied the brick building on the southeast corner, at 300 East Broadway. Weilemann lived next door at 304 East Broadway.

Frederick Weilemann's dry goods store

Weilemann provided eight bushels of corn for the Union cavalry horses and meals for twenty-six of Hobson's men. He received $7 in payment from the state.

Christian Loos operated a store and meat market. He lived at 401 East Broadway, at the northeast corner of Broadway and Vine. The raiders stole Loos's horse

HARRISON TO CAMP DENNISON

Christian Loos's house (c. 1860)

and emptied his whiskey barrel. They also took his cigars.

Many stores were looted; all manner of merchandise was taken. Bolts of cloth were frequently taken from stores in Indiana and Ohio. The raiders would tie one end of the bolts to their saddles, leaving the cloth to stream out behind them as they rode. They would then cut it away, only to pick up another bolt in the next town. In many instances, frugal women retrieved the cloth, washed it, and used it to outfit their families.

Morgan collected $1,000 from each of Harrison's three mills and its distillery. Mill owners across three states bought Morgan's costly insurance rather than watch their property go up in flames.

When leaving Harrison, Morgan sent two scouts dressed in farm clothes into Cincinnati. They were Captain Sam Burk Taylor and his cousin, 2nd Lieutenant John W. McLean (both serving with Company E, 10th Kentucky Cavalry). The men were nephews of President Zachary Taylor. Both men were familiar with the area, having lived in Cincinnati at one time. Their mission was to determine the strength and readiness of Union forces in the city. The scouts were to rejoin the main column at Bevis on the Colerain Pike.

The raiders cut the telegraph wires about 2:30 p.m., as they were leaving Harrison. Morgan's rear guard left town by 5 p.m., about an hour before Hobson's advance guard reached the smoldering ruins of the Whitewater River covered bridge. However, Colonel Lawrence S. Shuler's mounted 103rd Indiana Militia reached the burning bridge just in time to exchange shots with Morgan's bridge-burners. Shuler occupied Harrison until Hobson's troops arrived.

Return to your car. Continue on Harrison Avenue for 0.9 mile to New Haven Road.

In a feint toward Cincinnati, a contingent of approximately 500 raiders continued on Harrison Pike to Miamitown. There, they were to burn the bridge across the Great Miami River. *See Appendix A Alternate: Miamitown Feint Toward Cincinnati.*

While still in the Harrison area, the raiders met a funeral procession, which they stopped. The drivers of the carriages asked for permission to continue to the cemetery, after which they would return and surrender their horses. The raiders agreed; however, the drivers changed their minds and hurried home by another route.

Turn left onto New Haven Road and follow Morgan's main column. This segment of New Haven Road was rerouted when Interstate 74 was built. The 1863 road was in the shopping area to the right.

The raiders fanned out as they moved toward New Haven. Many of the men were searching for horses to replace their jaded mounts.

Go 1.4 miles to Baughman Road. Morgan's main column continued straight on New Haven Road. You may opt to take the New Haven alternate. It passes buildings of the Whitewater Shaker Community and a number of farms that incurred losses during the raid. *See Appendix C Alternate: New Haven Area.*

Raid claimants lived in the Oyler house (c. 1866)

Continue 0.6 mile on New Haven Road; the house on the left, at 9848 New Haven Road, was built after the war by George G. and John G. Oyler. John filed a claim for his losses during the raid; it included a watch, a pistol, clothing, jewelry, provisions, grain, and $50 cash.

It is 0.9 mile to Mt. Hope Road. Basil Duke placed his artillery near the intersection of New Haven Road and Mt. Hope Road. The guns were to protect his rear from a possible Union attack that never materialized.

A small flanking contingent rode south on Mt. Hope Road until it reached the Great Miami River. The soldiers raided many farms along the way. At the river, they turned north toward New Baltimore to rejoin Morgan's main column.

Drive 0.3 mile on New Haven Road. David H. Pottenger lived in the house on the left at 9220 New Haven Road. During the summer, the view of the house may be partially obscured by trees. Pottenger filed a claim for damages to a horse that was stolen, but later recovered, and for the loss of ten bushels of corn.

David H. Pottenger house (c. 1850)

Continue 0.3 mile to New Haven and bear right onto New Haven Road at the "Y" intersection with Oxford Road. The home of Doctor Samuel Gwaltney was located in the point of the "Y." It was reported that Morgan, Basil Duke, and other officers held a conference there. The house was razed in 1980. The raiders were in New Haven about 4 p.m.

The town of New Haven existed in 1863, but the area was designated as Preston Post Office. All raid claims from the area are filed under Preston Post Office.

A small company of raiders turned north from New Haven in a feint designed to convince Burnside that Morgan was headed to Hamilton. After traveling about eight miles, the raiders reached Venice (Ross Post Office), in Butler County. The raiders failed to burn the Great Miami River Bridge there. Near Venice at Cliptown, a riverside woolen factory contracted to make Union uniforms escaped the raiders' attention.

During this portion of the raid, Morgan's main column could use only improved roads, because the column included heavy artillery pieces, supply wagons, and ambulances. Following the loss of their guns and wagons at the Battle of Buffington Island on July 19, the raiders were able to leave the roads. They frequently rode cross-country and sometimes followed streambeds.

After going 2.4 miles, you will cross Paddy's Run. Some of the raiders rode north on Paddy's Run Road. Morgan's men also visited a number of nearby farms located along the stream to the south.

From Paddy's Run, it is 0.4 mile to SR 128 (Hamilton-Cleves Pike).

Moving south from Venice on the Hamilton-Cleves Pike, the men who had made the feint on Hamilton rejoined the main force here.

While at Venice, the rebels captured farmer James Poole who was in town on business. He was forced to serve as Morgan's guide to Bevis. At Bevis, the raiders released Poole, but kept his horse.

Some of the raiders, who had ridden through Miamitown, also rejoined the main force at this intersection.

Continue on the New Haven Road to New Baltimore; at 1.1 miles look to the right. This is Locust Street; in 1863, it was the approach to a covered bridge across the Great Miami River. A metal bridge spanning the site was closed in 2001 and has since been removed. A monument at the end of Locust Street tells about the truss bridge built in 1914, which occupied the same site as the covered bridge.

The 1914 bridge over the Great Miami River at New Baltimore has been removed.

It was about 5:30 p.m. on July 13 when the raiders reached New Baltimore.

According to eyewitness accounts, the Confederates stopped at the hickory pole in New Baltimore and hurrahed for campaigning Ohio gubernatorial candidate Clement Vallandigham. Hickory poles were erected in communities to serve as gathering sites for political rallies and events. Vallandigham was a popular Peace Democrat who had been ordered to be arrested and secretly transported to Tennessee by President Abraham Lincoln. From there, Vallandigham made his way to Canada where he continued his campaign for governor of Ohio. One of the raiders told the citizens, "If Old Abe Lincoln doesn't let Vallandigham come home soon, we will bring him back to Ohio."

After crossing the river, the Confederates burned the covered bridge. The 410-foot bridge was almost new and valued at more than $8,000. Morgan intended to burn three bridges across the Great Miami River in an attempt to delay the pursuing Union troops. The raiders failed, however, to destroy both the Miamitown and Venice spans.

Continue 0.2 mile on New Haven Road and turn right onto relocated Blue Rock Road. As you cross the new bridge, look to the right and the site of the old bridge.

At 0.3 mile, you cross East Miami River Road. James Radcliff lived within sight of the bridge in the house at the corner on the left. Morgan's men broke both of his guns to "prevent his bushwhacking the bridge burners." There is a written account that he was taken prisoner.

James M. Radcliff house (c. 1850)

Go 1.1 miles to a "Y," and stay on Blue Rock Road as it bears right.

Continue 1.2 miles and turn right on Blue Rock Hill Road. This was the original road; it continued straight to Schwing's Corner and a junction with Springdale Road. In 1863, Springdale Road was known as the Springfield-Taylors Creek Road.

Immediately on the left, at 5852 Blue Rock Hill Road, is the Jacob Westermann Store. Morgan's men looted the store, taking food and liquor.

Jacob Westermann store (c. 1840)

Turn around and return to the relocated Blue Rock Road. Turn right and go 0.5 mile. Turn left on the Springdale-Blue Rock Connector (just beyond the freeway). Go 0.2 mile to Springdale Road. Turn right on Springdale Road; then go 1.8 miles to Colerain Avenue (US 27).

As you approach the intersection with Colerain Avenue, note the house on the left at 3672 Springdale Road; it is across the road from the mall. This was the home of Mrs. Mary Hardin; she lost a horse, a blanket, and a whip to the raiders.

Mrs. Mary Hardin house (c. 1845)

The town of Bevis (the area also known as Bevis Post Office) was located just 0.25 mile north of the intersection. It had been chosen as the meeting site for the scattered troops before they would approach the railroad at Glendale.

Cross Colerain Avenue and go less than 0.1 mile. Park in the parking lot at the entrance to the shopping center on the right.

JOHN HUNT MORGAN HERITAGE TRAIL INTERPRETIVE SIGN #2

The nearby shopping complex, just south of the marker, stands on the site of the Methodist Meeting Grounds where Morgan's men rested.

This was also the location of Camp Colerain, a Union recruiting camp in the early part of the Civil War. Part of the 39th Ohio Volunteer Infantry (OVI) was formed here. Also, soldiers of the 28th Ohio Infantry, 1st Kentucky (U.S.) Infantry, and 2nd Kentucky (U.S.) Infantry regiments camped here for a brief period. The camp was abandoned sometime in August 1861. The campsite was part of the Martin Bevis farm.

While Morgan's main column rested, the detachment sent to Miamitown arrived. They had been thwarted in their attempt to burn the bridge there by a small force of Union scouts and militia serving under Major Bill Raney.

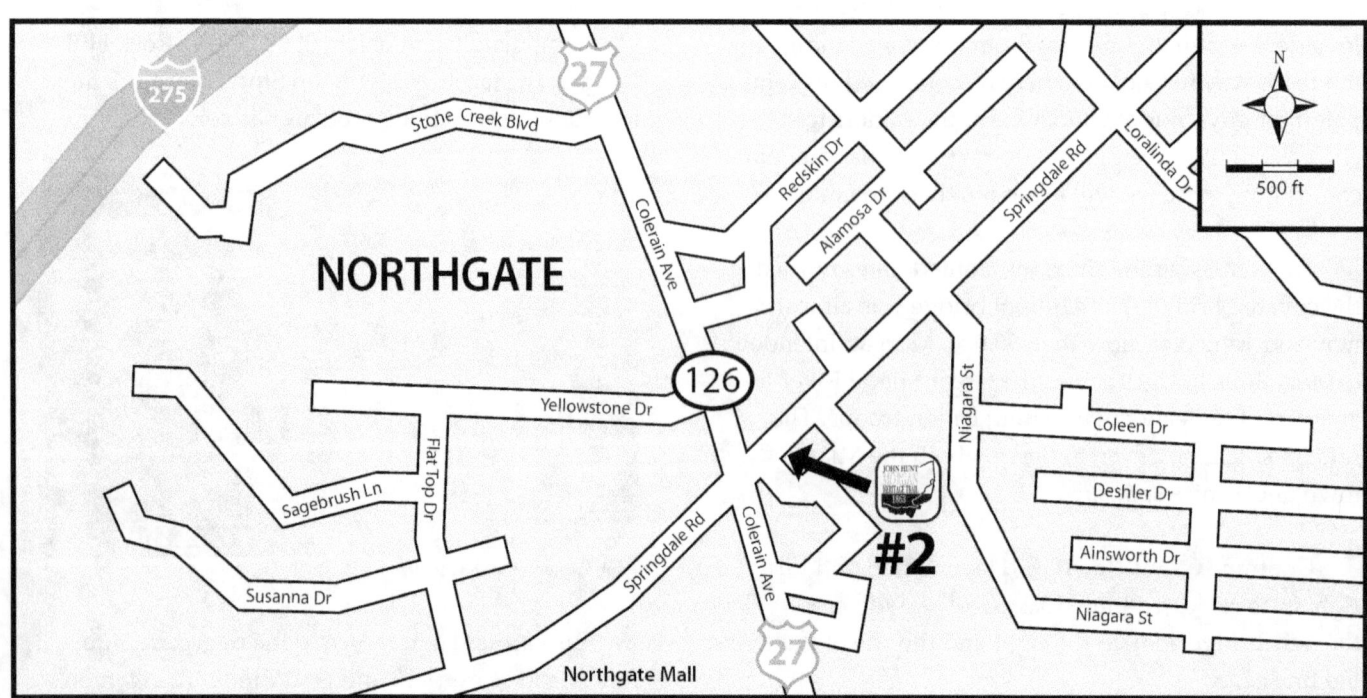

John Hunt Morgan Heritage Trail Interpretive sign #2 map

As Morgan led the column forward, Colonel Adam "Stovepipe" Johnson stayed behind to await the arrival of scouts Taylor and McLean. They arrived at the Meeting Grounds about 9:30 p.m., bringing word that the city was in a state of confusion and that it appeared no advance of Union troops against the raiders would occur that evening. With this information in hand, Johnson and Taylor rejoined Morgan at the head of the column. McLean was sent west to find Basil Duke's brigade and direct it to Bevis.

Among the many horses stolen in the Bevis community, Morgan's soldiers took three from Martin Bevis and two from Dr. John P. Waterhouse. The rebels overlooked the seventeen horses in James Bevis's nearby stable.

Drive 2.2 miles on Springdale Road and cross Hamilton Avenue (US 127). Go 0.1 mile to Burlington Road (the original Hamilton Pike). You are in New Burlington (also known as Transit Post Office).

The Hein Summe store was located in the building on the southeast corner of Springdale Road and Burlington Road. To appease one thirsty young rebel, Mrs. Summe filled the raider's canteen with whiskey from her jug in the house. By doing so, she hoped to prevent the man from finding the two barrels in the barn. She asked the soldier to keep quiet about the whiskey, which he said he would. She was skeptical, but the man kept his promise.

While in New Burlington, Morgan stopped at the home of Colonel J. Williamson. He was absent when Morgan arrived. His wife reported that Morgan asked for a light, which he used while studying a detailed Hamilton County map. Mrs. Williamson said that many of the rebel officers were riding in buggies, and some of them had female companions.

After leaving New Burlington, the raiders swung north through present-day Forest Park and Springdale.

Many of Hobson's pursuing force continued east, taking a more direct route to Glendale. They passed through what is now the Greenhills area. *See Appendix D Alternate: Greenhills Route.*

To follow Morgan's column, reset your odometer at the stop sign in New Burlington. Continue 0.6 mile on Springdale Road to Mill Road. The New Burlington Church site and Cemetery are located on the left. The church was razed in 2013. Many of the raiders rested their horses in the churchyard.

New Burlington Church & Cemetery (c. 1840)

The moonless night was very dark, making it difficult for the raiders to see. Morgan had ordered no torches be lit along the line for fear of being spotted by enemy troops. The advance raiders built a small bonfire in the cemetery to serve as a beacon and indicator for the cavalry to turn north on Mill Road.

Duke's account includes a vivid description of the problems encountered during this portion of the raid. His brigade groped its way through the dark, trying to follow Johnson's brigade. Tracking was a "nightmare."

Hein Summe store (c. 1850)

A large gap between the two brigades occurred when the men of Cluke's regiment riding at the rear of Johnson's brigade straggled and halted frequently.

Turn left on Mill Road and drive 0.3 mile. Cyrus Chadwick's house is on the left, at 10599 Mill Road. Chadwick and a neighbor, Oliver Brackett, claimed to have met Morgan on the road during the night. Chadwick lost a horse, saddle, and bridle to the raiders.

Cyrus Chadwick house (c. 1850)

Although a number of farmers in this area filed claims for horses and feed taken during the raid, Chadwick's house is one of the few surviving raid-related homes in the area.

Drive 1.6 miles to Mandarin Drive; turn right and go 0.1 mile. The old road continued straight to Kemper Road; it now dead ends. Turn left on Norbourne Drive, go 0.1 mile, and then turn right on SR 126 (West Kemper Road).

Tuesday, July 14, 1863

Continue on Kemper Road for 2.9 miles to Springdale. During the Civil War, Springdale was known as Springfield or Springdale Post Office.

As you approach Springdale, note the subdivisions on the right side of Kemper Road, in the area bounded by Kenn Road and Southland Road. They occupy the site of Charles Leggatt's farm, where Col. Adam Johnson halted his rear guard to allow Col. Basil Duke's brigade to catch up and close the gap that had formed between the columns during the night march. Duke's scouts, led by Major Theophilus Steele, made contact with Johnson's men at the farm around 1:30 a.m.

In Springdale, the butcher, John Watson, refused to make breakfast for the raiders with the excuse that he had no fire. He was told that it might be better for him to make the fire, because if the raiders made it, he might have trouble putting it out. He obliged. A witness reported that Morgan looked worn-out and aloof as he sat down for a brief rest. His brother, Dick Morgan, took a short nap in the butcher's bedroom.

Turn right on SR 4 (Springfield Pike). An **Ohio Historical Marker** describing Morgan's raid here is located on the southeast corner of Kemper Road and SR 4.

Go 0.4 mile to the Old St. Mary's Cemetery (Old Presbyterian Cemetery) at Springfield Pike and Cameron Road. Two exhausted raiders fell asleep in the cemetery. They were roused and taken prisoner in the morning by local citizens armed with rifles.

Old St. Mary's Cemetery in Springdale

Continue 0.6 mile on SR 4 to Sharon Road. Before turning left onto Sharon Road, note the Glenview Golf Course across Sharon Road on the right side of SR 4. The golf course occupies land that was part of the Jacob Riddle farm. The section of Sharon Road to the right did not exist at the time of the raid.

The Riddle farmhouse is gone. The remaining outbuildings were torn down in the last few years. One of Riddle's horses was taken by the raiders and one was confiscated by the Union cavalry.

HARRISON TO CAMP DENNISON

Jacob Riddle farm outbuildings (c. 1850)

The white frame depot of 1863 burned in 1879.

Turn left on Sharon Road and go 1.0 mile. Just before the old Cincinnati, Hamilton, and Dayton Railroad, turn right on Greenville Avenue toward the depot and historic Glendale square. Park at the depot.

JOHN HUNT MORGAN HERITAGE TRAIL INTERPRETIVE SIGN #3

The original white frame railroad depot burned in 1879. The Glendale Heritage Preservation Society has a small museum and gift shop located in the 1880 depot. It is open Thursday and Saturday from 11 a.m. to 3 p.m. Web site: *http://www.glendalemuseum.com/museum.html*.

The raiders passed through Glendale between 2 and 5 a.m. on Tuesday morning. During his ride around Cincinnati, Morgan's greatest fear was that Burnside would move Union troops from downtown Cincinnati to Glendale by train. Morgan's feint to Hamilton had worked; the Union troops had passed through en route to Hamilton, a half-hour earlier.

The rebels damaged the railroad, tearing up rails. "Lightning" Ellsworth used the Glendale railroad telegraph office in the depot to send out more misleading wires.

Side Note: Glendale, incorporated in 1855, is known as the first planned railroad commuter

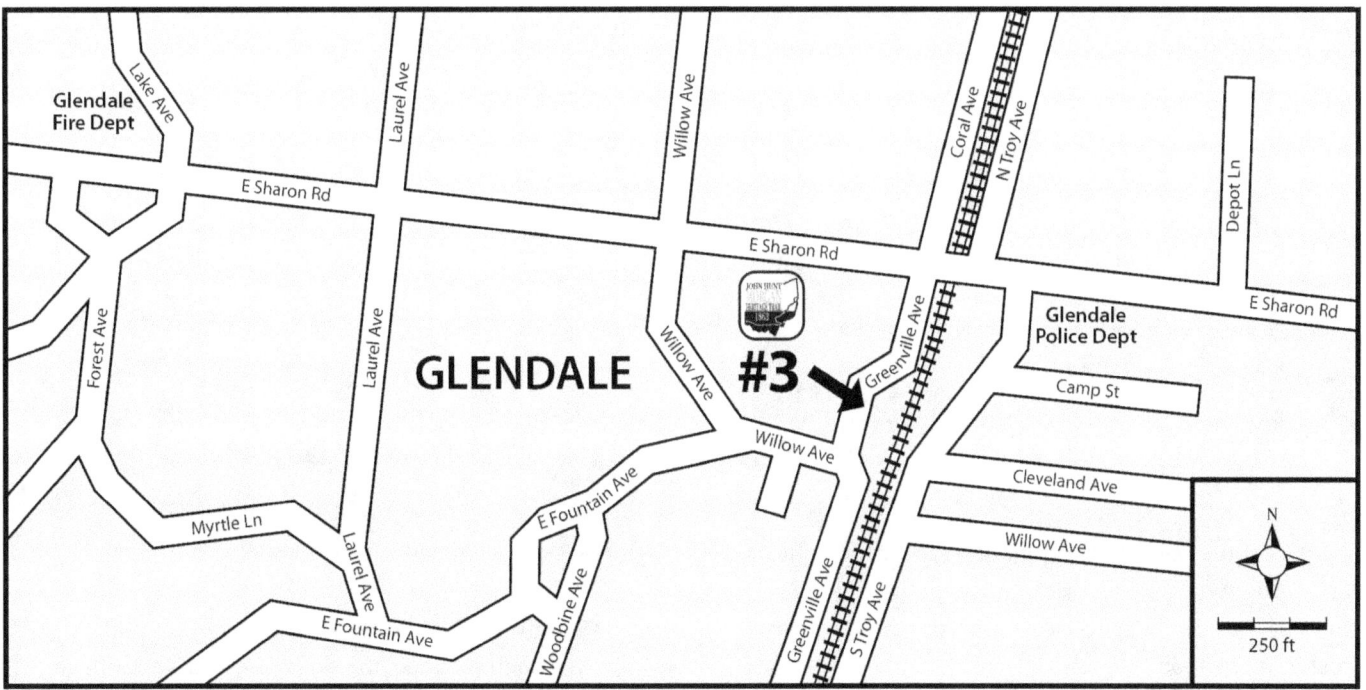

John Hunt Morgan Heritage Trail Interpretive sign #3 map

town in the country. Wealthy Cincinnati business and professional men welcomed the opportunity to move their families from the squalid downtown area to this beautiful park-like setting.

Exit Glendale Square from the rear and turn right onto Willow Avenue. Immediately bear left on East Fountain Avenue. There is a small oval park in the middle of Fountain Avenue. The house on the left, at 175 Fountain Avenue, was once the home of Colonel C. W. Moulton; his wife was Major General William T. Sherman's sister.

Keys-Moulton house (c. 1855)

Stay to the right on East Fountain Avenue. At the end of the park, the large house on the right, at 140 East Fountain Avenue, was the home of Judge John R. Wright.

Wright house at 140 Fountain Ave. (c. 1855)

Continue past the Wright house and turn right on Laurel Avenue. The brick house on the right was the Wright's carriage house. It was converted into a residence in 1935.

Wright's carriage house

Two village boys felt sorry for two of the exhausted young raiders. Unknown to Mrs. Wright, the boys hid the soldiers in the Wright's carriage house. When the sympathetic lady discovered them, she fed them until they were able to move on.

A number of other exhausted raiders, who had lain down to sleep by the roadside or straggled away from the main force, were captured. It was reported that Morgan's personal cook, a black man, was among those taken by the local militia near Glendale.

The fourth house on the left, the large white frame structure at 965 Laurel Avenue, was the Anthony Harkness home. Harkness owned a large Cincinnati foundry, famous for building steam engines. The family saved their team of prize carriage horses by hiding them in the smokehouse basement. The smokehouse is the small brick building to the left of the house.

Harkness house (c. 1852) and brick smokehouse

Continue north to the end of the block and Sharon Road. In 1863, the Glendale Female College

HARRISON TO CAMP DENNISON

Glendale Female College

was located on the northwest corner of Laurel Avenue and Sharon Road.

The young ladies remained inside while the raiders rode by and came out later when the Union forces arrived. Union Brigadier General James M. Shackelford wrote, "A host of young ladies who were attending Glendale College, were all out, standing in lines along the streets. In their hands were trays, baskets, dishes, and pitchers, all filled with both the substantials and luxuries of life, with which they served the troopers as they passed through, in their saddles. I never witnessed a lovelier sight."

Reset your odometer before turning right on Sharon Road. Drive 0.7 mile.

Benjamin R. Stevens's house (c. 1860) is on the right, before Glen Meadow Court. The post-Civil War picture shows Benjamin's wife, Jarusha, on the porch and his son Benjamin Jr. in the carriage. The Stevens's farm occupied land on both sides of Sharon Road.

Benjamin R. Stevens's family and farmhouse

Many of the raiders stopped to drink at Stevens's sulfur spring. The spring was across Sharon Road from the house. It was in the area where the sewage treatment plant is now located. In 1863, this area was the eastern outskirts of Glendale.

Stevens filed a claim for a horse, blanket, and bridle stolen, as well as for damages to two mares and his prized stallion, Sir Henry Bacchus. The stallion was valued at $4,000. Stevens informed the men pursuing Morgan that he was offering a reward for the horse's return.

The stallion was ridden by one of the rebel officers for the remainder of the raid. Following Morgan's capture, Captain A. C. Stockton of the 8th Michigan Cavalry recognized the value of the animal. The horse was separated from the mass of jaded mounts and was transported back to the Cincinnati area, where it was eventually recovered by Stevens. Stockton received the $250 reward offered by the horse's owner.

Continue on Sharon Road 0.8 mile to Canal Road. At this point, the bed of the old Miami and Erie Canal lay under Canal Road. The canal was filled in during the 1990s. The waterway was known as the Miami Canal in 1863. It connected Lake Erie at Toledo with the Ohio River at Cincinnati. The raiders burned the Sharon Road Bridge across the canal to delay their pursuers. A well-preserved but overgrown remnant of the canal parallels the western side of Canal Road about one mile north of Sharon Road.

The bridge across Mill Creek is just beyond Canal Road. The raiders also attempted to burn the wooden bridge there. Local residents were able to extinguish the fire before major damage was done.

Go 1.0 mile to the old town of Sharonville (Sharon, or Sharonville Post Office in 1863). The large brick structure, on the northeast corner of Reading and Sharon roads, was the Twelve-Mile House (Sharon Hotel); it was built in 1842.

Twelve-Mile House, built in 1842

Alonzo McGrew house (c. 1860)

JOHN HUNT MORGAN HERITAGE TRAIL INTERPRETIVE SIGN #4

Morgan's vanguard arrived in Sharon about 3 a.m. The Twelve-Mile House served as Morgan's headquarters. Tavern-keeper Christopher Myer was forced to feed Morgan and his staff. The Southern sympathizer provided food, drink, information, and a fresh horse; for his efforts Myer received $200 in "green-backs." Morgan's men raided most of the stables, stores, and kitchens in Sharon.

The Alonzo McGrew house is located several doors north at 11080 Reading Road. McGrew lost a horse and bridle, valued at $150, to the raiders.

Seven hours after the raiders left Sharon, the Union soldiers arrived there.

Safely past the feared railroad at Glendale, Morgan's men divided into two main columns, and these columns split into many small parties. As they fanned out, the raiders looted and took horses to replace their spent mounts. Morgan, riding with Adam Johnson's brigade, turned south toward Reading, while Duke's column moved east. *See Appendix E Alternate: Duke's Column Moved Through Northeastern Suburbs.*

Before leaving Sharon, Morgan and his officers selected Montgomery as their rendezvous point.

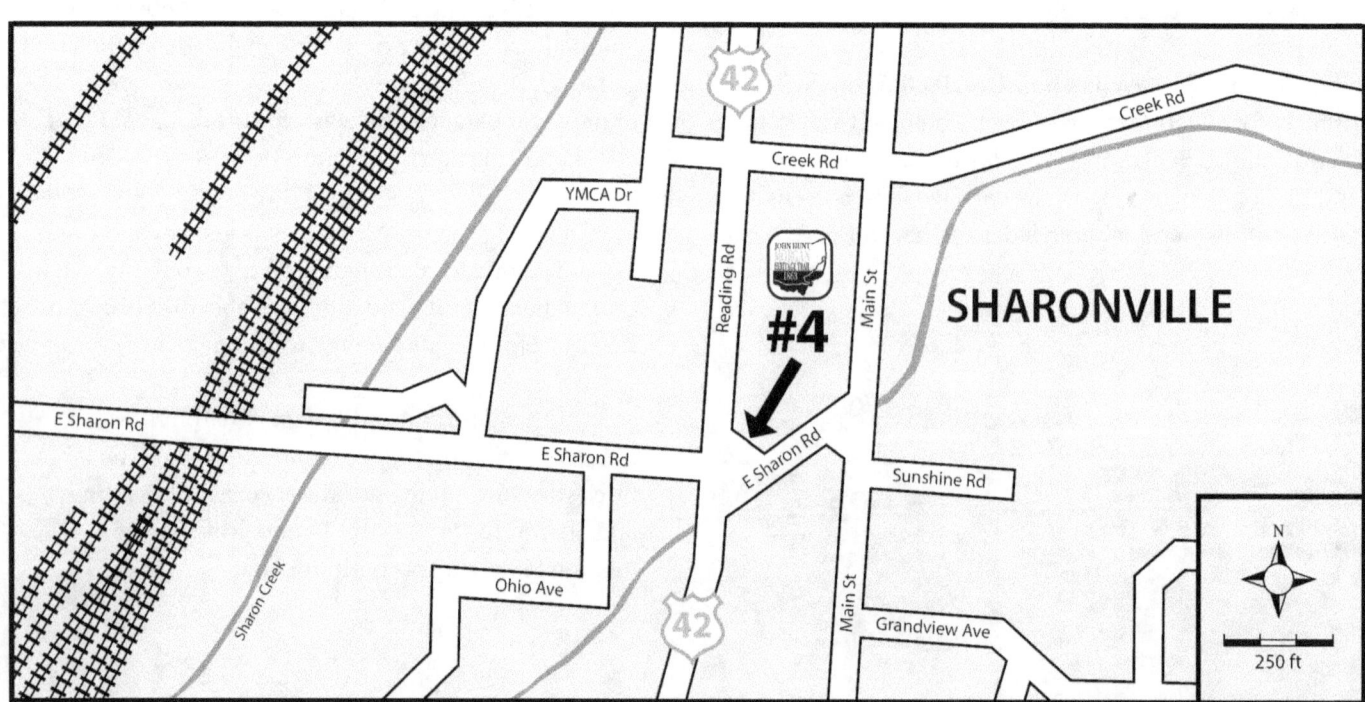
John Hunt Morgan Heritage Trail Interpretive sign #4 map

HARRISON TO CAMP DENNISON

Turn right and travel 1.7 miles south on Reading Road (US 42). Turn left on Gorman Heritage Farm Lane and go 0.1 mile to the Gorman Heritage Farm parking lot. To tour the farm buildings, enter through the museum. The farm's hours are Monday–Friday, 9 a.m.–5 p.m., and Saturday, 9 a.m.–3 p.m. It is open only on weekends during the winter.
Phone: (513) 563-6663;
Web site: *http://www.gormanfarm.org/*.

JOHN HUNT MORGAN HERITAGE TRAIL INTERPRETIVE SIGN #5

The village of Evendale operates the site as a working and educational farm open to the public.

A short trail leads to the house and farm buildings. During the Civil War, the property was owned by George Brown. The house, built from stone quarried on the property, has walls approximately thirty inches thick.

Nearby is the original bank barn, from which Morgan's men stole two horses. Brown later recovered one, but the horse had been harmed by extremely hard use. The State of Ohio allowed Brown's $150 claim for the lost horse, but rejected the $40 claim for damages

George Brown house (c. 1835)

Brown's banked barn (c. 1835). It is the only original barn in Ohio and Indiana raided by Morgan's men that is open to the public.

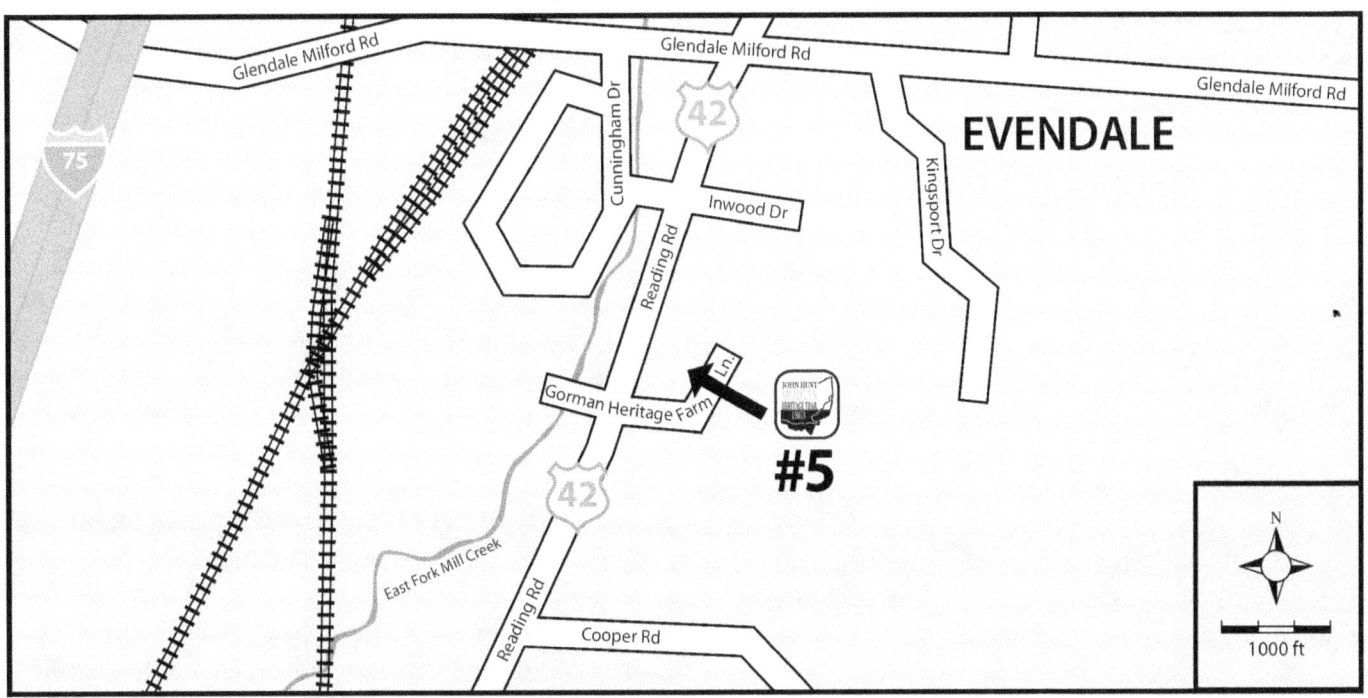
John Hunt Morgan Heritage Trail Interpretive sign #5 map

to the one he recovered.

The Brown family used the lower springhouse to store food and as a source of drinking water. The thirsty and hungry raiders enjoyed both.

Brown's lower spring house

Carpenter's Run Pioneer Cemetery

Return to Reading Road and turn left. Drive 0.4 mile to Cooper Road. Here, the main column turned east. A small company continued south to Reading. *See Appendix F Alternate: Flankers Through Reading.*

Turn left on Cooper Road. Thomas Spooner lived on the northeast corner of Cooper and Reading roads. He was the Internal Revenue Collector for the First District of Ohio. Spooner had received his appointment from President Abraham Lincoln in 1862. Spooner lost two horses to the raiders, but one was recovered before he filed his claim for the loss.

Spooner left an account in which he states it took Morgan's column one and three-quarter hours to pass his estate. He estimated Morgan's force to be 2,000 men. The soldiers were not wearing standard uniforms, and many of them wore linen dusters over their coats. Some of the men had new revolving carbines, while others were armed with sabers and revolvers. The men appeared very much fatigued, and pushed on rapidly in a northeastern direction.

Go 1.8 miles to Plainfield Road. Turn right onto Plainfield Road, passing between the two sections of Carpenter's Run Pioneer Cemetery.

The 1920s school building on the left side of Plainfield Road occupies the site of the log Carpenter's Run Baptist Church built in 1800. The church was dismantled in 1828. An eight-cornered log schoolhouse occupied the site at the time of the Civil War; it was later destroyed by fire. Some of the raiders rested their weary horses in the cemetery and the schoolhouse yard.

Drive 0.5 mile and turn right onto Reed Hartman Highway/Plainfield Road. Go 0.2 mile and turn left onto Hunt Road.

Drive 0.3 mile, round a sharp bend to the left, and turn left into the driveway of the John C. Hunt house.

John C. Hunt house (c. 1861)

JOHN HUNT MORGAN HERITAGE TRAIL INTERPRETIVE SIGN #6

The bricks used in building the John C. Hunt house were made from clay found on the Hunt farm. The lumber was cut from Hunt timber.

HARRISON TO CAMP DENNISON

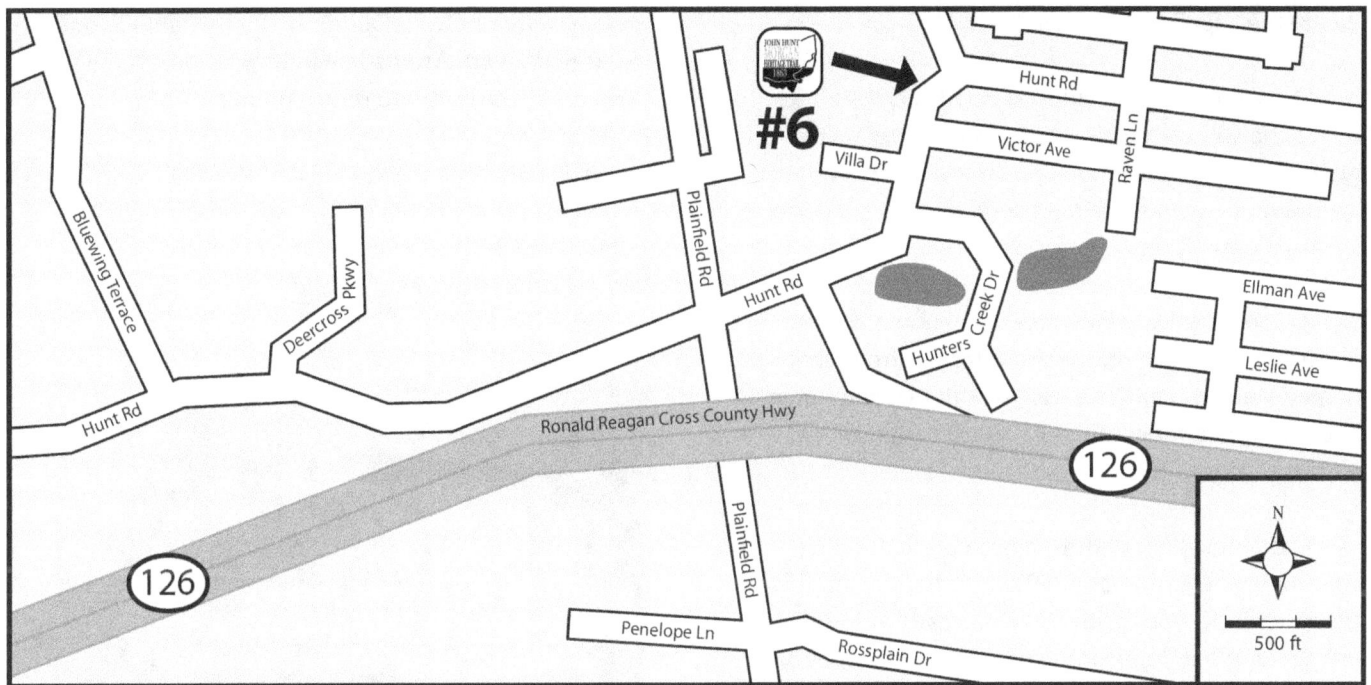

John Hunt Morgan Heritage Trail Interpretive sign #6 map

Ten-year-old Wilson Hunt, standing at an upstairs window, watched as the raiders led his father's six horses from the barn. Two were recovered when the raiders were captured. Hunt filed a $495 claim for the other four.

The house remained in the Hunt family into the twenty-first century, when it was acquired by the city of Blue Ash from Betty Hunt Bell, Wilson Hunt's granddaughter. The house now serves as a Blue Ash museum and meeting facility. It is open by appointment only. Phone: (513) 745-8550; Web site: http://www.blueash.com/content/87/195/2639/305/default.aspx.

*Side Trip to the Conklin House: From the Hunt house driveway, a left turn onto Hunt Road will take you on a loop drive passing the Conklin house. Go 0.4 mile and turn left onto Conklin Avenue. Drive 0.2 mile and turn right. The John T. Conklin house is located at 4658 Cooper Road. Conklin lost a horse valued at $125 to Morgan's men. The house was built by Isaac Conklin, about 1845. The porch was added after the Civil War.

John T. Conklin house (c. 1845)

Continue less than 0.1 mile to Railroad Avenue and turn right. Drive 0.2 mile back to Hunt Road. Turn right and go 0.8 mile to Plainfield Road. Turn left.*

To return to the main route from the Hunt house, turn right onto Hunt Road. Go 0.3 mile to Plainfield Road and turn left.

Drive 0.8 mile to Sycamore Road. We will continue on Plainfield Road as it angles right. After Morgan had breakfast at the Schenck home (described below) he returned to this intersection. His main column turned east on Sycamore Road to Kenwood Road. They rode a short distance south on Kenwood to Kugler Mill Road, where they again turned east.

Drive 0.7 mile on Plainfield Road and turn left onto Schenck Avenue; it is the second street on the left after crossing Galbraith Road. Go one block and turn right onto Lake Avenue. Go one-half block and turn left back onto Schenck Avenue.

In 1863, the Deer Park area was known as East Sycamore. Morgan's guide was a farmer from Sharon named William Landenburgh, whom Morgan's men had made a prisoner after he had exchanged shots with the raiders.

Landenburgh had directed the Confederate column on a circuitous route away from the intended place of rendezvous with Duke's brigade at Montgomery, Ohio. When Johnson's scouts entered East Sycamore a little before 5 a.m., they realized they had been duped. Fortunately for Landenburgh, Morgan did not carry out his threat to kill the guide if Landenburgh led his soldiers astray. Instead, Morgan forced the man to ride with them until they crossed the Little Miami River, at which time Morgan released him unharmed and took his horse. Union troops led by Captain J. Piatt later seized Landenburgh for suspicion of being a rebel. Piatt took the farmer to the headquarters of the commander of Camp Dennison, Lieutenant Colonel George W. Neff. After some interrogation, Neff allowed Landenburgh to return home.

The second house on the left, at 4208 Schenck Avenue, was the home of a prosperous farmer, John Schenck. The Schenck farm extended north, almost back to Sycamore Road.

John Schenck house (c. 1806)

JOHN HUNT MORGAN HERITAGE TRAIL INTERPRETIVE SIGN #7

Morgan had Tuesday morning breakfast at the Schenck house. During Morgan's visit the Schencks successfully hid their horses in the parlor.

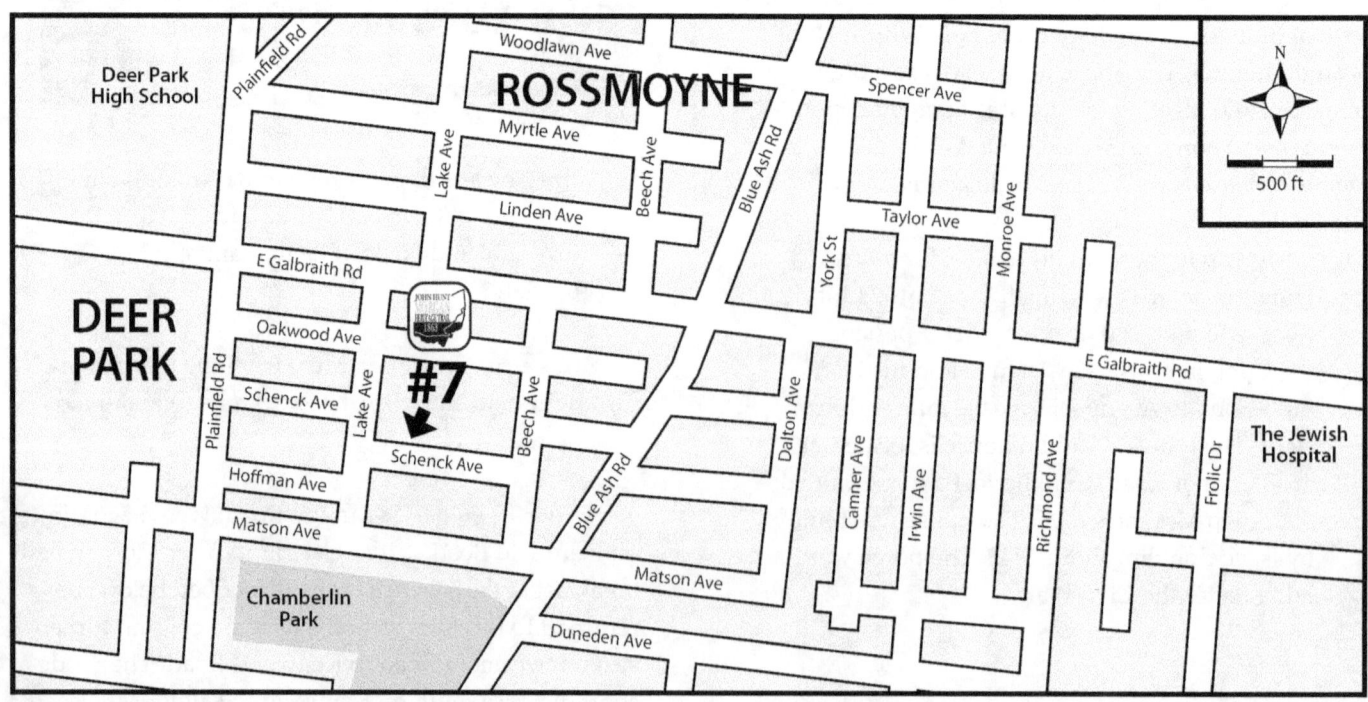

John Hunt Morgan Heritage Trail Interpretive sign #7 map

HARRISON TO CAMP DENNISON

It was also reported that Schenck hid members of the John Henry Thompson family. The family lived on Schenck property just south of Sycamore Road, in what would become known as the Rossmoyne community. John and his wife, Clara Jane, were ex-slaves from Virginia. Their master had transported them to Kentucky in the 1850s. The couple married and bore several children there, before the family escaped to Ohio sometime between 1861 and mid-1863. In later years, four of the nine Thompson children were recognized for their special abilities. One of the eldest, Garland Yancy, won awards for wood carving. A brother, Aaron Bedford, and two sisters, Clara Ann and Priscilla Jane, were published poets.

While Morgan was having breakfast at the Schenck house, some of his men, screening the column's right flank, continued several miles farther south through present-day Silverton to the Duck Creek (Pleasant Ridge) area. This detachment reached the closest point to the city of Cincinnati that Morgan's main force attained.

As we leave the Schenck house, we will be on post-Civil War roads. The present grid of streets did not exist in 1863.

Continue to the end of the block and turn left onto Beech Street. Go two blocks and turn right onto Galbraith Road.

Drive 1.7 miles and cross Miami Road. After the intersection, the road becomes Kugler Mill Road. We are back on Morgan's route.

As the raiders moved east, most of them used Kugler Mill Road. Others followed Euclid Avenue, several miles to the south. Raiders visited several homes in present-day Madeira.

Early Tuesday morning, Morgan, riding with Johnson's brigade, was approaching Camp Dennison. At the same time, Hobson's Union troopers were leaving Harrison. Their progress was delayed because Morgan's men had taken all the fresh horses. There were no replacements for the exhausted Union mounts.

Drive on Kugler Mill Road 1.3 miles to Loveland-Madeira Road. About 6 a.m., Morgan's advance troops reached this point and found a barricade of felled trees. The raiders encountered stiff resistance between this intersection and Camargo Road (Madisonville Pike in 1863), 0.1 mile farther east.

Lieutenant Colonel George W. Neff, commander of Camp Dennison, had ordered rifle pits dug on the approaches to the camp. Captain Joseph L. Proctor of the 18th U.S. Infantry was in command of 350 Union convalescents, Ohio militia, and civilians entrenched on the hill immediately east of the intersection of Loveland Road and Kugler Mill Road. The hill is visible directly in front of you.

(Note: In 1863, Loveland-Madeira Road did not exist. The Loveland Road at the time of the raid ran along the opposite bank of Sycamore Creek, where the railroad tracks are today. Contemporary accounts referred to Camargo Road as the Madisonville-Obanion-and-Camargo Pike.)

Proctor's men became involved in a skirmish with Morgan's advance troops around this intersection. Morgan unlimbered his artillery (two 12-pounder howitzers) on the road 0.25 mile behind you and shelled the rifle pits in an attempt to disperse the enemy, but to no avail.

This was as close as Morgan came to Camp Dennison during his approach from the west. He did not have time to become involved in a lengthy battle. Any delay would have decreased the distance between the raiders and the pursuing Union troops.

Stopped by the barricade, Morgan was forced to have Johnson's brigade backtrack along Kugler Mill Road. After going less than one-half mile, some of the men turned north on Blome Road. Morgan and the main column continued back to Montgomery Road, where they turned north to the town of Montgomery. There they met Duke's brigade.

From Montgomery, the main force followed Cooper Road and Spooky Hollow Road east to the Little Miami River. There was a ford at Porter's

(Hamilton's) Mill. The men crossed the river near the mill. Most of Duke's brigade used the same crossing.

To protect the division while crossing the Little Miami River at Porter's Mill, Morgan sent large detachments to screen the right and left flanks of the main column. The right flank column splashed across the river about 300 yards downstream from Porter's Mill while the left flank cavalry detachment forded the stream one mile southwest of Branch Hill. See Appendix E: Duke's Column Moved Through Northeastern Suburbs to view the fords at Porters Mill and near Branch Hill.

Coming up from the river, Duke led his brigade south toward Miamiville and the railroad bridge.

Morgan, riding with Adam Johnson's column, turned left on Beech Road. They followed it to Branch Hill-Miamiville Road and the Jacob Thompson farmhouse, which would serve as Morgan's headquarters.

Two bridges crossed the Little Miami River between Branch Hill and Miamiville. The wire suspension bridge at Branch Hill was guarded by the Loveland militia; the Camargo Road Bridge was controlled by Neff's men. Neither bridge was used by the Confederates.

We will stay on Kugler Mill Road to Camp Dennison. It is 2.7 miles to Camp Road and an area of flat open fields. On the west side of Camp Road, stretching from Kugler Mill Road to a point about one mile north, was the site of the Camp Dennison Hospital, which was established when wounded men from the Battle of Shiloh were transported to Cincinnati in 1862. With nearly 2,300 beds, this medical facility was one of the best the Union could offer. Both Union and Confederate soldiers were treated here.

It is 0.2 mile farther to the bike trail that was the Little Miami, Columbus and Xenia Railroad. Before you reach the bike trail, park in the soccer field parking lot on the left and walk to the Secrest Monument Park at the end of Kugler Mill Road. Secrest Monument Park is just beyond the bike trail.

JOHN HUNT MORGAN HERITAGE TRAIL INTERPRETIVE SIGN #8

The Secrest Monument honors the Union regiments formed at Camp Dennison during the Civil War.

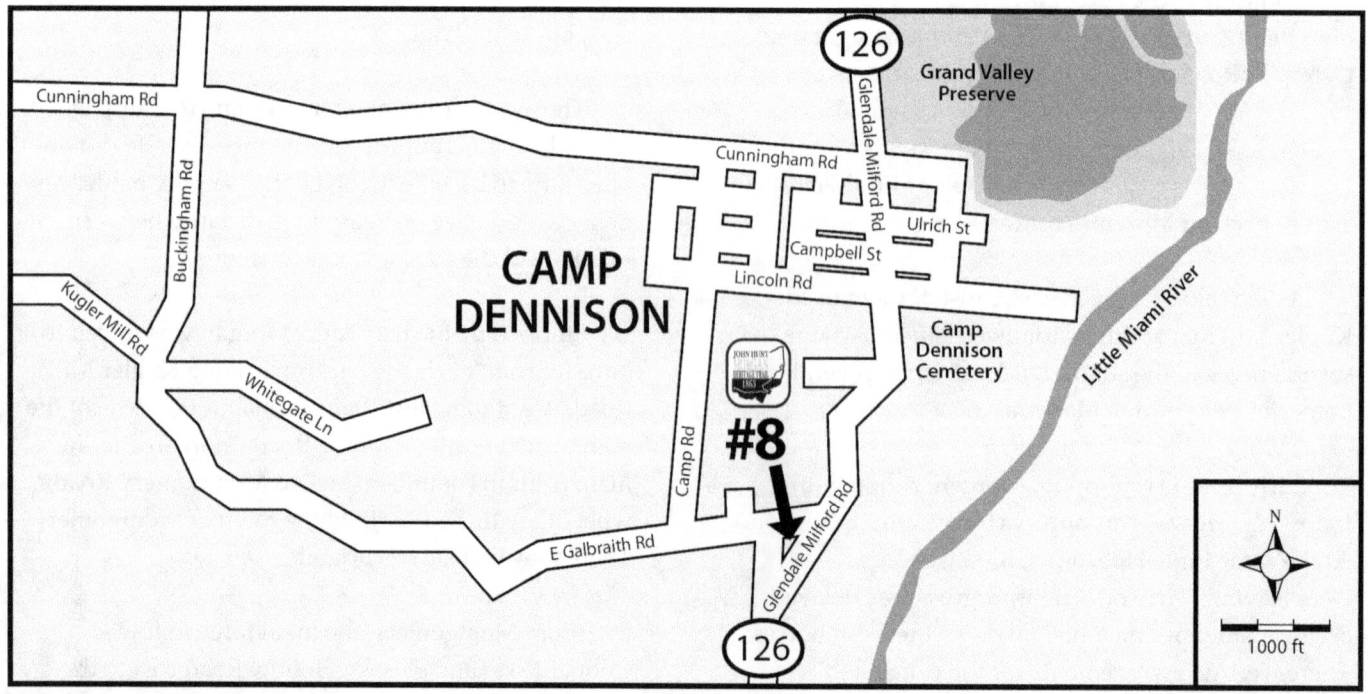

John Hunt Morgan Heritage Trail Interpretive sign #8 map

HARRISON TO CAMP DENNISON

Secrest Monument Park was dedicated in 1932.

The camp was named after Ohio's Governor William Dennison. The site was chosen by Major General George B. McClellan and laid out by Colonel (later General) William S. Rosecrans on April 27, 1861.

The camp was located on the Little Miami River near a town known as Germany before the Civil War. The Little Miami Railroad ran through the center of the camp. The name on the Germany depot was changed to Camp Dennison. After the war, the camp was dismantled, but the town was thwarted in its attempt to change its name to Grand Valley. The railroad refused to repaint the name on the depot and print new schedules.

Nearly 70 Union infantry, cavalry, and artillery units were established and trained at the camp between 1861 and 1865.

Encompassing more than 700 acres, the camp stretched from Kugler Mill Road to a point approximately one mile to the north, covering the plateau lying between the range of hills and the river.

In November 1861, new recruits constructed a line of 50 large and 17 small wooden barracks along the west side of Camp Road for use as living quarters, dining facilities, and storage houses. The large barracks, each designed to accommodate 98 men, were 25 feet wide, 120 feet deep, and 11 feet high, while the small barracks were 15.5 feet wide, 60.5 feet deep, and 11 feet high. A 40-feet-wide grassy corridor separated each structure. Behind the line of barracks, the soldiers built a row of buildings to house the commissioned officers.

A steam laundry was erected at the base of the hill on Kugler Mill Road (Galbraith Road), and a chapel was added near the center of the line of hospital wards. On the north side of Kugler Mill Road, just a few yards west of the Little Miami Railroad tracks (today's Bike Trail), a barn served as the

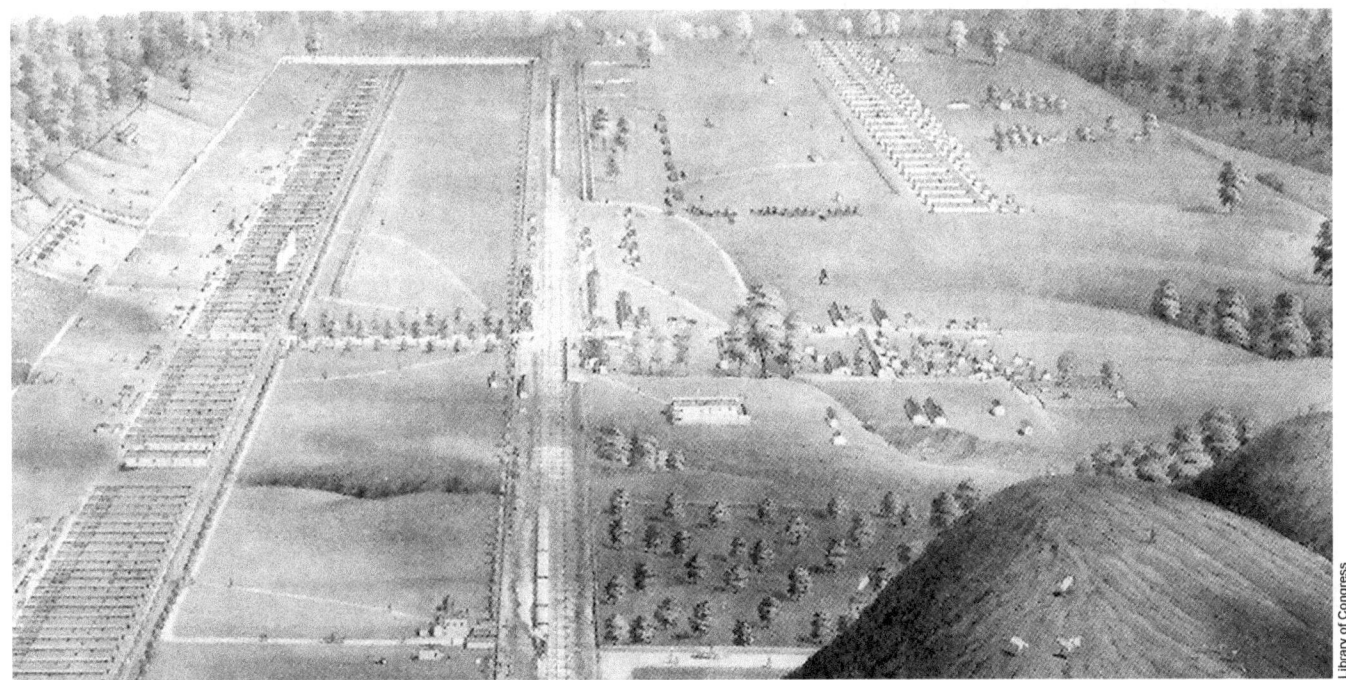

This lithograph of Camp Dennison, looking north, shows the hospital barracks on the left, the soldiers' barracks on the upper right, the railroad running through the center of the camp and the Little Miami River on the far right.

12th Division Hospital and Surgeon's Quarters.

Return to your car and turn left onto Kugler Mill Road; as you approach Secrest Park, bear left. Turn left onto Glendale-Milford Road (SR 126). It is 0.1 mile to the stone house that served as the camp's guardhouse. This stone building (c. 1805) is home to the Camp Dennison Civil War Museum. The museum is open on Sundays, 1–5 p.m., May–October. Web site: *http://www.waldschmidthouse.org/dar/waldmore.shtml* .

Stone house served as Camp Dennison guardhouse.

The Christian Waldschmidt house (c. 1804), located two doors north at 7567 Glendale-Milford Road, is open to the public as a museum. John Kugler owned the house during the Civil War. He and other property owners leased land to the State of Ohio for government use as a campsite. The house served as a temporary post headquarters for the camp commander. Museum hours are Sunday, 1–5 p.m., May–October, or by appointment via e-mail: *waldschmidt@ohiodar.org*; or phone: (513) 576-6327.

The Waldschmidt Cemetery became the camp's burial ground. The cemetery is located on the east side of SR 126, off Lincoln Road. Both Union and Confederate soldiers were buried there. Their bodies were disinterred after the war; many of them were moved to their permanent resting places in the three Civil War grave circles at Spring Grove Cemetery in Cincinnati. Most of the Confederate dead were moved to Camp Chase Cemetery in Columbus, Ohio.

Lt. Colonel George Washington Neff

George Neff, the post commander of Camp Dennison at the time of Morgan's Raid, was a thirty-year-old native of Cincinnati. As such, he knew the roads and terrain surrounding the camp very well. His father had been the first president of the Little Miami Railroad Company and had founded the Fireman's Insurance Company.

In 1861, Neff helped recruit Union volunteers for the 2nd Kentucky (U.S.) Infantry and was commissioned as the regiment's Lieutenant Colonel. At the Battle of Scary Creek, (West) Virginia, he was captured and sent to Libby Prison in Richmond, Virginia. He was exchanged on September 30, 1862, after 14 months of incarceration. Neff returned home on leave of absence, and on January 15, 1863, he accepted the appointment as Post Commander of Camp Dennison.

Neff had prepared for Morgan's arrival. Neff had ordered rifle pits dug and trees felled on the approach roads. In addition, he had rifle pits constructed on the hill southwest of the hospital.

Neff had transported most of the horses and mules, surgical instruments, medicine, and other vital supplies to Cincinnati. Fifty wagons containing

HARRISON TO CAMP DENNISON

saddles and supplies were taken to Camp Shady, several miles east in Clermont County.

Many of his men had been sent to guard the bridges across the Little Miami River at Milford, Miamiville, and other upstream locations. Because Camp Dennison had been designated as one of the rendezvous points for the Ohio militia, Neff received nearly 1,400 untrained men, who arrived by train and by foot throughout the day of July 13 and into the early morning hours of July 14. Unfortunately, Neff had no weapons to arm these reinforcements. General Burnside had failed to send the guns and ammunition that Neff had requested.

The lieutenant colonel sent his wife, with other officers' wives and their servants, to the William McGrew farmhouse located about three miles away on the road to Goshen. There, Mrs. Neff buried the family silver and the camp records. A party of raiders visited the farm, taking all the horses and stock. They offered no insults to the ladies and did not enter the house. They politely asked the women for water, which they received.

It is 1.3 miles from the Waldschmidt house to the SR 126 (Glendale-Milford Road) bridge across the Little Miami River. As you drive north from the village of Camp Dennison (known as Germany in 1863), note the gravel pits on the right between the road and the hills above the river. This area, now called Grand Valley Preserve, was the site of the Camp Dennison soldiers' barracks. Pull off on the right before crossing the river.

Chapter Two

CAMP DENNISON TO WILLIAMSBURG

Lithograph of the Little Miami Railroad Bridge looking west from the Fletcher farm on the south side of the river. The Oskamp farm was located on the north side. Raiders were attempting to burn the bridge from the north end, on the right.

Tuesday, July 14, 1863

After crossing the Little Miami River upstream at Porter's Mill around 7:30 a.m., Basil Duke led his brigade, with a portion of the 14th Kentucky Cavalry regiment, south along Glendale-Milford Road (SR 126) toward Miamiville. Eight mounted pickets (guards whose job it was to prevent surprise attack) from Captain Jacob Shuman's Company H, 11th Ohio Cavalry, guarded the Camargo Road (Madisonville Pike) Bridge over the river northwest of Camp Dennison. The Union pickets, unaware of the Confederate crossing at Porter's Mill and the subsequent train derailment a half-mile away, were playing cards on the deck of the bridge at the time of Duke's approach. The 14th Kentucky Cavalry detachment caught the bridge guards by surprise. Following a brief skirmish, the inexperienced Union troops scattered, and one man and eight horses were captured by the raiders. Duke posted pickets at the bridge before sending the rest of the raiders on toward Miamiville.

When the routed remnant of Shuman's pickets reported the enemy's capture of the Madisonville Pike Bridge, Captain Joseph Proctor prepared his Union troops at the Kugler Mill crossroads for a counterattack. Using the men he had left, he strengthened his patrols on all the roads leading north from the crossroads to the river. Their orders were clear: to prevent or delay any Confederate advances made south of the river.

At Miamiville, the raiders attempted to burn the railroad bridge from its north end. The wooden railroad bridge occupied the same site as the present-day metal bridge on your left (the Loveland Bike Trail Bridge).

The railroad bridge was guarded by a detachment of the 11th Ohio Cavalry, serving under Captain Shuman. His forces held the south end of the bridge (to the left). The skirmish began when the Confederates arrived at the north end. The bridge guards put up a good fight, but Duke's troopers outflanked them by crossing at a ford about 500 yards downstream. The raiders dispersed the Union defenders and captured most of them.

Lieutenant Colonel George Neff dispatched Lieutenant William H. H. Smith of the 21st Ohio Light Artillery, and 200 militiamen of Captain Guest's "Miami Volunteers," to the railroad bridge. The soldiers marched one mile at the double-quick on Glendale-Milford Road, from the Camp Dennison railroad depot to the bridge. When they arrived, the raiders were attempting to burn the bridge. After dispersing the arsonists, the militia fanned out along the south bank of the river to the left and right of the bridge. They used farm fences as barricades.

After Morgan heard the gunfire from his headquarters at a farmhouse on the Branch Hill-Miamiville Road, he forced the property owner, Jacob H. Thompson, to lead him to Miamiville by the most direct route. The two men soon reached the hill above town, from which Morgan could see the vast Camp Dennison laid before him. After reviewing the situation with Colonel Duke, the General ordered 2nd Lieutenant Elias D. Lawrence's section of Byrne's Battery to unlimber (prepare for action) on a hill on the Augustus Oskamp farm behind the center of the line. From there, the Confederate gunners shelled the soldiers' barracks, which stood where the gravel pits are today, northeast of the town of Camp Dennison. They also shelled the railroad bridge.

Morgan left the supervision of the skirmish in Duke's capable hands and galloped back to the main column to hurry it forward.

The ensuing engagement was a long-range firefight across the river that lasted until about 10:30 a.m., when Colonel Neff arrived with a squad of convalescents. Neff led his convalescents in a charge across the railroad bridge. The Confederates fell back, not wanting to get into a close-quarters fight with the enemy.

Convalescent Henry Meyers was killed in the charge across the bridge, four men were captured, and several men were wounded. One convalescent was reported missing.

By this time, Captain Proctor's men were at the Confederates' rear. They had moved north along Madisonville Pike from the Kugler Mill crossroads. They crossed the Camargo Road Bridge over the Little Miami River and turned east toward Miamiville. They opened fire on Duke's rear guard.

A small force of Duke's men held off the Union forces in the field adjacent to the Moses Robinson house while Duke led the rest of his troops north to Ward's Corner. The rear guard, mounted on fleet horses, soon followed.

The skirmish at the railroad bridge lasted almost three hours. Morgan's casualties included six men killed, four wounded, and seven captured.

Cross the bridge to Clermont County and turn left with SR 126. Immediately turn left and park in the blacktop drive that parallels the Little Miami Scenic Trail (Loveland Bike Trail). Visitors are not allowed to park in the lot of the adjacent deli store.

Lieutenant Charles H. Powell, of the 6th Kentucky Cavalry, was captured by Neff's convalescents when he was pinned under his horse, near the present-day parking area.

Two **Morgan Trail Signs** are located in the grassy area between the Loveland Bike Trail and the blacktop drive, at Bike Trail Milepost 47.59.

JOHN HUNT MORGAN HERITAGE TRAIL INTERPRETIVE SIGN #9

JOHN HUNT MORGAN HERITAGE TRAIL INTERPRETIVE SIGN #10

Park and follow the bikeway to the old railroad bridge (Bike Trail Milepost 47.80). Look downstream to the left and beyond the highway bridge. In the distance, you will see the river bend to the right. Above the bend is the bluff known as Devil's Backbone.

The gravel bar in the foreground was the extreme left of the Confederate line during the skirmish at Miamiville. The Fletcher farm was on the right bank. The bluff in the distant center is the Devil's Backbone.

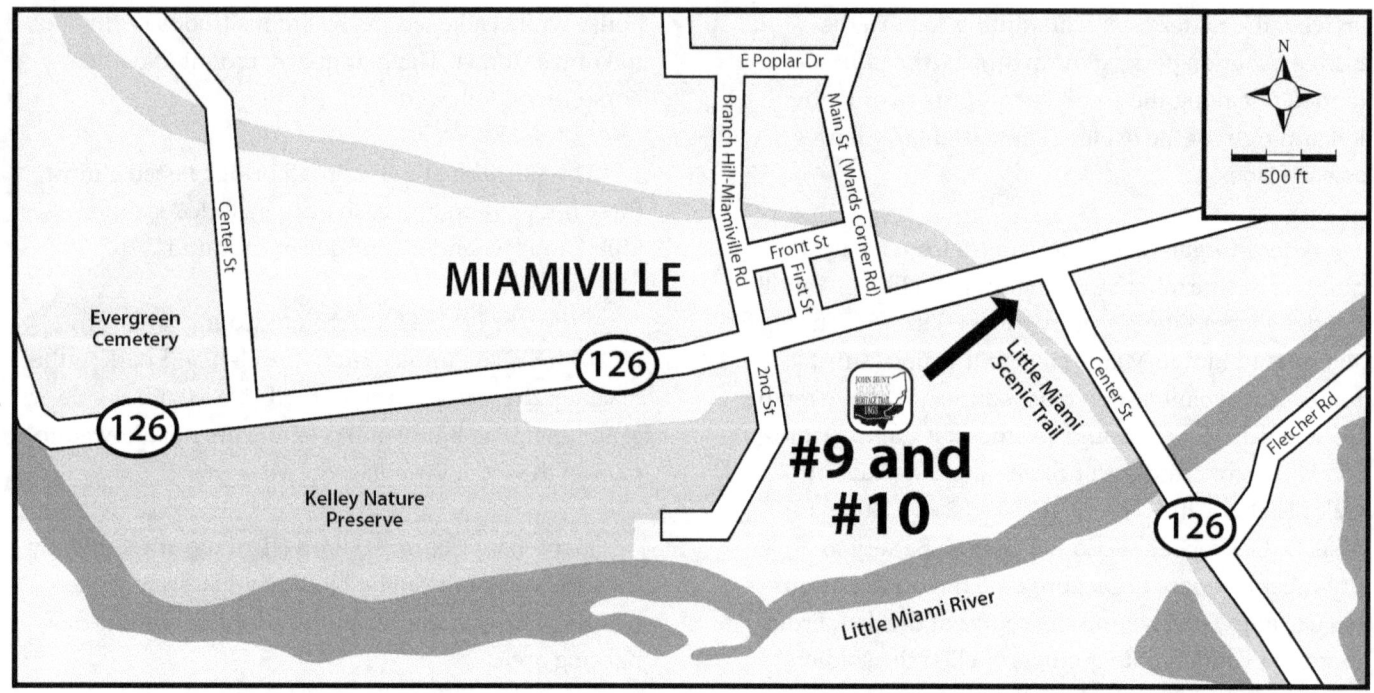

John Hunt Morgan Heritage Trail Interpretive signs #9 and #10 map

Union artillery men in training at Camp Dennison practiced firing cannon shots into the bluff. The area between the highway bridge and the bend is thought to be the area where the raiders "watered their horses in sight of the camp."

The Confederates tried to turn the Union right flank at the railroad bridge by making a foray across the river from the mouth of a nearby creek. The raiders charged into the open woods that bordered the west line of William Fletcher's farm, but after heavy skirmishing, the attack was beaten back by men of the state militia under command of Lieutenant Smith. Morgan's troopers retreated back across the river, taking two of Fletcher's horses with them.

Return to the parking area or take the following side trip.

Hike/Bike Side Trip: The Little Miami Railroad Bridge is at Bike Trail Milepost 47.80, and the parking area is at Milepost 47.59. To visit the site of the Kilgore derailment, continue north 1.15 miles on the Loveland Bike Trail from the parking area, through Miamiville, to the train wreck location. The raiders derailed the troop train bound for Camp Dennison at the curve at Milepost 46.44, after the raiders had hidden in a cornfield on the left between the curve and Dangerous Crossing (Beech Road), which is located at Milepost 46.01. Continue to Milepost 45.37, which was the site of the skirmish with Paxton's Scouts (Loveland Militia). You can read more about the derailment and Morgan's skirmish with the Loveland Militia later in this chapter. Return to the parking area.

As you leave the parking area turn left at SR 126. Main Street (Wards Corner Road) is just beyond the bike path. The red brick house on the southwest corner of SR 126 and Wards Corner Road occupies the site of the Susan Woodlief home. She lost two horses, a bridle, and $64 in grain to the raiders.

Turn right onto Wards Corner Road. Drive 0.1 mile. The field on the right side of Wards Corner Road, just north of the bike trail, was the site of the final engagement between Duke's rear guard and Neff's advancing troops.

Continue another 0.1 mile. The old stone house on the right side of Wards Corner Road, across from East Poplar Drive, belonged to Moses F. Robinson. Robinson filed a claim for the loss of a horse, damages to two others, 30 bushels of oats, and one-quarter ton of hay. Prior to the raid, Robinson was thought to be a Confederate sympathizer. That changed on July 14 when he was given the opportunity to contribute to the Confederate cause.

Moses F. Robinson house

The raiders involved in the skirmish at the railroad bridge left Miamiville on this road. Ward's Corner had been selected as a rendezvous point. There they would meet Morgan and Johnson's men who had moved around Branch Hill. The main driving tour does not follow Duke's route, which is described in the following side trip.

*Side Trip: It is less than 0.2 mile to the junction of Wards Corner Road with Lewis Road. At the junction, look to your right; Lawrence's battery of 3-inch Parrott rifles was deployed on the cleared hill on the right.

Continue just over 0.2 mile; "Indian Ripple" is on the right. It was the farm of Augustus Oskamp. The house has undergone extensive renovation since the Civil War.

"Indian Ripple," the August Oskamp farm

Oskamp's losses included 11 horses, 43 sheep, a carriage, harnesses, and $120 in grain. He filed for $2,772 in claims, but was awarded only $1,800. It was reported that a farm hand was shot while protecting the sheep.

Continue 1.2 miles on Wards Corner Road and look to the left. The house at number 582 was the 1863 home of John Fitzwater, Senior. He lost four horses and 145 bushels of grain to the raiders. Silas R. Hutchinson, a neighbor, lost three horses (one was later recovered) and 35 bushels of corn.

It is 0.3 mile farther to the site of the Artis and Lewis Fitzwater house on the right at 645 Wards Corner Road. The house was razed in 2011. The men lost two horses, two mules, and $90 in grain.

Artis and Lewis Fitzwater farm

Continue 0.3 mile to the junction with Branch Hill-Guinea Pike. The community of Ward's Corner developed around this junction. Turn around and return to Miamiville. At the northern edge of town, turn right onto East Poplar Drive.*

Turn left on East Poplar Drive and drive one block. At the corner, look to the right along Branch Hill-Miamiville Road. After Morgan crossed the Little Miami River at Porter's Mill Ford, he rode northeast to the Jacob Thompson farm on Branch Hill-Miamiville Road, 1.3 miles north of here, where he established temporary headquarters. We will visit the site later. Morgan viewed Camp Dennison from a spot near

Branch Hill-Miamiville Road on the hill overlooking Miamiville. Trees now obstruct the view.

Turn left onto Branch Hill-Miamiville Road. Cross the bike trail and turn left onto Front Street. Go one block and turn right onto First Street. It is one block to SR 126.

The house at the southwest corner of First Street and SR 126 was the Valentine Phillips home. His claim was for $17 for boots and shoes appropriated by Morgan's men.

Valentine Phillips home (c. 1860)

Turn right on SR 126; drive 0.5 mile and turn right into Evergreen Cemetery. One of Morgan's men, John H. Anderson, and Anderson's wife Katherine are buried here. The Anderson plot is at the beginning of the first driveway to the left after entering the main entrance. The grave is on the right side of the driveway. John met his future wife when the raiders stopped at the Deerwester home near Belfast, Clermont County. The smitten young man honored his promise to return after the war and marry Katherine. The Deerwester farm site can be seen when driving the alternate route, Appendix G Alternate: Company to Goshen.

John Anderson returned to Ohio to honor a promise.

Return to SR 126 and turn right. Where the highway makes a sharp turn to the right at the cemetery, the old Camargo Road Bridge abutments can be seen on the left and across the river. Because Neff had positioned a guard at the other end of the bridge, it was not used by the raiders, who knew that more Union troops were positioned to the south. It was, however, the site of the small skirmish with Company H, 11th Ohio Cavalry, in which Morgan's advance riders captured the bridge and held it until Duke's rear guard had passed.

Drive 0.8 mile; the area on the right borders the Loveland Bikeway. This area had been the farm of Horatio Buckingham. The section of track to the right, at the base of the hill, was straight; the derailment curve is a few yards to the south.

Raiders from Companies B and C of the 14th Kentucky Cavalry, coming up from Porter's Mill Ford, cut the telegraph wires and wedged railroad ties into a cattle guard around the bend of the railroad track approximately 0.43 mile south of the Beech Road crossing of the bike trail.

Barricade was around the bend.

When a train appeared half a mile north at Dangerous Crossing, the raiders hid in the cornfield, along the straight section of track, and waited. They fired at the train as it passed them, causing the engineer to put on more steam. This drove the train even faster into the obstruction; it was probably moving about 40 mph at the time of impact. The engine Kilgore and the tender (the car attached to the locomotive to supply fuel and water) jumped the tracks and rolled down the embankment. Miraculously, the baggage car and four passenger cars remained on the tracks and coasted to a stop.

Fireman Cornelius Conway (Cullinan) was killed. According to local legend, Conway's ghost still haunts the area. A lantern swinging in the dark has been seen at or near the site of the crash; sometimes a man is seen holding the swinging lantern.

The engineer, John Redman, was seriously injured. His $1,306 claim for doctor bills and loss of work resulting from the injuries was rejected by the state.

The passengers included 115 unarmed recruits bound for Camp Dennison. This group included a Columbus band with their musical instruments. The recruits were captured, taken to Morgan's headquarters, and then paroled. The parolees and train conductor W. H. Roberts were then allowed to continue on foot to Camp Dennison.

One of the civilians on the derailed train was William H. Clement, President of the Little Miami Railroad. After escaping unnoticed from one of the passenger cars, he ran toward Miamiville and soon flagged down another train heading north from Cincinnati. Confederate scouts spotted the second train and attempted to capture it, but Clement ordered the engineer to put the locomotive into full reverse. Barely outrunning the cavalrymen, the train retreated over the Little Miami Railroad Bridge and into the safety of the Federal line.

Loveland's Doctor Baen was taking the train to a bank in Cincinnati to deposit $700. He fled the scene to hide in an apple orchard on a nearby hill. He stashed his wallet in a cord of wood and crawled into a brier-covered hole where he remained until nightfall, when he slipped back to Loveland. He returned the following day and recovered his wallet.

It was after 7:30 a.m. when sixteen scouts from the Loveland militia, led by First Lieutenant Thomas B. Paxton, were sent out on a reconnaissance mission. They were dispatched because the raiders had cut the telegraph wires between Loveland and Camp Dennison.

About 9:00 a.m., they found the raiders burning the derailed train and tearing up the track. Sergeant Harry Ramsey and ten men attacked the raiders' left flank at the upper ford one mile south of Branch Hill. Morgan's larger force quickly turned back the militia but not before Ramsey wounded one of the raiders in the neck. The injured man was left at nearby Ward's Corner to die.

The scouts reported back to Captain Monroe S. Williamson in Loveland. Williamson and his force of 116 militiamen stayed to protect Loveland and Branch Hill from attack, while Paxton's scouts harassed Morgan's rear guard all the way to Mulberry.

Continuing on SR 126, the private drive on the left side of SR 126, just as the highway bends to the right, was the road to Porter's Mill Ford. As the raiders came up from the river, John Elliott's house was on their left. Elliott filed a claim for the loss of two horses and twenty-five bushels of corn.

Go 0.2 mile on SR 126 and turn right onto Beech Road. Drive 0.4 mile and follow the bend toward the right. After rounding the corner, look to the left. This was the site of the Benjamin F. Buckingham house. He filed a $150 claim for the loss of one horse and eighty pounds of meat.

It is 0.1 mile farther on Beech Road to the bike path; there is a **Clermont County Historical Marker** on the left. This place was known as Dangerous Crossing in 1863. Looking to the right, you can see the straight run leading to the derailment curve, which is located 0.43 mile to the south of here.

Cross the trail and drive 0.4 mile; the house on the left, at 295 Beech Road, was the home of John Thompson. He lost one horse to the raiders.

John Thompson farmhouse

Continue 0.2 mile to Branch Hill-Miamiville Road; turn left.

It is just over 0.3 mile to the Jacob H. Thompson house on the right at 6362 Branch Hill-Miamiville Road. The house, constructed of bricks, has been partially covered by siding. This house was Morgan's headquarters for the short time he was in the area. The recruits, captured at the train derailment site, were brought here to be paroled by Morgan.

After the raid, Jacob Thompson filed for the loss of one horse and $40 worth of grain.

Jacob H. Thompson house served as Morgan's headquarters.

Drive 0.6 mile. As you cross I-275, the 1863 road was off to your left; it comes back in at the street on the left just after the overpass.

Continue less than 0.2 mile; the house at 6504 Branch Hill-Miamiville Road occupies the site of flour merchant Elliott Armstrong's home. Armstrong's wife and daughter entertained some of Morgan's men and supplied them with food and drink. The daughter provided music by playing the piano and singing the song, *Rally 'Round the Flag*. One of the men told her he liked the music, but did not care for the words.

Go 0.4 mile to Branch Hill-Guinea Pike and turn right. The John F. Johnston house is located on the left at 6674 Branch Hill-Guinea Pike. Johnston lost one horse to the raiders.

John F. Johnston farmhouse

Drive 0.2 mile; the Aaron Thompson house once stood on the left just before Epworth Road. Thompson's horse was taken by the raiders along with fifty bushels of corn.

Continue 0.9 mile on Branch Hill-Guinea Pike to the intersection with Wards Corner Road. The community surrounding the junction was called Ward's Corner. Many of Morgan's men rested here for a brief time.

At Ward's Corner, Sarah Harrison was forced to cook dinner for more than 100 raiders. They repaid her by taking a ton of hay and her husband Joe's horse; they left a broken-down horse in its place. Sympathetic Unionists in Loveland offered the couple a barrel of flour to "mitigate the chagrin of having helped the rebels on their way." The Harrison house, now gone, stood in the yard immediately to the left (west) of the present-day Branch Hill Baptist Church parking lot.

The Confederate soldier who had been shot during the skirmish with Paxton's scouts near the upper ford was brought to Ward's Corner. Morgan told the local citizenry to give the fatally wounded young raider a Christian burial or he would return and burn their village. The citizens fulfilled the general's wishes. The body was later disinterred and returned to the South.

Morgan's rear guard later skirmished with Paxton's scouts from the Loveland militia near here.

Continuing straight on Branch Hill-Guinea Pike, it is 0.7 mile from Ward's Corner to Loveland-Miamiville Road. The farm on the left before the intersection was owned by Andrew J. Orr during the Civil War. Orr filed a claim for two horses lost to the raiders and one horse appropriated by Hobson's men; he received full compensation for his losses.

Drive 0.3 mile on Branch Hill-Guinea Pike to Paxton-Guinea Road. The house on the left before the junction occupies the site of the Hiram G. Leever home. Leever's two mules were taken by the raiders. Directly acoss the Pike, at 6345 Branch Hill-Guinea Pike, stands the George W. Apgar house. Legend says that General Morgan kindly held a sick, crying baby to allow mother Harriet and father George to prepare a meal for Morgan and his men.

Drive 0.4 mile on Branch Hill-Guinea Pike. The Henry W. Leever house is on the left at 6278 Branch Hill-Guinea Pike. His only claim was for a $7 saddle taken by a raider.

Henry W. Leever farmhouse

It is 0.5 mile to Weber Road. After you cross Weber Road, the first driveway on the left is the lane to the William Tudor farm. Continue 0.3 mile; the Charles P. Harker house is on the left at 6150 Branch Hill-Guinea Pike. Most of General Edward H. Hobson's cavalrymen camped on the Tudor and Harker farms on the night of July 14.

Charles P. Harker farm (c. 1820)

By the time Hobson reached Camp Dennison, Neff had received reports of the rebel activities at Camp Shady (present-day Mount Repose). It was also reported that the raiders had left Camp Shady (also called Camp Repose) and were headed toward Williamsburg.

Hobson followed Morgan's route through the Miamiville and Ward's Corner area. Hobson crossed the Little Miami River at the Camargo Road Bridge and moved southeast to the Harker farm.

The town of Mulberry was also known both as Newberry and New Salisbury. Mulberry is located at Business 28 and Elm Street, 1.5 miles west of present-day Mount Repose.

The town of Mt. Repose did not exist in 1863; the people living here were included in the Mulberry Post Office.

Arriving about 9 p.m., Hobson's exhausted men turned their horses loose to graze and dropped to the ground for a few hours of precious sleep.

Tudor filed claims for losses to Union cavalry for fifty bushels of corn, hay, and fodder, and damages to meadows, a cornfield, and an orchard. He also filed for damages to a horse that had been taken, but which he later recovered.

Harker filed claims for losses of ninety bushels of corn, eight acres of oats, hay, sixteen acres of meadow, and damage to a peach orchard. As an agent for Rebecca Cox, Harker filed claims for her loss of one and one-half tons of hay used by Union troops and a saddle and a bridle stolen by Morgan's men.

It is just over 0.3 mile to the George W. Ritter house on the right at 6111 Branch Hill-Guinea Pike. Ritter's losses were to the raiders, not the Union cavalry. He lost a horse and buggy, a harness, and $31 in bacon and hams. He also filed for damages to a stallion that was later recovered.

George W. Ritter house

Continue straight for 0.6 mile to the intersection with SR 28. There is a Frisch's Restaurant across SR 28 and to the left. During the excavation for the building's foundation, Camp Shady artifacts were uncovered.

Around 11 a.m. on July 14, Morgan's vanguard discovered the deserted Federal supply depot, located at the intersection of the Symmestown-Union Meeting House Road (present-day Branch Hill-Guinea Pike) and the Milford-Goshen Turnpike (SR 28). Much to the raiders' delight, they found a drove of U.S. horses and mules and a group of fifty U.S. Army covered wagons lined up in neat rows. Neff had been forced to leave the government supplies, wagons, and mules in the camp because he had not assembled enough teamsters to drive them to Cincinnati. While the men picked over the fresh mounts, Morgan ordered the wagons to be searched for needed items and then burned. As Neff's wagon park went up in flames, the raiders continued their march southeast.

Leaving Camp Shady, Morgan's main column followed the pike south toward Boston (present-day Owensville). Smaller groups traveled on parallel roads foraging in many Clermont County communities.

One small company of raiders rode northeast to Goshen. There, they turned south to rejoin Morgan at Williamsburg. To follow their route *See Appendix G Alternate: Company to Goshen.*

By 2 a.m. on July 15, the Union cavalry was on the move again. To follow their route *See Appendix H Alternate: Union Forces from Mulberry to Batavia.*

To follow Morgan's main column, turn right onto SR 28; immediately turn left at the light onto Woodville Pike. Drive 0.6 mile to a bridge over a small stream adjacent to Milford Christian Academy. The Emley Barber house stood on the right on the west bank. Barber lost a harness and a saddle to Morgan's men.

Continue less than 0.2 mile and turn right onto Deerfield Road. Some of the raiders continued straight on Woodville Pike before turning south to Simpkinsville (present-day Williams Corner).

When Deerfield Road ends in 2.6 miles, turn left on SR 131. Go 0.6 mile to Williams Corner and turn right onto SR 132. The two columns merged at this point.

It is 3.9 miles to US 50 at the edge of Owensville. The road to Owensville (Boston in 1863) was narrow, hilly, and twisting. Tuesday, July 14, was very hot. Many of the exhausted riders had been in the saddle since leaving Sunman, Indiana, before dawn Monday morning. The column pushed on, but riders were falling off their horses, lying down, and sleeping along the roadside. Many of these men awoke to find themselves captives of the militia.

CAMP DENNISON TO WILLIAMSBURG

Old Boston Methodist Episcopal Church

Turn left on US 50 and go 0.3 mile to the Old Boston Methodist Episcopal Church on the right side of US 50. There is a **Clermont County Historical Marker** beside the building. The church was erected in 1859.

The raiders arrived in Boston about noon on Tuesday. As they rode into town, an elderly man in the church steeple fired both barrels of his shotgun at them. It was reported that he was a veteran of the War of 1812.

Morgan ordered ten men to enter the church and capture the sniper. The raiders rode their horses into the sanctuary. They dismounted at the bottom of the stairs leading to the steeple and climbed to the steeple to capture the shooter. They returned with him, his gun, and a flag that he had placed atop the steeple. He was forced to accompany the raiders to Williamsburg. He was given a bony old nag to ride. The flag was tied to the horse's tail so that it dragged in the dust.

John M. Pattison was a sixteen-year-old working in his father's hardware store across the street from the church. The hardware store stood in the area that is now the IGA parking lot. Young Pattison became so angered by the raiders' actions that he enlisted in Company I, 153rd Ohio Volunteer Infantry (OVI) the following year. Forty-two years later, in 1905, John Pattison was elected Governor of Ohio. He served only five months before succumbing to pneumonia, the second Ohio governor to die in office.

Morgan stopped at the Malone house, next door to the hardware store. The Malones were a Quaker family and not involved in the fighting. Mary Ann Malone was forced to prepare lunch for the general.

Malone house is no longer standing.

While eating, Morgan noticed an American flag painted on the ceiling. He told Mrs. Malone the only reason he did not burn the house was because they were Quakers. When the raiders left town they took three of Malone's horses. The incidents involving the Malone family were recorded years later by John Walter Malone, who was five years old at the time of the raid. Malone was the founder and first president of Malone College, in Canton, Ohio.

In addition to individual's homes, the raiders looted the Boston stores, taking not only what they needed, but also many absurd items that they would never use.

Ulrey house/store, built in 1838; razed in 1961.

Ulrey's store and residence were located in a large brick building at the southeast corner of Broadway (SR 276) and Main (US 50). Mrs. Ulrey, alone in the store, had hidden the family horses behind a curtained doorway leading into the residence. Several raiders entered the store. When they started toward the residence, Mrs. Ulrey blocked an officer's way, saying, "Confederate officers are gentlemen, and gentlemen do not enter where they are not invited. And you, sir, are not invited into my parlor." The officer and his men left without discovering the horses hidden in the parlor.

The raiders stayed in Boston only about an hour. When they left, they took local men to serve as guides to Williamsburg.

Continue on to the corner and turn right onto SR 276 (Broadway Street).

The large, white, brick house on the left at 410 South Broadway (just beyond Gauche Park Drive, or Cherry Alley) was the Pattison home.

Boyhood home of Ohio Gov. John M. Pattison

Go 0.1 mile to the "Y." An old brick house, located in the "Y" intersection between SR 132 and SR 276, has been incorporated into the present building.

Brick house at the "Y"

A small company of 80–100 raiders took the Batavia Road to the right of the "Y." They would rejoin Morgan later at Williamsburg. For a description of both Confederate and Union activities in the Batavia area see Appendix H Alternate: Union Forces from Mulberry to Batavia.

To follow the route of the main force, continue down the road to the left of the "Y" toward Williamsburg (SR 276). In 1863, this was a plank road consisting of split logs laid side-by-side with their flat-side face up. The road's washboard effect created a bouncing ride that no springs could soften; it was a torment to the sick and wounded in the buggies.

It is 5.6 miles to the junction of SR 276 with SR 133 on the outskirts of Williamsburg. Beyond the intersection on both sides of SR 276/133 was the area known as "The Big Field." It had been cleared by James Kain in 1795. The "Big Field," which bordered on Kain's Run, served as a campsite for many of Morgan's men on the night of July 14.

Drive 0.1 mile on SR 276/133 (Main Street); on the left side of the road is **Trail Sign #11**.

JOHN HUNT MORGAN HERITAGE TRAIL INTERPRETIVE SIGN #11

Continue straight for 0.5 mile to the **historical marker** embedded in the curb across from the old high school.

Local legend credits Morgan with scratching the following inscription into the doorsill of the John Lytle home: "John Morgan, July 14, 1863, 3000 men." Although Morgan's force numbered nearly 3,000 men as it left Tennessee, by the time it reached Williamsburg it had been markedly reduced due to heavy losses in Kentucky, the capture of Davis's men when they attempted to cross east of Louisville, and daily attrition resulting from small skirmishes, snipers, and exhaustion.

Colonel Adam "Stovepipe" Johnson and several other officers spent the night in the Lytle home. One of them probably was responsible for the graffiti.

CAMP DENNISON TO WILLIAMSBURG

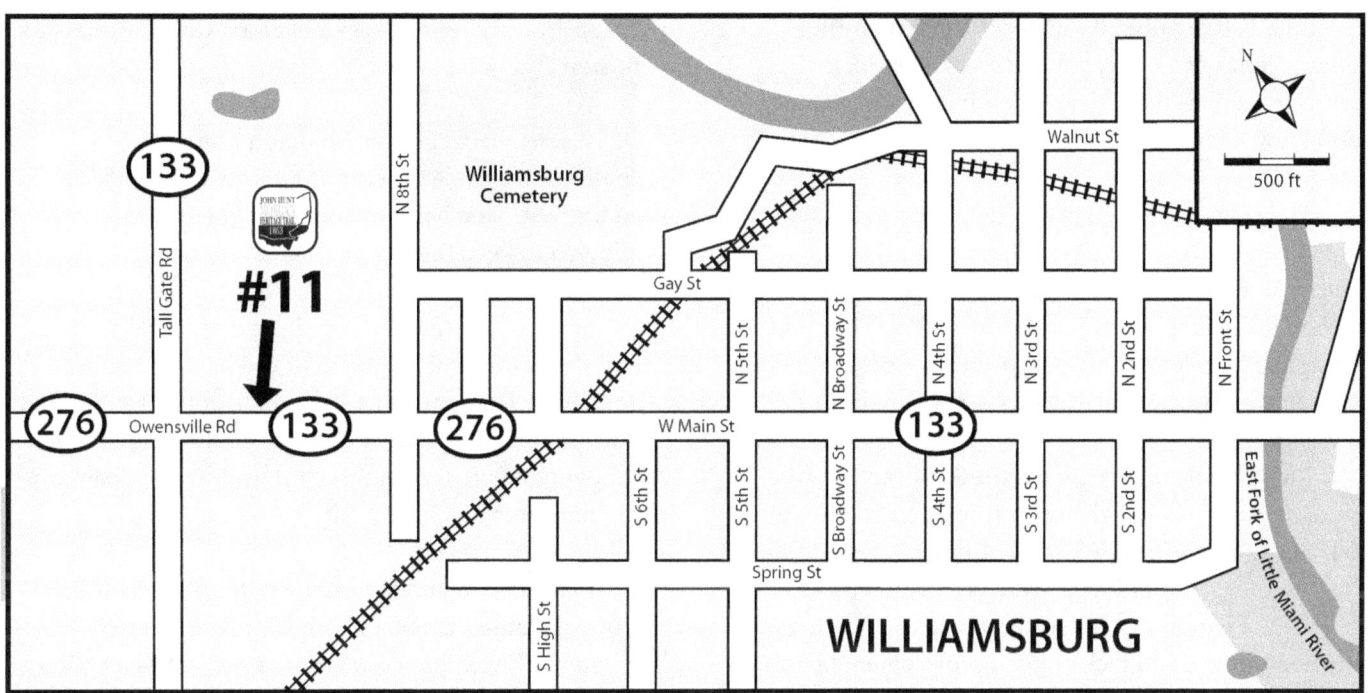
John Hunt Morgan Heritage Trail Interpretive sign #11 map

Doorsill from the home of John Lytle

John Lytle house

The Lytle home was razed about 1950. Lytle filed a claim for losses of corn, hay, and thirty shocks of wheat. He also sought reimbursement for damages to his orchard and fences.

Morgan's advance guard arrived in Williamsburg about 4 p.m. Their arrival was no surprise to the townspeople, who had watched the cloud of dust stirred up by Morgan's horses from the time the riders had left Boston.

The raiders' advance guard would check the safety of a town before the main column arrived. They were led by several horsemen, who rode with reins slack and a revolver in each hand. The guns were pointed at the buildings on both sides of the road as they passed.

The rebels gave notice that nobody would be harmed or injured if the raiders were not fired on or molested. The men following them would split off and ride down and back each side street. The main column would enter town shortly after the advance guard had "checked things out."

The companies that had ridden to Goshen and Batavia arrived in Williamsburg several hours later.

Small companies of foragers visited many other Clermont County towns. See Appendix I, which describes their visits to Withamsville, Amelia, and New Richmond.

The exhausted raiders finally "dropped" to rest at Williamsburg about 5 p.m. They had ridden eighty-five miles since leaving the Ferris School near Sunman, Indiana, thirty-five hours earlier. They had completed the longest non-stop ride of a cavalry division through enemy territory in American history.

Many of the men were too tired to prepare anything to eat. They just dropped from their saddles and fell asleep on the ground, still holding the reins to their horses. Morgan didn't post pickets at Williamsburg. He felt the Union cavalry would be delayed by the burned bridges and lack of good replacement horses.

Continue on Main Street for two blocks to Third Street. Morgan's headquarters on Main Street was one door from the northwest corner of Third and Main at the village tavern owned by John Wesley Kain. Kain's staff was kept busy preparing meals for 136 raiders. Morgan stayed in room number nine of the adjoining Kain House Hotel. While at the hotel, he went through the Willliamsburg mail that his men had confiscated. He was looking for news of military importance and cash.

Kain House Hotel & Tavern (c. 1816) were razed in 1907.

Six of Morgan's officers slept at the Kain Hotel. Many of the officers camped with their men. While many of the raiders bivouacked in the "Big Field," others camped east of town along the Bethel Road between the bridge and the hill. A few camped in town, while other raiders slept along the roads to Boston and Batavia.

A gutsy local farmer, Solomon Mershon, challenged a raider attempting to steal his horse to a fair fight. Mershon won the fist fight and was allowed to keep his mount.

Some of the raiders looted the dry goods stores and shops and exchanged their old hats and boots for new ones. They carried away whole bolts of calico and muslin, tying one end of the cloth to their saddles and dragging the material in the dirt as they rode back to their camps.

Before the first rebels arrived in Williamsburg, a travel-stained Union soldier slipped into town. Lieutenant Archibald Carson was serving as a Union scout in Kentucky when he was captured by the raiders. He had been forced to ride with them through Indiana and into Ohio, but he escaped near Williamsburg. Carson was seeking refuge until the raiders passed, after which he intended to join Hobson's force.

Carson was hidden in the cellar of Lewis Ellis's shoemaker residence on Main Street, where he was forgotten. Some of Morgan's men searched the area but were unable to find their missing prisoner.

After the raiders and their Union pursuers were gone, Ellis's daughter, Lizzie, remembered the soldier she had hidden in the cellar. Carson, who had visions of serving time in Libby Prison, was glad to be given a horse, which enabled him to rejoin his regiment, the 8th Kentucky (U.S) Cavalry, the next day.

While the raiders stopped early and enjoyed their first good night's sleep in weeks, Hobson's men rode until 9 p.m. before going into camp. They spent the night near present-day Mount Repose, nearly fifteen miles from Williamsburg.

The following night, a gang of scalawags rode into Williamsburg. They reported that Morgan's men were headed back to burn the town and murder all the citizens — men, women, and children. The panicked citizens gathered their prized possessions and fled to

CAMP DENNISON TO WILLIAMSBURG

the woods. Many of these people left town on Pignut Alley (present-day South Third Street). The following morning they returned to their homes after hearing that the news had been false.

Go two blocks and turn left onto Front Street, the last street before the bridge. John Atchley's hotel and store stands on the northwest corner of Front and Main streets. Atchley lost two horses, a wagon, hay and grain, and $140 in goods from his grocery store.

John Atchley's hotel and grocery store (c. 1854)

After going one block, look off to the right. At its eastern end, Gay Street dead ends at a "dug-away" that leads to an old ford across the East Fork of the Little Miami River. Long before the Civil War, it was a fording spot on the Bullskin Trail, one of the most important Indian trails in Ohio. The ford was used by Simon Kenton and Daniel Boone.

Dug-away and ford

Wednesday, July 15, 1863

When the Union cavalry arrived in Williamsburg, the men were diverted down Gay Street to the ford, rather than down Main Street. The townsfolk had prepared food and beverages for them. They lined the street and handed food to the soldiers as they rode by. Williamsburg residents claim that their town was "the first ride-through fast-food service."

Hobson's men reached the river and began fording about 1 p.m. on July 15.

Turn left onto Gay Street. John Williams's house is on the right at 112 Gay Street.

Colonel John Williams's house

Confederate artillery Captain Joseph E. Harris, a Northern student at the Nashville University in Nashville, Tennessee, had been caught up in the war fervor and enrolled, with the rest of his senior class, in the Confederate army. After the Battle of Shiloh, his battery was assigned to Morgan.

Harris was looking for an opportunity to break away and return to the North. His father was a Union Navy paymaster and friend of General Burnside. With the aid of Bryon Williams, Harris hid in the attic of the Williams home. The house belonged to Bryon's father, Colonel John Williams.

Three Confederate officers, Captain A.W. Ray, Captain Thomas Hines, and Chaplain Thomas J. Moore, spent the night in the second-floor bedroom on the left-front corner of the house. Their room was directly below the attic where Harris was hiding. When the raiders left the Williams home, they took a horse, a locket, and $4.

After the raiders had gone, Harris confided in Williams that he had only three rounds of ammunition left for his four cannons. The following day, he dressed in a plain black suit that he had appropriated from a store in Indiana. His old jacket, left with his host, became a prized memento of the raid. Doctor S. S. Walker and Frank A. Warden accompanied Harris to Cincinnati. There, he turned himself in to Burnside, and then took an oath to the Union. Soon after, he was sent abroad due to ill health. He died at sea and was buried in England.

Continue down Gay Street to Second Street. Doctor Leavitt T. Pease's eight-room home stands on the northeast corner of Gay and Second streets. Pease, a political and social leader in the Williamsburg community, helped runaway slaves on the Underground Railroad as they moved north to the Quaker community in Clinton County. He lost corn, a horse, and a spring wagon to Morgan's men.

Dr. Leavitt Pease house (c. 1840)

During the night while the exhausted rebels slept, Pease slipped into their camp trying to locate his horse. He was unable to find his own horse, but he did locate and release a horse belonging to Doctor E. C. Sharp.

Turn left onto Second Street. When you return to Main Street, turn left to leave Williamsburg.

Chapter Three

WILLIAMSBURG TO LOCUST GROVE

Wednesday, July 15, 1863

The raiders' well-earned rest ended with a 3 a.m. reveille. The advance riders were on the road by dawn. By 8 a.m., the last of Morgan's men were gone.

Before leaving Williamsburg, the raiders broke up the pigpen at the John Harvey Wright farm; it was located on the left just before the covered bridge. Wright was away, serving with the Union army. The raiders whittled shavings off the boards and piled them up in key areas of the bridge to serve as kindling. After crossing the East Fork of the Little Miami River, they burned the bridge. The nearby Wright home was threatened by the flames. Townsfolk hurried to the site and saved the house. They were unable to save the almost-new bridge, the pride of their community. The burning of the bridge was a waste, as the river was almost dry: Fording it posed no problem for the Union pursuers.

Bridge built in 1864 to replace bridge burned by raiders.

Soon after Morgan's rear guard crossed the river, Sergeant John Quincy Park, of the 2nd Ohio Cavalry, arrived. The local man was serving with Hobson and had been sent ahead. He was to check on his family and assure the townsfolk that the Union forces were coming. Although many pantry shelves had been emptied in providing meals for the raiders, local citizens lost no time in finding and preparing food for Morgan's pursuers.

Hobson had lost precious time by riding through Batavia. His main force arrived in Williamsburg about 1 p.m. The men paused only long enough to eat.

Reportedly, a Union teamster was mortally injured when he fell under the wheels of a battery wagon. The accident occurred near Kain's Tavern. The soldier was carried to the tavern's office where he was placed on a table. He died during the night and was buried in the town cemetery. Later, relatives disinterred the body and moved it to his home.

Cross the bridge over the East Fork. Some of the raiders camped on this side of the stream.

A small company of raiders turned left and rode two and a half miles to the community of De La Palma, near the Clermont-Brown County Line. The citizens of that community filed claims for the loss of twelve horses, eight to the Rebs and four to the Yanks. From De La Palma, the raiders turned east, moving along a road that paralleled Morgan's route. They passed through Buford and Sinking Spring in Highland County.

Farther north in Brown County, at St. Martins, the Ursuline Sisters at the girls' school shuttered the windows and kept night watch. They heard the distant thud of horses' hooves as the raiders passed to the south.

After crossing East Fork, drive 0.3 mile to the junction with SR 133. One of Morgan's brothers, Colonel Richard (Dick) Morgan, took the road to the right (SR 133). His regiment, the 14th Kentucky Cavalry, passed through Bethel and Georgetown en route to Ripley on the Ohio River. When his scouts determined there were Union troops and gunboats at Ripley, the raiders turned away from the town. They moved northeast to rejoin the main column at Locust Grove.

See Appendix J for more information about Dick Morgan's ride to Ripley. This interesting alternate route includes Georgetown and Ripley, an abolitionist stronghold. The John Rankin House, a state historical site located on the hill overlooking Ripley, is open to the public.

To follow Morgan's main column and the designated Morgan Trail, continue straight on the old plank road (Tri-County Highway/Old SR 32). It is 6.8 miles

WILLIAMSBURG TO LOCUST GROVE

to the traffic light at US 68 in Mt. Orab. Along the way, you will enter Brown County, where Union general and future president of the United States, Ulysses S. Grant, spent most of his childhood. Our tour includes a side trip from Mt. Orab to Georgetown, the boyhood home of Ulysses S. Grant. Turn right on US 68. Drive 9.4 miles and turn right on Mt. Orab Pike.

Drive 0.5 mile on Mt. Orab Pike to a cemetery on the right. The cemetery has a history related to Grant. Local accounts credit young Ulysses Grant with moving a large stone from White Oak Creek to a home at the corner of Main and State streets for the purpose of using the stone as a porch step. In 1906, the house was torn down, and on its site the brick Public Building was built. The stone was relocated to the cemetery at that time. The stone later was moved from the cemetery to the backyard of the Grant Homestead, where the stone resides today.

Continue 1.4 miles on Mt. Orab Pike/North Main Street. The house at 421 North Main Street was the home of a "War Democrat," U.S. Congressman Chilton White. His support of Lincoln's war efforts angered the Confederates (mostly Democrats), who thought their Northern party members were turning their backs on them in support of the "Black Republicans." Raiders searching for his home were told by residents, who lied, that White lived miles to the west. The raiders, expecting their Union pursuers to approach Georgetown from that direction, decided not to pursue the matter. The house still stands unharmed.

U.S. Congressman Chilton White's house

Continue 0.2 mile to downtown Georgetown. Georgetown was the boyhood home of Ulysses S. Grant. The Grant family moved from Point Pleasant to Georgetown soon after his birth.

Turn left on Grant Avenue. A life-size gray, granite statue of Grant, Georgetown's most famous resident, stands on the northeast corner of Grant Avenue and Main Street. Its black granite base displays laser art pictures of Grant as the commander of all Union forces and as the eighteenth president. This man, best known for waging war, left us with his most famous quote, "Let us have peace."

The Brown County Courthouse is on the right. **Trail Sign #12** stands at the northwest corner of the Courthouse Square lawn.

Brown County Courthouse (c. 1851)

JOHN HUNT MORGAN HERITAGE TRAIL INTERPRETIVE SIGN #12

Arriving in Georgetown about 9:30 a.m., the raiders stayed approximately three hours. Some of the men picketed their horses around Courthouse Square. Others rested their weary mounts at the fairgrounds; squads were sent out to secure food.

Dick Morgan's men met with little resistance. Most of the town's able-bodied men had gone to Ripley, where the raiders were expected to attempt a crossing. Only one Union soldier was in the village. Lieutenant William H. Hannah of the 4th Ohio Independent Cavalry Company was home from Vicksburg to recruit. He went to the Square in his new Union uniform to see what was going on with all the horses. He was met

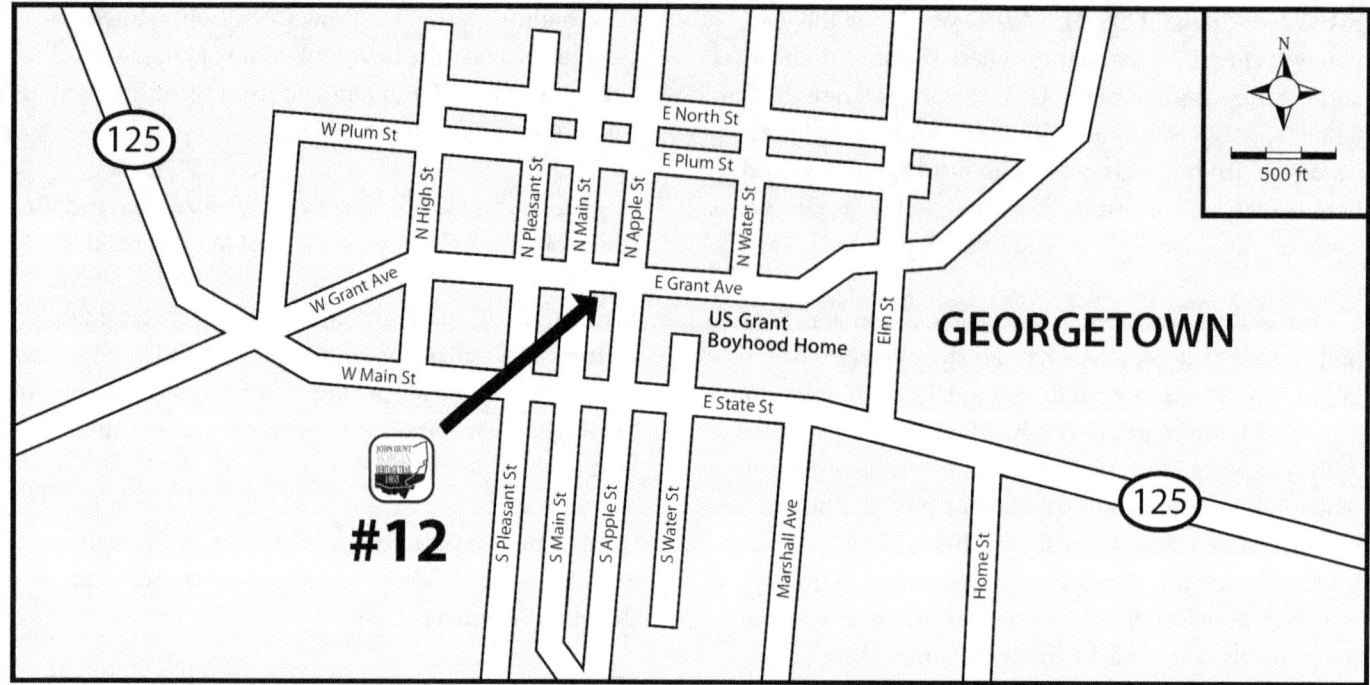

John Hunt Morgan Heritage Trail Interpretive sign #12 map

with gunfire and fled. To this day no one knows how he avoided capture. It is suspected he hid in an outhouse pit because he would never divulge his secret. Following the war, Hannah returned to Georgetown and became a pharmacist and a leader in the local GAR (Grand Army of the Republic).

The raiders looted the stores of Evans & Woodward, Cyrus Newkirk, Adam Shane, Charles Theis, and Charles Zaumseil. The Confederates not only took boots and shoes from the shop of George Woodward, but they also took the owner's overcoat.

While the raiders usually took what they wanted from stores and left the rest of the stock alone, that changed at Colthar's grocery store at the southeast corner of Cherry and Main streets. The raiders broke open a full barrel of molasses and poured it over a large pill of clothing and other items they didn't want.

The raiders visited the Henry Brunner home and cobbler shop in Federal Row, across Apple Street from the courthouse. Brunner repaired the rebels' boots while his wife cooked for the hungry men. In return, they were allowed to keep their horses. The intruders didn't find the family silver that had been lowered into the well. Union General Jacob Ammen lived as a boy in the house next door at number 115.

Henry Brunner cobbler shop and residence

While in Georgetown, Dick Morgan investigated the rumor that the Georgetown bank contained large deposits of gold, shipped there by Kentucky banks at the onset of the raid. He posted guards at the bank and sent Lieutenant Leeland Hathaway and several other raiders to locate the cashier. They found him at home. The cashier was able to convince the raiders that the rumor was unfounded. He then invited Hathaway and his men to share his dinner.

F. J. Phillips, one of the owners of the King-Phillips bank, sent his elderly black janitor to bury the bank's $60,000 in gold coins in the woods. The raiders forced the man to go with them when they left Georgetown, claiming that he was an escaped slave.

The bank's money was never found. Five years after the war, a black couple, with the same last name as the old janitor, walked into Georgetown. When they left a few days later, they had sufficient gold to purchase a team of horses and a surrey.

Some of the Georgetown residents welcomed the rebels. There were many "Peace Democrats" and Southern sympathizers living in the area. It was reported that several local Confederate sympathizers joined Morgan's men when they left the area.

Another column of horsemen dressed in blue, with stars and stripes flying, arrived in town later in the day, and after a few hours rest on the fairgrounds, they continued their pursuit of the Confederates.

The men of Company E of the 7th Ohio Volunteer Cavalry were the vanguard of the Union pursuit through Brown County because Colonel August Kautz, who had grown up in Brown County, understood that these boys knew the roads of their native county. Company E was commanded by Captain R. C. Rankin, son of Reverend John Rankin, and was made up of men from every township of Brown County. The pace of the pursuit was so hurried that the cavalrymen would see a loved one along the route, but instead of stopping to talk, they would swing the person up behind them in the saddle and visit for a mile or two. Then the passenger would be lowered back to the ground to make his or her way home on foot, and the pursuit pressed on.

To visit Georgetown's Grant sites, continue on Grant Avenue, crossing Apple Street. The first school that Grant attended is on the right.

Grant's boyhood home is located on the left at 219 East Grant Avenue. He lived here until the age of seventeen, when he left to attend West Point. His five siblings were born in the Georgetown house.

Grant's boyhood home

The Grant Boyhood Home is owned by the Ohio Historical Society; check their Web page for information, or contact the Bailey House Bed and Breakfast at 112 North Water Street, Georgetown, Ohio (phone: (937) 378-3087; Web site: *www.baileyhousebandb.com*). The Grant Boyhood Home is open Wednesday–Sunday, noon–5 p.m., Memorial Day through Labor Day; Saturday and Sunday, noon–5 p.m., September and October. Phone: (877) 372-8177; Web site: *http://www.ohiohistory.org/museums-and-historic-sites/*.

The house across the street was once part of the building that housed Jesse Grant's tannery. Young Ulysses was expected to help his father at the tan-

Grant attended this school at 208 E. Grant Avenue in 1827.

Part of Jesse Grant's tannery building (c. 1823)

nery. He did so reluctantly; he preferred working with horses. Grant was remembered by many in Georgetown for his skill with horses.

Turn left on Water Street. The large, white, Greek Revival house on the right was the home of Dr. George Bailey, the first physician in Georgetown. His son Bart, a friend of Grant's, flunked out of West Point. This provided the opportunity for Grant to receive an appointment to the academy.

Dr. George Bailey house (c. 1830)

Turn left onto Plum Street and then left again onto Apple Street. Drive four blocks and turn left onto State Street (SR 125).

Immediately turn right onto Water Street. The Grant School House is located at 508 South Water Street. It is maintained by the Ohio Historical Society; the hours of operation for the school house are the same as those for the Grant Boyhood Home. Phone: (877) 372-8177; Web site: *http://www.ohiohistory.org/museums-and-historic-sites/*.

Grant attended this two room school (c. 1829) on Water Street.

Turn around; return to SR 125 and turn right. Go 1.6 miles to US 68. To rejoin John Morgan and the main force at Mt. Orab, turn left.

Drive 1.2 miles on US 68, and then turn left onto Camp Run Road (CR 37) for less than 0.1 mile. Turn right onto Veterans Boulevard; drive approximately 0.5 mile to the Ohio Veterans' Home. There is a life-size statue of General Ulysses S. Grant on the front lawn.

Grant statue

A 12-pounder brass, Napoleon cannon is located in front of the main building. It was forged in Cincinnati in 1864 and was placed in service at Johnson's Island Confederate POW Camp near Sandusky, Ohio, where Basil Duke was held.

Twelve-pounder brass, Napoleon cannon from Johnson's Island

WILLIAMSBURG TO LOCUST GROVE

Return to US 68 and turn left. Drive 6.2 miles. The covered bridge on the left was built after the Civil War at the site of the bridge damaged by the raiders. It is 172 feet, the longest single-span covered bridge in Ohio.

New Hope Covered Bridge (c. 1878)

Continue 0.2 mile on US 68 and turn right onto New Hope-White Oak Station Road; then immediately bear left onto New Hope Street in the town of New Hope.

The large brick building on the left was a hotel, tavern, and store at the time of the Civil War.

Hotel, tavern, store (c. 1846)

Some of Morgan's men shot a volley into the hillside behind the town, terrifying the citizens. It was reported farmer Milton Patton walked behind the tobacco warehouse on the east side waving a white table cloth.

The citizens of New Hope filed claims for the loss of twelve horses — eleven were taken by the raiders and one by a Union man. Several guns were also stolen.

Turn right onto Walnut Street and then turn right again. The New Hope Methodist Church is on the left. Some of the raiders rested their weary horses in the churchyard.

New Hope Methodist Church (c. 1851)

Continue on New Hope-White Oak Station Road through the stop and turn right onto US 68.

It is 4.6 miles to East Main Street/Tri-County Highway (CR 24B) in Mt. Orab; turn right. Thirty-six claims were filed by residents here. Forty horses were reported stolen. Rebels looted the stores and emptied several huckster wagons before moving on. Oscar Dunn filed for the loss of 150 pounds of pork, two shirts, a razor, and the fifty cents he paid for the release of his fiddle.

Drive 2.0 miles on Tri-County Highway (CR 24B); the present highway curves right. The original road (now closed at the tracks) continued straight. The railroad and White Oak Station did not exist in 1863.

Go 0.6 mile; you will cross the North Fork of White Oak Creek. The original road was off to your left. Morgan's men burned the 115-foot North Fork covered bridge built in 1852.

Reset your odometer; continue 2.6 miles. The field on the left was the site of the home of Noah and Elizabeth Hite and their twelve children. Sam, the youngest, was four years old. The family was sitting down to eat when hungry raiders arrived and took their food. One Confederate soldier struck up a conversation with young Sam. He told him he had a son at home about his age, and his son had no shoes.

Noah Hite home no longer stands.

Dr. Isaac M. Beck's office and residence

He asked for Sam's shoes. Sam gave him his shoes, and the soldier gave him candy in return.

Sam lived his whole life in this house; he married, raised five children, and died here. His descendents still have a painting of the nearby covered bridge burned by Morgan's men.

It is 0.2 mile to the Tri-County Highway bridge across the East Fork of White Oak Creek. A Sardinia man hid his cash high in the rafters of the covered bridge located here. The raiders burned the 115-foot bridge and with it the man's fortune.

East Fork of White Oak Creek

Brown County trustees filed a claim for $3,380 for the loss of the two bridges. The state awarded them only $2,064.

Continue 0.8 mile to the stop sign in Sardinia. The building (c. 1835) on the northeast corner of Winchester and Main served as the office and residence of Dr. Isaac M. Beck. It was also an important station on the Underground Railroad.

Dr. Beck, an ardent abolitionist and temperance advocate, was forced to give up to the raiders a horse, harness, $50 in cash, and many of his surgical instruments. Union forces later took the rest of the instruments.

The raiders looted the Sardinia stores. Thomas Davis lost a horse and $350 worth of assorted goods from his country variety store. Stephen Feike filed a large claim of $2,625 for dry goods and other merchandise stolen. Hugh Kennedy and Ellison Purdy were awarded $600 for the loss of boots and shoes. William Henderson filed two claims, one for the loss of merchandise and whiskey to the rebels, and the other for 100 meals served to Union troops.

Hobson's troopers arrived in Sardinia around 11 p.m. and made camp in and around the town. They were on the move again by 4 a.m.

In the Sardinia area, the raiders stole twenty-one horses and the Union cavalry appropriated ten.

As they moved east, Morgan's men found Buckeyes to be more formidable than Hoosiers. The raiders' progress was hampered by felled trees and small skirmishes. Basil Duke reported, "Small fights with the militia were of daily occurrence. They hung around the column, wounding two or three men every day and sometimes killing one. We captured hundreds of them daily, but could only turn them loose again after destroying their guns."

Drive two blocks (0.2 mile) and bear right onto Winchester Street (Tri-County Hwy/CR 24C). It is 2.3 miles to Five Points. Turn left, then immediately bear

WILLIAMSBURG TO LOCUST GROVE

right at the "Y" intersection onto Five Points-Fincastle Road (CR 82). At 0.4 mile, cross SR 32 and drive 1.7 miles to the intersection with Heaton Road.

Ahead at Fincastle, Morgan's scouts skirmished with the home guard. With Hobson's men close behind, Morgan had no time to lose. He turned the main column aside and headed to Winchester (Scott in 1863).

The raiders stopped Charles Dietrich on his way to market in Fincastle. They not only took his produce, but they also took his huckster wagon and three horses. In the Fincastle area, 13 more horses were taken by raiders and 10 more by Union pursuers. James Records lost a winter harness with sleigh bells.

Turn right on Heaton Road (TR 74). Go 1.4 miles to Tri-County Hwy (CR 24C/SR 74); turn left. It is 5.1 miles to SR 136 (Main Street) in Winchester, Adams County. You are entering town on South Street. If possible, park on the right side before the stop sign.

During the Civil War, the population of Winchester was approximately 500 people. The citizens had been warned of Morgan's approach by fast-riding Will McClanahan, a young man who lived between Winchester and Fincastle.

The township treasurer had time to bury the town's funds by a fence post north of town. However, there was insufficient time for the citizens to hide their horses. The advance riders arrived about 9 a.m.; they galloped into town, cheering and firing pistols. This demonstration was intended to throw the citizens into panic and confusion. The advance men also ordered the townswomen to begin cooking. The food would be ready by the time the main force arrived.

The building that stood on the left at the northwest corner of Main and South streets was owned by Elizabeth Eyler. The Masonic Hall occupied the second floor. Israel H. DeBruin's dry goods store was located on the first level.

DeBruin was away, serving as quartermaster of the 70th Ohio Volunteer Infantry (OVI). After discovering the store was owned by a Mason, the raiders did not loot indiscriminately. Morgan and many of his men were Masons. There are a number of documented incidences in which raiders respected the rights and property of fellow Masons. The raiders paid for their purchases with Confederate money, although it had no value. After the war, DeBruin filed a claim for $858.66 for his losses. The building burned in the fire of 1917.

A Union officer, Lieutenant Hines, had been captured at Bardstown, Kentucky. He had been forced to ride with the raiders. When they arrived here, Hines was taken to the Norval Osburn house, where he was held captive. The Osburn house stood on your right, at the southwest corner of Main and South streets. It has been moved to Washington Street.

Hines, feigning illness, sought and was granted permission to go to the drugstore. He slipped through a gate in a board fence and moved to the back of Jerome DeBruin's home. His home was located next door to his brother's dry goods store. Jerome directed Hines to his parents' home.

Turn left on Main Street; the elder DeBruin's brick home was located on the left, three doors north of South Street.

Rebecca & Hyman I. DeBruin's house is gone.

Hyman Israel DeBruin was born in Holland. He immigrated to the U.S. in 1819. By 1833, he had married and moved to Winchester, where he became a prominent businessman. In 1844, he renounced the Jewish religion and became a member of the Methodist Church. He died in 1871; his tombstone, in the Winchester Cemetery, is inscribed, "Born a Jew, lived a life of faith, died a Christian."

When Hines arrived at DeBruin's house, Grandma Rebecca DeBruin took him to the cellar. She removed several loose stones so he could crawl under the house. She sat calmly in her rocker while Confederates searched her home and the neighboring houses. The next day, Hobson arrived and issued Hines a pass to return to his home in Kentucky.

The Union general used the DeBruin house as his temporary headquarters. He and his staff spent several hours there, dining and scanning dispatches, before rejoining the troops.

Raiders broke into Johnny Frow's combination grocery, drug store, and post office. The brick building still stands on the right, at 19262 Main Street, three doors south of Washington Street.

Continue north on Main Street to Washington Street. On the far right corner is **Trail Sign #13**.

John Frow's grocery, drug store, and post-office (c. 1837)

JOHN HUNT MORGAN HERITAGE TRAIL INTERPRETIVE SIGN #13

Morgan made the Nicholas Bunn Hotel his temporary headquarters. It was a large two-story building with an upstairs balcony extending over the sidewalk. The hotel, located on the right on the southeast corner of Main Street and Cross Alley (between Washington and Jefferson streets), burned in 1886.

Bunn was compelled to provide 155 meals for the rebel officers, who also took feed for their horses from the hotel livery stables.

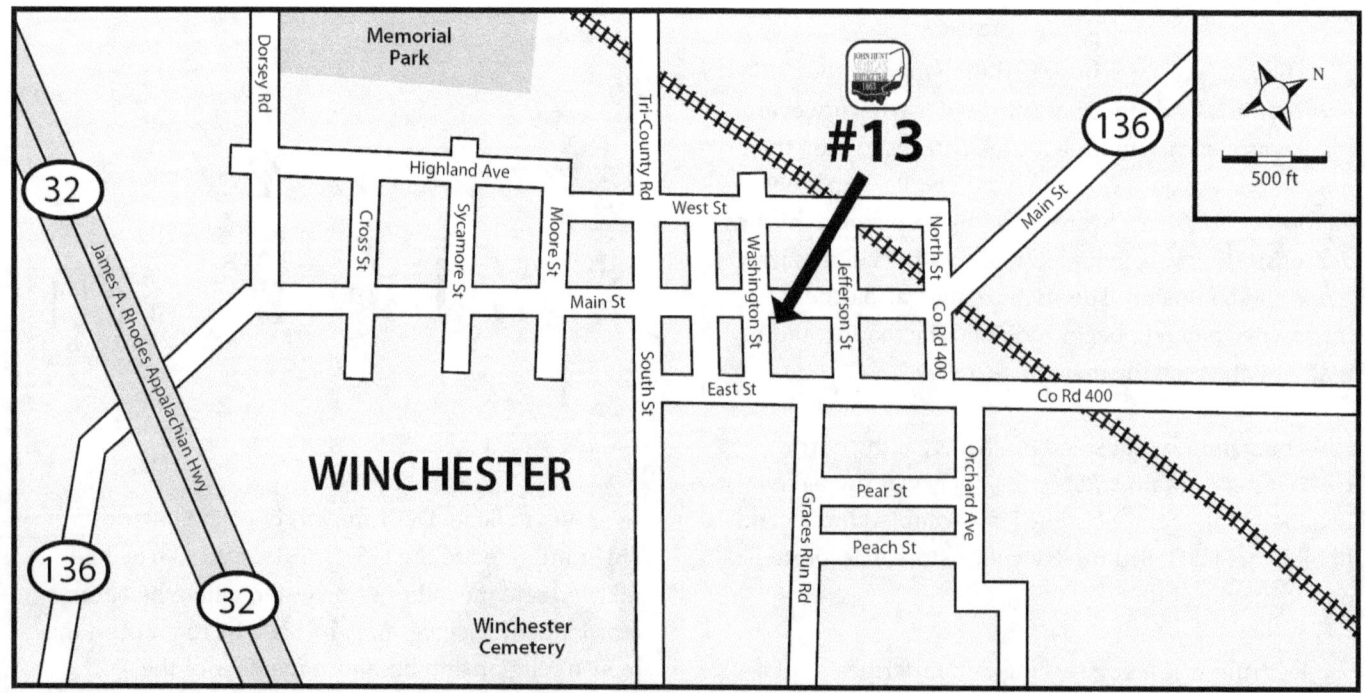

John Hunt Morgan Heritage Trail Interpretive sign #13 map

WILLIAMSBURG TO LOCUST GROVE

Bunn House Hotel occupied this site.

Here, Morgan waited for the Aberdeen-Hillsboro Stage that was carrying the mail and Cincinnati newspapers from Ripley to Hillsboro. Tired of waiting, he sent men southeast of town to meet the stage. They forced the driver, Gilbert Paul, off the coach and brought it into town.

A Winchester resident and passenger on the stage, Mrs. Mary Lockwood, saved her money by hiding it in her petticoats.

While Morgan waited, his men found other things to do. Some broke the muskets of the home guard; others tied American flags to mules' tails and chased them through the streets. The raiders rode up and down the streets, dragging bolts of cloth and blowing on the stolen instruments of the Winchester Saxe-Horn Band. Many exhausted raiders rested under the locust trees along Main Street and at the old Winchester cemetery.

Housewives were required to bake bread and biscuits, and fry ham and chicken for the hungry men. Many of the officers ate at White's, the only restaurant in town. Quantities of hay, oats, and corn were taken from the mill, livery stables, and barns. Businessmen lost more than $40,000 worth of merchandise, including 15,000 cigars taken from the Anderson Havens store. The biggest loser was the store of E. E. Wilkins and N. R. Thompson; looting there amounted to $8,800.

When Postmaster Frow realized the incoming mail pouches had been diverted to Morgan's room at the Bunn Hotel, he went there representing the U.S. government and demanded to be allowed to sort the mail. Morgan informed him that he was the government that day and would sort the mail himself. He offered to assist Frow down the stairs with the toe of his boot.

As he read the newspapers, Morgan's concern grew. He gave orders for the entire command to assemble at the cemetery southeast of town. Go one more block on Main Street and turn left onto Jefferson Street, then left onto West Street, and left again onto Washington Street. The relocated Norval Osburn house, in which Lieutenant Hines was held, is on the left.

Relocated Norval Osburn house

Go one block and turn right onto Main Street. It is one block to South Street.

*Side Trip: Continue 0.3 mile south on Main Street (SR 136) to view the Morgan's Raid **Ohio Historical Marker**. It is on the right side before the junction with SR 32. Return to Winchester and turn right onto South Street.*

Turn left onto South Street. Proceed less than half a block. The large two-story brick house on the right was Doctor Abel C. Lewis's home. Lewis, a staunch abolitionist, was forced to provide food, a horse, and fodder to the raiders. The house, with its secret passageways, served as a station on the Underground Railroad.

Continue on South Street to the cemetery. Here, Morgan addressed his men, stressing the urgency of the situation: Hobson was closely pursuing them, and Union gunboats were patrolling the Ohio River. He acknowledged that the situation was becoming critical.

Doctor Abel C. Lewis house (c. 1845)

After Morgan spoke to his men, they followed the old Grace's Run (Jacksonville) Road through the cemetery and across Elk Fork to a junction with the present-day Grace's Run Road. The old road now dead-ends beyond the cemetery.

By 4 p.m., the raiders were on the move. Hobson's force arrived early the next morning. The tired men in blue stopped only long enough to enjoy the food and coffee prepared by the local women.

The Winchester Cemetery contains the remains of more than 100 Civil War soldiers.

Raiders left Winchester on old road through cemetery.

Return to the stop sign at East Street and turn right. Go two blocks to Grace's Run Road (CR 1) and turn right. Reset your odometer.

At 1.0 mile cross SR 32 and continue 3.5 miles on Grace's Run Road to the junction with SR 137. The road to the right was used by Dick Morgan's force coming from Ripley. When they reached this junction, most of his men turned right on Grace's Run Road. From here, they followed the same route used by General Morgan's main column.

Turn left onto SR 137 and immediately turn right. Follow Grace's Run Road for another 1.9 miles to the Harshaville covered bridge. The bridge spans the Cherry Fork of Ohio Brush Creek. The raiders crossed the bridge but failed to burn it.

Harshaville Bridge (c. 1855) survived the raid.

Harshaville was not a post office at the time of the Civil War. Claims from the Harshaville/Unity area are filed as being from Wheat Ridge.

Cross the bridge and look to the left. This was the location of George A. Patton's store and residence. He filed a claim for $1,559 for loss of merchandise and one horse.

1909 photo of Patton store and residence

In 1863, Harshaville was a thriving town. It had been settled by Paul Harsha, a bricklayer from Pennsylvania. In 1846, Harsha, intent on changing occupations, purchased the Wright grist mill and log cabin on Cherry Fork Creek. This was the beginning of the

WILLIAMSBURG TO LOCUST GROVE

Sketch from Caldwell's atlas. William Buchanan Harsha's house was on the left, and the mill was across the road on the right.

town which soon included a number of homes, several stores, a tavern and a hotel. The mill closed in 1925; only a few of the buildings remain.

Pull into the dead-end road on the right. This was the setting for the sketch from the *1880 Caldwell's Atlas of Adams County*. The old brick house in the field on the left was the home of William Buchanan Harsha, Paul's oldest son, who lived there at the time of the Civil War. He lost two horses, a saddle and two bridles to the raiders. They did not enter the house itself, but visited the cellar. They found several stoneware jugs, containing what they thought was sweet apple cider. Lifting the jugs to their lips, the thirsty men soon discovered it was vinegar.

"Hillcrest", the Paul Harsha home (c. 1848)

Harsha lost seven horses valued at $780 to Morgan's men. When the raiders arrived at Hillcrest, his wife, Martha, had just finished making several jars of preserves and jelly. Martha put the "goodies" in a cupboard and seated several grandchildren on the floor in front of it. Morgan's men entered the house but did not disturb the small children playing on the floor.

Return to the main road; its name changes from Grace's Run Road to Wheat Ridge Road after passing through the bridge. Turn right and go 1.6 miles to the stop sign in Unity.

William Buchanan Harsha's house (c. 1853)

Paul Harsha's home, "Hillcrest," still stands on the hill overlooking the town. It is hidden by trees and cannot be seen from the road. His son, nineteen-year-old Nathan, died in the Civil War.

Seven miles away at West Union, the townspeople were expecting the raiders and were in a state of panic. Citizens felled trees on the approach to the Adams County seat. The County Treasurer, George Moore, buried $7,000 of county funds in his father's pigsty. All manner of precautions were taken, but Unity was as close as the raiders would come to West Union.

Continue straight on Wheat Ridge Road, passing through the Wheat Ridge community.

It is 4.2 miles from Unity to Dunkinsville, which sits on the old Zane's Trace. The Trace (SR 41) was an early road laid out in 1797 along Shawnee Indian trails. It ran from Wheeling, West Virginia, to Maysville, Kentucky. The road was sponsored in part by the federal government, which issued land grants to Colonel Ebenezer Zane to develop the route. It was the only major road in Ohio until after the War of 1812.

As you turn left onto SR 41, note the Dunkinsville church on the right. The bell tower shown in the early photo has been removed. Many of Morgan's men rested their horses in the churchyard.

Early photo of Dunkinsville church

While the raiders were in Dunkinsville, they took groceries, dry goods, and other merchandise from the Phillips and Eakins stores.

Drive 4.0 miles to SR 781 and turn right; then go two blocks and turn right onto Old SR 41 (Jacksonville Road).

Jacksonville (Dunbarton Post Office, or Jack Town) was named in honor of Andrew Jackson who had traveled through on the Trace and spent the night there.

The village sits high on a hill with an excellent view of the surrounding countryside. The original road entered the town from the south. It was abandoned in 1978, when the new bridge and bypass were completed.

At the time of the raid, the town consisted of two stores, a tavern, a small hotel, a tannery, a livery stable, and a few houses.

Morgan was reported to have spent the night at Kilpatrick's Inn. It stood on the right, in the middle of the first block, before Lilly Alley. The sign at the inn bore a Masonic emblem, which provided the establishment some degree of protection from rebel depredations.

Kilpatrick's Inn in Jacksonville has been razed.

Mrs. Kilpatrick cooked for the general and his officers. Before leaving, Morgan gave her his cape in appreciation for her services. She treasured the cape and wore it to church for years.

Many of the raiders bivouacked in the Jacksonville area; some slept in the village square. The advance troops rode six miles ahead to Locust Grove. Other raiders camped along the road between the two towns.

A local Jacksonville legend has an elderly man fearlessly attacking some of Morgan's men. The raiders brought out a rope and prepared to hang the man. Several locals ran to the inn and brought Morgan back to the square. He confronted the condemned man and asked what was going on. The feisty old fellow said, "You can hang me, but you can't stop me from fighting you until then." Morgan ordered him released, saying, "If we had just 100 men of this caliber in the Southern army, we could lick the whole North."

Riders were sent into the surrounding countryside looking for horses; many of the horses, carefully hidden by their owners, were found and confiscated. The stores of Joseph Wisecup and Wesley Thoroman were looted.

Another local legend is the story of raider John Barnes, who was favorably impressed with the Jacksonville area. Before leaving the next morning, he told some of the townsfolk of his intention to return someday and make the town his home. No one believed him. Ten years later, the Barnes family arrived and was welcomed into the community.

Drive the loop around the public square and return to the stop sign at SR 781. Turn left. Continue straight to the junction with SR 41. Reset your odometer and turn right onto SR 41.

It is 3.0 miles to Elm Street in Peebles. The town did not exist during the Civil War. In 1863, local residents traveled northeast to the village of Palestine to get their mail.

Continue 0.7 mile on SR 41. On the left is the historic Aerl Inn, another wayside inn on the Trace. Its construction is part stone, part frame, and part brick.

Stephen and Mariah Reynolds owned the old inn at the time of Morgan's Raid. A group of rebel soldiers bivouacked in the field on the left side of the house; they left early the following morning. Reynolds filed a claim for $201; it included losses for one horse, ninety bushels of wheat, harnesses, and food appropriated from the kitchen.

Continue 0.2 mile north on SR 41. A lane on the left once led to the two-story Mitchell/Anderson home. The house was destroyed by heavy winds in the late 1980s. At the time of the Civil War, the house was owned by William Mitchell.

Mitchell lost six horses, more than one hundred bushels of wheat, four tons of hay, a saddle, and a bridle to the rebels.

According to legend, many of the local men, afraid of being taken prisoner, fled the area and hid in the nearby hills and hollows. Their wives and mothers congregated on the upper porch of the Mitchell house. From there, they watched the movements of the enemy, and when the raiders had departed, signaled their "brave" men to return home.

It is 0.9 mile to the old Wickerham Inn on the right. The inn was built during 1800–01 by Peter Wickerham, a Revolutionary War veteran. It was used as an overnight stagecoach stop and tavern on Zane's Trace until the 1850s. In 1863, the community surrounding the inn was known as Palestine.

Wickerham Inn (c. 1801)

In 1863, the Aerl Inn was owned by Stephen Reynolds.

Henry Clay and Andrew Jackson are reported to have stayed at the inn, while traveling from Kentucky and Tennessee to Washington, D.C. Runaway slaves hid here when the Underground Railroad was in operation.

Some of Morgan's men spent Wednesday night at the inn. It was reported by Peter Noah Wickerham, the old man's grandson, that on the night of July 15–16, the brick house was abandoned to the rebels, clusters of whom were sleeping on the floor.

Continue 1.5 miles to SR 73 in Locust Grove, where Morgan's advance troops camped for the night. At the northeast corner, next to the firehouse, is **Trail Sign #14**.

JOHN HUNT MORGAN HERITAGE TRAIL INTERPRETIVE SIGN #14

The residents of Locust Grove knew the pursuing Union forces were close behind Morgan. At the time of the raid, David and Martha Eylar were operating the old Cannon Hotel. Women there were busy preparing food and hiding it until the Union troops arrived. The advance raiders arrived before the bread was hidden. They consumed the bread and ordered the women to keep baking.

One of the raiders entered the kitchen and shot the lock off the sugar safe drawer. He ran his hands through the precious sugar searching for silver. The silver was not there, but safely hidden in a bucket under some berry bushes.

Raiders also visited the Kilpatrick house, which stood on the northeast corner of SR 41 and Locust Street. The Kilpatrick house was built in 1849. Following the Civil War, David Eylar bought the property, added the north wing and kitchen, and operated it as a hotel, renaming it the Grove House. The old hotel was razed in 1985, prior to construction of the firehouse.

Kilpatrick house (c. 1848) was converted to the Grove House Hotel at the end of the Civil War.

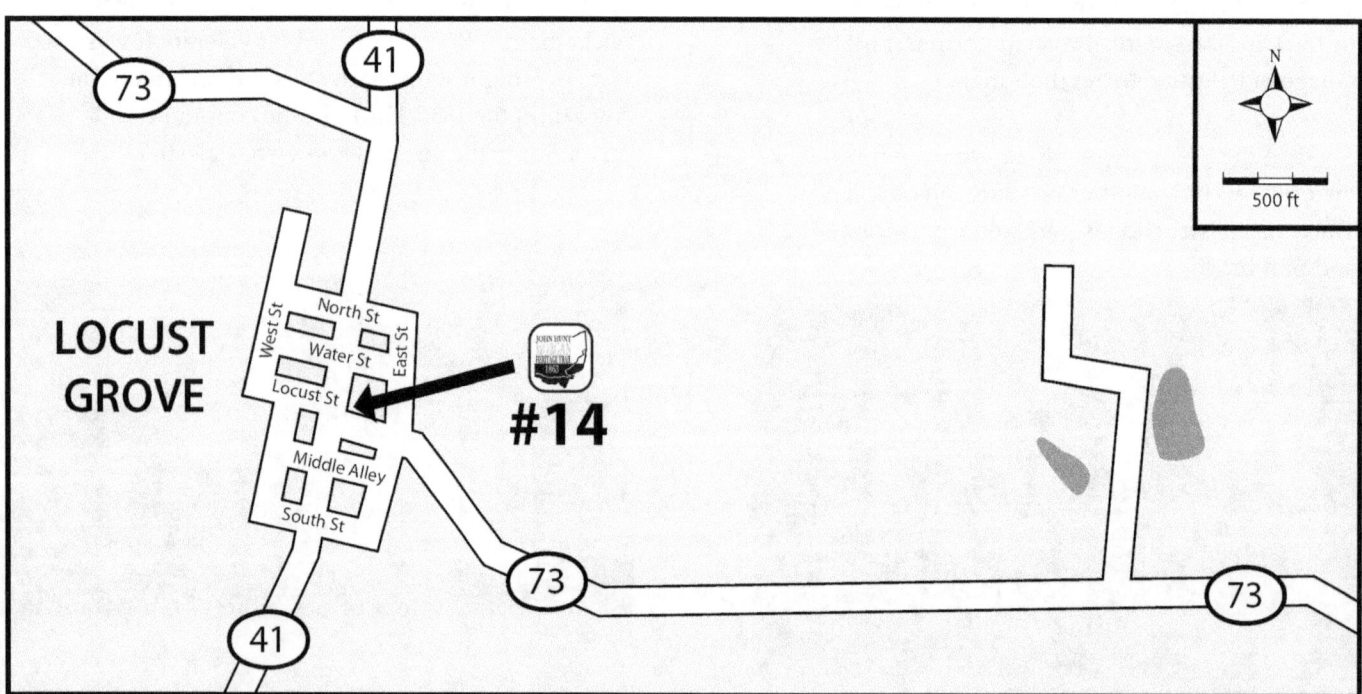

John Hunt Morgan Heritage Trail Interpretive sign #14 map

Hosteller David Eylar lost a buggy and an overcoat to the raiders.

Dr. Newton Richards's surgical instruments and stock of medicines were confiscated by Morgan's men. His horse was one of more than seventy-six taken by the raiders from the town and the surrounding Locust Grove Post Office area.

Joseph A. Wickerham and Peter Wickerham reported losses of $700 in merchandise from their general store. Other Locust Grove storekeepers, George Reddick, Jacob Copeland, and Elisha Kelley also filed claims for losses incurred during the looting that occurred that night and the next morning.

Side Note: George Reddick, one of the storekeepers, was the father of Corporal William Henry Harrison Reddick.

William Reddick's sword in Southern Museum of Civil War and Locomotive History at Kennesaw, Georgia

Two months prior to Morgan's Raid, the young soldier had returned to Locust Grove to receive a hero's welcome and a fine presentation sword, which is now on display at the Southern Museum of Civil War and Locomotive History at Kennesaw, Georgia. Phone: (770) 427-2117; Web site: *http://www.southernmuseum.org/*.

In April 1862, Reddick, a member of Company B of the 33rd OVI, volunteered to join the group we know as the Andrews Raiders. Their mission was to go behind enemy lines, steal a rebel train, and cut an important railroad line between Atlanta, Georgia, and Chattanooga, Tennessee.

Cpl. William Henry Harrison Reddick

The mission, known forever after as the Great Locomotive Chase, failed, and the leader, James Andrews, and seven of his men were hanged as spies. Reddick and several of his comrades were paroled. The survivors, who were greeted by President Lincoln, became the first recipients of the Medal of Honor.

Chapter Four
LOCUST GROVE TO JACKSON

Thursday, July 16, 1863

The raiders began to move out of Locust Grove shortly after dawn. A small party moved southeast to Rarden in Scioto County as a feint on the city of Portsmouth. The main force moved northeast.

Three men who were too ill to ride were left behind. The Platter family cared for them until they were able to travel. When they reached their homes in the South, they wrote to their hosts, thanking them for the hospitality they had provided.

Edward L. Hughes was a well-respected and prosperous local farmer. He was especially proud of his fine horses. When Duke's men appropriated two of them, he appealed to General Morgan for their return. When that failed, he volunteered to serve as Morgan's guide to Jackson, hoping to recover the horses.

On reaching Jackson, Hughes, a large Irishman, became drunk and boisterous. Morgan dismissed him. Not only did Hughes fail to recover his horses, but when Hobson arrived, Hughes was arrested and sent to jail for treason. Out on bail, he fled to Montreal, Canada. After Lincoln's Amnesty Proclamation in 1863, Hughes returned to Locust Grove and took the loyalty oath. He soon discovered that he was no longer welcome in Adams County; he left the area and moved west.

Leave Locust Grove by turning from SR 41 onto SR 73 East. Go 0.9 mile; where SR 73 bears to the right, take CR 16 (Hackelshin Road) to the left.

In 1863, most of Morgan's men used a road that no longer exists; known as the Chillicothe Road, it ran northeast from here to the Poplar Grove Road. Morgan used the Chillicothe Road instead of the Piketon Road in order to deceive Federal authorities into thinking that he intended to attack Chillicothe. This feint worked well. Go 1.6 miles to Poplar Grove Road (CR 47) and turn left. Drive 1.0 mile; the road used by Morgan's main force would have angled in from the left; continue 0.3 mile to a "Y." Take Poplar Grove Road to the right.

Side Note: Immediately after passing the "Y" intersection with Conaway Road (CR 17B), the area on the right side of Poplar Grove Road is the site of the Battle of Scioto Brush Creek (Wethington's Spring), the last battle between the whites and the Indians within the Virginia Military District, prior to the signing of the Greenville Treaty in 1795. At this spot, in July 1795, General Nathaniel Massie and approximately 60 militiamen defeated a band of Shawnee warriors who had refused to go to Fort Greenville to negotiate a treaty with General "Mad" Anthony Wayne. After an hour-long engagement, the warriors fled from the field, leaving behind several of their dead and many of their horses. One militiaman was wounded in the fight.

Drive 0.6 mile to a "Y" intersection with Betty's Creek Road; bear right, staying on Poplar Grove Road.

It is 2.9 miles to Poplar Grove in Pike County. The first road on the right is Union Road. A small company of scouts rode up Union Ridge and around to Smith Hill.

Turn right on the second road, Chenoweth Fork Road (CR 23). Reset your odometer. We will follow the route taken by Morgan's main column as it moved along the creek toward Jasper and the Scioto River.

The Kendall farm was located between Poplar Grove and Arkoe. The raiders took fresh bread from Mrs. Kendall's oven. It is 4.2 miles to Arkoe. Near Arkoe, the raiders took Lewis Beekman's horse and 20 pounds of honey from his hives.

Just beyond Arkoe, families named Shanks lived on both banks of Chenoweth Fork. Joseph Shanks hid his horse and that of his neighbor and sister-in-law, Cynthia Shanks, in the woods. The raiders stopped at the farms and took food and a saddle from Cynthia. Joseph lost fifty bushels of corn, seventy-five pounds of bacon, and some flour.

Continue on Chenoweth Fork Road for 4.1 miles to Elm Grove. The large two-story house on the right was

LOCUST GROVE TO JACKSON

William Henry home in Elm Grove

the William Henry home. It served as a station on the Underground Railroad.

Mr. Henry took his livestock to the woods. Not intimidated by Morgan's men, his sixty-six-year-old wife, Jane, drove the raiders out of her house and flower beds with a broom stick. After they showed her the respect due her, she fed them and let them water their horses in the creek behind the house. She then requested and received a receipt for her services. While the captain was writing the receipt, another raider slipped into the barn and took a saddle, four bridles, two halters, and a horse blanket. When Mr. Henry returned home, he was not impressed with his wife's account of her dealings with the raiders.

It is 1.3 miles to SR 32; turn right. Go 0.3 mile and turn left on SR 772; after 0.1 mile turn left on Tennyson Road (CR 85). The original junction of Chenoweth Fork and Tennyson roads was lost when SR 32 was improved.

Morgan's men became frustrated by the number of trees felled across the roads. Governor Tod had called forth the axe brigades of southern Ohio, and they were responding. Downed trees were not a major problem for the riders, but they delayed the wagons and artillery pieces.

Near Tennyson, Benjamin Chestnut, his brother, and his son Isaac had just felled a tree across the road, at a spot where the road dropped off on the left side.

Confederate scouts, hearing the tree fall, hurried ahead, captured the local "woodsmen," and ordered the trio to cut up the tree. One of the rebels gathered up the men's horses while another confiscated Benjamin's money pouch. The three dismounted axmen climbed to the top of the hill and watched as Morgan's main column rode by them.

Go 0.8 mile on Tennyson Road and stop before crossing the bridge over Sunfish Creek. The Stewart Alexander mill and residence were located downstream on the right.

Two of the miller's older sons were ordered to help clear downed trees from the road.

Three of the younger children had gone berry picking and returned home to learn that Morgan's raiders were approaching. The younger children were sent to hide in nearby woods, while their parents remained to face the intruders. One of the boys made it no farther than the chicken house. A raider opened the door but did not discover him. The raiders broke into the mill and took all the wheat flour and cornmeal. They opened the grain bins and fed their horses.

When the children returned home from the woods, the raiders were gone, and so were their berries. Alexander lost a barrelful of honey from the cellar, his gun, and one of his horses to Morgan's men.

The raiders crossed and burned the nearby 125-foot covered bridge over Sunfish Creek.

Some accounts credit the raiders with burning the mill. However, an account written by Alexander's granddaughter, Lina Silcott Shoemaker, refutes the claim. She wrote that as soon as the raiders left,

Citizens felled trees to impede the raiders.

Alexander collected corn and wheat from the neighbors and started milling. He knew his customers would need flour and meal to replace that lost to the raiders.

After preparing corn cakes for her family's evening meal, Mrs. Alexander began cooking for the hungry Union troops that would soon arrive.

Go 0.2 mile. Here, Morgan sent a company right on Long Fork Creek Road. The men passed over Yankee Hill and followed Long Fork toward the Scioto River. *See Appendix K Alternate: Over Yankee Hill to Jasper.*

Continue 1.2 miles on Tennyson Road and cross SR 32 on SR 124/772. After 0.1 mile, turn right onto Jasper Road (CR 43). Go just over 0.3 mile and pull off on the right, near the crest of Stoney Ridge. Here, the valiant men of Jasper made their stand.

JOHN HUNT MORGAN HERITAGE TRAIL INTERPRETIVE SIGN #15

News of Morgan's approach reached Jasper several hours before the raiders arrived. Andrew Kilgore was the chairman of the Pike County Military Committee. He was assisted by Jasper storekeeper, Samuel Cutler. The committee was responsible for recruiting in the area and for the defense of the county in an emergency.

Some of the Pike County Volunteer Militia had been called to Camp Chase to help protect Columbus; other members were sent to aid in the defense of Chillicothe and Portsmouth. The militia was fully armed and could be called up at an hour's notice by the governor. It would later become the National Guard.

The home guard could be called out only to defend their local area in case of attack. On July 16, it fell to Kilgore's men to protect Jasper. Kilgore chose this spot on Stoney Ridge, about four miles west of Jasper, for the construction of a barricade. From here, the forty citizen-soldiers would have a clear field of fire down the road.

The town's doctors, lawyers, clerks, and clergymen had joined farmers and laborers behind the barricade. The nervous men waited for Morgan's charge. They were prepared to defend their town even though outnumbered four to one.

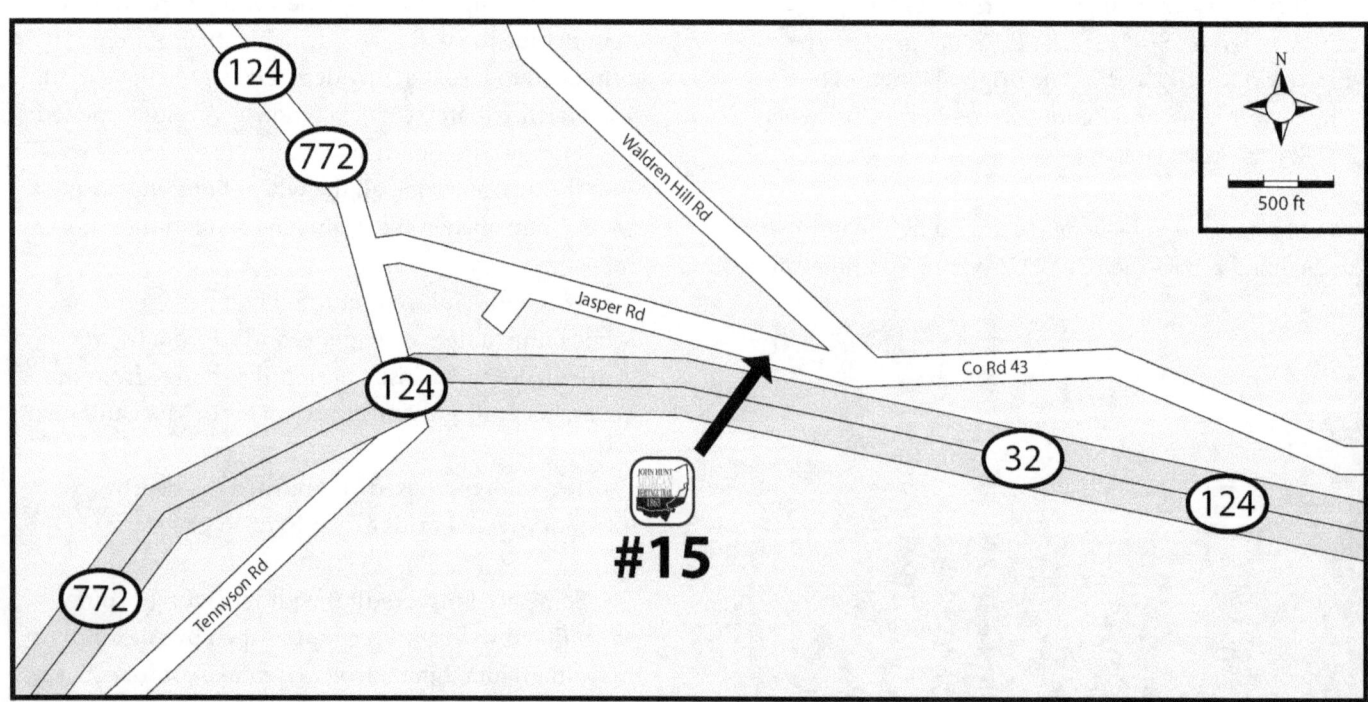

John Hunt Morgan Heritage Trail Interpretive sign #15 map

LOCUST GROVE TO JACKSON

View from the site of the Jasper barricade.

Old Jasper Methodist Church

Morgan's scouts arrived about 1 p.m. They notified him of the barricade. Morgan realized that he would probably lose men in a direct charge. He ordered several companies of the Second Brigade to dismount and fire a volley at the barricade.

The surprised defenders were not expecting the dismounted attack. After firing several rounds, they surrendered. The captured men were marched at gunpoint back to Jasper.

Go 3.2 miles to the edge of Jasper and park. There is an abandoned church on the hill to the left. On the right is **Trail Sign #16**.

JOHN HUNT MORGAN HERITAGE TRAIL INTERPRETIVE SIGN #16

During the march back to town, the prisoners suffered verbal abuse from Morgan's men. Most of the prisoners said nothing. Forty-seven-year-old Joseph McDougal, a staunch Unionist schoolteacher, made some disparaging remarks to his captors.

Because Morgan could not take the prisoners with him, he assigned Captain James W. Mitchell the task of paroling the home guard. Before paroling the men, Mitchell asked for directions to the Scioto River ford. No one volunteered the information.

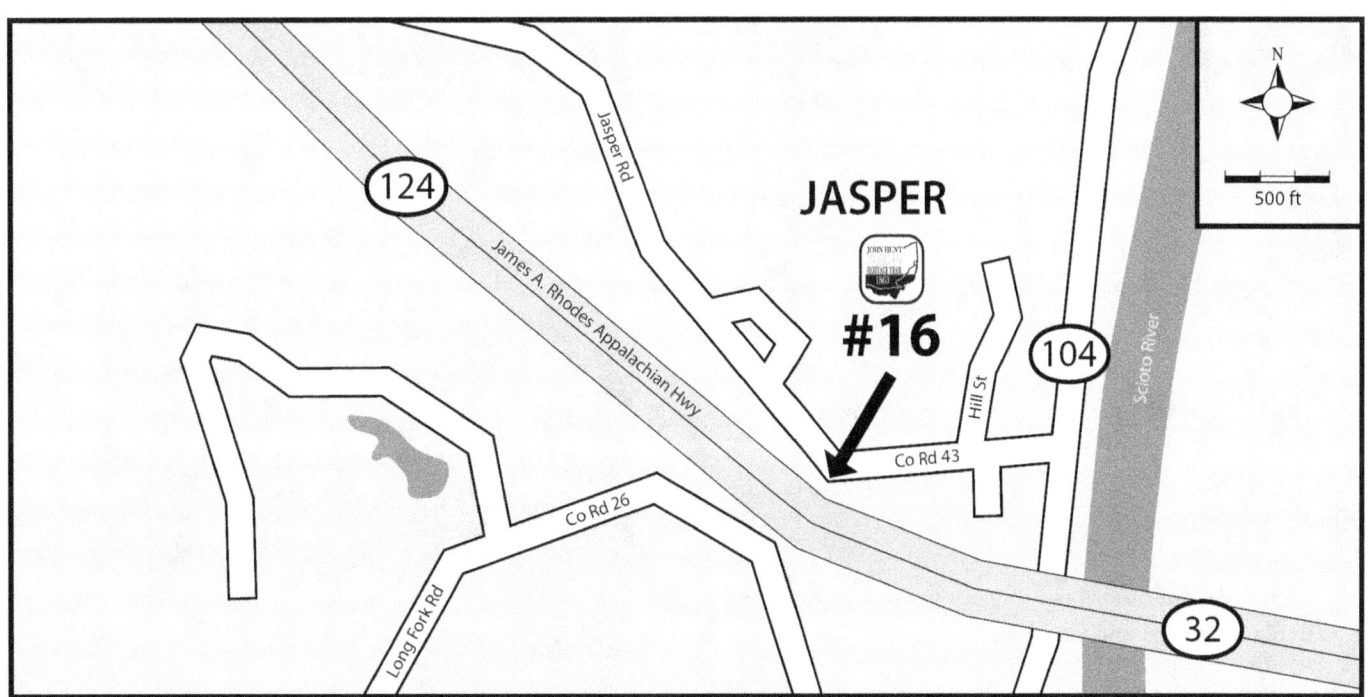
John Hunt Morgan Heritage Trail Interpretive sign #16 map

We do not know what happened next. Written accounts of the incident vary. We do know that McDougal was pulled from the group of prisoners and bound. Captain Mitchell ordered him placed in a small boat on either the Ohio & Erie Canal or the Scioto River. He ordered two of his men to shoot McDougal, who was struck below the right eye and in the chest.

We do not know what provoked the raiders to take this action. Very few civilians were killed during the raid, and then only if they fired on the raiders first.

Joseph McDougal is buried behind the old Jasper Methodist Church at the top of the hill on your left. The broken tombstone inscription reads: *Joseph McDougal was shot by John Morgan's men July 16, 1863, Aged 47 ys.7 ms.9 ds*. The grass-covered lane leading to the cemetery is located beyond the church and behind the trailer home.

Joseph McDougal grave

McDougal was survived by his wife, Elizabeth, and five children, ranging in age from one to seventeen years. Before leaving town the raiders stole one of the widow's horses.

A number of other Jasper residents had horses and valuables taken by the raiders.

Ohio & Erie Canal from bridge in Jasper.

Drive 0.2 mile to the bridge over the abandoned Ohio & Erie Canal. In 1863, Jasper was a bustling canal town of about 160 people. The town's stores served both canal traffic and local farmers.

Angered by the citizens' resistance at the barricade, the raiders were violent in their looting and destruction. They burned all manner of buildings: barns, stables, and mills.

They torched the Charles Miller sawmill and lumberyard, located between the canal and the river. They also burned Miller's canal boat. An attempt to burn his private bridge over the canal failed.

Ohio & Erie Canal at Cutler's Store in Jasper (c. 1900)

Jonathan Gray's new canal boat, outfitted with equipment and tools, was ready for launching. It was burned in the stocks.

The C. K. Marquis & Company's two steam engines and other machinery were damaged when their storage shed was burned. In addition to the claims Marquis filed for those losses, he asked to be reimbursed $5.80 for meals served to 29 rebels.

Storekeeper Andrew Kilgore claimed losses of $5,400 worth of merchandise. The raiders took little from Samuel Cutler's store, but destroyed a storage barn containing his buggy and fifteen plows.

William Truesdell, a twenty-five-year-old disabled veteran, lost $3,300 worth of merchandise, in addition to having his stable and outbuildings burned.

After spending several hours in Jasper, the raiders crossed and burned the county bridge across the canal.

Drive to the stop sign. Morgan's men turned left and rode approximately one-half mile upstream to the Scioto River ford.

Before leaving Batavia, Hobson realized that his artillery and wagons were slowing his progress.

Colonel August V. Kautz

He sent Colonel August Kautz and his best men ahead on the fastest horses in an attempt to catch Morgan. The men were from the 2nd and 7th Ohio Cavalry regiments. At Jasper, Kautz's men were delayed for six hours rebuilding the canal bridge. Exhausted from their hard ride, they encamped in town from 2 a.m. to 8 a.m. on July 17.

Five men from Pike County were riding with the Union cavalry. Several of these men were from the Jasper area. After viewing the destruction there, they had increased incentive to capture the rebels.

Turn right onto SR 104; turn left onto SR 32 and cross the Scioto River. Go 1.3 miles to the junction with US 23 and turn left (north).

Drive 1.0 mile and turn left onto West Street in Piketon. Go 0.3 mile north to Second Street; the dead-end street on your left was the road used by the raiders coming up from the Scioto River ford.

The raiders arrived in Piketon about 3 p.m. on July 16. The Piketon home guard had erected a log barricade but when the rebels arrived, the militiamen dispersed without a struggle. As a result, Piketon did not suffer the heavy damages that had occurred in Jasper.

Some of the businessmen lost merchandise and horses. Doctor Edward Allen lost a large stock of drugs and medicines. Buggy and wagonmaker, William Patterson, lost a new buggy, harness, and blacksmith tools. Charles Cissner made harnesses and ran a small livery. The raiders took all his harnesses and saddles, as well as a horse and the grain from the stable. Andrew Kellison, the town shoemaker, lost nearly $200 worth of boots and shoes.

Continue on West Street one block and turn right on Main Street. Drive six blocks and cross Middle Street. The second brick building on the right was the Pike County Courthouse until 1861, when the county seat was moved to Waverly. Raiders stole a flag here.

Turn right on the next street, which is Market Street. The stone building on the right was the old county jail.

Old Pike County Courthouse

While he was in Piketon, Morgan read a disparaging article in the Republican *Jackson Standard* newspaper. This account with the press would be settled when Morgan reached Jackson.

Morgan sent a small company up the river road to Waverly. There, at about 4:30 p.m., they burned the Scioto River Bridge, built in 1861 for $10,000. James Emmitt, the builder of the bridge and president of the Scioto Bridge Company inflated his claim to $12,000. When claims commissioners discovered the actual cost, they allowed him only $8,000. The bridge was on the road that is now SR 220. A Union soldier and a civilian were killed at Waverly.

To the north, Chillicothe was the military headquarters for Ross, Pickaway, Muskingum and Fayette counties. The militia poured into the town; about 7,000 men were gathered there. On July 15, Colonel Benjamin Piatt Runkle arrived and took command of the assembled force. On July 17, some of these men would encounter Morgan east of Jackson at Berlin Crossroads.

Lucy Hayes, wife of Colonel Rutherford B. Hayes, was staying at the home of her parents in Chillicothe. She wrote a detailed account of the frantic activity in the town. Morgan would encounter Hayes and his 23rd Ohio Volunteer Infantry two days later in Meigs County.

"Lightning" Ellsworth tapped out a misleading telegraph report that Morgan's men were headed to Chillicothe. Terrified citizen-soldiers burned the $10,000 bridge across Paint Creek, although water below the bridge was only inches deep. Morgan's men never reached the area.

Federal forces were catching up, so Morgan ordered another night ride. To prepare for the long ordeal, his men ate well before leaving Piketon.

Go straight on Market Street; reset your odometer when you cross US 23. You will be on Zahns Corner Road (CR 78). Take Zahns Corner Road up Pike Hill.

The people along this road were primarily of German descent, much more comfortable with the German language than with English. For some reason, they had not hidden their livestock. Always in need of horses, the raiders took all they could find. From Piketon to Beaver, hardly a horse was spared.

It is 2.1 miles to "Friendly Grove," the Governor Robert Lucas mansion, on the left. The house was built in 1824. Lucas no longer lived here in 1863. Conrad Vallery was living here at the time of the Civil War. He lost two horses, wheat, hay and 50 pounds of sugar to the raiders.

"Friendly Grove," the Governor Robert Lucas home

Continue 0.5 mile to Zahn's Corners located at the intersection with SR 220. Jacob Zahn's blacksmith shop stood on the northeast corner. He lost corn, provisions, two featherbeds, and $68 worth of horseshoes and nails. The raiders used the featherbeds to reduce the jolting effects on the sick and wounded who were lying in the wagons and ambulances. Frederick Zahn lived nearby and lost three horses. Several other men in the area lost horses.

The raiders, who had ridden from Piketon to Waverly to burn the bridge, rejoined the main column at Zahn's Corners.

Continue straight and drive 0.5 mile. The road now jogs to the right to meet with East Beaver Creek Road; the old road continued straight. The Hamman Church, founded in 1849, is just ahead on the old road; raiders rested their horses in the church yard and cemetery.

Hamman Church

The Phillip Hamman family lived across the road from the church. Phillip lost two horses. The road continued past the farms of George and Peter Hamman; both were forced to provide the raiders with grain and provisions. William and John Theobold both lost horses to the raiders.

Turn left onto East Beaver Creek Road and drive 1.0 mile to SR 32. Here there was a fork in the road. The north fork went east to Givens. The south fork turned on Germany Pike. The fork was originally in the area now under the railroad overpass on the left; the railroad did not exist in 1863.

Bill Givens kept a horse in a small stable located in the fork. Givens loaded his gun and waited in the stable; no raider would take his horse. It was about 6 p.m. when the raiders arrived. Givens had expected only one or two men, not hundreds. Remaining quiet, he watched as his horse was led out of the barn. As they left, the raiders set fire to the stable. Things got quite warm for Givens before the last rebel rode away, giving him the opportunity to escape.

When he reached his house, he found the raiders had taken clothes, provisions, household goods and two bee hives.

Turn right onto SR 32 and drive 0.6 mile to Tipton Lane. Make a U-turn at this intersection and follow SR 32 East for 0.6 mile back to East Beaver Creek Road. Look to the right before you reach the overpass and you will see the relocated section of Germany Pike. A party of raiders rode down Germany Pike collecting horses. Some of them headed east on present-day Coal Dock Road to the Beaver Pike, where they rejoined Morgan's main column. Others continued farther south before turning east on present-day Adams Road.

Continue another 0.6 mile on SR 32 and turn left onto Beaver Pike. This area is known as Givens. The small, now dead-end road immediately to the left is Givens Road. George Givens lived on the north side of that road. He was robbed of his money as well as two horses. His wheat and oats fields were also damaged. His neighbor, Adam Rader, had his watch stolen.

Bear right on Beaver Pike. Samuel Givens lived on the left side. He lost one horse, one hundred bushels of corn, clothes, provisions, and $86.

It is 5.7 miles to Beaver (Beaverton in some accounts). Morgan's advance guard passed through Beaver about 7 p.m. They ordered the women to prepare food for the men to come.

The main force soon arrived. The citizens of Beaver offered little resistance; the raiders did little damage. They were tired and hungry; they had been in the saddle since 7 a.m. when they left Locust Grove. They were not ready to camp for the night, but they were ready for supper.

They took $700 worth of merchandise from the stores of John and Jacob Kuntzman. The raiders also stole eighteen pocket knives from Andreas Kern's store. Spangler, a local blacksmith, repaired and replaced the horseshoes on the rebels' mounts. The grateful raiders offered to pay Spangler for his work. Charles Buehler served glasses of wine to Morgan and many of his men.

Other thirsty raiders stole a total of $163 worth of liquor from three local merchants.

As they left Beaver, a small company of raiders, traveling along a parallel road to the south, stopped at the farms of Milton Smith and John Coles. Raiders passed through the neighboring towns of Cove and Petersburg.

By 10:30 p.m., the last raiders had passed through Beaver and out of Pike County.

July 16, the day Morgan's command spent in Pike County, had been very discouraging for the raiders. Felled trees had slowed their progress. Militiamen hiding in the hills had taken shots at the passing rebels. Several men had been wounded.

What Morgan did not yet know was that General Burnside now realized Morgan was moving eastward. For the first time, Burnside could anticipate Morgan's moves and order troops to intercept him. The net was beginning to tighten.

Earlier in the day, Colonel Rutherford B. Hayes had persuaded Brigadier General Eliakim Parker Scammon, commander of the Kanawha Division, to allow him to take two regiments down the Kanawha River to the Ohio River in an effort to stop Morgan. Scammon later decided to follow with two additional regiments and an artillery battery.

That afternoon and evening, as Morgan moved from Piketon to Jackson, Brigadier General Henry M. Judah debarked three regiments of cavalry and several batteries of artillery from 10 transports at Portsmouth. Judah's force consisted of the 5th Indiana Cavalry [90th Indiana Regiment] (Lt. Col. Thomas H. Butler), the 14th Illinois Cavalry (Col. Horace Capron), one company of the 11th Kentucky U.S. Cavalry (Major Milton Graham), Company I of the 8th Michigan Cavalry attached to Companies C and K of the 9th Michigan Cavalry (Col. James I. David), two rifled guns of Battery L of the 1st Michigan Light Artillery [11th Michigan Battery] (Capt. Charles J. Thompson), two 3-inch Ordnance rifles attached to the 5th Indiana Cavalry (Lt. Charles H. Dumont),

four 12-pounder mountain howitzers attached to the 14th Illinois Cavalry (Lt. DeRiley Kilbourne), and two six-pounder brass 3.67-inch cannons of Henshaw's Illinois Independent Battery Light Artillery (Capt. Edward C. Henshaw). Mounted militiamen also joined Judah at Portsmouth and Oak Hill. After detaching the Michigan battery to the *Allegheny Belle,* Judah led his 1,300 men east on the old Pomeroy stagecoach road toward Portland and the Buffington Island Ford, 90 miles from Portsmouth.

Colonel Runkle's large force of militia at Chillicothe was prepared to board trains and move on short notice.

Capturing Morgan was to be a combined operation, utilizing not only the army, but also the brown-water navy (boats used in rivers). Lieutenant Commander Leroy Fitch's fleet of tinclads and transports was charged with conveying Union forces upstream, denying the raiders use of the Ohio River fords, and preventing Morgan from capturing boats that he could use to ferry troops and horses across the river.

Morgan was losing more and more men each day to exhaustion. Kautz's Brigade began capturing stragglers from Morgan's force as soon as they started down Chenoweth Fork. After being captured, a straggler's behavior was often like that of a sleepwalker. Before he was captured, one of the stragglers wounded Union Sergeant William P. Cowan, 2nd Ohio Cavalry. The wounded man was left in the care of Doctor Thomas Rose in Jasper, where he died ten days later.

The following day, July 17, Colonel Kautz's 400 men would make better time than the raiders. His men were met with cheers and fried chicken as they moved across Pike County. They did not have to contend with downed trees and barricades. By the time they reached Beaver, they were only twelve hours behind the Confederates.

Leaving town, continue straight on Beaver Pike (CR 57); it is 1.3 miles to the Jackson County line, where the road becomes CR 76.

LOCUST GROVE TO JACKSON

Reset your odometer and drive 8.1 miles to a railroad track. Just before the tracks, the old road veered off to the left. As we continue 0.2–0.3 mile toward Jackson, look across the tracks on the left and you can see the tree line along the old road. The road became Main Street as it entered Jackson.

Fence and tree line are along the Old Piketon Road.

Continue 1.5 miles on CR 76 and turn left onto High Street. Go 0.3 mile to Main Street. Look to the left; this was the route used by the raiders.

Turn right onto Main Street to enter Jackson with Morgan. Go 0.5 mile to the top of the hill at Portsmouth Street; the Gibson House stood on the right at the corner of Main and Portsmouth streets, until it was razed in the early twenty-first century.

Some of the raiders slept at the Gibson House. Levi Gibson's claim included the cost for meals for 100 Confederate and 150 Union troops.

Gibson House Hotel

Park in the next block of Main Street (SR 93) and take a short walking tour of raid-related sites in the downtown area. On the left side of Main Street in this block is **Trail Sign #17**.

JOHN HUNT MORGAN HERITAGE TRAIL INTERPRETIVE SIGN #17

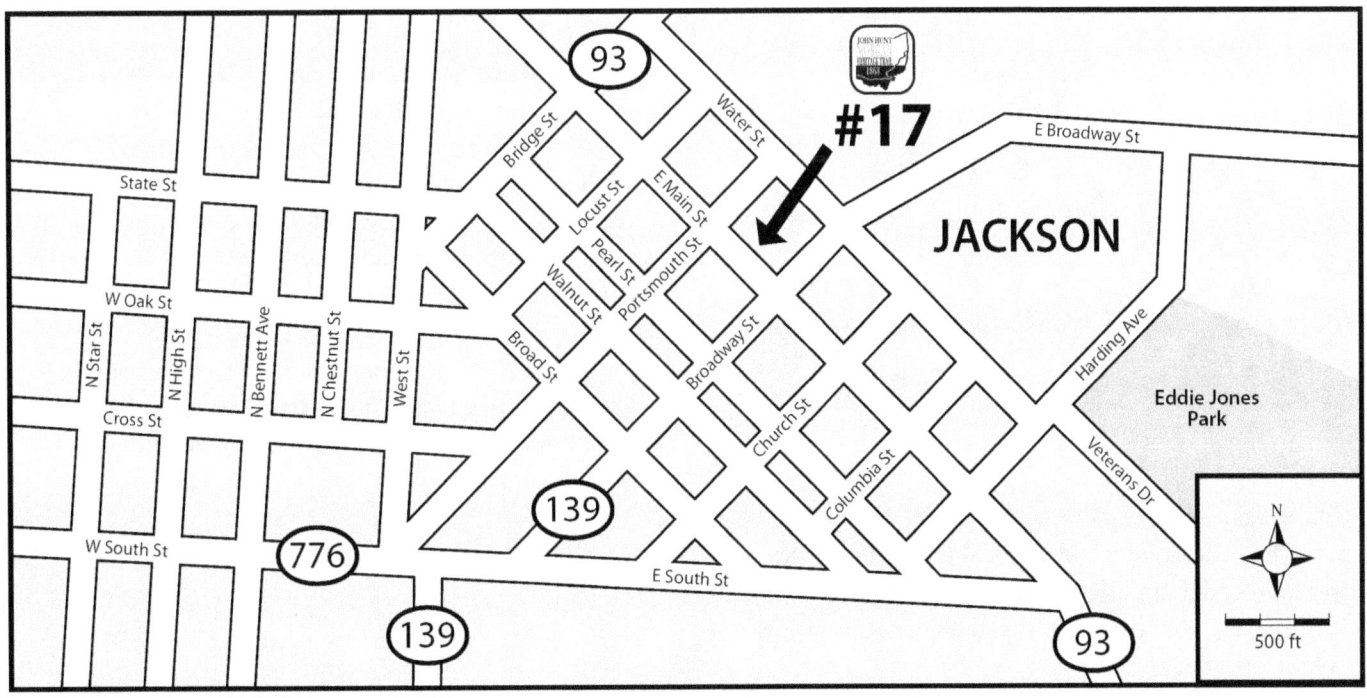
John Hunt Morgan Heritage Trail Interpretive sign #17 map

The present courthouse was built after the Civil War. Its predecessor burned prior to the raid.

In 1863, the population of Jackson was about 1,000. Most of the Jackson and Vinton County Militia had been sent to Portsmouth, where Morgan was expected to attempt a crossing. Old men and boys remained to protect the town.

Joshua Sheridan, who lived near Jackson, owned a fine pedigreed stallion, one of the fastest horses in the area. Sheridan volunteered to ride as a scout to the Beaver area. When he encountered the raiders, they demanded he surrender his horse. Instead, he spurred the horse to a gallop, and the chase was on, with the rebels firing at Sheridan. Sheridan outdistanced them after several miles, and they abandoned their pursuit. Sheridan carried the word back to Jackson that Morgan was coming. Minutes later, Morgan's advance riders arrived.

About 9:30 p.m., Provost Marshal C. W. Selfridge and a group of men were trying to organize a tree-felling party near the Isham House on Main Street. They scattered as Captain Neil Helm and the advance raiders appeared on the crest of the hill in front of the Gibson House.

Cambrian Hotel stands on the site of earlier Isham Hotel.

Morgan arrived with the main force around 10 p.m. The raiders captured all the men on the street and marched them down South Broadway to the old fairgrounds. The rebels destroyed all the guns found in Jackson.

Edward L. Hughes, Morgan's guide from Locust Grove, was dismissed after he became drunk and boisterous.

Morgan acquired two new guides in Jackson, James Nelson and Peter Hartinger; both men were known "Copperheads" (Confederate sympathizers). Nelson owned a tavern on Broadway, which he opened to entertain his guests from Kentucky.

Morgan, his brother Dick, and several other officers stayed at John French's Isham House. The proprietor had locked the door when he received word of Morgan's approach. When the General demanded admission, French hesitated only seconds before opening the door. Morgan and his staff registered like regular guests and retired to their rooms, where hotel porters were soon serving them food and drinks.

The building was razed in 1900 and later replaced by the Cambrian Hotel. Many of the raiders fed their horses at the Monahan Livery Stable at the rear of the Isham House.

Duke and about fifty raiders spent the night at the Valley House, which stood on the southeast (southernmost) corner of Portsmouth and Pearl streets (the hotel was razed in the 1920s).

Small groups of raiders that had been out foraging rejoined the main force at Jackson.

During the night, the raiders burned the depot, turntable, engine house, freight cars, and several railroad bridges of the Portsmouth branch of the Marietta & Cincinnati Railroad.

Other men broke barn door locks on a search for horses. Some farsighted residents succeeded in hiding their horses in outlying areas before the raiders arrived.

Friday, July 17, 1863

Early in the morning, County Treasurer Thomas B. Dickason saved the county's $20,000 by hiding it in a briar patch east of town. The raiders attempted, without success, to batter open the empty safe.

The Confederates looted the businesses of Jackson, including the store of David D. Dungan and Alanson Robbins. Later, on August 6, the enterprising merchants ran this advertisement in the *Jackson Express*.

The Cheapest Store.

If "John Morgan does come," or if "John Morgan don't come," D. D. Dungan will keep on hand the largest and cheapest assortment of Dry Goods, Fancy Goods, Notions, &c., &c., in Jackson county. This is a fact. Morgan's men stole a large lot of goods; but Dave has plenty left. Go along, every body, and examine his stock, avail yourselves of the opportunity now offered you for great bargains and unequaled goods. Come from every part of the county—far and near—and see his goods!

Dungan's August 6th ad

From the Henry H. Fullerton millinery shop, the raiders took ribbons that they tied into bows and placed on their hats. They also took womens' blue veils to wear as protection from the sun and dust.

Doctor I. T. Monahan, well-known for his Southern sympathies, lost to the raiders $500 worth of items from his drugstore.

Copperheads throughout Indiana and Ohio expected special treatment from Morgan and his men, and "special treatment" was often their reward. The raiders had no sympathy for these men living in comfort as civilians in the North while professing to support the Confederacy. The raiders would thank them for their donations to "the Cause" as they rode away on their stolen horses.

There were many Southern sympathizers living in Jackson County. The citizens of the northern townships were primarily Democratic or of the Copperhead persuasion. The people of the southern townships were Republican and staunch Unionists.

Some of Morgan's men entered the Masonic Lodge on the second floor of the Gratton Block (211 Broadway). The structure has a new facade and is now the Carrington building. The raiders came out wearing Masonic robes. They were reprimanded by Morgan and told to return the items.

Masonic Hall was on 2nd floor.

The flour mills in Jackson were saved when the owners paid the $2,300 ransom demanded by the raiders to spare the buildings.

The raiders destroyed the office and press of the Republican *Jackson Standard*, which was located on the third floor of the Commercial Block on Main Street, adjacent to the present Cambrian Hotel. Their actions were in response to the "bad press" the paper had given Morgan and his men. The editor had referred to them as "scum of the South." The rebels threw the type out the upstairs window and smashed the press with a pickax. This was the only instance where Morgan's men attacked a newspaper.

Jackson Standard building

Jackson Express building

That night, Union forces, acting in retaliation, would pitch the type, supplies, and records of the Peace Democrats' *Jackson (Iron Valley) Express* out a second-floor window. The paper's office was located in the Sternberger Block, across Main Street from the Gibson House. The building is still standing, but it has undergone extensive renovations.

Drummer William A. "Berry" Steele of Company C, 53rd Ohio Volunteer Infantry (OVI), was one of the boys who claimed to be "the drummer boy of Shiloh." On April 6, 1862, the first day of the Battle of Shiloh, Steele was struck a glancing shot on the left side of his head and ear, which rendered him unconscious.

He was subsequently discharged. Regaining his health, he rejoined the army and continued to serve as a drummer for the remainder of the war. Steele was home on leave at the time of the raid. Raiders found his drum hidden under his bed and destroyed it; they did not find Steele, who was hiding nearby. The Steele home at 208 Water Street is still standing.

*Side Trip: You may choose to visit the 1863 locations of the depot, Salt Creek Bridge, and fairgrounds, which are key sites of Morgan's Raid on Jackson.

Continue three blocks south on Main Street (SR 93); turn left onto Harding Avenue (Railroad Street in 1863). Drive one block to the railroad tracks.

The depot was located on the right. It was a large red building 100 feet long and 50 feet wide. The track passed through the center of the building. Two local men were sent to guard the depot with orders to shoot anyone attempting to burn the building. After firing at the approaching raiders and wounding one, the two guards beat a hasty retreat to the nearby woods. They were later captured and taken to the fairgrounds.

LOCUST GROVE TO JACKSON

Site of the Marietta & Cincinnati Railroad depot.

Continue two blocks to Main Street and the courthouse square. Cross Main Street and drive 0.3 mile to South Street. This was the route traveled by Morgan's prisoners as they were marched into captivity at the fairgrounds on Thursday night. The old fairgrounds was located at the end of South Broadway. We will drive the streets bordering the old fairgrounds. Turn right onto South Street; left onto Vaughn; left onto East Huron and left onto Dickason.

Salt Creek Bridge

The old fairground was located in the wooded area to the right of the track.

Turn left onto Water Street and drive three blocks to East Broadway; turn right. The bridge over Salt Lick Creek is just beyond the railroad tracks. Beyond the bridge over Salt Lick Creek, the area on your right was the village of Jamestown.

At the time of the raid, East Broadway connected to the Berlin Road. This was the route a portion of Morgan's main column followed when leaving Jackson.

Turn around and return to the Salt Lick Creek Bridge. When several raiders set fire to the bridge, Mrs. John D. James and Mrs. J. L. Ramsey pleaded with them not to destroy the span. When that failed, Mrs. James shamed them into extinguishing the flames by asking them what their mothers would think of such a deed.

The men of Jackson were held under guard all night at the fairgrounds. Early Friday morning, Cornelia Hoffman Long took coffee to the prisoners in a big pot, and when it was empty, carried away some of the men's watches and wallets for safe keeping.

Around noon the 300 captives were marched from the fairgrounds to the corner of Main and Church streets. There they were paroled by Morgan before he left town.

Continue to the end of Dickason and turn right on South Street. Immediately turn left onto Church Street and return 0.2 mile to Main Street.*

The raiders either destroyed or carried away all the guns discovered in Jackson.

Part of the parole ceremony involved taking an oath not to bear arms against the Confederacy. James Tripp and W. K. Hastings disliked taking the oath. Fortunately, a dog fight erupted in the middle of the street and, while the guards were distracted, the men slipped away into the crowd.

After paroling the prisoners, the rebel columns moved out. One of the horses taken in Jackson was "Old Bob," a Kentucky thoroughbred. The previous year, he had been appropriated by Lieutenant Benjamin Trago of the 7th Ohio Cavalry serving in Kentucky. Trago had given the animal to his father-in-law, John French, who kept him at the Monahan Livery Stables. When the raiders entered the stable, one of them instantly recognized the horse.

By 2 p.m., all the raiders were gone. Confederate Curtis Burke kept a diary of the raid; he wrote in it that Jackson was a good-looking place with fine homes.

It was not until evening that the advance Union forces entered Jackson. The women of Jackson prepared a hearty meal for the Union soldiers who had arrived there. The ladies carried the food to the central market, where they served the hungry troops.

Chapter Five

JACKSON TO BUFFINGTON ISLAND

Friday, July 17, 1863

The first of Morgan's men left Jackson about 10 a.m., singing, yelling, and shouting as they moved out. It was several hours until all the raiders were gone.

The raiders split into two groups as they left Jackson. Morgan rode with Duke's 1st Brigade as it moved northeast through Jamestown toward Berlin Crossroads. Adam Johnson's 2nd Brigade moved southeast toward Vinton, in Gallia County. Both groups were headed toward the Middleport-Cheshire area and the Ohio River.

Sergeant Mark Sternberger was a member of the 129th Ohio Volunteer Infantry (OVI), stationed at Camp Taylor near Cleveland, Ohio. At the time of the raid, he was in uniform and serving on special duty as an army recruiter in Jackson County. On learning of Morgan's approach, Sternberger fled Jackson and hid in the woods northeast of town.

At daybreak, he went to the Jamestown home of Elias Long with the hope of obtaining food and rest. The house was deserted. The exhausted man lay down and was soon asleep. He awoke to the sounds of voices and horses going by. Peering out a window, he saw raiders going toward Berlin. He quickly hid his uniform and jumped into bed. Soon, several raiders entered and questioned him. In a very weak voice he lamented that his family had fled, and he was too ill to go with them. He heard them report there was nobody in the house but a sick man. He remained in bed until the sound of the raiders' horses faded away in the distance.

Because the route through Jamestown to the old Berlin Road has been abandoned, we will leave Jackson by following the route used by most of the main column. You may also choose to follow Colonel Adam Johnson's brigade as it marched through Keystone Furnace and Vinton. *See Appendix L Alternate: Johnson's Column Passed Through Vinton en Route to Middleport.*

Take SR 93 North by turning left from Church Street at Main Street (SR 93). Go four blocks, then turn right onto Bridge Street. It is two blocks to the junction with SR 788 (Athens Street); turn right at SR 788.

Reset your odometer and go 2.3 miles to Petrea. When SR 788 turns left; bear right onto CR 78 (Fairgreens Road). It is 2.5 miles to Keenan Road (TR 928), which was the original road to Berlin Crossroads; bear right on Keenan Road.

Raiders followed Keenan Road to Berlin Crossroads.

As Morgan's main force approached Berlin, his scouts reported a heavy concentration of Union forces on the heights behind the town. They could not determine whether the Union force included artillery; Morgan assumed that it did and acted accordingly.

Drive 0.7 mile to the intersection with Fairgreens Road (CR 78). As you approach the stop sign, notice the hill on your left. Morgan placed his guns here; the battery overlooked the town of Berlin Crossroads.

Morgan placed his battery on this hill overlooking Berlin.

Before leaving Berlin, the raiders burned a buckeye crib and the large steam-powered flour mill of Rufus Hunsinger & Company. Hunsinger's claim for $5,700

JACKSON TO BUFFINGTON ISLAND

was the largest single loss in Jackson County. At the stop sign, look to your right; the mill was located just east of the railroad embankment, on the right side of Fairgreens Road, before the bridge over SR 32.

Turn right on Fairgreens Road into the town of Berlin Crossroads; the town was known as Berlin or Berlin Crossroads in 1863. Due to anti-German sentiment during World War I, the name "Berlin" was dropped and the village became simply Roads. Recently, the town's original name was restored. The town was located on a branch of the Marietta & Cincinnati Railroad in 1863.

Doctor William Sylvester's house stood on the left, about 30 yards before SR 327. The building survived the skirmish at Berlin Heights but was razed in 2003.

Continue straight on Fairgreens Road to the junction of SR 327. Here, at the old crossroads, Fairgreens Road becomes Salem Road (SR 124). Turn left on SR 327 and go one block to the church parking lot on the left.

JOHN HUNT MORGAN HERITAGE TRAIL INTERPRETIVE SIGN #18

Dr. William Sylvester's house was razed in 2003.

Colonel Benjamin Runkle commanded a force of 1,700 militia assembled at Chillicothe. They had been moved by rail from there to Hamden Station, arriving between 2 and 3 a.m. At dawn, the men marched six miles south to Berlin.

Colonel Runkle had about 1,500 untested militia occupying Berlin Heights, the high ground behind the town. He had no artillery. Runkle's men were prepared to offer the raiders stiff opposition. It was his mission to delay Morgan five or six hours until Hobson's regular troops could arrive. Runkle positioned his infantry regiments as follows: the 1st Ross on his right, 1st Pickaway on his left, 2nd Pickaway and 1st Fayette

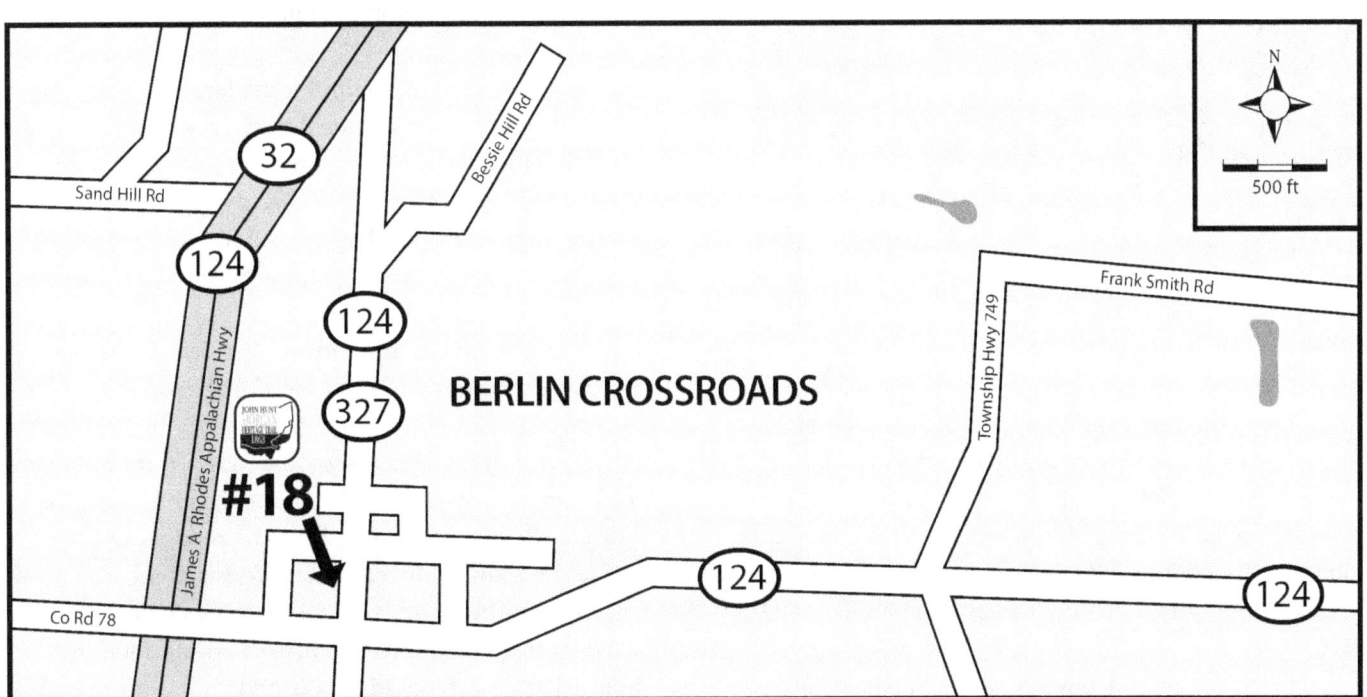

John Hunt Morgan Heritage Trail Interpretive sign #18 map

in reserve, and the Muskingum Rifles on his right rear.

Before the "Battle of Berlin Heights," rebel scout leader Tom Murphy, "the Wild Irishman," and two companions approached Berlin. When a militia picket ordered them to halt, Murphy whirled over to fire his weapon from under the neck of his horse. The picket fired, seriously wounding Murphy. The other men escaped and returned to the main force.

When Morgan's men departed from Berlin, they left the wounded scout behind to die. He surprised everyone and lived. Murphy was taken care of in a private home until his wounds healed; then he was sent to Rock Island Military Prison Camp in Illinois. In March 1865, he was exchanged, and he returned to Confederate service.

William McGhee resided in Berlin; he was nearly blind. He was riding his horse and carrying his cane under his arm. The raiders spotted him from a distance and believed the cane to be a gun. They fired two shots at McGhee; the shots struck and killed his horse.

Runkle's men were positioned on high ground in center.

Heavy shelling from Morgan's battery, placed on the ridge west of town, caused the militia to fall back behind the brow of the hill. After less than an hour, Morgan called off the artillery barrage. Duke's brigade attacked Runkle's position and succeeded in pushing the militia farther back, opening the way east to Wilkesville.

Hoped-for reinforcements had not arrived, and Runkle could hold no longer. Runkle delayed Morgan for only about three hours — not enough time for

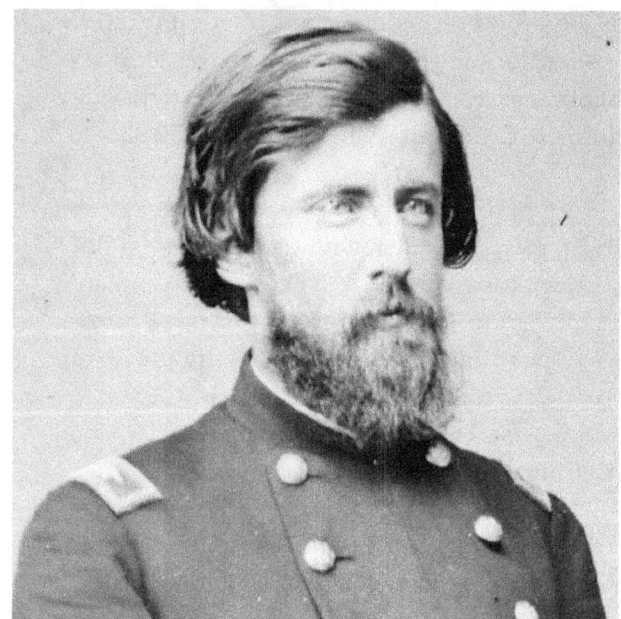
Col. Benjamin Runkle

the Union regulars to arrive, but nevertheless, a three-hour reduction in Morgan's lead. Morgan's men broke off the fighting and left Berlin about 2 p.m.

Accounts vary as to the number of Confederate casualties; they range from four to twelve raiders killed, with more than a score wounded. There are no records of the Union casualties.

In addition to the claim for the losses at Hunsinger's Mill, other claims in the Berlin Crossroads area included the loss of sixteen horses; saddles, harnesses, clothing, dry goods, and merchandise from the local stores; guns; grain for the horses; food for the troops; and damages to property resulting from the skirmish.

As the main column moved east, felled trees along the route continued to slow their progress.

Return to the old crossroads. Reset your odometer and turn left (east) onto SR 124. Go 0.5 mile; Latrobe Furnace Road was on the right. The road, now closed, led to the charcoal furnace that produced the iron used in casting "The Swamp Angel," the 8-inch Parrott gun used by the Union forces to fire on Charleston, South Carolina, from Morris Island.

JACKSON TO BUFFINGTON ISLAND

The Latrobe Furnace Company filed a claim for lost wheat: twenty-five bushels at $1 per bushel and eighteen sacks worth $9.

Go 0.4 mile and bear right onto Old Salem Road (TR 178). It is 1.0 mile to Salem Church on the right. The present church, built in 1915, replaced the original log structure built in 1834. The old log church served as Morgan's temporary headquarters while the men and horses rested in the churchyard and at the nearby Ramsey farm. Many of the raiders roasted and ate fresh corn appropriated from Ramsey's field.

Men and horses rested in the Salem churchyard.

It is 0.5 mile to the stop sign at the western edge of Middleton (also known as Dawkins Mills Post Office in 1863). We will enter town with the raiders. Turn right on SR 124, and then make an immediate left on Old Salem Road (TR 178). Continue less than 0.1 mile to the crossroads at Kisor Road (TR 184).

The old brick house on the left served as the Dawkins Mills Post Office during the period from 1874 to 1897. The original road, now abandoned, continued straight for about 0.1 mile to the present highway.

Middleton was the home of Francis Smith before he moved to Jackson. Smith, an avid abolitionist, predicted the terrible war and its eventual outcome. When Lincoln made the call for 75,000 men in 1861, sixty-two-year-old Smith was the first man in Jackson County to enlist in Captain J. J. Huffman's Company. When his three-month term was up, he joined the 53rd OVI. Fighting at the Battle of Shiloh in April 1862, Smith became the first man from Jackson County to be killed by the Confederates. At his request, he was buried on the field where he fell.

Claims were filed for eleven horses taken in the Dawkins Mill area.

Turn right at the crossroads, then left onto SR 124. It is 9.6 miles to the stop sign at Wilkesville, where you will turn right. Drive 0.1 mile; there is an **Ohio Historical Marker** in the small park on the left.

Warned of Morgan's approach, Cornelius Carr, father of the village postmaster, hurried to hide the American flag and other valuables in a nearby field. He failed to note the location and was never able to retrieve the money. Morgan and his men came into the post office and took mail and newspapers.

The raiders arrived in Wilkesville before dark. The home guard offered only token resistance.

Go 0.1 mile and park; the brick house straight ahead, as SR 124 bends sharply to the left, was the postwar home of Doctor William C. Cline.

Brick building served as post office.

Post-war home of Dr. William C. Cline

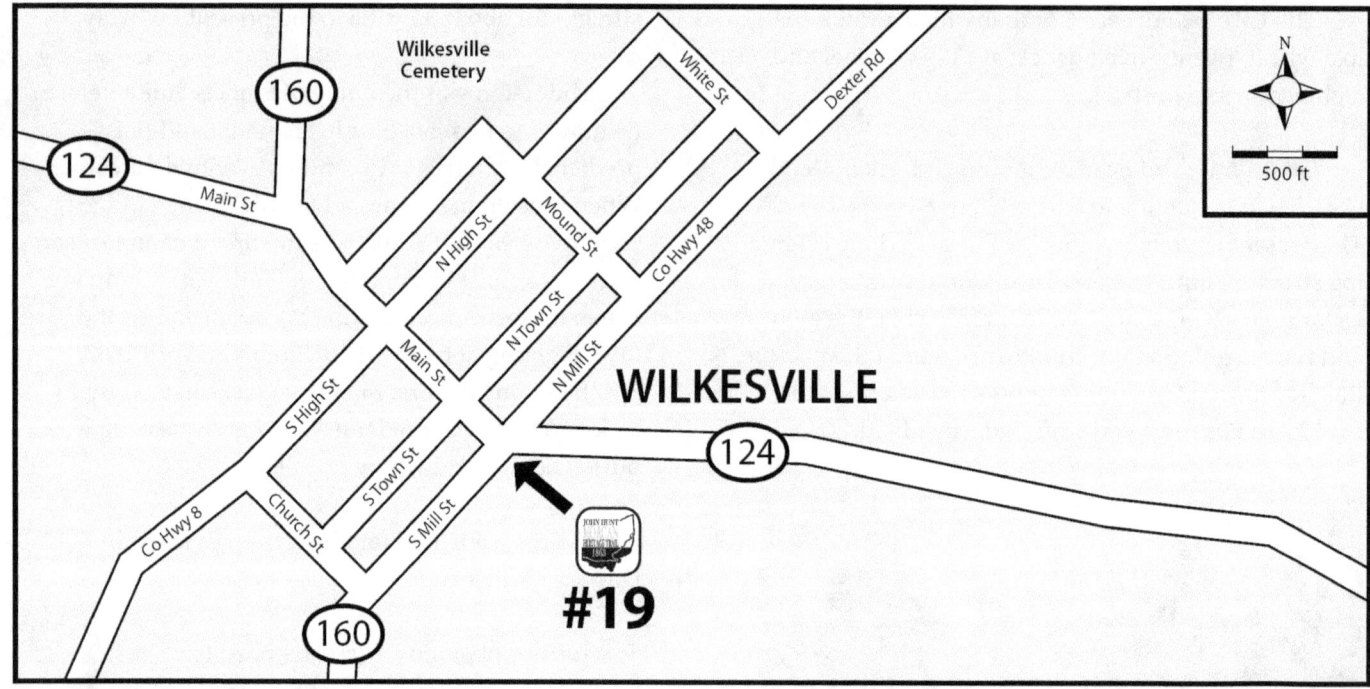

John Hunt Morgan Heritage Trail Interpretive sign #19 map

JOHN HUNT MORGAN HERITAGE TRAIL INTERPRETIVE SIGN #19

During the Civil War, Cline lived in a nearby two-story frame house, which was described as the finest house in town. The doctor was one of the wealthiest men in Vinton County. His holdings included 1,400 acres of land, a drugstore, and a general store across the road from his home.

Morgan established the Cline house as his headquarters; a heavy guard was placed around the building. The general read through the stolen mail to look for military information.

That evening, the raiders plundered the J. N. Douglas store and imbibed in hard spirits at the Douglas Tavern. Some of Morgan's men camped at the village square. Approximately 40 raiders slept in and around the John Levis house on Yankee Street. Eliza Levis baked biscuits and cooked for her visitors.

Abraham Morris, a local farmer, had been pointed out as an "Underground Railroad operator." He was captured by raiders who threatened to hang him. Morris escaped and hid in a stack of wheat behind Dr. Cline's house.

A local legend: Cline's wife Ruth Virginia Althar Cline was Morgan's cousin, and Morgan had visited their home before the war. When he left Wilkesville, he asked the Clines to hold a large share of his ill-gotten gains until he could return for it. He never returned, and that money paid for the Cline's large brick home.

Another local legend: During the night, Box, Morgan's negro valet, stole the General's wallet and saddlebags, which contained a large amount of cash. One version of the story has the slave using the stolen money to pay Cline to aid in his escape. Another version credits Abraham Morris and the good Dr. Cline with helping the slave escape to Carpenter, a nearby town in northern Meigs County.

While Morgan's main force spent the night in Wilkesville, his advance scouts camped in Rutland.

Saturday, July 18, 1863

Before leaving Wilkesville, the raiders emptied the feed bins in Dr. Cline's barn. They looted his stores, taking more than $1,000 worth of drugs, notions, and dry goods. After the raid, Cline submitted a claim that included the loss of two horses and a buggy.

Other raiders ransacked the home and burned the barn of Fred Carr, located on the edge of town.

One seriously ill raider was left at the home of James Blakely, where he succumbed several days later. He was buried in the Wilkesville cemetery; his remains were later disinterred and moved south.

The raiders began to move out about 3 a.m. As the raiders left Wilkesville, a small force of several hundred men took the Dexter Road northeast through Dexter and Harrisonville. Along the way, the raiders confiscated horses and other items. Three Harrisonville citizens submitted claims for expenses incurred when they were forced to feed the men. When the raiders left Harrisonville, Robert Combs was taken to serve as their guide.

Morgan and Duke rode with the main column and continued east on present-day SR 124. They intended to turn south on the Old Stagecoach Road near Pomeroy and meet Adam Johnson's column at Middleport, the location of an Ohio River ferry. Cheshire was several miles downstream, and the ford there, at Eight Mile Island, provided another option for the raiders to cross the Ohio River.

Reset your odometer at the Cline house. Soon after leaving Wilkesville on SR 124 East, you will enter Meigs County. Within the next mile, you will cross and follow along Strongs Run Creek.

It is 4.0 miles from Cline's house to Salem Center. The John Williams farm was located on the outskirts of Salem Center. The musical Williams family lost a drum and a fiddle to the raiders. Morgan's troops passed through Salem Center about 5 a.m. The four-mile trip from Wilkesville took nearly two hours because the raiders experienced many delays due to felled trees.

A group of nearly 100 home guards, serving under Major David Harkins, assembled at Salem Center. As the large Confederate force neared the town, the town's defenders fled, burning a bridge on the road to Rutland as they departed. Morgan's men fired at the fleeing men.

The raiders threatened a crippled old man by pointing a bayonet at his chest and demanding the names of the bridge burners. The old man told his captors he had but a short time to live, anyhow, and told them to do their worst. They released him unharmed.

The old man was Thomas P. Fogg, a well-known abolitionist. His house stood on the edge of Salem Center. Originally from New England, Fogg had moved here long before the Civil War. A group of Virginia slave owners had placed a price on his head: $2,000 Dead or Alive. Luckily for him, Morgan's men had no idea who he was.

Fogg's home stood near the edge of Salem Center.

East of Salem Center, the raiders took $30 from Benjamin Gorby. He had received the money from his sons, who were serving in the Union Army.

It is 5.4 miles to Langsville. When the main force reached Langsville, they were delayed. The home guards had cut trees to block the road and had burned the covered bridge over Leading Creek near McMaster's Mill. It is now a small creek, but in 1863 the mill's dam made the creek quite deep.

Morgan sent men across the dam, and citizens were captured and forced to build a makeshift bridge for his wagons and artillery. Morgan ordered other local men and boys to clear the felled trees from the road leading to Rutland. He threatened to burn the mill and rip out the dam. Jabez Hubbell, the miller, offered to open the dam gates, lowering the water level to make it easier for the men and horses to ford the stream.

Captain William McKnight was with a few of the 7th Ohio Cavalry left behind in Kentucky. When the raiders approached the McKnight house in Langsville, his wife attempted to flee with their two-week-old twin daughters. Morgan ordered them back to their house and assured McKnight's wife that the family would be protected. True to his word, Morgan waited in the McKnight home while the bridge was being built.

As the raiders left town, citizens on the hill shot at the rear of of the column. A very young raider was mortally wounded and buried nearby. His widowed mother was later notified, and she stated her intent to have the body returned to Tennessee; however, she never sent for the body. The exact site of the unmarked grave is unknown.

Joe Pickering, a Union soldier, was home on leave and waiting for orders. He and a friend followed the raiders as they left Rutland. They were able to capture five stragglers and turn them in to the militia.

Drive 2.0 miles. The brick house on the right was built in 1820 by John Miles. The Miles Cemetery is located on the left beyond the house.

Miles/McQuigg house was built in 1820.

Miles's youngest daughter, Electa, married John McQuigg. In 1863, the McQuigg family was living on the homestead. Southern soldiers visited the home and looted as they moved from room to room. One of them took a gold dollar belonging to one of the children.

Go 1.2 miles to Rutland; SR 124 turns right. After making the turn, reset your odometer. When the main force rode into Rutland about 8 a.m., the men's breakfast was ready. Before leaving town earlier that morning, the advance guard had ordered the local women to begin baking for the main force, which would be arriving soon. The well-fed raiders rewarded the women's efforts by looting the town.

The residents of Rutland were particularly apprehensive because the town had been a major station on the Underground Railroad. Morgan was in a hurry, however, and did little damage.

Hobson's men rode into Rutland five hours after the last Confederate left. The townswomen, who had been forced to feed the raiders earlier, gladly provided food for the rebels' pursuers.

Leaving Rutland, Morgan took blacksmith Joseph Giles as a guide. Stay on SR 124; it is 3.1 miles to the intersection with Bradbury Road (CR 5). Along the way, you will drive through a gap in the hills. This area was known as Cook's Gap. The intersection is a mile beyond the gap. There is an **Ohio Historical Marker** at the Bradford Cemetery entrance, 0.1 mile south on Bradbury Road.

Two civilians, P. Holliday Hysell and his neighbor, Doctor William Hudson, were mortally wounded near here. The intoxicated sixty-five-year-old Hysell was shot for cursing the rebels. Hudson, who was shot when he went to aid the old man, died a week later.

Drive 1.0 mile to SR 7 and turn right. Look to the left; the Old Stagecoach Road runs parallel to the highway. Morgan turned right on the old road and headed toward Middleport.

Bradbury Hill and the Old Stagecoach Road on the left.

Morgan had sent men to scout the fords of the upper Ohio River before leaving Tennessee. He knew there was a ford located below Middleport, near Cheshire. Morgan's guide, Joseph Giles, had also told him there was a ferry at Middleport.

At 0.6 mile, the high ground on your left is Bradbury Hill, known as Jacobs Hill during the Civil War. When Morgan arrived here, he found Johnson's troops involved in a skirmish with enemy troops positioned on the hill.

As Morgan moved east across Ohio, Captains R. B. Wilson and John Schreiner, in command of the Middleport militia, had been sent to Camp Marietta. With Morgan threatening Meigs County, they hastily returned to Middleport. The approximately 120 men and one cannon were positioned on Bradbury (Jacobs) Hill. Captain Wilson sent out George Womeldorff, a local scout, to locate the raiders. He found them and was captured by them. Womeldorff escaped and rode back to warn the militia Morgan was coming.

The militia was in a nearly impregnable position of superior elevation in dense woods. Morgan did not know whether he was facing militia or Judah's men. He knew that Judah's force had been brought upriver to Portsmouth and might be in the area. Unsure of the nature and strength of his enemy, Morgan broke off the action and headed back up the Old Stagecoach Road.

Continue down the hill; go left on Bradbury Road (CR 5), where you can safely turn around. Return to SR 7, turn right and reset your odometer. It is 1.6 miles to Union Avenue. Morgan's men found Union Avenue blocked west of Pomeroy by Union militia under Captain Charles W. Smith. There were five gunboats and transports in Pomeroy, and the rebels could see their smoke plumes rising above the hills.

Denied access to the Middleport ferry, the Eight Mile Island crossing, and Pomeroy, the raiders headed upriver toward Portland and the Buffington Island Ford. Wilson's Middleport militia and Smith's Pomeroy militia and Trumbull Guards followed Morgan.

*Side Trip: To visit the scenic old river town of Pomeroy, turn right onto Union Avenue. When Union Avenue ends, turn right on Mulberry Avenue and follow it to the downtown area.

After the Battle of Buffington Island, many of the approximately 900 captured Confederates from the surrounding region were brought back to Pomeroy. Awaiting the steamers that would carry them to Cincinnati, 227 raiders were held in the Meigs County Courthouse. Generals Hobson and Judah and other Union officers used the Grand Dilcher Hotel at 106 E. Main Street as their headquarters. An **Ohio Historical Marker** stands next to the courthouse.

Meigs County Courthouse built in 1848. Portico and columns added during extensive remodeling in 1877.

The Meigs County Historical Society Museum is located at 144 Butternut Avenue. Museum hours are Tuesday–Friday, 10 a.m.–3 p.m. Open on Mondays by appointment only. Phone: (740) 992-3810; Web site: *www.meigscohistorical.org*.

To return to the main route, take Mulberry Avenue back to Union Avenue; turn left and continue up the hill. Turn right onto SR 7.*

It is 0.4 mile to the junction with SR 143. Beyond the junction is the bridge over Thomas Fork. Pull off on the right.

The company that passed through Harrisonville came down the road on your left to rejoin the main force. The men invited themselves to Samantha Smith's wedding party here at Thomas Fork. They ate breakfast and stole wedding gifts before making a hurried departure when Morgan's main column arrived after having been turned back at Bradbury Hill.

We are at the beginning of a three-mile stretch of road known as "The Gauntlet." As the raiders moved through the ravine, there were concentrations of militia at each crossroads, as well as men posted along the sides of the ravine. Morgan's men were under constant fire from Captain Horace M. Horton's Meigs County militia and Smith's Trumbull Guards.

Go 0.7 mile to Hiland Road (CR 75) and turn right. Immediately turn right again onto Hiland Road and go less than 0.1 mile; there is an **Ohio Historical Marker** on the right. Turn around; in less than 0.1 mile, after passing straight through the intersection, you are on Laurel Cliff Road. Proceed 0.9 mile on Laurel Cliff Road to Burdette Road. **Trail Sign #20** stands at the intersection, adjacent to a modern brick church on the left.

JOHN HUNT MORGAN HERITAGE TRAIL INTERPRETIVE SIGN #20

Laurel Cliff Road was the wartime road. The East Branch of Thomas Fork is on your right. The raiders suffered heavy losses as they moved through this area.

The militia on Bradbury Hill delayed Morgan for one hour. The delay allowed Brigadier General Eliakim Scammon and Colonel Rutherford B. Hayes time to position their troops near the end of "The

Col. Rutherford B. Hayes

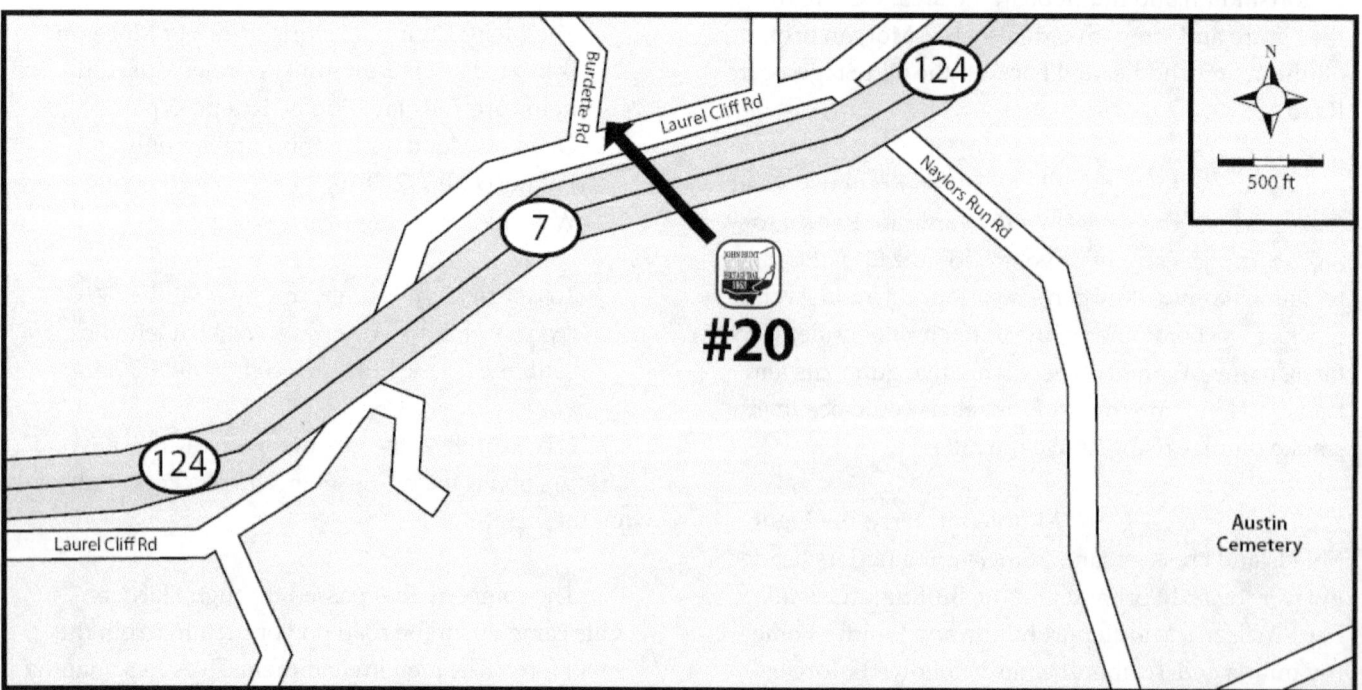

John Hunt Morgan Heritage Trail Interpretive sign #20 map

JACKSON TO BUFFINGTON ISLAND

Gauntlet." Their force consisted of the 23rd OVI and the 13th Virginia (U.S.) Infantry, which had been brought up from the Kanawha Valley of West Virginia.

The men from the Kanawha Division joined the Meigs County militia on the slopes and at the crossroads. They fired down on the raiders as they galloped by. Colonel J. Warren Grigsby and the 6th Kentucky Cavalry were in the lead. Major Thomas Webber and the 2nd Kentucky Cavalry brought up the rear as they made their dash through the ravine.

Webber and his men had their hands full. After the main column passed, the members of the Middleport militia made short dashes to attack the rear. The rebels drove them off, but at high cost. According to Union records, at least three of Morgan's men were killed and sixteen wounded during the five-mile ride around Pomeroy. One soldier of the 23rd OVI was wounded.

Continue on Laurel Cliff Road. When the section of original road ends in 0.7 mile, turn left onto SR 7. Drive 0.8 mile on SR 7 and turn right at the sign for CR 25 and 20 (Meigs County Fairgrounds). Immediately turn left onto CR 25 (Pomeroy Pike), and then turn left again onto Crew Road, passing under the highway. Turn left one more time at the first road after the underpass (Rock Springs Road). Reset your odometer. Go straight at the stop sign. You will be driving parallel to SR 7 on the unmarked Rock Springs Road (CR 20). It is 0.3 mile to Rock Springs Park on the right. The park is adjacent to the Meigs County Fairgrounds.

JOHN HUNT MORGAN HERITAGE TRAIL INTERPRETIVE SIGN #21

This marks the end of "The Gauntlet." The raiders emerged from the ravine near here, and there were no Yankees to greet them. They stopped briefly to rest, water their horses, count their losses, and regroup. There is an **Ohio Historical Marker** at the site.

Raiders regrouped at Rock Springs.

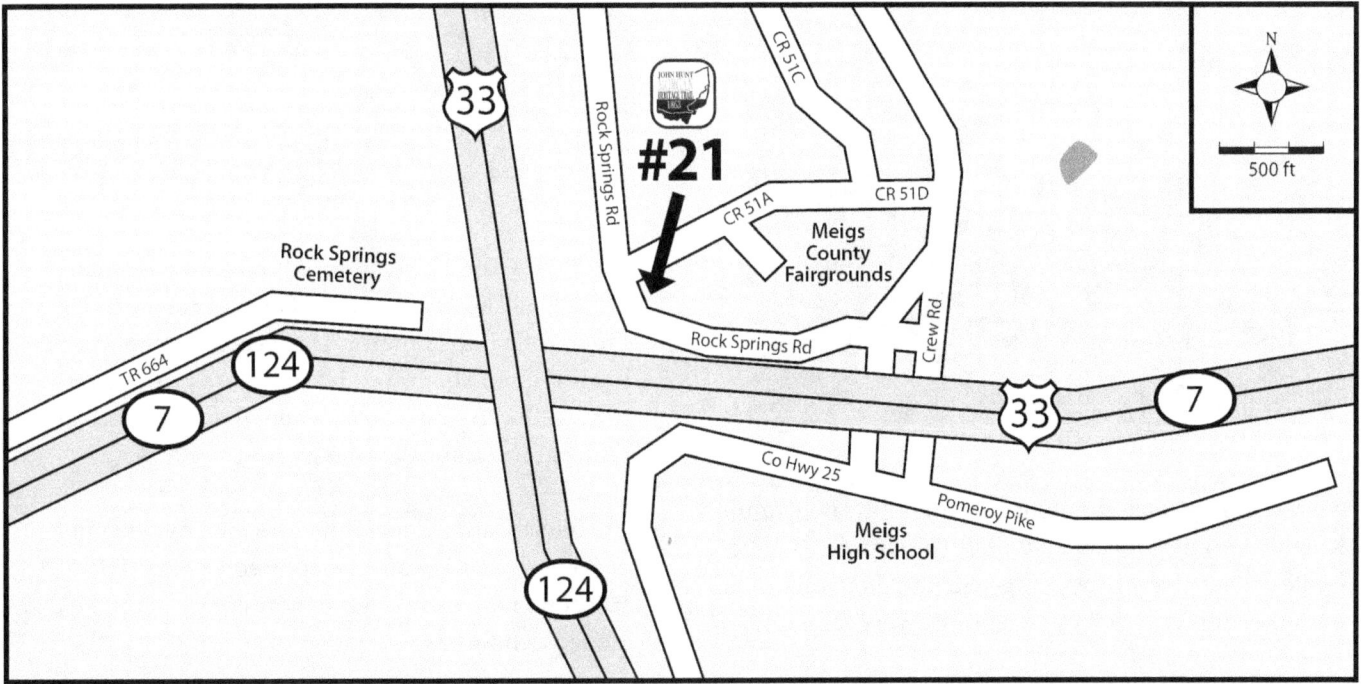

John Hunt Morgan Heritage Trail Interpretive sign #21 map

While at the springs, the raiders captured two civilians. When they tried to escape, Isaac Carleton, Jr., was shot in the back and left for dead. He eventually recovered. His companion escaped with just a few bullet holes in his clothes.

Turn around. To retrace your route back to SR 7, go through the stop sign and make four right turns. Reset your odometer as you make the fourth turn onto SR 7 East.

Drive 0.7 mile to CR 25 (the old Chester Road) and turn left. It is 4.7 miles to the intersection with SR 7. Go straight through the intersection and cross the Shade River Bridge. The road becomes SR 248 before the bridge.

Enter the town of Chester and park on the right side of the street. In 1863, the town had a population of several hundred people. Its buildings included a hotel, several stores, a grist mill, a rolling mill, and an academy.

The bridge you crossed occupies the site of the wooden covered bridge burned by the raiders on July 18. Remains of the original bridge abutments can be seen beneath the present-day bridge, which was built in 1926.

Shade River Bridge built on site of covered bridge.

On the right are the stone remains of the Benjamin Knight Carding Mill and Sawmill. The structures were ignited when the nearby bridge went up in flames. Both the mills and the covered bridge were rebuilt.

Chester mills and covered bridge

Morgan arrived in Chester about 1 p.m. The raiders were expecting to be attacked at Chester; it did not happen.

As you come up the hill from the Shade River, note the white two-story building on the right. This building served as Morgan's headquarters and is believed to be where Morgan sat with his feet propped on the porch railing. He was reported to have said to Adam Johnson, "All our troubles are now over... tomorrow we will be on Southern soil."

Porch where Morgan waited during search for a guide.

How wrong he was. Five hours after Morgan arrived in Chester, Brigadier General Henry Judah's forces rode into Pomeroy. His weary men and jaded horses rested about four hours before pushing on toward Buffington Island, where they expected the raiders to attempt a crossing.

Shortly after General Judah's men moved out of Pomeroy, Union scouts reported General Edward Hobson's men were passing north of town on the Old Stagecoach Road.

JACKSON TO BUFFINGTON ISLAND

The Ohio River was running higher than usual, allowing Lieutenant Commander Leroy Fitch to move his tinclad gunboats upriver. General Burnside's net was closing.

While Morgan rested on the porch, some of his raiders looted the local stores while others scoured the surrounding countryside for horses.

From Morgan's headquarters, it is 0.1 mile on SR 248 to the Chester Village Commons on the right. Here, some of the exhausted men rested while their horses grazed.

The oldest courthouse in Ohio, built in 1823, overlooks the commons. The Meigs County seat was moved to Pomeroy in 1841. The nearby Chester Academy was built in 1839. There are two **Ohio Historical Markers** across the road from the commons.

JOHN HUNT MORGAN HERITAGE TRAIL INTERPRETIVE SIGN #22

Joseph Giles, Morgan's guide from Rutland, escaped in Chester. Morgan wasted more than 90 minutes trying to find a replacement to lead him to Buffington Island Ford. This delay for rest and to

Old Meigs County Courthouse and Chester Academy

locate a guide cost Morgan the opportunity for a daylight crossing.

Continue on SR 248 for 1.0 mile. At the top of the hill where SR 248 turns left, bear right on Riebel Road (TR 113). Reset your odometer. There is a church and a pond on the right. Horse Cave is located on private property in the hollow below. Horses may have been hidden in the cave by Chester residents during the raid, but the name Horse Cave predates the Civil War.

Between here and the Portland Bottoms, the roads may not be well marked; it is important to follow the driving instructions and watch your odometer.

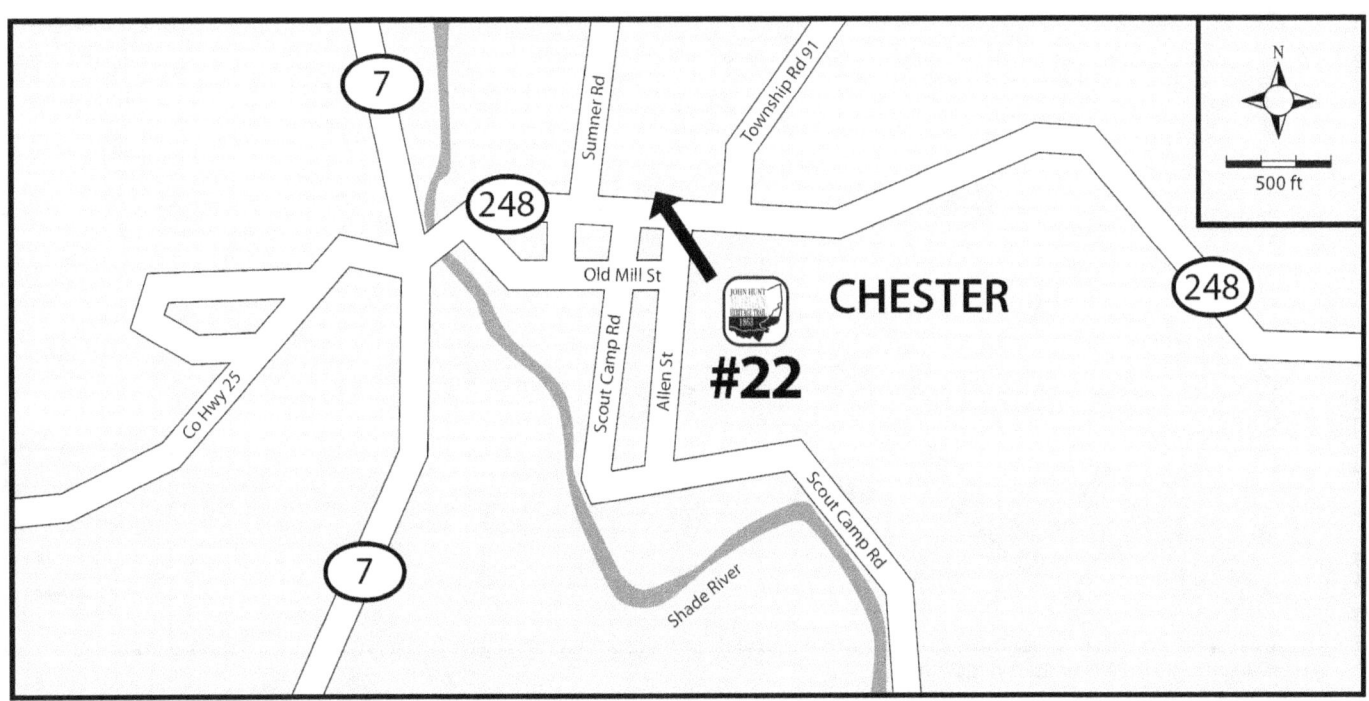
John Hunt Morgan Heritage Trail Interpretive sign #22 map

After 0.3 mile, bear right on Oak Hill Road (TR 59). Continue for 1.7 miles, bear left on Scout Camp Road (TR 112), and cross Shade River. This section of road has changed little since 1863.

Go 1.4 miles to a stop sign and turn left onto Eagle Ridge Road (CR 32). Another 0.6 mile will bring you to a "T" intersection. Turn right onto Bashan Road (CR 28) and you are in old Bashan. There is an **Ohio Historical Marker** in front of the firehouse on the left.

JOHN HUNT MORGAN HERITAGE TRAIL INTERPRETIVE SIGN #23

After the Battle of Buffington Island on Sunday, July 19, Colonel Richard Morgan and approximately 180 raiders escaped and followed primitive roads toward Bashan Church. Near here, in the fields on the east edge of town, they engaged in a skirmish with Union cavalry serving under Brigadier General James M. Shackelford and Colonel Frank L. Wolford. The skirmish lasted approximately one hour. Outnumbered and out of ammunition, the raiders surrendered.

Short-story writer, newspaperman, and satirist Ambrose G. Bierce was born on Horse Cave Creek near Bashan on June 24, 1842. The exact site is not recorded. His family moved to Kosciusko County, Indiana, where Bierce spent his childhood. His experiences as a Civil War soldier were the basis of much of his postwar writing. Bierce participated in the battles of Shiloh, Chickamauga, and Missionary Ridge. His best-known work is probably the short story, "An Occurrence at Owl Creek Bridge," from his book *Tales of Soldiers and Civilians* (1891).

Leaving Bashan in route to the Buffington Island Ford, General Morgan's advance troops skirmished with a small company of militia, which they quickly routed.

Continue on Bashan Road (CR 28) for 0.7 mile. There is a lane on the left leading to an old cemetery. Depending on the foliage, it may be possible to see some of the grave stones. The story is told that Morgan encountered a funeral procession on the way to the cemetery. The raiders dumped the coffin in the road and took the hearse and horses.

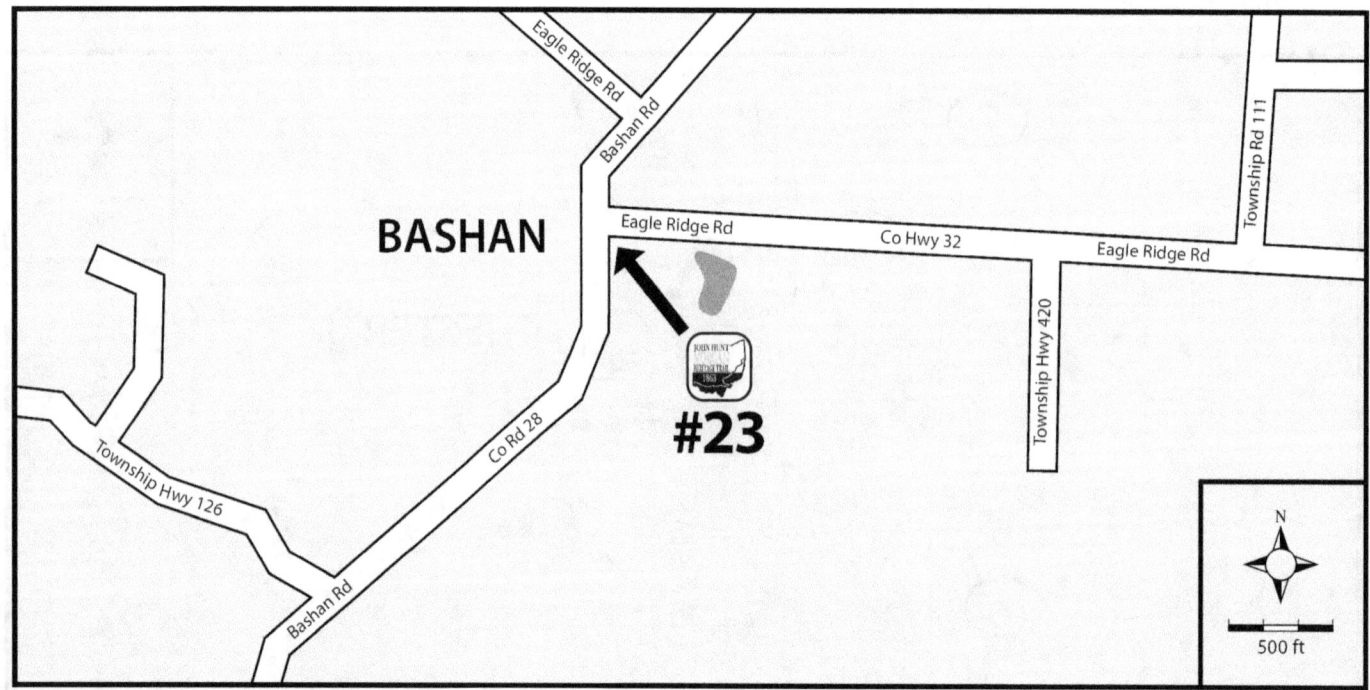

John Hunt Morgan Heritage Trail Interpretive sign #23 map

Continue another 0.3 mile and turn left onto Bald Knob-Stiversville Road (CR 31). At 1.9 miles, stay on CR 31 as it bears right. It is 1.9 miles to the high ground where Morgan posted his pickets on the night of Saturday, July 18.

Stay on CR 31; it is 0.6 mile to Stiversville. Just beyond Stiversville, the road begins its descent to the Ohio River valley. It is less than 1.5 miles to the edge of the woods where the raiders came out on the valley floor near Portland.

Chapter Six
BATTLE OF BUFFINGTON ISLAND

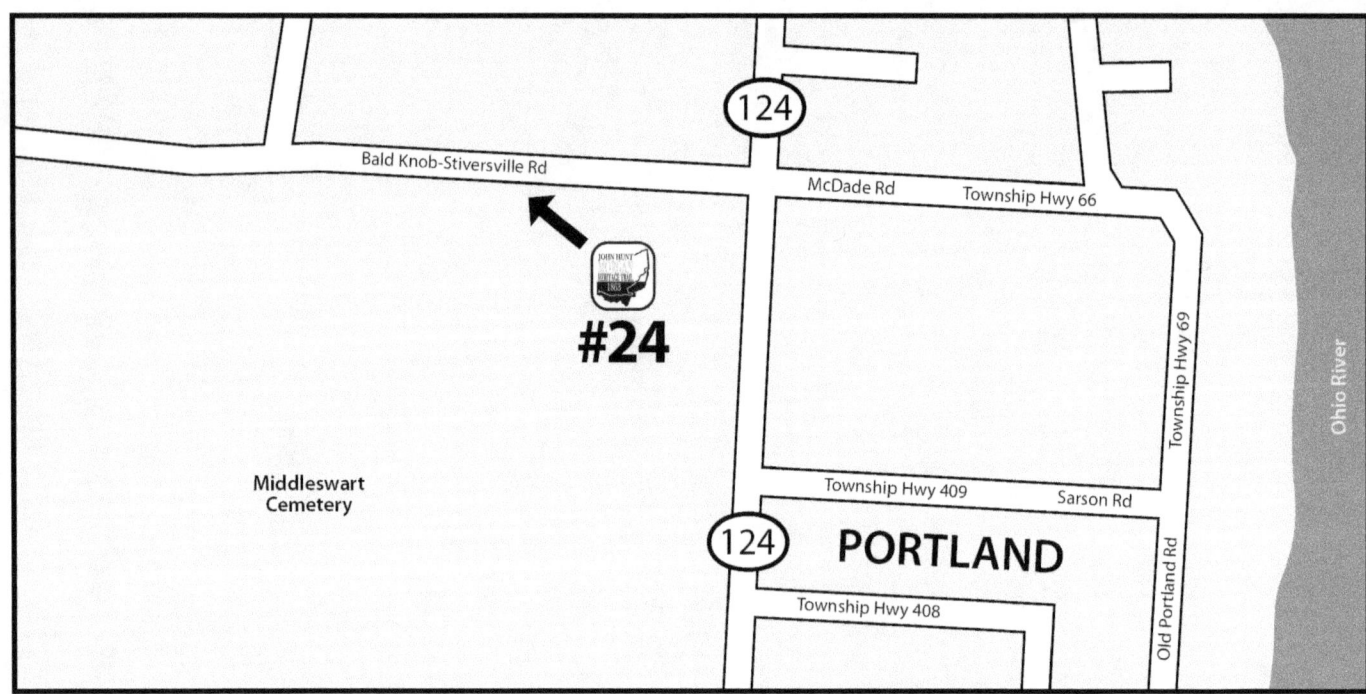

John Hunt Morgan Heritage Trail Interpretive sign #24 map

Saturday night, July 18, 1863

As Morgan's 1,930 raiders came out of the woods near Portland, the sun was setting on a valley of wheat and corn fields. **Trail Sign #24** is on the right side of CR 31, a quarter of a mile before SR 124.

JOHN HUNT MORGAN HERITAGE TRAIL INTERPRETIVE SIGN #24

The Buffington Island Ford and the southern end of the battlefield are to the right. Duke's last stand and Morgan's retreat route are to the far left. At the time of the battle, the area immediately to the left was open fields. It has since been mined for gravel.

About 8 p.m., scouts were sent ahead to reconnoiter the Buffington Island Ford. In early September 1862, Brigadier General Albert Gallatin Jenkins and his 350 troopers had used this ford to enter Ohio on a raid through eastern Meigs County. Morgan intended to use the same ford to exit the state.

In the fading light on the 18th, the Confederate scouts could see the earthwork fortification and Union militia guarding the ford. The raiders could not tell how many defenders were in the redoubt (the fortification).

The earthworks were manned by Ohio militia troops under Captain D. L. Wood, 18th U.S. Infantry; they had been sent from Marietta. The force included approximately two hundred men, fifty mounted scouts, and two guns.

Morgan's scouts could also see the river level was high. In midsummer, the water was normally boot-top high at the Buffington Island Ford. In mid-July of 1863, however, recent heavy rains in Pennsylvania and West Virginia had raised the river level to between five and six feet at the ford.

The high, swift waters would make for a dangerous crossing. After consulting with his officers, Morgan decided a night crossing was too risky. They would wait until dawn.

A portion of Colonel Adam Johnson's command, consisting of the 7th and 10th Kentucky Cavalry regiments, camped in this area. They would hold this position until morning, when they were attacked by Colonel August Kautz's and Colonel William Sanders's Federal troops. Greatly outnumbered and running out of ammunition, the Confederates would be forced to fall back.

BATTLE OF BUFFINGTON ISLAND

Basil Duke moved toward the river and followed the Old Portland Road south (right) to within 400 yards of the militia redoubt. He intended to storm the earthworks at daybreak, clearing the way for the river crossing.

Morgan rode to Tunis Middleswart's farm, located between here and the river. Morgan used the farmhouse as his headquarters, and many of his men camped in the surrounding area.

When the junior officers checked the ammunition supplies, they found that many men had no more than two or three rounds left. The raiders were not overly concerned, however, because the next day they would be across the river and safe in West Virginia (formerly Virginia).

The women of Portland were put to work preparing food for the rebel officers. Most of the troopers were not so lucky. Afraid to light fires, the men munched on whatever cold rations they could find. Meanwhile, back at Chester, Hobson's main force was treated to fresh-baked biscuits and quick bread served with butter, fresh milk, and preserves from the local spring houses.

The exhausted raiders had trouble falling asleep. Musicians brought out their instruments, and soon many of the men were singing and playing sentimental songs. Weariness finally overcame the men, and they drifted off to sleep. While they slept, others, both Union and Confederate, did not.

Kautz led the advance Union troops, consisting of the 2nd and 7th Ohio Cavalry regiments, from Chester to a position several miles back on the Bald Knob-Stiversville Road.

A Union force commanded by Brigadier General Henry M. Judah spent the night marching from Pomeroy. They were approaching the battlefield from the south along the road through Racine.

Under cover of darkness, Captain Wood's militia spiked both of its field pieces, pushed them into the river, and abandoned the redoubt.

Lieutenant Commander Leroy Fitch's gunboat, USS *Moose*, had been towed upstream from Portsmouth by the dispatch boat *Imperial*. Unable to navigate in the narrow chute between the island and the Ohio shore after dark, the boats anchored off the foot of Buffington Island. *Allegheny Belle* joined them.

Confederate Lieutenant Leeland Hathaway took a patrol upriver and found several ancient flatboats and skiffs. His men spent the night repairing the boats, so that they would be available to transport the sick and wounded during the crossing in the morning.

Drive 0.2 mile to the stop sign at SR 124 and turn right. In 1863, this road did not exist; Old Portland Road along the river was the primary north-south road in the valley. It is 0.7 mile to the Buffington Island Battlefield State Memorial Park.

JOHN HUNT MORGAN HERITAGE TRAIL INTERPRETIVE SIGN #25

Trail Sign #25 is a **Trail Point of Entry Sign**, located in the informational kiosk. Other signs in the kiosk provide an overview of the Battle of Buffington Island and of Morgan's Indiana-Ohio Raid. Near the Indian mound is a **stone monument** commemorating the battle.

Monument at Buffington Island Battlefield State Memorial Park

Three **Ohio Historical Markers** here also honor the Union regiments and gunboats, the Confederate regiments, and the citizens of 1863 Portland. Another **Ohio Historical Marker** describes Jenkins's Raid of September 1862.

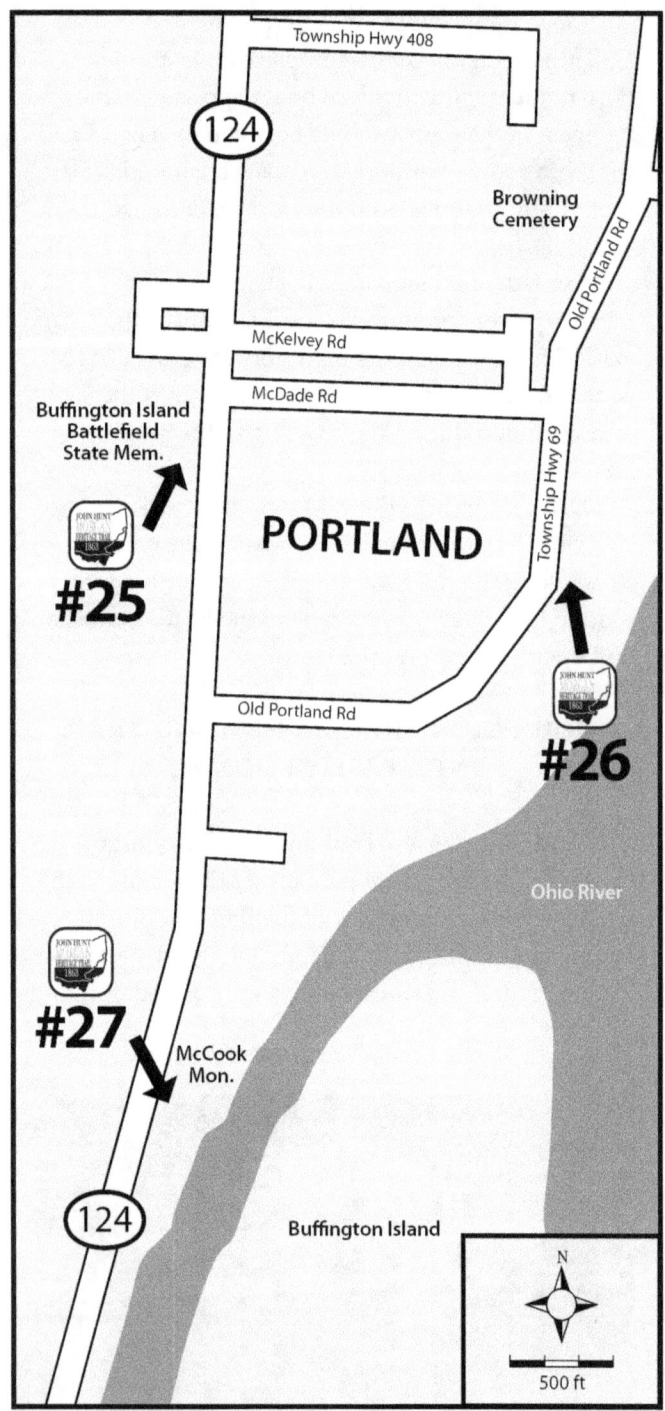

John Hunt Morgan Heritage Trail Interpretive signs #25, #26, and #27 map

stone monument in the park. The guns overlooked the southern end of the Portland Bottoms. Captain Edward P. Byrne placed two howitzers in position to protect the approaches to the ford.

After viewing the visitors' kiosk, leave the parking lot and turn left (north) onto SR 124 and drive 0.7 mile to McDade Road. Turn right and continue straight on McDade Road for less than 0.2 mile. The site of the Middleswart house, which served as Morgan's headquarters, was on the high ground on the right. Continue 0.1 mile to Old Portland Road and bear right.

Tunis Middleswart's house is no longer standing.

It is about 0.5 mile to the site of Civil War-era Portland. All that remains are a few abandoned buildings. The town was moved to higher ground to escape frequent flooding.

Continue about 0.4 mile; the redoubt occupied the high ground on the right. At dawn, the valley lay under a blanket of dense fog. Duke's troops under Colonel D. Howard Smith assaulted the redoubt guarding the ford and were surprised to find it empty.

JOHN HUNT MORGAN HERITAGE TRAIL INTERPRETIVE SIGN #26

The site of the Buffington Island Ford is on the left. The ford crossed the river from northwest to southeast. Although the nature of the river has changed drastically since the 1860s with the construction of dams and dredging, if you look downriver, you should be able to see the end of Buffington Island. In 1863, the island was much longer, its head reaching almost back to the ford.

The ground for the park was donated by descendants of the Price family. Price descendants still farm the land at the northern end of the battlefield.

Sunday, July 19, 1863

Before dawn, Lieutenant Elias D. Lawrence's men moved Morgan's two Parrott guns to a position on the bluff about 400-500 yards southwest of the present-day

BATTLE OF BUFFINGTON ISLAND

After viewing **Trail Sign #26**, go 0.3 mile to SR 124 and turn left. Drive 0.9 mile and turn around at Berringer Ridge Road, which marks the end of the Portland Bottoms. Judah's skirmishers deployed here.

It is approximately 0.6 mile back to the **McCook Monument** and **Trail Sign #27**. As you drive, look to the right; you may be able to see Buffington Island and the chute through the trees. The picture shown here was taken from a private road leading down to the river.

Buffington Island (on the left) and chute

Major Daniel McCook

The island, near the Ohio shore, belongs to West Virginia. Located at the site of a key ford, it had served as a station on the Underground Railroad. Although the action in the valley is referred to as "the Battle of Buffington Island," no fighting occurred on the island.

Park your vehicle at the small McCook Monument State Memorial Park.

JOHN HUNT MORGAN HERITAGE TRAIL INTERPRETIVE SIGN #27

The park monument honors Major Daniel McCook Sr., who was mortally wounded 0.2 mile south on SR 124; the exact location is unknown. Daniel McCook Sr. was the patriarch of the "Fighting McCooks" from Carrollton, Ohio.

At age sixty-five, he volunteered to serve as paymaster with Judah's army. He blamed the Confederates for the murder of his son, Brigadier General Robert L. McCook, who was killed in cold blood by Confederate guerrillas near New Market, Alabama, in August 1862. The old man wanted to settle the score.

McCook was one of the first men wounded in the initial contact between Smith's and Judah's men on the south end of the battlefield.

Morgan had placed pickets several miles back on the Bald Knob-Stiversville Road to watch for the approach of Hobson's men. Although he was aware there were other Union forces in the area, Morgan failed to place pickets on the Pomeroy Road entering the valley from the south.

This allowed Judah's men, who had marched from Pomeroy during the night, to arrive at the southern end of the valley without warning. Judah's force consisted of approximately 1,000 men, including a brigade of cavalry and several batteries of artillery.

Stand with your back toward the monument. Leaving the abandoned redoubt, the raiders moved south to belatedly secure the Pomeroy Road. It was about 5:30 a.m. when the fog lifted, and Smith's men found themselves facing the advance guard of Judah's Union force. Both sides were equally surprised. The rebels charged into Judah's men on the highway approximately 0.2 mile south of here, on your extreme left. This is where the battle began.

Smith's men won the initial skirmish, routing the Federal forces and nearly capturing Judah. Daniel McCook fell mortally wounded in the highway. The raiders captured 30 men and one of the Henshaw Independent Battery's guns. The action lasted about 20 minutes. Judah's men fell back and regrouped.

Now, look slightly to the left across the road. Recent archeological studies suggest the area near the utility pole was the site of Judah's first counterattack against Duke's men of the 5th and 6th Kentucky Cavalry regiments, serving under Colonel D. Howard Smith.

Site of first action of Judah's counterattack against Smith's men.

Judah, having regrouped his force, rejoined the battle. The turning point occurred when fifty men of the 5th Indiana Cavalry, led by Lieutenant John O'Neil, charged ahead of Judah's main force and captured Lawrence's artillery. They turned the captured guns on the raiders.

Colonel J. Warren Grigsby's attempts to retake the Confederate guns proved futile. Judah ordered his artillery pieces into action. The 5th Indiana Cavalry and 14th Illinois Cavalry, along with the detachments of the 11th Kentucky (U.S.), 8th Michigan, and 9th Michigan Cavalry regiments, began a slow advance, pushing Duke's men back up the valley.

Look across the fields to the high ground and the Confederate artillery position up the valley on the right. From there, Lawrence's two Confederate Parrott guns could cover the ford and the southern approach road from Pomeroy. Between here and the Confederate artillery position, Judah's troopers fought Duke's men on foot. The fighting became heavy. Judah later set up his artillery in the farm lane located across the highway, just over 0.1 mile south of the McCook monument.

Confederate artillery position is marked by the arrow.

Several things happened that quickly altered the battle. First, when the action opened between Kautz and Johnson, Judah became aware there were other Union forces present. Second, Captain John Grafton returned. During the initial skirmish, Grafton, a member of Judah's staff, was separated from his unit. He had narrowly escaped capture and made his way to the river, where he was picked up by a gunboat.

Lt. Commander LeRoy Fitch

BATTLE OF BUFFINGTON ISLAND

Early in the morning, the USS *Moose* had steamed up the chute between the island and the Ohio shore. The naval contingent was under the command of Lieutenant Commander LeRoy Fitch, a twenty-seven-year-old Regular naval officer.

The armed transport *Allegheny Belle* also moved into place. Eighteen-year-old Nathaniel Pepper was the son of the captain of the *Alice Dean*, a steamboat Morgan's men had burned after they had used it in crossing the Ohio River at Brandenburg, Kentucky. Pepper manned the *Belle's* forward gun. Trailing behind the gunboats was the dispatch boat *Imperial*.

Captain Grafton was able to point out the exact position of the rebel units to the captain of the *Moose*. The gunboat's 24-pounder Dahlgren guns would soon be devastating the Confederates.

James Williamson's house is in center; J. Ritchey house lies at the highway bend (left, in distance). McCook fell between the two houses on the highway.

The J. Ritchey house served as a field hospital.

The large frame house on the left belonged to James Williamson. It served as a field hospital for both Union and Confederate wounded. Farther down the road, just before the sharp bend in the highway, is the J. Ritchey house, which was also used as a field hospital. The house was later bought by the Williamson family. The fifty-seven Confederate dead are thought to be buried nearby.

The Confederates were greatly outnumbered and running low on ammunition. They were caught up in a crossfire from three directions. Judah's force attacked from the south and pushed Duke's men back. Colonel Kautz's men, attacking along the Bald Knob-Stiversville Road, drove back Johnson's brigade.

Brigadier General Edward H. Hobson, who had sent Kautz ahead, now arrived with Colonel Sanders's brigade and moved men and artillery into place on the hill overlooking the battle. Lieutenant Cyrus Roys's two guns from Battery L, 1st Michigan Light Artillery (also called the 11th Michigan Battery), opened up on Johnson's men with shell and canister shot.

The *Moose* had arrived while the first of the raiders were crossing the river. Shots from the boat's bow gun killed several men and sent the others already in the river scurrying to the nearest shore. Approximately 140 men, including Captain Edward Byrne and Colonel J. Warren Grigsby, succeeded in crossing the river before the gunboats arrived.

If the *Moose* had not been there, Morgan could have organized a rear-guard action and escaped. Morgan had not taken gunboats into account, because his scouts had informed him the upper Ohio was too shallow for navigation in July. Later, Portland area residents claimed the July river level had not been this high in twenty years.

After reading **Trail Sign #27**, continue 1.1 miles north on SR 124 to McDade Road. Turn right and drive less than 0.3 mile; this time, turn left onto Old Portland Road and follow it less than 0.9 mile to SR 124; pull over on the right.

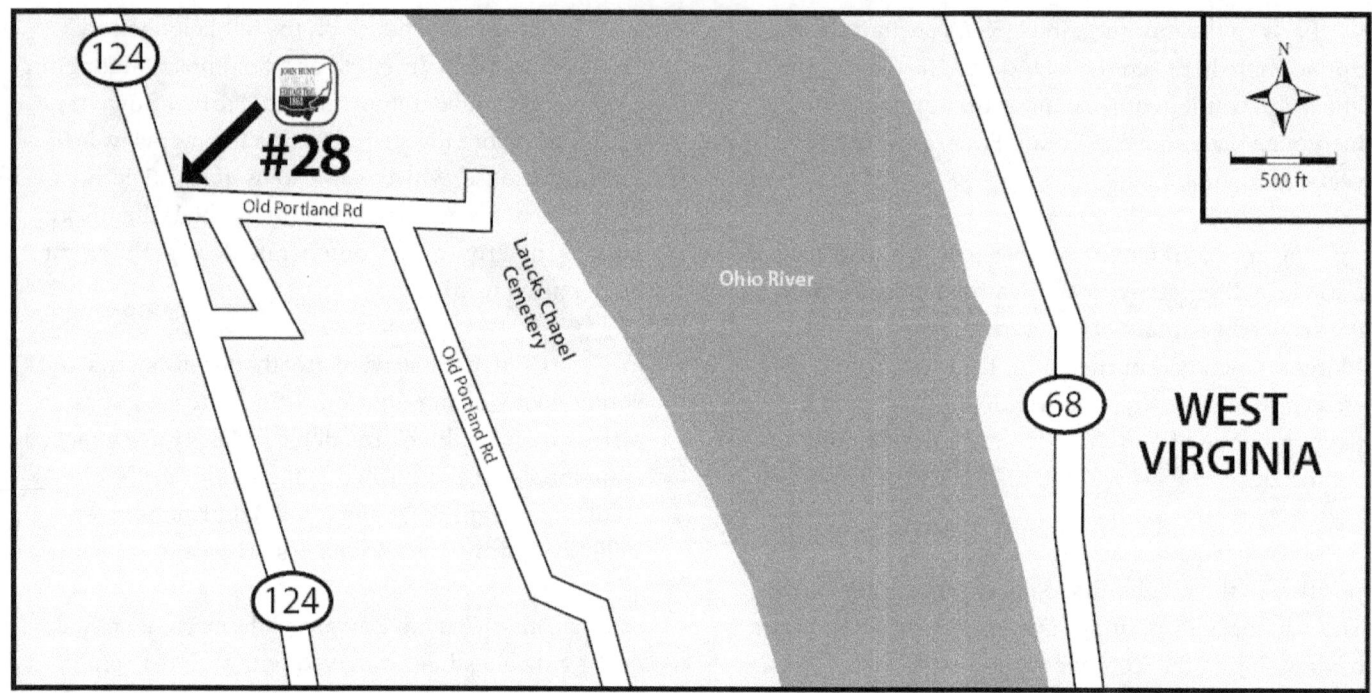

John Hunt Morgan Heritage Trail Interpretive sign #28 map

JOHN HUNT MORGAN HERITAGE TRAIL INTERPRETIVE SIGN #28

Along the Old Portland Road, you will pass a white house with a green roof on the left. It is the Price family home, built shortly after the Civil War. In 1863, the family lived in a nearby log house.

At the stop sign, look to the right and the trees in the distance. In 1863, the Ohio River flowed along the base of a steep hill just north of there, making travel along the riverbank almost impossible. While a few Confederate soldiers made their way upstream along the bank, most followed Lauck's Run Road.

Post-war Price family home

Lauck's Run Road

Now, look straight ahead down the grassy strip located across SR 124. That is the original road; it ran across the field and then turned right following Lauck's Run. The tree line across the back of the field borders on the creek and ravine.

BATTLE OF BUFFINGTON ISLAND

As Judah's men pushed Duke's men north toward Portland, Hobson's men pushed Johnson's men east across the Portland Bottoms. The brigades ended up positioned in the shape of a giant "L." Duke's line extended east-west to face Judah's men attacking from the south. Johnson's brigade was aligned north-south to face Hobson's force advancing from the west.

Shells lobbed on the battlefield from the Union gunboats added to the mass confusion. Old Portland Road was a scene of pandemonium, as the rebels sought to escape the deadly Union naval fire. Morgan's supply wagons, ambulances, and other vehicles were strung along the Old Portland Road. Panicked men, downed horses, and overturned wagons blocked the road. Artillery, wagons, horses, and men tumbled to the bottom of Lauck's Run ravine and came to rest in a heap.

Confederate Major James B. McCreary wrote, "Shells and minnie balls ricocheting and exploding in every direction, cavalry were charging, and infantry with its slow, measured tread moved upon us, while broadside after broadside was poured upon our doomed command from the gunboats…."

The outnumbered Confederates, desperately low on ammunition, under attack from the south and west, and under fire from the gunboats to the east, were forced to retreat north.

Morgan began an orderly withdrawal of about 400 troops to the north, taking the road along Lauck's Run. After crossing the bridge over the run, Morgan followed wagon roads leading first northwest and eventually northeast back to the Ohio River.

Colonel Richard Morgan led approximately 200 of his men west on a primitive road leading out of the bottoms and back to the Bald Knob-Stiversville Road. They made their way back toward Bashan, where they were captured after a brief skirmish with Shackelford's men.

After seeing that General Morgan had made his escape, Duke and Johnson agreed to a slow and simultaneous withdrawal north.

The area where Spencer cartridges were found. This photo was taken from the old road before it turns right to follow Lauck's Run.

Duke's and Johnson's men, fighting as they retreated, gave up ground slowly. About to be flanked by Hobson's men, they decided it was time to mount up and pull out. The remnants of Johnson's brigade took the lead, escaped, and followed Morgan's route back to the river.

With landowner permission, it is possible to park here and follow the abandoned township road to Lauck's Run ravine and Duke's "last stand."

Archeological work performed under the direction of Michael Pratt of Heidelberg University in Tiffin, Ohio, located a line of Spencer carbine cartridges near the back of the field, suggesting it was the area from which the 8th and 9th Michigan Cavalry regiments fired down on the fleeing rebels in the ravine.

A tour group winding its way down to Lauck's Run.

The old township road wound down the ravine, crossed the run, and connected with a road leading west out of the valley and another primitive road eventually leading back to the river.

The old road is blocked beyond this bridge over Lauck's Run.

Duke's "last stand" was along Lauck's Run. Under fire from the gunboats on the river and surrounded by men of the Michigan Cavalry, Duke and approximately fifty of his men surrendered just after 7:30 a.m. in a ravine located beyond the bridge over Lauck's Run.

The rear-guard action that resulted in the capture of Duke and his men allowed Morgan, Adam Johnson, and the larger force of approximately 1,100 men to escape.

The gunboats were shelling in the blind. They continued to shoot, even after Duke's surrender. The Michigan forces under Colonel William P. Sanders sought refuge in the ravine with their captives.

After the surrender, the dusty, exhausted troopers of the North and South bathed together in the Ohio River. The victors shared their fried chicken with their hungry prisoners.

Brigadier General Henry M. Judah was Brigadier General Edward H. Hobson's senior commander. Their relationship was strained, due primarily to Hobson's independent nature and his practice of offering unsolicited advice to his commander.

General Burnside, dissatisfied with Judah's failure to prevent Morgan's breakout from Kentucky, had placed Hobson in command of an independent provisional cavalry division and had given him orders to pursue and capture Morgan. Hobson had pursued Morgan since he left Lebanon, Kentucky.

Brigadier General Edward H. Hobson

Brigadier General Henry M. Judah

BATTLE OF BUFFINGTON ISLAND

Following the Battle of Buffington Island, Union troops took the field, and General Hobson set up his headquarters in the Tunis Middleswart house.

Hobson was issuing orders for the pursuit of Morgan when General Judah rode up and asserted his command over Hobson and his force. Hobson was denied the opportunity to personally lead the pursuit and capture of Morgan. Brigadier General James M. Shackelford and Colonel Frank Wolford were ordered to continue the chase of Morgan and the remnants of his command.

Hobson insisted the matter be referred to Burnside. When Judah received Burnside's response commending Hobson's performance, he was furious. Judah left the field and returned to Pomeroy. Hobson took charge of burying the dead, caring for the wounded, and marching the prisoners to Pomeroy.

The captives were transported by boat from Pomeroy to Cincinnati. From there, they were sent to prison camps. Many of the men ended up at one of the four camps in the region: Camp Morton (Indianapolis), Camp Douglas (Chicago), Camp Chase (Columbus), or Johnson's Island (Sandusky).

Hobson returned to Kentucky as a division commander. During Morgan's "Last Kentucky Raid" in 1864, Morgan captured Hobson at the Battle of Keller's Bridge. Hobson died in 1901 while delivering a speech at a Grand Army of the Republic convention in Cleveland, Ohio.

The Battle of Buffington Island resulted in heavy Confederate losses: 57 men killed, 150 to 200 wounded, and approximately 520 captured at various places on and off the battlefield in eastern Meigs County. One hundred of the wounded were also counted among the captured. In addition, Morgan lost his four artillery pieces and his wagon train.

Union casualties were estimated at 55 killed and wounded.

Booty was strewn over the battlefield. A newspaper correspondent described the battlefield after the action ended:

> The battlefield and roads surrounding it were strewn with a thousand articles never seen on a battlefield before. One is accustomed to seeing broken swords, muskets and bayonets, haveracks, cartridge boxes, belts, pistols, gun carriages, cannons, wagons upset, wounded, dead and dying on the battlefield, but besides all these on the battlefield at Buffington Island, one could pick up almost any article in dry goods, hardware, house furnishing or ladies or gentlemen's furnishing line. Hats, boots, gloves, knives, forks, spoons, calico, ribbons, drinking cups, buggies, carriages, a circus wagon, and an almost endless variety of articles, useful and all, more or less, valuable.

This concludes the Buffington Island battlefield tour.

Turn right onto SR 124 North to continue on the Morgan Heritage Trail and the guidebook tour route.

Chapter Seven
BUFFINGTON ISLAND TO NELSONVILLE

Sunday, July 19, 1863

The Battle of Buffington Island was over. Duke covered the Confederate retreat while Morgan and Johnson led about 1,100 men upriver. A number of smaller squads escaped. Most of them were later captured, but a few eventually made it back to the Confederacy.

Colonel Richard Morgan and approximately 180 men were captured near the Bashan church. Three of Morgan's senior officers were among those captured: Colonels Richard C. Morgan, D. Howard Smith, and William W. Ward. Smith was captured with Duke near Lauck's Run, while Dick Morgan and Ward surrendered at Bashan. Lieutenant Colonel John Huffman and Captain Thomas Hines were captured not far from the Buffington Island battlefield.

Other raiders managed to swim the Ohio River only to be picked up on the West Virginia shore by the 23rd Ohio Volunteer Infantry (OVI), which served under Colonel Rutherford B. Hayes, the brigade commander.

One company of eighty men hid in the woods until after dark, and then headed for the sandbar at Wolf's Riffle. While trying to cross the river at Bowman's Run between Syracuse and Racine, they were captured by Captain Wilson and the Middleport militia. The militia was on its way home after the battle. Thirty-two raiders were captured while attempting to cross the Ohio at Guyandotte, near Huntington, West Virginia.

To continue the driving tour, turn right from Old Portland Road onto SR 124 and go 0.5 mile. There you will cross the ravine of Lauck's Run. Reset your odometer. We cannot follow Morgan. The old road that crossed Lauck's Run, upstream near Duke's last stand, has been abandoned. The present road did not exist in 1863.

Note the sheer bluffs on your left and the close proximity of the river on your right. It was reported a few of the raiders escaped down this narrow corridor.

Before the battle, 110 raiders, mostly from the 9th Tennessee Cavalry, crossed the river here and at the ford. They used skiffs and flatboats that they had repaired during the night. They planned to take a position on the West Virginia shore and cover the crossing of the rest of the men. Helplessly, these men watched the battle and then started their long trek back to the Confederate lines in Virginia.

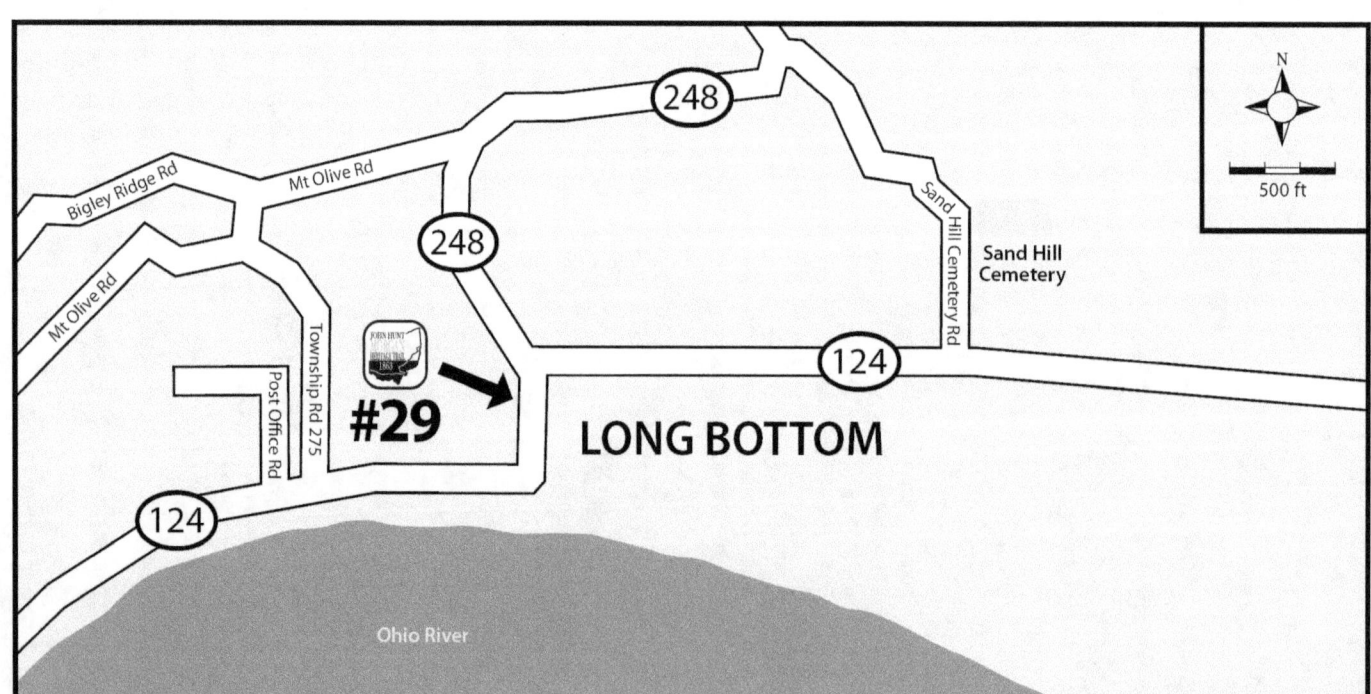

John Hunt Morgan Heritage Trail Interpretive sign #29 map

BUFFINGTON ISLAND TO NELSONVILLE

Note: The section of SR 124 between Portland and Long Bottom is frequently closed due to portions of the road sliding into the river. In the event you need a detour, return to SR 248 near Chester, turn right, and continue to Long Bottom.

It is 5.0 miles from the ravine at Lauck's Run to the post office at Long Bottom. Proceed around the bend of SR 124 toward the left; **Trail Sign #29** is on the left side of the road, before its intersection with SR 248.

JOHN HUNT MORGAN HERITAGE TRAIL INTERPRETIVE SIGN #29

When Morgan reached Long Bottom, he realized there were no close Union pursuers. He waited for Johnson and the rear guard to arrive. Morgan assessed his losses and reorganized his troops.

Morgan retained the two-brigade system. Adam Johnson retained the command of his brigade. Major Thomas "Iron Man" Webber was given command of the remnants of Basil Duke's brigade. Morgan bestowed on Webber an immediate field promotion to Brevet Lieutenant Colonel, a rank that would not become permanent unless Webber could return to Confederate lines.

The loss of the guns and wagons would allow the raiders to follow streambeds and ride cross country in the miles ahead. They were no longer committed to traveling on improved roads.

Drive 4.5 miles on SR 124 to the Belleville Dam fishing access. Park and follow the lane to the river.

The citizens of nearby Reedsville had been warned of Morgan's approach, and the whole town hid themselves in the brush-choked gully located behind the livery stable. However, two adventurous boys, Lewis Spencer and his thirteen-year-old companion, James H. Randolph, did not follow them. To get a closer look at the dreaded Morgan and his men, the boys snuck away from the crowd and climbed into a large tree that leaned over the main road.

When the raiders trotted into town, they spotted the two boys in the tree. The scouts asked them if they knew the way to the nearest river ford. James replied negatively, but Lewis answered that he knew. They told Lewis to come down and lead them to the ford. Lewis quickly rode off with the raiders while James ran into the gully.

When evening came and Lewis had not returned, all feared the worst. However, the next day, a tired but unharmed Lewis walked into town, much to the relief of his family. Lewis told how he had guided Morgan's men to Reedsville Ford (located at today's Belleville Dam fishing access) and to Lee Creek Ford, and then inland to Flatwoods, where he had stayed the night with them and had listened to their exciting tales of the raid. In the morning the rebels let Lewis go home.

About 350 yards below Belleville Dam, near the fishing access lane's first bend, was the Belleville Island Ford, also known as Reedsville Ford. The ford was submerged with the construction of the dam. Belleville, West Virginia, is on the opposite shore.

About 330 raiders succeeded in fording the Ohio River there before the gunboat USS *Moose* arrived. Johnson led those making the crossing. Because the river was flooded, the water level was up to the necks of the horses and riders. Many raiders drowned swimming their horses across the river. Morgan was almost across when the gunboat arrived. He returned to his approximately 800 men trapped on the Ohio shore. At Morgan's side was his telegrapher, "Lightning" Ellsworth. When Morgan turned back, he instructed Ellsworth to continue on and save himself.

A large group of raiders rode north on present-day SR 681 from Reedsville to Flatwoods. Morgan's column would meet up with this group later that evening at Flatwoods.

Proceed 0.9 mile on SR 124. Turn into Barr Hollow Road on the left to safely pull over.

JOHN HUNT MORGAN HERITAGE TRAIL INTERPRETIVE SIGN #30

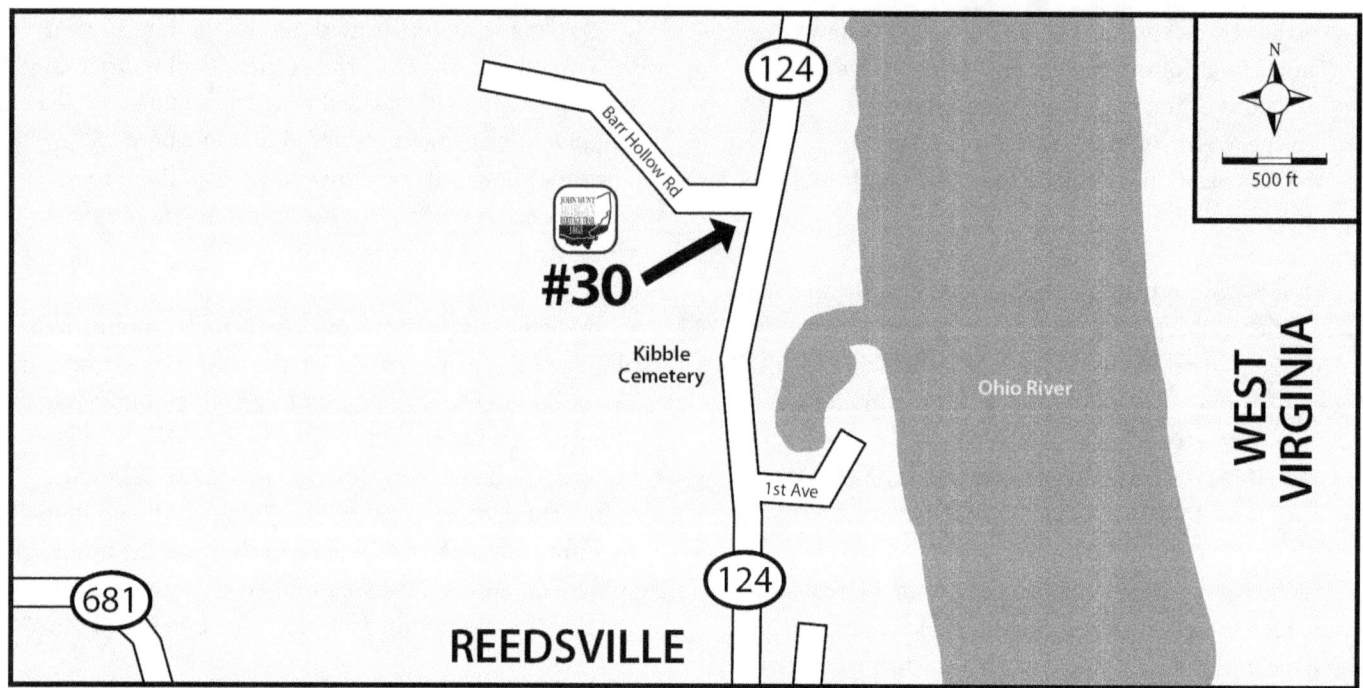

John Hunt Morgan Heritage Trail Interpretive sign #30 map

The large white house on the side of SR 124 facing the river is the Philip Hetzer house; it was built on the site of a wartime structure. The smaller white building, near the road, was here during the Civil War. Sarah Hetzer was called on to feed some of the raiders.

Hetzer House built on the site of 1863 house.

Drive about 1.0 mile on SR 124 and look upriver; you can see a stream entering from the opposite shore. That is the area of Lee Creek Ford. About twenty men made it across, before the USS *Moose* arrived.

Approximately thirty other raiders hid in the wooded area at the creek's mouth and fired, hoping to pick off some of the gunboat crew. The crew quickly ended this action by shelling the woods.

Lee Creek enters the Ohio River at the site of the ford.

Go 1.3 miles to Eden Ridge Road (CR 50). Morgan's men did not turn onto Eden Ridge Road. Instead, they continued along the river toward Hockingport. The following side trip allows you to follow a portion of Morgan's route in that region.

*Side Trip: From the Eden Ridge Road intersection, drive 0.7 mile on SR 124 to the approximate site on the right where the T. Parker house stood. Parker's Hill derived its name from this hilltop farm.

Go an additional 0.3 mile to the SR 124 crossing over Indian Run (look closely for what appears to be a pond at the bottom of the hill on the left side of the highway). About 0.1 mile farther, pull over to the side of the highway. Look back at Parker's Hill to see the view that Lieutenant Commander Leroy Fitch and his gunboats had of the raiders. This flat section of SR 124 did not exist during the war; the road ended at the mouth of Indian Run, where there was a low-water ford of the Ohio River.

Parker's Hill (right) and the mouth of Indian Run (center)

The Union gunboats shelled Morgan and his advance guard as they rode down the hill to inspect the ford. Without artillery, Morgan could not contest Fitch's guns. Morgan ordered a retreat from the river in the hopes of finding another ford. Later, several companies of the 23rd OVI disembarked from steamboats at this point to begin their search for the elusive raiders.

Turn around at a safe place. When you return to the SR 124 bridge over Indian Run, reset your odometer. Go slightly farther than 0.6 mile and turn right onto Deeter Road, a narrow and steep gravel road. This is the road Morgan and his column took when they were turned back by the gunboats at Parker's Hill.

Drive slightly farther than 0.7 mile along Deeter Road to a point where it forks. The left road at the fork is a dead end, private lane that follows the creek, and the right road leading up the hill is Indian Run Road. Indian Run Road parallels the old Civil War era road that headed toward Hockingport. After Confederate scouts had reported that Ohio troops blocked the road to Hockingport and the roads leading to the Hocking River, Morgan was forced to turn west onto the private lane which, at that time, led to the village of Flatwoods two miles from here.

Morgan followed Deeter Road up Indian Run.

Turn around and return to SR 124. Turn right at SR 124 and drive 0.3 mile; turn right onto Eden Ridge Road.*

Turn left onto Eden Ridge Road. This is a dangerous turn; go to the crest of the hill before turning.

Go 2.4 miles on Eden Ridge Road to the intersection with Coolville Road. During the Civil War, this intersection was the center of the village of Flatwoods. After the war, Flatwoods was first renamed as Fayal, and later renamed as Joppa.

Bear left on Eden Ridge Road. In 0.2 mile is the stop sign at SR 681. This point marks the center of Morgan's camp on the night of July 19.

With Adam Johnson safely across the Ohio River, Morgan had to reorganize again. Roy Cluke, his only remaining colonel, was given command of the 2nd Brigade; Brevet Lieutenant Colonel Thomas Webber continued as the acting leader of the 1st Brigade.

Turn left onto SR 681; drive slightly farther than 0.8 mile. Turn right into Flatwoods (Joppa) Cemetery.

Morgan's rear guard camped near Flatwoods Cemetery.

JOHN HUNT MORGAN HERITAGE TRAIL INTERPRETIVE SIGN #31

Morgan's rear guard camped in the fields surrounding Flatwoods Cemetery and on both sides of SR 681. At one time the first Methodist church in Flatwoods stood directly across the highway from here. The cemetery contains the graves of several Morgan's Raid claimants, including George Landon, Moses L. Flanders, and George Hetzer.

Turn around; take SR 681 for 0.8 mile back to Eden Ridge Road. Turn right onto Eden Ridge Road. In 0.2 mile, reset your odometer and turn left on Coolville Road. West of here stood the house of Michael Heiney, a Southern sympathizer. On the night of July 19, he hosted a dance for many of Morgan's raiders in his home. Heiney was well known for his excellent fiddling abilities and for his love of entertainment and dancing.

The raiders rested until about 11 p.m., when Morgan had them mount up for a night ride to escape Shackelford's trap. The last troopers left Flatwoods by 1 a.m.

Monday, July 20, 1863

In 0.3 mile is the location of the Hockingport fight between Morgan's raiders and Lieutenant Colonel James M. Comly's 23rd Ohio Infantry on the morning of July 20. Before dawn, Comly met a citizen who had been forced to guide Morgan's men earlier that morning. The citizen directed Comly and his regiment to follow Indian Run to Morgan's camp at Flatwoods.

When they arrived at the Confederate camp, Comly deployed Company C to cover the road from the river, and he sent Company A around to the right to block the Coolville Road and seal off escape on the north side of the camp. Comly personally led Company F on a five-mile journey in which they marched back to the river and then turned west on

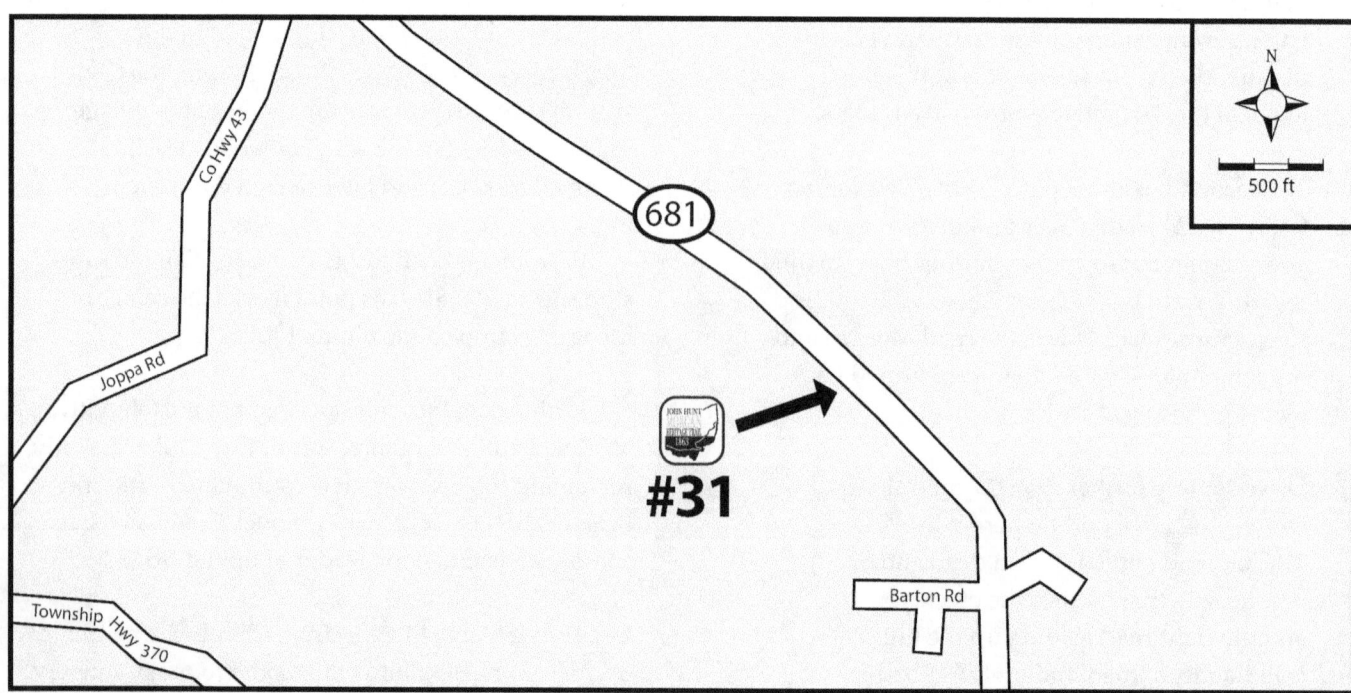

John Hunt Morgan Heritage Trail Interpretive sign #31 map

BUFFINGTON ISLAND TO NELSONVILLE

Location of Morgan's camp and Hockingport fight.

Eden Ridge Road. When they neared the intersection of Eden Ridge Road with Coolville Road, he deployed Company F's skirmishers to cut off the enemy's retreat south and east. When within thirty yards of the raiders' camp, the Union infantrymen opened fire, but the raiders immediately surrendered without firing back.

To Comly's great dismay, he discovered that General Morgan and the majority of his cavalrymen were gone. Only six officers and forty-three men, mostly wounded and dejected, were manning the Confederate camp. They had volunteered to stay behind and stoke the camp fires, giving the Union army the false impression that all of Morgan's command had been camped there all night. Morgan's old campfire trick had been successful!

Go approximately another 0.4 mile. As the Coolville Road bends to the left, you can see the remains of an old dirt road entering on the right, on which Morgan led his men from the river to Flatwoods. This is the point where Companies A and C of the 23rd Ohio attacked the camp.

Proceed 0.7 mile; look to the left to see the view of the valley in which Shackelford's skirmishers deployed during the night of July 19. Union Brigadier General James M. Shackelford's pursuit force contained approximately 600 cavalrymen supported by four mountain howitzers of Law's Mountain Howitzer Battery. Another 500–700 reinforcements were expected to join them during the evening and into the following day. The Union troopers camped on the ridge in the

Brig. Gen. James M. Shackelford

distance. They could clearly see Morgan's campfires from there. Conducting a personal reconnaissance, General Shackelford led Colonel Wolford and several other officers to within 300 yards of Morgan's camp. With the coming darkness, Shackelford concluded that it would be impracticable to make an assault through the dense woods and steep terrain. He decided to delay his attack until dawn.

Continue 0.2 mile and turn left onto Rice Run Road, a well-maintained gravel road. Reset your odometer again. Morgan's scouts forced Ezra T. Mills, a local resident, to guide them to the Hocking River ford. Mills had a bad leg, and he tried to use that fact to excuse himself from the task. It did not work: Morgan's men lifted him onto a horse, and they rode northward. When they neared the river and noticed Union troopers guarding the roads, the raiders offered to send a soldier to accompany Mills on horseback to his home. Mills readily refused the offer, saying that he would prefer to limp back home.

In just over 1.0 mile, take note that the old northbound road — possibly the hog path described by Shackelford — is the private driveway of 51488 Rice Run Road, which is visible on the right as Rice Run Road makes a sharp bend to the left. This path led northwest to Bethel Church in Athens County. Shackelford's pickets did not patrol this intersection, thus allowing Morgan's men to slip quietly past the sleeping Union troops during the night.

Continue on Rice Run Road for another 0.7 mile to the campsite of a large portion of Shackelford's troops in the fields on both sides of Rice Run Road. On the night of July 19, Union troops encamped on farms surrounding the town of Tuppers Plains, thus blocking all of Morgan's avenues of escape leading west or south. Brigadier General Eliakim Scammon's troops guarded all the Ohio River crossings and all the roads leading northeast from Flatwoods. Furthermore, a detachment of the 7th Ohio Cavalry guarded the roads to the Hocking River. However, Shackelford failed to close the door on the remote area in Athens County lying between Coolville and Tupper Plains.

Drive another 0.2 mile to the stop sign at SR 681. Reset your odometer. Turn right on SR 681. At 0.1 mile, the Lewis Dodderer house, 50600 SR 681, stands at the right near the intersection with Brooks Road. The Union troopers, who camped all over Dodderer's farm fields on both sides of Brooks Road, took 50 bushels of wheat, two tons of hay, and one hog, and destroyed Dodderer's fences and bee hives.

Lewis Dodderer house (c. 1821)

Proceed another 0.9 mile and turn right onto SR 7. Several wounded raiders were left behind in the Tuppers Plains area. They were treated by Doctor Edward Tiffany before they were turned over to the Union military authorities.

Go 1.8 miles to Garton Lane (TR 468E). On the way, you will cross into Athens County. Turn right onto Garton Lane. Go to the stop sign at Old 7 Road. The hog path that Morgan used to escape from the trap at Flatwoods is Rawley Lane (TR 158), seen ahead and a little to the left. This lane is private.

Turn left onto Old 7 Road (TR 468C). You are back on the Morgan Trail.

In less than 0.4 mile is Bethel Church on the right. It was built around 1824. Morgan passed this Methodist church on his ride around Shackelford during the night of July 19–20.

Bethel Church (c. 1824)

The first road on the left just beyond Bethel Church is Brister Road (TR 468D/TR 120). Turn left. At the stop sign with SR 7, reset your odometer. Cross over SR 7 to continue on Brister Road (TR 120).

Go 1.5 miles to a stop sign. Reset your odometer. Turn right onto Vanderhoff Road (CR 65). Note that Morgan went straight on Brister Road, but today Brister Road dead-ends and the old road no longer exists. Morgan followed West Robinson Road from Brister Road.

BUFFINGTON ISLAND TO NELSONVILLE

In 2.8 miles turn left onto a feeder road called Varner Road (TR 117) that parallels the divided highway SR 32 for about 0.4 mile. At the end of this feeder road, turn left onto old Varner Road.

In just over 0.4 mile, veer left onto Kincade Road (TR 116A). Kincade Road becomes Blackwood Road (TR 116) and turns to gravel. At the stop sign in 1.9 miles, turn right onto West Robinson Road, where we will rejoin Morgan's path. Use caution on this narrow, steep, and often rutted gravel road.

Drive a few yards to the stop sign at Lottridge Road (CR 53). Reset your odometer and turn left. In 1.2 miles, just beyond the Orange Church, the Ebenezer M. Young house is on the left at 176 Lottridge Road. Morgan's men confiscated two horses and five sheep from Young, and took sixty bushels of wheat from his barn to feed their hungry mounts.

Ebenezer M. Young house

Continue 0.7 mile; bear left onto Lottridge Road (CR 41) and re-enter Meigs County. Drive another 0.6 mile on Lottridge Road to the intersection with Woods Road (TR 240), a gravel road. Before reaching Woods Road, you will pass Buck Lake Road. Morgan sent a flanking detachment along Buck Lake Road toward the town of Garden in Athens County. The group raided the farm of William Kyle before turning southwest on Blackwood Road to rejoin the main column near Bearwallow Church.

Turn right onto Woods Road. Go 0.5 mile. Turn right onto Carr Road (TR 231), which is also a gravel road. Reset your odometer.

At just over 0.6 mile, the Sardine Guthrie house is on the right, at 44886 Carr Road, across the street from a barn. The raiders rode away with Guthrie's $500 stallion and $100 mare.

Sardine Guthrie house

Go 0.8 mile farther to cross the single-lane bridge over the Middle Branch of the Shade River. Continue 0.9 mile to see the William McConkey house on the left along Carr Road. McConkey lost a horse valued at $75 to the Confederates.

William McConkey house

Just beyond the McConkey house, at the stop sign, bear right onto the paved Elk Run Road (CR 238). This is the village of Bearwallow Church, where Morgan's flankers from Garden returned to the column. Go 0.9 mile to a stop sign and turn right onto Bearwallow Ridge Road (CR 37). Continue on Bearwallow Ridge Road (CR 37) for 2.4 miles. Turn left onto US 33 Business.

Immediately turn right onto Burlingham Road (CR 40). Reset your odometer.

The old town of Burlingham, once called "Bungtown," is 0.1 mile farther down US 33 Business. During the Civil War, the Burlingham Road ran directly into town along the bottom of the hills to your left. Morgan sent a flanking column south along US 33 Business into Millersburg (present-day Darwin), where they turned west to merge back into the main column at the intersection of White Oak and Gold Ridge roads.

In 0.3 mile, you will pass the Leroy Jones house on the right at 40780 Burlingham Road. An old schoolhouse stands behind the home. Morgan's troopers took two horses, saddles, bridles, and an overcoat from Jones. The old road merged into the present-day road here.

Leroy Jones house

Drive another 0.2 mile. You will pass Burlingham Cemetery and Church, which stood here when Morgan and his men rode by on the morning of July 20. Established in 1843 at this site, Burlingham Church originally served the Baptist denomination in this community of settlers who came from Massachusetts and Vermont. The original church burned in 1887; the current, restored structure dates to 1888.

Burlingham Church (est. 1843)

Proceed 1.2 miles. The old road to Harrisonville turned through the field on the left to connect to Gold Ridge Drive. Present-day Burlingham Road continues straight to a stop sign at the junction with SR 681. Here, General Morgan sent flankers northwest along Chase Run Road to the village of Woodyard Post Office in Athens County. From Woodyard, the group turned directly south, rode through Pageville (Downington Post Office), and rejoined the main column just north of Harrisonville.

Turn left at SR 681. In 0.3 mile turn right onto Gold Ridge Drive (CR 40). This is a well-maintained gravel road. Reset your odometer and pay close attention to your mileage, because the next few intersections can be confusing.

At 1.3 miles, turn left onto Gold Ridge Road (TR 130). Immediately turn right onto White Oak Road (TR 145), a gravel road.

In about 0.3 mile, the David Gilkey house stands on the right at 40155 White Oak Road. The Confederates took one of Gilkey's horses, which he claimed was worth $60; however, the State of Ohio awarded Gilkey only $40.

David Gilkey house

Go 1.7 miles to the end of White Oak Road. Turn right onto Mohler Road (TR 238). This road becomes gravel after passing Landaker Road. There were many farmers who filed raid claims in this area, including John S. Landaker, Nicholas Stanart, William Hudnall, Isaac Moler, and Jonathon Hinds. The Hinds house still stands at 39694 Landaker Road.

Go 1.1 mile on Mohler Road to the intersection with Vance Road (TR 259). The original road continued straight to the Pageville Road.

Turn left on Vance Road. Drive 0.5 mile. At the stop sign at Pageville Road, reset your odometer. Turn right onto the gravel Pageville Road (TR 142).

At 0.2 mile is the Jacob Cuckler house, on the right at 37437 Pageville Road. Morgan's men took Cuckler's horse and some provisions, and they broke his gun. Later that day, Shackelford's Union troopers arrived and confiscated seven bushels of corn and three meal sacks.

Jacob Cuckler house

Continue 1.0 mile and turn left onto Weaver Road (also known as Horner Hill Road, TR 141). It is gravel. In 1.2 miles, you will reach a stop sign at Vance Road. Turn right onto Vance Road and drive 0.9 mile. Vance Road ends at SR 684 (New Lima Road). Reset your odometer and turn left at SR 684 into the town of Harrisonville. You may wish to park somewhere in town and walk around to get a feel for this historic village. Many of Harrisonville's buildings date back to the Civil War period.

The Confederate column arrived here about 9 a.m. Morgan's men looted the stores and grabbed horses from the residents. The raiders dispersed the small home guard, which scattered at the first sight of Morgan's advance troopers charging into town. Elza and Presley Turner were late in reaching Harrisonville for home guard duty. They were quickly captured, and their fresh horses became Confederate property. The raiders bent the Turners' guns around trees to prevent

Morgan's men entered Harrisonville at its north end.

the weapons from being used again. Reverend Thomas A. Welch, a future member of the Ohio senate, lost both of his horses but escaped capture. Martin Dye ran so fast that when his backside struck a post, he thought he had been shot and sprinted immediately to Dr. Day's office. Residents Frank White and Selim Tope tried to flee the scene, but when Morgan's men ordered them to halt, they continued to run. Shots rang out, and Tope caught a bullet in his heel. Tope did not recover from his wound.

About 10 a.m., Morgan's column moved out on the Rutland Road. Three of Morgan's rear guardsmen stayed a little too long at Joseph Magoon's store in downtown Harrisonville. While two of them picked over the goods in the store, the third stayed outside to hold the horses and watch for the enemy. Suddenly, the lookout saw Shackelford's advance riders galloping into town. The raiders hopped onto their horses and prepared to fight. The Union cavalrymen saw them and charged down the main street with drawn swords. The three men wisely chose to surrender to the vastly superior enemy force without a shot being fired. One of the raiders, a teenager, said to his captors, "Well, I don't care; I'm tired of this anyhow. Now, I'll get to go home to Mother."

Mary Farley Folden of Dexter, who was 14 years old at the time of the raid, was visiting Harrisonville on the morning of July 20 when Morgan's column arrived. She witnessed the raiders' actions and the "gallant charge of the Union men." Shackelford's cavalrymen were dirty, worn out, and hungry. They decided to rest for a bit. The break allowed time for the townswomen to bake apple pies for their heroes in blue.

This was not Harrisonville's first encounter with Morgan's men. Two days earlier, as the raiders left Wilkesville in Vinton County, Morgan had sent a flanking force of several hundred men northeast to Harrisonville. Along the way, they had foraged from many Columbia Township and Scipio Township farms west of town before they struck SR 684 near the Vance Road intersection and rode into the village. Three Harrisonville citizens submitted claims for expenses incurred when they were forced to feed the men that day. When the raiders had left town, Robert Combs had been taken to serve as their guide.

Go just over 0.5 mile to the intersection with SR 143, which marked the south end of town during the war. On July 18, the Confederate detachment turned here and rode southeast toward Pomeroy, where they met Morgan's column on their way to Buffington Island. On July 20, however, Morgan chose to head directly south toward Rutland and Cheshire. He also sent a detachment south along Dye Road to protect his right flank.

Continue straight on New Lima Road (CR 3). Reset your odometer.

At just under 0.9 mile is the Jane Lee house on the hill on the left at 37416 New Lima Road. After damaging her gun so that she could not turn it on them, the rebels rode away with three of her horses. When Shackelford's men came through, she cooked meals for 60 soldiers and provided feed for their horses. She also allowed the Union cavalrymen to stable 14 horses overnight in her barn.

Jane Lee house

Drive another 0.2 mile and look to your left. Zion Road approaches from the left. The house on the knoll about 100 yards distant is the John Bradfield house at 45175 Zion Road. He lost two horses and their bridles to Confederate cavalrymen.

John Bradfield house

Continue straight on New Lima Road, and in another 0.1 mile is the Hiram Chase house, on the left at 37120 New Lima Road. The rebels departed from this farm with two horses and two guns. The state later reimbursed Chase $213 for his losses.

Hiram Chase house

Go 1.0 mile; turn right onto Loop Road (CR 60). Reset your odometer. During the Civil War, this was the direct road leading to Rutland.

In 0.5 mile, bear left on Loop Road. In another 0.4 mile, where Loop Road makes a sharp turn to the left, the old road continued straight until it reached present-day McCumber Hill Road.

BUFFINGTON ISLAND TO NELSONVILLE

Drive for 0.4 mile and turn right onto McCumber Hill Road (CR 4). In less than 0.2 mile, reset your odometer and turn left onto the gravel-covered Whites Hill Road (TR 58). You are back on the Morgan Trail.

At 0.5 mile, on the left, is the Israel Stansbury house at 34810 Whites Hill Road. Stansbury lost two horses and a saddle to the passing rebel column. In addition, Stansbury quartered Confederate prisoners for eight weeks in his house before they were sent off to a prisoner-of-war camp. The government did not pay out anything toward Stansbury's claim.

Israel Stansbury house

Proceed 1.8 miles to the end of Whites Hill Road. At the stop sign, turn right onto New Lima Road (CR 3). Go 0.5 mile.

You will enter the village of Rutland, which Morgan had passed through on July 18. At the stop sign in downtown Rutland, go straight and follow SR 124 East.

Morgan rode through Rutland twice.

Go 0.6 mile on SR 124 and turn right onto Leading Creek Road (CR 3). Drive 0.6 mile and turn left onto Nichols Road (TR 176), which is paved in gravel. Reset your odometer.

Just past the 0.7 mile mark, look to the right; you can see remnants of the Civil War road, which turned southward and crossed Leading Creek, and then merged onto the modern Paulins Hill Road at the Meigs-Gallia County line.

Continue another 0.8 mile to the stop sign at Leading Creek Road. Turn right and go 0.9 mile to the intersection with Wells Road (TR 352). You will pass underneath a railroad bridge along the way. The railroad was built after the war.

Reset your odometer on reaching Wells Road. Turn left on Wells Road, which will become Paulins Hill Road in about 0.1 mile. Continue straight on Paulins Hill Road (TR 360) and drive a little over 0.1 mile. Just beyond Keller Road, the Benjamin S. Williams house (35857 Paulins Hill Road) is perched on the hill on the right. Morgan's men took one horse and several horseshoes and bridles from Williams's barn. Williams also provided food for Shackelford's pursuing cavalrymen and kept twenty of their exhausted horses for the night.

Benjamin S. Williams's house

Drive 0.6 mile farther. The road Morgan's main column followed entered Paulins Hill Road from the field on the left, along the creek bottom. Just beyond this point, you will cross into Gallia County.

Continue straight on Paulins Hill Road for 1.5 miles, to a stop sign. Go straight and drive for another 0.5 mile to the stop sign at the intersection with SR 554. Look to your right. The old town of Kygerville is nearly 0.8 mile away. Morgan avoided Kygerville (present-day Kyger) because Shackelford's advance troopers were hot on his tail. It is thought that about 100 men who had escaped from Buffington Island reunited with Morgan's column near here. Also, on July 18, Brigadier General Henry Judah's Union forces passed this point and proceeded south along SR 554 to Cheshire, where they turned north to follow the Ohio River toward Pomeroy.

Reset your odometer. Turn left on SR 554. The old road to Cheshire passed through the fields on the left, paralleling the current highway. One of the farms along here belonged to the Rife family. When the Confederates took Emy Rife's grandfather's horses, her grandfather went to General Morgan and explained to him that the horses were too old and would not be able to survive hard riding. The plea must have worked; Morgan returned the horses.

During the raid, Howard Shuler's father, William, lived as a boy on a farm near here. His mother Anna was surprised that when Morgan's advance guard came up to the house looking for horses, they wore Federal blue uniforms.

In this vicinity, at about 1:30 p.m., Colonel Frank Wolford's Union brigade caught up with Morgan's rear guard, under the command of Lieutenant Colonel Cicero Coleman of the 8th Kentucky Cavalry. A running skirmish began that did not end until the Confederates made a stand three miles south of Cheshire.

Capt. Lorenzo Hockersmith of the 10th Kentucky Cavalry recalled how young Dr. H. S. Jones, a member of the rear guard, volunteered to use a few men to slow Wolford's advance:

> When he [Jones] saw the dust rising in the distance from the pursuing enemy he wanted to stop, fire on the enemy, and thus retard their approach. This method was opposed by some of the officers. But Jones was

Col. Frank L. Wolford

Capt. Lorenzo D. Hockersmith

determined and he and a few men faced the enemy, directed their pistols in the faces of the approaching army, wheeled, and retreated joining the command. The surprise caused the advancing pursuers to halt for a short time, and Jones and his men soon joined their command.

At about 2.4 miles, as you pass Roush Lane, look to your right. The old road to Cheshire veered off to the right and followed the banks of Kyger Creek until it reached present-day Gravel Hill Road.

In another 0.6 mile, Gravel Hill Road comes into SR 554 from the right. You are now back on Morgan's route. Continue straight on SR 554; we'll come back to this point later.

The open areas on either side of SR 554, from here to the edge of town ahead, were the farms of Peter Swisher, George Knapp, and Peter Knapp. Their fields were the site of Shackelford's camp on the night of July 20, and later became a camp for hundreds of Confederate prisoners of war before they boarded steamboats for Cincinnati and, from there, to prison camps throughout the North.

Go another 0.6 mile to the intersection with SR 7 in the center of the town of Cheshire. As you pass the intersection of SR 554 with South 3rd Street, look to your right. The school building sits on the site of Cheshire Academy, whose dormitory was used to house Confederate officers after their capture on July 20, 1863. At the stop sign, go straight across SR 7. Park in the parking lot at the end of the street.

Cheshire town

A village park provides beautiful views of the Ohio River and the Eight Mile Island Ford. The river was much shallower here in the 19th century before the river was dammed. Eight Mile Island is located where the power lines reach the opposite bank slightly downstream of the park.

Eight Mile Island Ford

Morgan and his advance riders lined the Ohio River bank here to ford at Eight Mile Island. Two columns started to wade across the river to both tips of the island. Unexpectedly, they saw the steamboat, *Condor*, approaching from around the bend upstream. They mistook the side-wheel towboat for a Union gunboat. With the disaster at Buffington Island still fresh in his mind, General Morgan aborted the attempted crossing. Only a couple men had made it across the river successfully. Morgan ordered the remainder of his troopers to about-face and ride south on Gravel Hill Road so that the cannons on the gunboat would have difficulty firing on them.

Alvira Nye Gate's family, who lived in a large brick house on the south edge of town just opposite Eight Mile Island, had heeded the early warnings that Morgan was heading their way. They had led their horses to the woods and had hid their jewelry and silver in the ash hole of the fireplace and the ash pit in the cellar. Alvira had stuffed her money among the baby's clothes.

Morgan's advance riders forced two locals, a boy named Swishes (Swisher) and an old man named Galbreth, to act as guides to the Eight Mile Island Ford. During the confusion following the appearance of the *Condor No.3*, Swishes slipped away and sought refuge at Alvira's house. She hid him in the cellar behind a meat cask.

When the raiders arrived in Alvira's yard, they asked the family for food and horses. Alvira gave them bread and pies, but the horses were nowhere to be found. While some of the butternut-clad raiders quickly downed the bread, others washed their faces at the well. ("Butternut" refers to homespun clothes dyed brown with butternut extract.) After a few minutes, the Confederates remounted their horses and hurried southward. They took the pies in their pans and wrapped them up in handkerchiefs "to go." Swishes escaped detection.

Morgan's rear guard became separated from Morgan's main column during the confusion of the retreat from the river and the attack of Wolford's advance on the rear. Morgan's rear guard turned left (south) onto SR 7, and Wolford's men followed them. Meanwhile, the rest of Morgan's force, led by the general himself, rode south on Gravel Hill Road, out of close range of the cannon from the Union gunboats.

We will follow Morgan's main column from the river.

Note: In the spring of 2002, the town of Cheshire essentially ceased to exist. The town of 221 citizens was bought out by American Electric Power for $20 million. The EPA and the citizens of Cheshire had sued the company because of the medical problems that developed among the townspeople as a result of living in close proximity to an AEP power plant.

Return to your car and drive back to SR 7. Go straight across SR 7 and follow SR 554 West for 0.6 mile back to Gravel Hill Road. Turn left onto Gravel Hill Road (CR 13). Reset your odometer.

At just over 0.3 mile, the road makes a sharp turn to the left. It was here that the old Cheshire Road intersected with Gravel Hill Road during the Civil War. Morgan's main force turned south here and followed Gravel Hill Road.

Continue on Gravel Hill Road for 1.3 miles to an intersection; go straight on Little Kyger Road (CR 15). Drive another 0.6 mile to where Oliver Road (now a private entrance to a quarry) enters from the right. It was used by Shackelford to surround Coleman's troopers. Just beyond, Little Kyger Road goes under a ten-foot clearance railroad overpass. Drive slowly with caution, as this is a one-lane road here with a sharp, blind curve.

Proceed 0.4 mile on Little Kyger Road from the Oliver Road intersection; pull off onto the right side of Little Kyger Road wherever safely possible.

Accounts of what happened here were written by Captain Lorenzo D. Hockersmith, 10th Kentucky Cavalry, and Captain Thomas M. Coombs, 5th Kentucky Cavalry, who were later imprisoned with John Hunt Morgan in the Ohio State Penitentiary. Major James B. McCreary, 11th Kentucky Cavalry, was also present here and later recorded his experiences.

As Lieutenant Colonel Cicero Coleman's men neared Cheshire about 2 p.m. on Monday, July 20, Colonel Frank Lane Wolford's Union cavalry, who had been skirmishing with them off and on since Kygerville, came up on them again.

Suddenly, around 2:15 p.m., the 45th Ohio Mounted Infantry renewed their attack against Coleman's column, which wavered at the bank of the swollen Ohio River while the menacing *Condor* hovered nearby. The bewildered raiders fled south from Cheshire with Wolford in hot pursuit, but they used the Old Stagecoach Road (present-day SR 7) instead of Gravel Hill Road. Captain Coombs, who was riding with Coleman, wrote, "Confusion took the place of order, and Officers could not control the men, and thus every man for himself, we again commenced to retreat down the river. In the confusion, the general part of Duke's and Cluke's regiments became separated from the rest of the command."

Instead of joining the main column, Coleman's group of about eighty officers and men turned on the 45th Ohio. After the raiders crossed over the

Old Stagecoach Road covered bridge, which in 1863 spanned Kyger Creek at the present-day location of the SR 7 bridge over Kyger Creek to your left, they noticed a rail fence that ran diagonally from the bridge and across Coal Hill. It was an inviting spot to make a stand. They rode up Coal Hill on your right for 300 yards, dismounted, hitched their horses in the woods, marched back to the fence, and concealed themselves in the fence corners where bushes and briars had grown. The field on your left was the site of the Confederate line.

Cheshire (Coal Hill) battlefield and surrender site. Confederate skirmishers deployed in this field, while Union cavalry attacked from the foreground. The Old Stagecoach Road and fence line ran from the lower right to the Wesley Rothgeb house at left center. Coal Hill rises above the Rothgeb house.

The Confederates fired a volley at the 45th Ohio as the Union cavalrymen galloped across the bridge, sending them scurrying back to the opposite side of the creek. When the Confederates fired on the 45th Ohio, Hockersmith recalled that "it seemed as if one great big gun had been turned loose on the enemy. The surprise to the enemy was so great and so complete that the whole of the attacking command was for the time being completely at a loss to know what to do." Hockersmith believed that if he would have had fifty men on either side of the bridge, the raiders could have captured Wolford and his men. But the Confederates did not, and they had just fired their last round of ammunition.

Coleman's gallant band held the bridge for almost an hour until Colonel Adams's 1st Kentucky U.S. Cavalry and Captain Ward's company of the 3rd Kentucky U.S. Cavalry outflanked the right of the Confederate line and took possession of the

BUFFINGTON ISLAND TO NELSONVILLE

Old Stagecoach Road 0.2 mile south of the present-day intersection of SR 7 and Little Kyger Road. This movement blocked the raiders' only escape route. To avoid being crushed between the two Union cavalry lines, the raiders retreated to their horses, mounted up, and climbed to the crest of precipitous Coal Hill, which rises abruptly above the right side of Little Kyger Road. There Coleman reformed his line.

Major James B. McCreary

Meanwhile, the rest of Shackelford's troops followed present-day Oliver Road to complete successfully the encirclement of Coleman's small group. Around 4:30 p.m., Shackelford sent a flag of truce to Morgan demanding his immediate and unconditional surrender. Making their way down Coal Hill to this vicinity, Coleman, Hockersmith, McCreary, and other officers requested a personal conference with Shackelford to discuss the proposed terms. The terms allowed field officers to retain their side arms and horses, and all others could keep their private property. Shackelford allowed them 40 minutes to decide whether to give up or fight. Coleman held a council of war with Coombs,

McCreary, Hockersmith, Joseph Tucker, and the other officers. With their men exhausted, out of ammunition, and surrounded, they had no other choice but to surrender their command. Only a few men from both sides were wounded during the skirmish.

Although Shackelford later claimed he captured 1,000 men at Cheshire, in reality only eighty Confederate prisoners were taken. Some historians believe Shackelford inflated the numbers to hide his embarrassment for allowing Morgan and most of his men to escape yet again. Shackelford reported that Morgan was there on the battlefield and had escaped under a flag of truce. It was claimed that even the Confederate officers believed Morgan and the other 700 men were included in the surrender. Recent research has found that Morgan was riding near Addison at the time of the skirmish and may not have known about the rear-guard stand until it was too late.

Shackelford's victorious, worn-out troopers spent the night in Cheshire and in the fields west of town. Wolford and his men, including the "Wild Riders" of the 1st Kentucky U.S. Cavalry, were assigned to guard the prisoners. Out of respect for their fellow Kentuckians, they provided food to the hungry Confederates.

After being captured at Coal Hill, the commissioned Confederate officers were allowed to stay at the hotel and the school dormitory in Cheshire and were given the freedom to move about town. All the other prisoners were forced to camp in the meadows west of town.

Continue another 0.1 mile. On the right, at 199 Little Kyger Road, is the Wesley Rothgeb house. Wesley Rothgeb's son, Samuel Vinton Rothgeb, was 13 years old at the time of the fight here. He lived in this house until his death in 1932. Samuel Vinton Rothgeb witnessed the Cheshire skirmish swirling around his house and finishing a short distance up the slope of Coal Hill behind his home. According to Rothgeb's account and William Griffith's 1874 *Illustrated Atlas of Gallia County, Ohio,* the Confederates surrendered on the Wesley Rothgeb farm. Although the exact location of the surrender site is unknown, we know it occurred between a bridge over Kyger Creek and the base of a hill. It is therefore most likely the surrender occurred in the field to your left, between the Wesley Rothgeb house and the present-day SR 7 bridge over Kyger Creek.

Wesley Rothgeb house

The SR 7 bridge crosses the creek at the site of the covered bridge from 1863. The section of SR 7, leading north from Little Kyger Road to the present SR 7 bridge, did not exist in 1863; the Old Stagecoach Road (SR 7) intersected Little Kyger Road directly in front of the Wesley Rothgeb house. The Old Stagecoach Road was rerouted to its present location in the mid-20th century.

After the raid, residents searched Coal Hill for items left by the raiders. They discovered discarded guns and bolts of cloth lying on the ground or leaning against trees. The locals and their descendants also looked for buried treasure, even as late as 1937, but never found any.

Go 0.2 mile to the end of Little Kyger Road and reset your odometer. Turn right on SR 7. The field on your left, as you travel south along SR 7, was the scene of fighting during the skirmish.

In 0.4 mile, the large brick house on the right, at 4743 SR 7, was owned by Samuel Rothgeb at the time of the raid. The house was built around 1830. Samuel lost one horse to the raiders as they rode quickly south to Addison. He also gave up forty bushels of corn to Shackelford's hungry horses following the fight at Coal Hill.

Samuel Rothgeb house (c. 1830)

In about 0.2 mile, turn right onto Honeysuckle Drive. This is the Civil War era road. Drive with caution as you pass beneath the railroad bridge, as it is only one lane. You may also choose to follow SR 7 to the Addison Pike, as Honeysuckle Drive parallels SR 7 for a mile.

In just over 1.0 mile, you will reach the Addison Pike (CR 1) and the center of the town of Addison. Reset your odometer. Supposedly, when General Morgan and his men rode by, an Addison citizen yelled to them, "Halloa! How did you get here? Did you all come in the same litter?"

Turn right on Addison Pike and cross the railroad tracks. In 2.0 miles, turn left onto Brick School Road (TR 305). After turning, glance to your left. The original road cut across the field on your left and reconnected with this road near the entrance to the elementary school parking lot.

In about 1.1 mile, at a sharp bend to the left, the road Morgan followed continued straight over the hill to Possum Trot Road. We will briefly follow a postwar route by taking Brick School Road to its end.

At the stop sign 0.6 mile farther ahead, turn right onto Johnson Ridge Road (CR 9) and go 0.2 mile to the next stop; turn right onto Addison Pike (CR 1). In 0.5 mile, veer left at the fork onto Possum Trot Road (CR 17). You are back on Morgan's path.

In 1.0 mile, turn left at the intersection with Blazer Road in order to continue on Possum Trot Road, which becomes gravel along the way. In 0.9 mile, Possum Trot Road merges into Greentree Road (TR 315). Yield to cross-traffic here. The road Morgan's men followed continued straight; that section of the road to Porter was closed by 20th-century strip-mining operations. The former road followed the top of a ridge and then plunged down a steep ravine to meet up with present-day Reeves Road, which you will see later.

Look to your right. The old Campaign Church stood close to the intersection. It was founded in 1840, and Morgan's raiders passed it on the evening of July 20. The church is now gone. The Confederate rear guard camped for the night near here and along roads running several miles northwest of here. Morgan's camps were not always contained to just one or two farms. He often stretched out his camp over several miles in order to provide more forage for his men and to allow adequate time for the majority of his troopers to coalesce in case any part of the camp was attacked.

Campaign Church (c. 1840) has been razed.

Turn left onto Greentree Road. Morgan sent a large group of his raiders on Greentree Road to act as flankers and to forage for food, horses, and other necessities. The drive down the steep hill on Greentree Road affords a beautiful vista of the Campaign Creek valley below. The view has not changed much from the way it looked in 1863.

At the bottom of the hill, turn right at the stop sign onto Bulaville Pike (CR 3). In 0.8 mile, on the left, at 8373 Bulaville Pike, stands the James F. Irwin house. When Morgan's rear guard camped here on the night of July 20, they foraged Irwin's horse, saddle, bridle, twenty bushels of oats, fifteen bushels of corn, and a pair of pants. The rebels also took Irwin's shot gun.

James F. Irwin house

David Summers house

However, the Morgan Raid Commission denied Irwin reimbursement for his losses, estimated at $181.

Continue 0.3 mile. Just before crossing the narrow bridge, turn right to the gravel-based Campaign Road (TR 465). Reset your odometer.

At 0.6 mile, Campaign Road makes a sharp turn to the left before it crosses over a one-lane bridge. On the right is Reeves Road, which Morgan and his men used to ride down the tall ridge on the right. The house (636 Campaign Road) on the right at this intersection is the William Reeves house. Morgan's rear guard camped here, too, and at several farms along Campaign Road. Reeves lost two horses and a saddle to the raiders.

In 0.8 mile, the house on the left within the curve at 1451 Campaign Road is the Henry Rothgeb home. The house has been greatly modified in the past century, but the core structure dates back to the war. Rothgeb lost two horses to Morgan's men the night they visited his farm.

Continue another 0.7 mile to the stop sign at SR 554. Check your odometer and turn left onto SR 554. Morgan's men camped the night of July 20 all along this road to Porter.

At 1.4 miles is the David Summers house on the right at 13622 SR 554. His son, Andrew, supposedly lost $25 cash to the raiders.

About 0.3 mile beyond the Summers house is Porter Road, located in the heart of downtown Porter.

Turn right onto Porter Road, which becomes Airline Road at the next stop sign. Go straight on Airline Road.

This area had seen military activity previously: On July 18, during their pursuit of Morgan, Brigadier General Henry Judah's Union cavalry brigade rode from Portsmouth through Porter and proceeded east along SR 554 to Kyger.

The center of Morgan's camp on July 20 was situated at Porter. The camp stretched north for two more miles. Following the debacle at Eight Mile Island and the loss of comrades at the Cheshire skirmish, the morale among Morgan's troopers was at an all-time low. Most were without guns or ammunition. All were hungry and tired. It was reported that most of Morgan's men were ready to surrender to Union forces the next morning.

That night, approximately 100 raiders left Porter and rode south toward the Ohio River. It is unknown whether the group deserted, or whether General Morgan gave them permission to leave, but this detachment weaved its way throughout the night and the next day toward Rankin's Point, also known as Rankin's Landing, where today's Crown City is located. They passed through Adamsville, Rodney, Wales, Gallia Furnace, and McDaniel's Crossroads before entering Lawrence County. After riding south through Waterloo, they turned southeast at Arabia and reached present-day Crown City. As the exhausted raiders rested on the north bank of the Ohio River, they were surrounded and captured by a group of Gallia County militia under Captain Jacob Riggs on July 21.

BUFFINGTON ISLAND TO NELSONVILLE

Tuesday, July 21, 1863

At Cheshire, General James Shackelford called for 1,000 volunteers "who would stay in their saddles as long as he would, without eating or sleeping, until they captured Morgan." Nearly all volunteered, but they could find only 500 serviceable horses among them.

The resulting 500-man force was a kaleidoscope of detachments from different regiments belonging to Hobson's and Judah's former makeshift divisions. Shackelford's volunteers included 157 men of the 14th Illinois Cavalry (Colonel Horace Capron) and detachments of the 3rd Kentucky U.S. Cavalry (Captain Edward W. Ward), 5th Indiana Cavalry (Captain Powers), and other regiments. Also under Shackelford's control were the redoubtable Colonel Frank L. Wolford and his reduced-size brigade containing 40 men of the 2nd Ohio Cavalry (Captain William H. Ulrey) and elements of the 1st Kentucky U.S. Cavalry (Adjutant William D. Carpenter), 2nd East Tennessee (Mounted) Infantry (Maj. Daniel A. Carpenter), and 45th Ohio (Mounted) Infantry (Lieutenant Colonel George E. Ross). No artillery accompanied them because of the lack of fresh horses.

Later in the morning of July 21, after learning of Morgan's movements, Shackelford led his small division north from Cheshire toward Porter. He would attempt to head off Morgan's raiders before they could reach the Ohio River again.

As Morgan's remaining force broke camp at Porter on the morning of July 21, the raiders prepared to burn the town's mill. Several women pleaded with General Morgan, asking him to save the mill, saying that it provided necessary food for their children. Morgan ordered the mill to be spared.

Airline Road ends at Cindy Drive. Turn left onto Cindy Drive. At the stop sign, check your odometer and turn right on SR 160.

The residences along the valley through which SR 160 passes over the next several miles were heavily hit by Morgan's troopers. Spending the previous night on farms adjoining either side of the highway, the raiders were able to replenish their supplies and obtain fresh horses.

Side Trip: To see a farm that was used for camping by both armies, go 1.5 miles on SR 160 from Cindy Drive and turn left onto Summit Road. In just over 0.3 mile, on the left, sits a log cabin; an old house is located approximately 100 yards beyond the cabin. This is the Samuel M. Lewis farm at 435 Summit Road. When Morgan's men camped here on the night of July 20, they confiscated from Lewis an axe, a saddle, and $15 worth of food for horses and men. Lewis also hosted 75 Union soldiers pursuing Morgan. They damaged his cornfield, and their horses feasted on two tons of hay, seven acres of oats, and three acres of wheat. The soldiers took a fat sheep and $10 worth of provisions. Turn around at the next intersection and return to SR 160. Turn left to rejoin Morgan's main column.

Log cabin on the Samuel M. Lewis farm.

Samuel M. Lewis house

At 2.5 miles from the Cindy Drive intersection, SR 160 curves to the left. Here, the road to Ewington continued straight, roughly following today's Head Road.

Continue on SR 160. In 1.2 miles, turn right at Morgan Center Road (CR 11). SR 160 leads into Vinton, Ohio. On the morning of July 21, Morgan's men decided not to enter Vinton. Besides, Adam Johnson's men had foraged that town and had burned the covered bridge there three days prior! Instead, Morgan headed straight for Ewington, which his men had not entered.

In just over 0.5 mile, Head Road (a private lane) merges into Morgan Center Road from the right. We are back on Morgan's path. Continue toward the left on Morgan Center Road and drive 0.4 mile. At the stop sign, go straight on Spires Road (CR 121).

Go 1.5 miles to a junction with SR 325. The Civil War road went straight into the woods ahead until it reached Adney Road.

Turn left onto SR 325. In approximately 0.6 mile, turn right on Adney Road (CR 133). Reset your odometer. Where the road turns into gravel is approximately where the old road merged from the right into Adney Road.

At just over 1.2 miles, just after passing Andrews Road, bear left onto Adney Road at its intersection with Strong Run Road. Morgan and his men followed Strong Run Road a short distance before turning west across the fields, crossing over present-day Adney Road, and eventually entering Ewington just north of the Ewington Cemetery.

Continue 0.8 mile on Adney Road and look to your left. A lone chimney marks the site of the George A. Ewing house. Ewing was amongst the Gallia County militia captured at Ewington. A couple days later, he wrote a letter to his brother describing the incidents of Morgan's Raid that occurred in Ewington and other parts of Gallia County. This is also where the Civil War road crossed the present-day Adney Road.

In approximately 0.3 mile, Adney Road stops at SR 160. Turn left onto SR 160. Go 0.7 mile and turn right onto Ewington Road (CR 149) in the village of Ewington. Reset your odometer.

At 0.1 mile, the Ewington Academy is on the right. Turn into the building's driveway to read an **Ohio Historical Marker** describing the building's history. The Academy was the site of an unusual Civil War event — a double surrender of Union and Confederate troops on the same day and at the same spot.

Ewington Academy (c. 1859)

On July 20, Lieutenant Colonel Louis Sontag and 450 men of the 1st Scioto Militia boarded a train at Portsmouth, with the mission of intercepting Morgan in northern Gallia County. Sontag was a saddler from Minford, Ohio, (Harrisonville in 1863) who possessed some military experience. To cover more territory, Sontag ordered his second-in-command, Major Daniel F. Slane (Slain) from Pike County, to take 200 men to Jackson, while Sontag and the rest of the militia disembarked at the station at Oak Hill, where they would begin their march east to the designated rendezvous point at Ewington. Sontag's detachment reached Ewington and encamped there for the night.

Meanwhile, Slane's detachment detrained at Jackson, ate dinner, and requisitioned wagons and ambulances for the journey. At 3 p.m., the group finally set out on foot toward Ewington via Berlin Crossroads. Slane claimed that his militiamen, mostly furnace men and farmers, were untrained and unfit, and could march only as far as Latrobe Furnace, 7.5 miles from Jackson. While they spent the night at Latrobe Furnace, Slane sent couriers to

Ewington to communicate with Lieutenant Colonel Sontag. None of the couriers returned; all were captured by Morgan's scouts.

In the early morning hours of July 21, Morgan's column of approximately 600 men entered Ewington from the north. Because Sontag had failed to post pickets, his troops were completely surprised by the Confederates' sudden arrival. Assuming Morgan had at least 1,000 men with him, Sontag surrendered his 250 militiamen without a shot being fired. He also told Morgan of the approximate position of Slane's detachment. Sontag's militiamen stacked their French rifled muskets on the lawn of the Ewington Academy.

While General Morgan and his staff wrote paroles for the Union soldiers, the raiders sought out horses and food from Ewington's residents. Eight-year-old Isaac Ewing held the general's horse while about forty rebels took food from his family's cellar. A few Confederates amused themselves by shooting at the fan-shaped ventilator in the gable of the Ewington Academy.

After issuing the paroles, Morgan assembled his men at the Academy and spoke to them. He offered them the opportunity to surrender to Lieutenant Colonel Sontag if they could not, or wished not, continue on the raid. Only 54 of the roughly 600 raiders took up the offer. These Confederates who were "tired of raiding" handed over their usable weapons and horses to their comrades and then officially gave themselves up to an unparoled militiaman, John T. Miller. Morgan obtained Sontag's promise to treat these men with the proper respect given to prisoners of war, and Sontag kept his word.

While Sontag and his odd contingent of unarmed militiamen and former raiders marched off toward Oak Hill, Morgan led more than 550 cavalrymen northwest. Morale would not be a problem within Morgan's command for the rest of the raid; these remaining men were determined to get back to the Confederacy with Morgan as their leader.

Reset your odometer and continue straight (west) on Ewington Road. In 1.3 miles is a stop sign. Bear right to continue on Ewington Road (TR 813).

Drive another 0.4 mile; turn right onto Franklin Cemetery Road (TR 809). This is a single-lane, rough gravel road, so drive slowly and with caution.

In 0.6 mile is a stop sign. Reset your odometer. Turn left onto the asphalt-paved Alice Road (CR 151). Much of the region here has been strip mined since the Civil War.

In about 1.5 miles, as you cross into Vinton County, Alice Road turns into Minerton Road (CR 26). Go another 0.7 mile. On the right is the Thomas J. Cardwell house, at 46550 Minerton Road. He lost one horse with its saddle and bridle to Morgan's men.

Thomas J. Cardwell house

Continue 0.9 mile, at which point you will pass the site where the road from Buckeye Furnace came in from the left. It was here that Major Daniel F. Slane surrendered his detachment of Ohio militia to the advance guard of Morgan's column. It is just over two miles from this point to Buckeye Furnace. In the postwar mining days, the old road to the furnace was rerouted to Morris Road, located a quarter-mile ahead.

Major Slane and his 200 militiamen broke camp at Latrobe Furnace at dawn on July 21. They marched to Buckeye Furnace, where the residents reported to Slane that Morgan's scouts had been spotted nearby. Being cautious, Slane sent mounted pickets ahead as his column proceeded on the road to Ewington. Around two miles out of Buckeye Furnace, near this spot, Major Slane's advance guard was approached by Morgan's scouts under a flag of truce.

Slane was informed of Sontag's surrender earlier that morning, and that Morgan had 1,800 men positioned around Slane's detachment. Lieutenant Jones, one of Slane's captured pickets, confirmed the situation. With this convincing information in hand, Slane and his officers held a short consultation and surrendered their men without a shot. Morgan paroled Slane and his militiamen, took their arms and equipment, and sent them marching back toward Jackson. During their return, Slane and his men suffered more embarrassment by taking the wrong road and getting lost in the coal fields.

The commander of the Ohio militia at Camp Portsmouth, Colonel Peter Kinney, preferred charges against Sontag and Slane for their actions, but no court of inquiry was ever convened.

Proceed for 1.2 miles. Turn left onto Buckeye Branch Road (CR 26A). Morgan and his main column went straight from this intersection on a road that has been closed for many years by mining operations. The road wound its way north along the border between Vinton and Jackson counties. We will follow a postwar road to head north through this heavily mined terrain.

Proceed just over 0.7 mile to the Hickory Ridge Road (TR 173) intersection. Note: Buckeye Branch Road becomes Buckeye Furnace Road (CR 58) near this point. We are now in Jackson County.

*Side Trip: Buckeye Furnace State Memorial Park is just ahead off of Buckeye Furnace Road (CR 58). Slane's militia passed through the furnace town on their way to Ewington via Ridgeland Road and Johnson Mine Road.

From the Hickory Ridge Road turnoff, go straight on Buckeye Furnace Road for 1.0 mile. Turn left at the Buckeye Furnace State Memorial Park sign onto Buckeye Park Road (TR 167). Drive 0.6 mile; the restored 1852 Buckeye Furnace is on the left. Continue 0.1 mile to the public parking area on the right. You can park here.

Buckeye Furnace (c. 1852)

The company store is across the street, and there is a trail back to the furnace buildings. There are interpretive signs throughout the park to help explain the significance of this rich mining region and its impact on the Union war effort during the Civil War. The museum is open Saturday and Sunday, noon–4 p.m., June–October. Phone: (740) 384-3537 or (800) 860-0144; Web site: *http://www.buckeyefurnace.com/*.

From the parking lot, take Buckeye Park Road back to Buckeye Furnace Road and turn right. In 1.0 mile, turn left onto Hickory Ridge Road (TR 173) to follow Morgan's route.*

Turn right on Hickory Ridge Road (TR 173). As you travel north on Hickory Ridge Road, the old road ran parallel to it by following the county line about a quarter mile to the east.

Hickory Ridge Road becomes Tower Ridge Road (TR 30) along the way. When you reach the stop sign at SR 124 in 2.4 miles, pause for a moment. We cannot follow Morgan's actual route here. Morgan's path went straight across SR 124 onto Hawk Station Road a short distance before turning west on Tower Ridge Road, a private lane that at one time joined with Mulga Road about a mile to the west.

Reset your odometer. Using extra caution, turn left (west) onto SR 124. In over 1.1 miles, turn right on Mulga Road (CR 39). At the creek crossing about 100 yards north of SR 124, the old road once entered into Mulga Road. You are back on the Morgan Trail.

In approximately 0.9 mile you will pass the intersection with Kriebel Road. Morgan's column rode along Kriebel Road to Iron Valley Furnace. Several farms on Kriebel Road, now gone, were raided. However, the current road dead ends into a quarry.

We will continue on Mulga Road until it stops at SR 32 in another 1.2 miles. Reset your odometer. Turn right onto SR 32.

At just over 1.0 mile, turn right onto Charles Bierhup Road. Reset your odometer. Immediately after the turn, there is a fork with three roads. Take the left-most road, which is Charles Bierhup Road. The middle and right roads are private roads for the quarry.

At 0.3 mile, Charles Bierhup Road bends to the left. At the bend you will pass an abandoned path on the right with a wire fence gate; this was once the other end of Kriebel Road, but it is now cut off and restricted by the quarry. You are now in the center of what was once the company town of Iron Valley Furnace. Morgan's 550 men passed this point around dinnertime on July 21.

Pause where Charles Bierhup Road straightens out after the bend, and look into the woods on your right. When the foliage permits, you can plainly see through the trees what appears to be a cave approximately 100 yards from the road. This cave is actually the remains of the Iron Valley Furnace. The furnace lies on private property; please do not trespass.

Iron Valley Furnace was constructed between 1853 and 1855. The cold-blast charcoal furnace was carved into the steep hillside as a cave-like structure with a tunnel leading from the ceiling of the cave up to the top of the cliff. Nearby Mulga Run may have supplied the power for the bellows. The operation initially produced an average of twelve tons of pig iron per day. William McGhee and William Ratcliff owned the lease for the furnace during the Civil War. In 1863, McGhee

Iron Valley Furnace (c. 1853)

purchased the partnership from Ratcliff and renamed it Lincoln Furnace. Years later, McGhee called it Cornelia Furnace in honor of his only daughter. The furnace was closed in 1885 with the economic decline of the industry.

Approximately sixteen raiders stopped at the Richard H. and Rachael A. Kirkendall home nearby and demanded food. The women in the home, who prepared breakfast for the raiders, asked the men to be quiet, because there were a sick woman (Rachael) and a newborn baby in the house. The raiders complied. One man even held the baby boy, who reminded him of his baby back in Kentucky.

Approximately 100 yards straight ahead, turn around at the dead-end road on the left. At this point, look across SR 32 toward the northwest. This is roughly where the road led that Morgan's main column took to get to Vinton Furnace. That road was removed in the 20th century by strip mining.

Return to SR 32 by the same way you came. Turn right on SR 32, heading east. We will follow Morgan's right-flank detachment, which rode along a trail that SR 32 covers up. Occasionally, you will see remnants of that road paralleling either side of the highway. We will cross into Vinton County on the way.

Go 5.0 miles and turn left onto SR 160. Reset your odometer. Morgan's flankers also turned north onto SR 160.

In 0.4 mile, you will pass through the village of Radcliff. This village did not exist in 1863, but John

Booth, who lived on a farm near here, recalled meeting the raiders on the afternoon of July 21, 1863, when a group stopped by his home looking for food and horses. One Confederate used his rifle and bayonet to lift the half-bushel basket out of Booth's hands. The raider then asked for Booth's vest, which the farmer reluctantly gave up, along with $10 he had stuffed in a pocket.

From Radcliff, continue north on SR 160 for 2.8 miles. When you reach that point, look to the left. A private lane leads into the woods. Near the gate, you can see all that remains of the Eagle Furnace. The stone wall on the left side of the lane above the gate was the back face for the cold-blast charcoal furnace.

This is the center of the ghost town of Oreton (or Eagle Furnace). During the Civil War, it was a vibrant community that produced eight to nine tons of pig iron per day for Northern foundries, which turned that iron into cannon and other war materiel for the Union army. In the late 1800s, the iron-smelting industry in Ohio collapsed, and most of the state's furnaces went to ruin.

Remains of Eagle Furnace (c. 1852)

Brick vault of the Eagle Furnace company store.

In 0.1 mile farther ahead, a small brick structure, which is the remains of the brick safe of the company store at Eagle Furnace, stands on the right.

Continue 0.5 mile; here, the flankers joined with the main column, which headed north on a road that turned right along the small creek that SR 160 crosses as the highway bends left. That road was lost to strip mining many decades ago.

Drive another 0.9 mile and turn right onto SR 324. Drive 4.3 miles on SR 324 to Dundas. Outriders searching for food and fresh horses reached the communities of Dundas and Puritan. Turn right on CR 24 before reaching the railroad.

It is 3.2 miles to US 50 and Vinton Station. Turn right and go 0.7 mile to Stone Quarry Road (TR 8) on the right. This road leads to Vinton Furnace. It is now closed about 1.9 miles south, before the furnace site.

A hiking trail leads to the furnace ruins, which are located at the base of a hill on the south bank of Elk Fork. It is now within the Vinton Furnace Experimental Forest. Contact them at (740) 596-4238 for information regarding the trail, furnace history, and historical photographs. The furnace dates to 1853.

The Elk Fork of Raccoon Creek is on your right. The raiders rode along the fork after they left Vinton Furnace and turned northwest.

When the raiders left Vinton Furnace, Morgan forced the furnace manager, Isaac Brown, to ride with him as a guide.

Turn around unless you are interested in visiting the furnace site.

*Side Trip: The route to the furnace trail may not be well marked or well maintained. We suggest calling the Vinton Furnace Experimental Forest number before visiting the furnace.

BUFFINGTON ISLAND TO NELSONVILLE

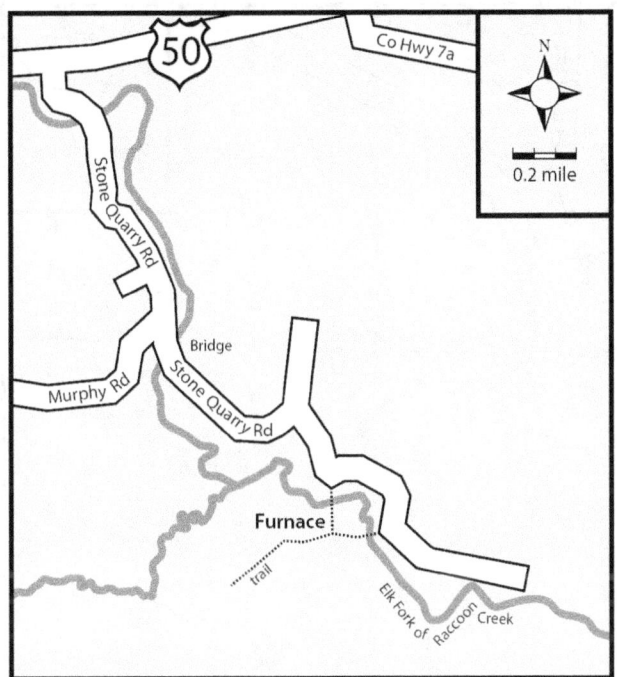
Vinton Furnace trail map

Take Stone Quarry Road 0.7 mile to a "Y" intersection and follow the road to the left. Go 0.2 mile and bear left, and then in 0.1 mile, cross a rickety bridge. Go 0.5 mile to another "Y" intersection and take the road to the right. Follow it 0.6 mile and park on the right side of the road.

An abandoned bridge is on the right. The bridge has been closed for many years and the flooring is not sound; use caution. It may be possible to ford Elk Fork in periods of low water. The abandoned road on the other side of the bridge is the original road; it leads to the hiking trail. Follow the trail to the left and uphill to the Vinton Furnace ruins.

Well preserved post-war Vinton Furnace coke ovens.

The best-preserved portion of the furnace ruins are the Belgium coke ovens on the hill. They were built about 1875 and are believed to be the only ones in the U.S.

Turn around and retrace your route back to US 50.*

After turning around at Stone Quarry Road, drive 0.7 mile west on US 50, and after passing the railroad tracks, pull over at the intersection with SR 677 (Powder Plant Road). Look back toward the railroad tracks.

JOHN HUNT MORGAN HERITAGE TRAIL INTERPRETIVE SIGN #32

In 1863, these tracks belonged to the Marietta & Cincinnati Railroad. A spur line ran from here to Vinton Furnace.

Look to the left along the tracks; the area a quarter of a mile to the north of US 50 was Vinton Station. When the raiders arrived here about 7 p.m., they cut the telegraph wire and damaged several telegraph posts.

The John Dowd farm was located near Vinton Station. The two oldest Dowd sons were serving in the Union Army, and their ten-year-old brother was helping his father with the farm. Once warned that Morgan was coming, Dowd sent the boy to hide their horses in the woods. Later, after the horses had been brought back to the fields, Dowd learned the approaching Union army also was confiscating horses. Once again, he unhitched his horses and told the boy to hide them in the woods.

Before the boy and horses reached those woods, a Union patrol spotted the boy, who was riding one of the horses and leading the other. A trooper yelled at him to stop; the boy kicked the horse and kept going. The troopers raised their guns and began firing at him. The furious father raised hell with the cavalrymen: "I have two sons serving in the Union army, and now Union troops are trying to shoot my other son."

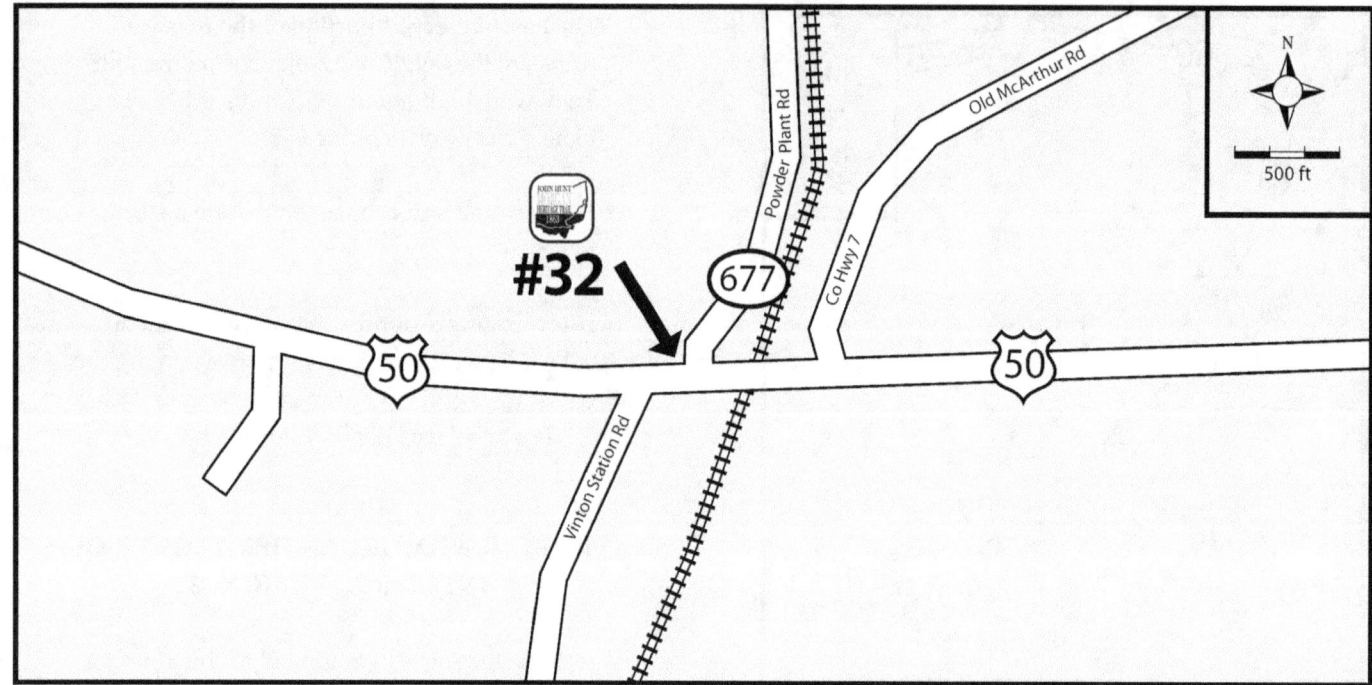

John Hunt Morgan Heritage Trail Interpretive sign #32 map

Morgan's guide, Isaac Brown, lied when he warned the general that many Union soldiers were in McArthur. Morgan had no intention of encountering an armed force, if it could be avoided. So the raiders followed Elk Fork northwest, skirting the town.

Go 1.9 miles west on US 50 and turn right onto Morgan Road (TR 11). At 0.3 mile, stay on Morgan Road (TR 11) as it turns left. Go 1.8 miles to a stop sign and turn left onto Infirmary Road (TR 14). It is 0.3 mile to SR 93.

Turn right on SR 93 and go 3.3 miles to the outskirts of Creola; turn left onto Dunkle Creek Road (CR 34). After turning, glance to your left as you round the sharp bend ahead. The vacant lot next to the road was the site of the Cornelius Karns house.

Tuesday night, Morgan stayed at the Cornelius Karns house, while his men camped nearby, including at the site of the present-day chapel. Captain Cornelius Karns, who was sixty-one years old at the time of the raid, was a Civil War veteran who had been honorably discharged from Company F, 114th Ohio Infantry, in February 1863. Mrs. Karns cooked food for the raiders in a big iron pot in the yard. The hungry men ate in relays. Cornelius Karns's log house has since been razed.

The townspeople's horses were hidden nearby in the Karns grove, where they escaped the raiders' attention. John Karns, who lived south of town, lost his horses.

Creola did not exist at the time of the Civil War. Cornelius Karns founded the town of "Karns Grove" after the Civil War in his effort to bring the railroad here. The railroad venture failed, but the town remained and was later renamed Creola.

Follow around the curve and immediately turn left on Karns Avenue. Continue past the chapel and cemetery on Karns Avenue and follow the street as it makes a sharp bend to the right. This will take you back to Dunkle Creek Road.

Wednesday, July 22, 1863

The raiders were on the road before sunup. One of them forgot two cartridge boxes, which remained in the Karns family for generations as a souvenir of the raid.

The raiders rode north from the Karns farm on a road that roughly followed modern-day SR 93; the Civil War era road no longer exists.

BUFFINGTON ISLAND TO NELSONVILLE

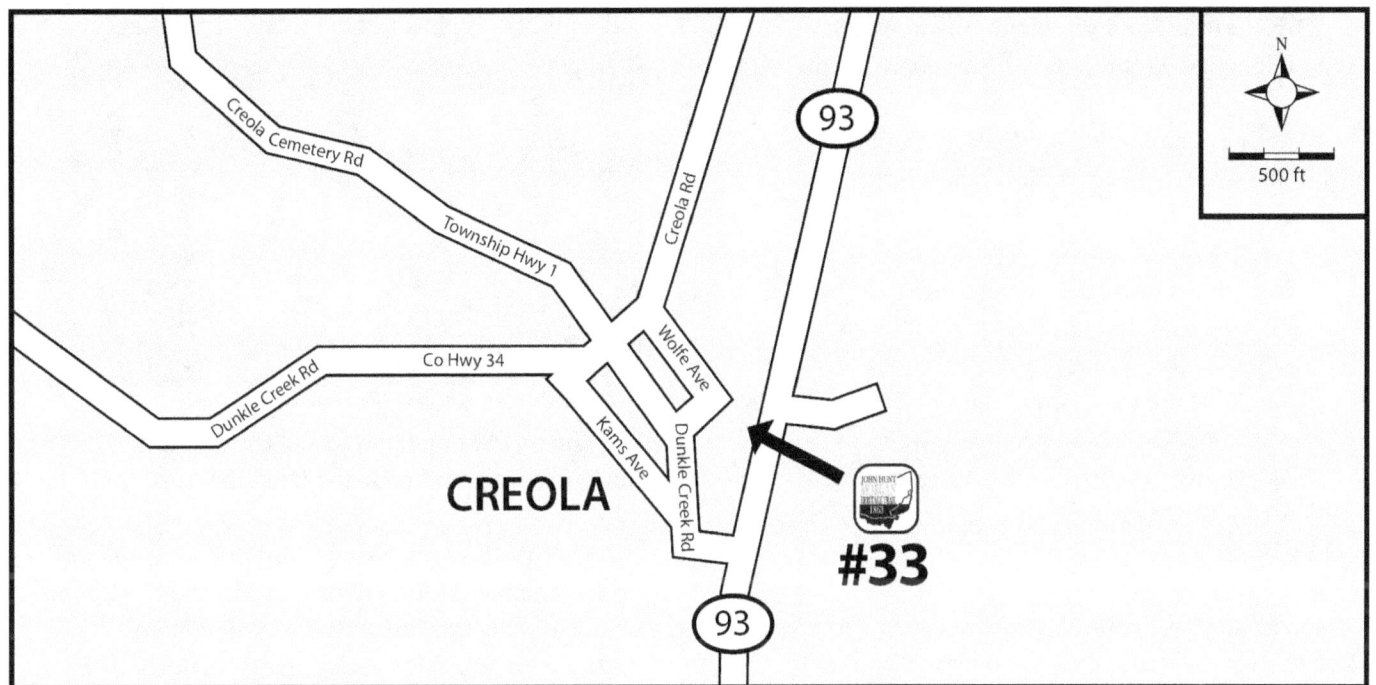

John Hunt Morgan Heritage Trail Interpretive sign #33 map

Turn right onto Dunkle Creek Road. Go 0.2 mile to the stop sign at SR 93; turn left. We have rejoined Morgan's route.

Go 0.1 mile and turn left at the next driveway. **Trail Sign #33** is near the parking lot.

JOHN HUNT MORGAN HERITAGE TRAIL INTERPRETIVE SIGN #33

Return to SR 93 and turn left. It is 1.2 miles to Airport Road (CR 22); turn right. At 0.5 mile, when Airport Road turns right, continue straight onto Pumpkin Ridge Road (CR 32). Follow the ridge road 5.0 miles to the stop sign in Orlando. Turn right on SR 56.

It is 1.3 miles to New Plymouth. The sun was up by the time the raiders reached here. Henry Ornduff Harden, a nineteen-year-old New Plymouth farm boy, was away serving as a private in Company G, 90th OVI. In just eight days, he would be escorting Morgan to the Ohio State Penitentiary.

Drive 2.4 miles to Oneal Road (TR 314). You will enter Hocking County along the way. Look to the right across the pond located before the intersection.

The core of the house on the right is a log cabin built by Henry O'Neill, in 1810.

During the Civil War, one room of the house served as the Starr Post Office, and a blacksmith shop was attached to the house. Lavina Eggleston, the postmistress at Starr, was warned the raiders were coming. She took down the U.S. flag and hid it.

Starr Post Office (c. 1863)

Morgan stopped at the post office and went through the mail while the blacksmith performed emergency shoe work on some of the raiders' horses. Other rebels were scouring the area for new mounts; they found twelve.

Drive 0.1 mile and you are in downtown Starr. The raiders passed through this area about 7 a.m.

Another 1.2 miles will find you in front of the Coonville Church. Go 0.6 mile; at this point Morgan split his forces.

Side Trip: A small detachment turned north on Laurel Run Road (CR 26) and followed along the East Branch of Raccoon Creek for 0.6 mile. There they turned right on Sanner Road (CR 325) and followed it 2.2 miles to SR 278. Turn around and retrace your route back to SR 56 near Coonville Church. Turn left on SR 56.

To follow the main column, continue 2.2 miles to SR 278. Turn left onto SR 278 and drive 2.6 miles to Mt. Zion Church on the left.

The church was organized in 1863, but the building was not constructed until 1868. It was built beside the Bollinger School, which stood where the church parking lot is located today. In July 1863, summer session was being held for children too small to walk to school in the winter.

Bollinger School site next to Mt. Zion Church.

Lodema Skinner, the school teacher, rode her horse to school and picketed it nearby during the day.

That Wednesday, Skinner responded to a knock on the door, and found herself facing one of Morgan's men. He said, "Ma'am, we mean you no harm. I'll trade my horse for your horse." He unrolled a blanket on the floor and ordered the students to empty their lunch boxes onto it. With no more ceremony than that, he departed with the teacher's horse and the students' lunches.

Continue 5.4 miles on SR 278 to the Hocking River at Nelsonville, Athens County. Drive to the far end of the bridge and pull over on the left before the railroad tracks.

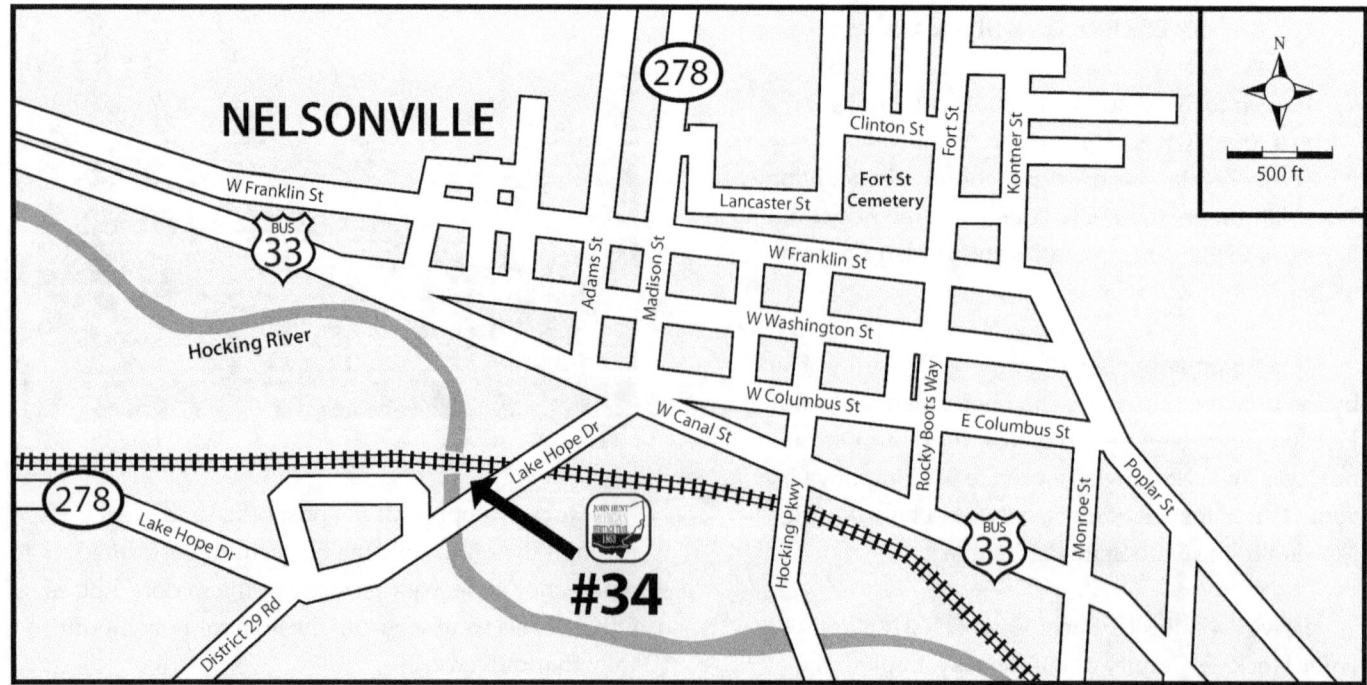
John Hunt Morgan Heritage Trail Interpretive sign #34 map

BUFFINGTON ISLAND TO NELSONVILLE

**JOHN HUNT MORGAN HERITAGE TRAIL
INTERPRETIVE SIGN #34**

When the raiders were attempting to burn all the bridges before they left town, they built a fire in the covered bridge at the location of the present-day highway bridge. The townspeople were able to put the fire out before serious damage was done.

Morgan arrived in Nelsonville between 10 and 11 a.m. Because the town was unprotected, the mayor immediately surrendered. All the able-bodied men had gone to Athens, where they were expecting the raiders to strike.

Continue on SR 278 to the stoplight at US 33 Business. Turn right on Canal Street (US 33 Business) and reset your odometer. Go just over 0.2 mile to the intersection with Rocky Boots Way. The area on the left, before reaching the Rocky Boots Way intersection, was the site of the Hocking Street Canal basin.

Hocking River and Canal at Nelsonville. The railroad (1869) and Robbins Store (1866) on the left were built after the Civil War. The intersection in the foreground is Fulton and Washington streets. The canal was filled-in and is now Canal Street (US 33 Business).

The basin filled most of the northwest corner lot on the left. The raiders burned ten canal boats in the basin: the *Forest Rose, Swan, Comstock, Hibernia, Ontario, Fame (Fatue), Eureka, Quebec, Valley,* and *Virginia*.

The *Custer* was spared when Betty Stewart, the owner's wife, stood on the deck holding their infant daughter in her arms, while her husband, Charles, convinced Morgan's men it was a houseboat and not used to carry coal.

This area of the Hocking Valley had rich coal deposits. Large-scale coal mining was done in this area, and the canal boats were used to transport it.

Sparks from the burning boats spread the fire to the nearby Lorenzo Poston Coal Works on the south side of the canal. The blaze, which was extinguished after the raiders departed, did considerable damage to the coal hopper.

After tearful pleas from Mrs. Steenrod, the raiders did not burn the Steenrod Mill located on the north bank of the canal. The Robbins flour mill located on the Hocking River also escaped the torch.

The Steenrod Mill is on the left beyond the trees. The Hocking Canal, seen here, is US 33 Business today.

It was lunchtime when the raiders arrived. They helped themselves to all the food the Nelsonville women had cooked and asked them to cook more. They opened dozens of jars of preserves. It was reported Morgan stopped at the Butt home, when he smelled fresh berry pie. He not only ate the requested pie, but also devoured an entire meal before leaving.

Morgan's men looted the stores of Charles Ashton and William B. Brooks. Ashton's losses included cigars, clothing, tobacco, shoes, and boots. He filed a claim for $694. Brooks filed a claim for $384 for miscellaneous goods taken from his store. Four saloon keepers filed claims for lost liquor; all claims for liquor were rejected.

The raiders took forty-seven horses in the Nelsonville area and the Union forces confiscated seven more.

After the war, the Hocking Canal fell into disuse when the railroad became the primary form of transportation in the region. Eventually, the canal was drained and filled in, and Canal Street was built on top of it. However, a nicely preserved section of the Hocking Canal can still be seen at a roadside park located 3.0 miles west of town on Diamond Brick Road/Haydenville Road (CR 25).

Before leaving Nelsonville between 1 and 2 p.m., the raiders set fire to both covered bridges over the Hocking River and the bridges over the Hocking Canal. The citizens hurriedly extinguished the flames. When Shackelford's men arrived that evening around 5 p.m., they were treated to a large dinner prepared by the women of Nelsonville. The meal was served on tables in the public square. While the exhausted Union soldiers dallied over the meal, Morgan's men pushed on to the valley of the Muskingum. Continue on US 33 Business for 0.8 mile to Burr Oak Boulevard. Turn left on Burr Oak Boulevard.

Chapter Eight
NELSONVILLE TO OLD WASHINGTON

Wednesday, July 22, 1863

After leaving Nelsonville on US 33 Business (Canal Street), turn left onto Burr Oak Boulevard and go 1.3 miles to a stop sign. Turn right, and then make an immediate left turn onto SR 78. It is 5.2 miles to the junction with SR 216 in Murray City. En route, you will pass through Buchtel, just beyond which you will enter Hocking County. Neither Murray City nor Buchtel existed in 1863.

Bear left on SR 216 for 0.5 mile; turn right onto Salem Hollow Road (TR 21). The raiders used this road, which closely follows Snow Fork (Snow Fork Branch of Monday Creek).

The Snow Fork Branch of Monday Creek is on the left.

It is 2.0 miles to Salem Cemetery. Some of the men rested their horses in the churchyard.

Salem Cemetery

In 1863, at the point where Salem Hollow Road enters Perry County, the raiders turned northeast on a road that led directly to Hemlock; that road no longer exists.

Go 2.9 miles and turn right onto CR 17 (Salem Hollow Road). Go 0.7 mile, and continue on CR 17 as it turns left.

Go another 0.7 mile and turn right onto TR 392. Drive 0.7 mile and bear left; it is 0.3 mile to SR 155. Turn right at SR 155.

Drive 2.3 miles and turn right onto Main Street in Hemlock. You will cross the West Branch of Sunday Creek. Follow Main Street (TR 257) for 0.9 mile. TR 257 is the Civil War road that Morgan's main column used to reach Hemlock. The path leading from Salem Hollow Road intersected TR 257 on the left. Only faint remnants of that road are visible today.

Hemlock

Turn around and enter Hemlock, as Morgan's men did. In the Civil War period, the town was officially designated Whipstown Post Office. Several claims for stolen horses were filed by residents of this town: six horses taken by the raiders and one confiscated by the Union.

Return to SR 155 and turn right. It is 0.4 mile to **Trail Sign #35** on the right, which is located near the Southern Local Schools' garage and maintenance building. Park next to the Trail Sign.

JOHN HUNT MORGAN HERITAGE TRAIL INTERPRETIVE SIGN #35

The Benjamin Sanders house, razed in 2003, stood across the road 75 yards west of the Trail Sign. The post-war barn stands on the south side of the road.

NELSONVILLE TO OLD WASHINGTON

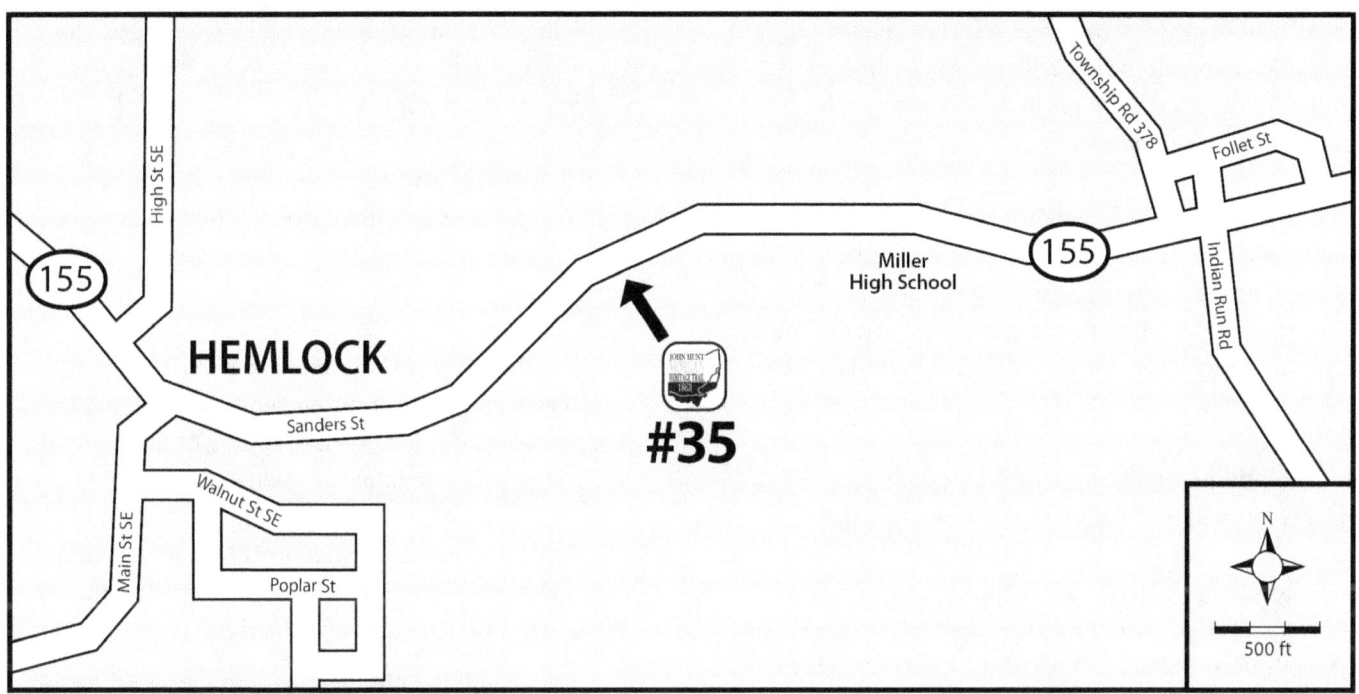

John Hunt Morgan Heritage Trail Interpretive sign #35 map

The Benjamin Sanders farmhouse was razed in 2003.

The raiders stopped there to water their horses. They took all the "ready" food in the house.

Susannah Sanders gave one of her best quilts to a young raider after he showed her his horse's saddle sores. She had three sons serving in the Union army in the South and hoped that some Southern woman would treat them kindly. When Morgan's men left Hemlock, they took the Sanders's three horses and a mule with them. Benjamin followed the raiders at a distance and, after nearly a week, was able to recover two of his horses after Morgan was captured.

Drive 2.8 miles on SR 155. Morgan's men arrived in Millertown early in the afternoon and stayed until about 5 p.m. Nineteen claims were filed from the town and the surrounding area of Buchanan Post Office. The area included the communities later known as Drake and Corning. Losses to the raiders included ten confiscated horses and damages to nine others, later recovered.

While in Millertown, the raiders fed their horses and ate the locals' food. Joseph Rodgers served meals to fifty men. The rebels looted the stores and confiscated whiskey. Adam Gift's store lost $700 worth of clothing, dry goods, shoes, and boots, and $306 cash.

Ten miles away at New Lexington, the Perry County seat, the citizens waited for the raiders. A rider from Vinton County had arrived with a warning that Morgan was coming. Horses and valuables were hidden. Because most of the able-bodied men were away on military duty, two men were sent to meet Morgan and surrender the town. Following an anxious night, the citizens learned that Morgan had bypassed their town.

Three men from New Lexington, D. W. Marsh, Sill Colborn, and James Carroll, rode out to discover the raiders' whereabouts. About daybreak they rode into the rebel camp at Island Run. Marsh escaped, but Colborn and Carroll were taken prisoners. They were forced to ride with the raiders for forty miles before they were released and allowed to make their way home on foot.

Shackelford's exhausted men arrived during the night and camped at Millertown. It was almost 10 a.m. the following morning before the last soldiers left. Several men "gave out" and were unfit to continue the pursuit. They were taken to New Lexington for rest and recovery.

Continue east 0.5 mile on SR 155 and cross SR 13. Go two blocks and turn left onto Corning Street.

Reset and rely on your odometer; a number of roads will be unmarked. You will go 0.3 mile up a very steep hill. At the top of the hill turn left onto TR 291. Go 0.4 mile and turn right with TR 291.

Drive almost 0.3 mile and bear right at Chapel Hill Road (CR 50). It is 1.5 miles to a "Y" intersection; bear left on Irish Ridge Road (CR 16).

Go 0.2 mile to Chapel Hill.

The town was originally named Thompsonville in honor of its founder. When Thompson applied for a post office, another town already bore the name "Thompsonville," so he renamed the primarily Irish Catholic settlement Chapel Hill.

A log mission had been established here by the Catholic Church in 1825. The stone St. Francis Assisi Church replaced it in 1839.

Chapel Hill was a business center for the area before the coming of the railroad. It had a doctor, a general store, a harness shop, several taverns, and a hotel.

The church was abandoned in 1898. By then the businesses and most of the citizens had left the area. The town was doomed by the coming of the railroad and the establishment of the town of Corning.

When Morgan arrived, many of his men rested their exhausted horses in the churchyard. The ruins of the church are in the trees on the right.

St. Francis Assisi Church ruins

The George Thompson General Store and Post Office were next door to the church. The raiders confiscated $10 in postage stamps, $140 from the money box, four saddles, several bridles, other leather goods, and all of Thompson's whiskey. Six horses were taken from the community.

St. Francis Assisi Church at Chapel Hill

Chapel Hill Cemetery

Continue 0.1 mile on Irish Ridge Road. Decaying remains of other buildings can be seen through the trees on both sides of the road. The Chapel Hill Cemetery is on the left.

Continue 0.1 mile to a "Y" intersection and bear left on CR 16. It is 0.7 mile to Alabama Hill.

Turn right on Santoy Road (CR 37) and follow it 1.0 mile to a "T intersection". Stay on Santoy Road as it turns left. Drive 0.5 mile and bear right at the "Y"; it is 0.7 mile to the junction with SR 555.

Turn left and drive 1.4 miles to SR 37. Turn left and drive through Portersville. The raiders passed through the town at dusk. Six horses were taken from this community. Morgan forced Henry Koons, a Perry County resident, to serve as his guide. Koons was released later near Rokeby Lock.

When SR 37 turns to the left after 0.5 mile, continue straight on SR 555 for 0.2 mile.

Turn right on TR 453 (Timberman Road); it soon becomes CR 51, and you are in Morgan County. The Thomas Pettit family lived near the county line. The Pettit women had baked fourteen pies to feed the family and boarders. When the raiders arrived and discovered the pies, they were distracted and failed to look for Pettit's horses.

Continue on Timberman Road (CR 51) for 2.1 miles to a "T" intersection. Turn left onto TR 189 (Pletcher Road). It is 0.8 mile to the next "T"; turn right onto Triadelphia Road (CR 3).

After 0.5 mile, turn left onto Stoneburner Road (CR 54). Drive 0.5 mile; the John Weaver house stood on the right at the break in the trees lining the road. The farm was located near the head of the South Branch of Island Run.

Morgan pulled a "straw tick" mattress off one of the beds and slept on the floor of the two-story log house. Before he retired, he ordered Susanna Weaver to bake bread for his men, who were camped in the orchard and surrounding fields. The raiders helped themselves to Weaver's stock of wheat and hay in the barn.

The Weaver house no longer stands on Island Run.

The old log house has been moved to Dublin, Ohio, where it has been restored. It now serves as part of The Morgan House Gift Shop and Restaurant at 5300 Glick Road (Web site: *http://www.morganhse.com/*).

During the night, Morgan's men captured ten Northern scouts from the Zanesville area. They included Colonel Z. M. Chandler, Reverend J.N. McAbee, and Judge Ezra E. Evans. The captives were forced to ride with the raiders and were paroled the next afternoon near Zeno.

Thursday, July 23, 1863
Morgan forced Weaver to serve as his guide to the Muskingum River ford. They rode down Island Run; sections of the original road along the run no longer exist.

Drive 0.9 mile to the bridge over the South Branch. Continue less than 0.2 mile; at the "Y" intersection bear left on CR 54. At this point we leave the raiders. They followed the abandoned road along the north bank of the South Fork to Helmick Mill.

Go 1.3 miles and turn right on Hivnor Road (TR 194). Drive 1.2 miles and ford Island Run.

The road becomes TR 193 (Deaver Road) as it follows along the run. Go 1.1 miles to a "Y" at Helmick Road (TR 269). This area was known as Helmick Mill. After the Civil War, the bridge was built near the mill.

John Hunt Morgan Heritage Trail Interpretive sign #36 map

Wednesday night, six armed citizens from Deavertown captured five Confederates near here. They held Private M. M. Brownard and the other four men overnight in the mill, and the militia turned them in to Union authorities at Zanesville the next day.

At this point the raiders took the road to the left following along Island Run to Fisher's Mill and Rokeby Dam on the Muskingum River. When they reached the river, Morgan told John Weaver to walk back home. The road along the run is now closed.

Bear left to continue on Deaver Road. Go 0.2 mile to another "Y" intersection and bear left onto Bush Road (TR 201). Morgan and his men followed the right fork, which is now a dead-end private lane. Drive 1.5 miles on Bush Road to the stop sign at SR 669. Turn left onto SR 669. In 0.4 mile, turn right into the parking lot of the Soloman Lutheran Church. Trail Sign #36 is next to the parking lot.

JOHN HUNT MORGAN HERITAGE TRAIL INTERPRETIVE SIGN #36

Soloman Church, established in 1820, stood here during the Civil War. A flanking detachment of raiders passed by here on July 23rd.

Turn around and go 0.4 mile on SR 669 to Bush Road. Turn right onto Bush Road and drive 1.5 miles to Deaver Road. Bear right onto Deaver Road; go 0.2 mile and turn left onto Helmick Road (TR 269).

Cross the Helmick Mill Covered Bridge on Helmick Road (TR 269). Go 0.4 mile to the top of the hill and make a sharp left turn onto Lemon Hill Road (CR 74). Reset your odometer. This road follows the ridge; the raiders rode down the valley off to the left.

Helmick Mill Bridge (c. 1867).

Adventurous, ten-year-old Lawson (Lon) Woodward wanted to see the raiders. His friends refused to join him, so he made his way alone to Lemon Ridge.

NELSONVILLE TO OLD WASHINGTON

From its brow, he could watch the raiders as they made their way down Island Run. He heard a shot from a squirrel rifle. Peering through the leaves, he saw his father, John F. Woodward, aiming at the raiders. Then, the raiders fired back at their assailant. Suddenly the area was peppered with rebel carbine fire. His father beat a hasty retreat.

Lon traveled parallel with the raiders as they continued eastward down the run. The ridge turned into a hogback (a sharp ridge with steep sides) that terminated at a point below the ford. Safely hidden among the trees, he watched the skirmish and the river crossing play out as if they were a scene set on a stage.

It is 1.1 miles to the "Y" intersection at the cemetery; bear left on Lemon Hill Road. Go another 2.4 miles to SR 669 and turn left.

At 0.6 mile, Island Run comes in from the left. Morgan's men approached on the road along the north bank of the run.

Continue 0.4 mile and park. Rokeby Dam is on the right. The dam and lock were built in the 1840s as part of a system designed to improve navigation on the river.

Rokeby Dam and Lock, built in the 1840s. Morgan's men forded the river here.

The ford was 150 to 200 yards downstream from the dam, at the head of Bald Eagle Island.

Local men and boys with hunting rifles and flintlocks gathered along the bluff on the east bank to cover the ford and prevent the raiders from crossing. The defenders fired at the Confederates, who were on the west bank, but the citizens' guns lacked sufficient range to be very effective.

Some of Morgan's men dismounted and returned the fire. Shots were exchanged for about one and a half hours. A young raider was buried in McElhiney's Hollow. He was probably wounded during this action. His companions tied him to his saddle, and he

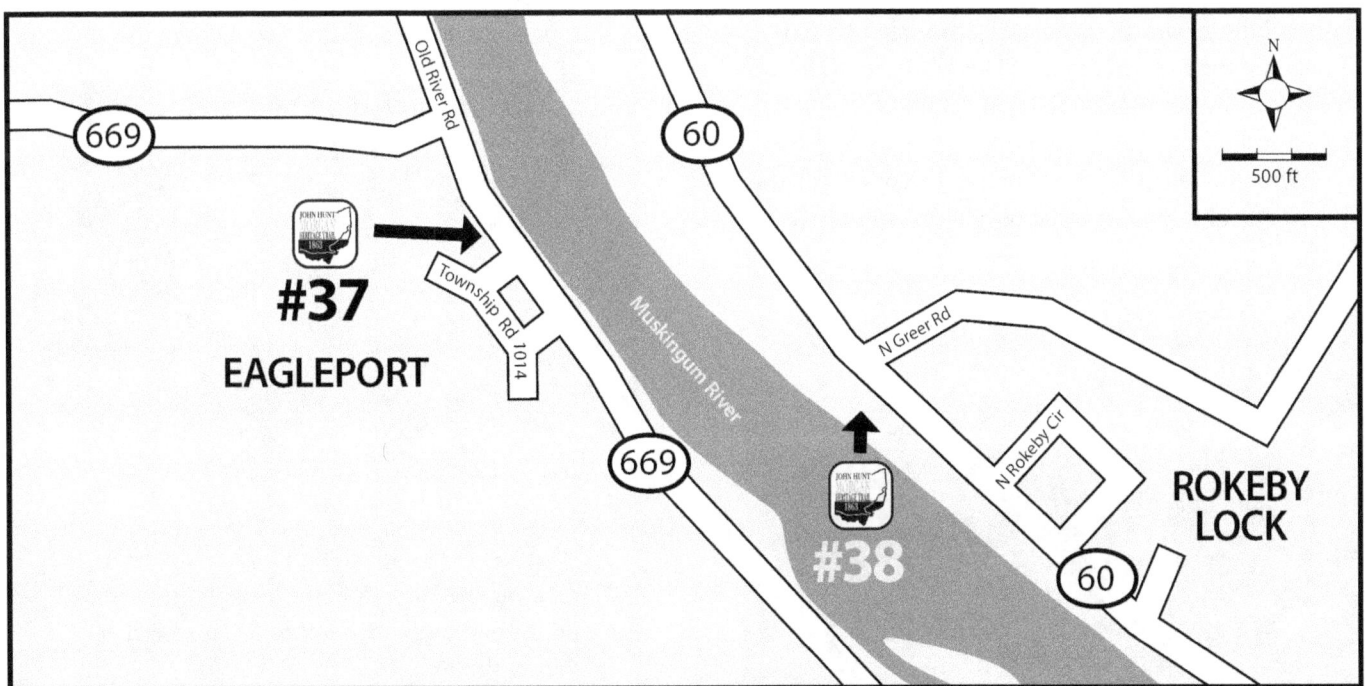

John Hunt Morgan Heritage Trail Interpretive signs #37 and #38 map

managed to survive the river crossing, but died shortly thereafter.

About 8:30 a.m., a party of raiders captured Hiram Winchell's ferry flatboat above the dam and used it to gain a foothold on the east bank. As these men moved down toward the lock, the hostilities ceased and the defenders fled to nearby cornfields.

By 9 a.m., Morgan's main force was crossing the Muskingum River ford. Lock tender David Power served as the guide. He was forced to make many trips piloting the men across the narrow ford.

Continue north 0.4 mile to the church on the left.

JOHN HUNT MORGAN HERITAGE TRAIL INTERPRETIVE SIGN #37

This is the center of the old town of Eagleport, founded in 1837.

Henry Kelly, a citizen of Logan, was killed near here. He and a companion had been following Morgan since Nelsonville, taking shots at the Confederates along the way. Acting as a sniper, Henry had killed several of Morgan's men while standing on a knob above the stone quarry. As he took aim again, three bullets hit him simultaneously. He was shot by five rebels standing on the steps of Devol's store. Kelly was survived by a wife and five young children.

After the rebels looted Dalphon Devol's store, they forced Devol to row them across the river in his skiff.

The ferry crossing above the dam at Eagleport.

At Eagleport, a terrified resident, Mr. Forgrave, hid in a pigpen. When detected by a raider, he was asked, "Did you all come from the same litter?"

Proceed 0.1 mile north on SR 669. Where SR 669 turns left, turn around. Follow SR 669 south along the west bank for 7.5 miles to Malta and a bridge across the Muskingum River.

At this point, you have an option to cross the bridge and continue north to Rokeby Lock, or to take the alternate route through Malta and McConnelsville. The alternate route brings you back to the east side of the bridge.

*Alternate Route: Malta has a monument honoring one of her native sons. Confederate Brigadier General Otho French Strahl grew up in Malta. After passing the bar, he moved to Tennessee to practice law. He was one of six Confederate generals to die on the field of battle at Franklin, Tennessee, on November 30, 1864.

To visit the **Strahl Monument**, do not cross the 7th Street (SR 78) bridge; instead, continue straight on Main Street for three blocks. The monument is on the right in front of the town hall.

Malta native son, Confederate General Otho Strahl

Drive just over a block and turn left onto Third Street. Turn right onto Front Street and immediately turn left onto Third Street to cross the river.

NELSONVILLE TO OLD WASHINGTON

You are in McConnelsville. Turn right onto Main Street (SR 60/78); it is three blocks to the town square and the Morgan County Civil War Monument.

Morgan County Civil War Monument and courthouse

There is a painting by a local artist of the skirmish at Eagleport, hanging in the main hallway of the Morgan County Courthouse.

The Morgan County Historical Society Museum is located at 142 East Main Street. It contains a Morgan Raid exhibit and relics from the raid. The hours are Friday, 1–3 p.m., and Saturday, 10 a.m.–3 p.m. Phone: (740) 962-4785; Web site: *http://www.historicalmorgancounty.com/*.

The museum's raid-related items include the stone that served as the original marker for the grave of Tommy McGee, the young Confederate killed near Eagleport, and a piece of barn siding with a cannonball hole in it. The siding was taken from the Meloy barn when it was dismantled.

Original Tommy McGee grave marker, now at Morgan County Historical Society Museum

Turn around at the square and take Main Street (SR 60/78) 0.5 mile west to the second bridge across the river. Reset your odometer and continue north on SR 60.*

If you did not take the Alternate Route, then after crossing the river, turn left at SR 60 and reset your odometer.

As Morgan was crossing the Muskingum at Eagleport, Union forces closed in. General Shackelford's men were in close pursuit.

Lieutenant Colonel Robert W. McFarland and approximately 400 men from Companies D, E, G, and H of the 86th Ohio Volunteer Infantry (OVI) came downriver from Zanesville on the steamer *Dime*.

Colonel Joseph Hill, 500 militiamen, and two 12-pounder Napolean cannons (from Lieutenant William Dustin's section of the 19th Ohio Battery Light Artillery) came upriver from Marietta on the steamer *Jonas Powell*. Hill did not seem particularly anxious to find Morgan. He had ordered the boat to tie up early the evening before at Stockport, ten miles below McConnelsville.

In the morning, while Morgan was crossing the river at Rokeby Lock, Hill was marching his forces up to McConnelsville.

Go 6.1 miles north on SR 60 to the community of Rokeby Lock.

The Richard McElhiney house is on the right. The raiders came out of the river just north of the house.

Richard McElhiney house (c. 1822)

During the skirmish at the crossing, bullets hit both the McElhiney house and the neighboring home of Theobald Weber.

When they heard the first shots, Richard and his wife grabbed a few valuables, gathered the children, and fled to a nearby field. The McElhiney house still has bullets imbedded in the walls. The house has been in the same family since the 1820s.

McElhiney acted as the banker for the area. He hid $1,400 in a cigar box and buried the box in the potato patch. After the raid, he could not recall the box's exact location and had to dig for some time to locate the money.

The raiders battered open a locked chest of drawers looking for money and jewelry. The chest is still in the family. The river-soaked raiders took all Richard McElhiney's dry clothes and all the "ready" food in the house.

Next door, a bullet whizzed over Mrs. Theobald Weber as she bent down to make a bed in the front room. Her husband and most of the able-bodied local men were in Marietta serving with the militia. Mrs. Weber was at home with her eight children. The youngest, Louis, became a McConnelsville judge and later wrote the history of the raid at Eagleport. The Weber house stands at 8916 SR 60 on the east side of the highway, next to the dam at Rokeby Lock.

After crossing the river, Morgan moved about two miles upriver toward Gaysport (Blue Rock). Where the river bends to the east, he encountered the steamer *Dime* with Lieutenant Colonel McFarland and the 86th OVI on board.

Morgan turned back toward Rokeby Lock and took Greer Road east. After less than one-half mile the road turned north. Another mile brought the raiders to the Eli Barr farm. The farm was on a hill overlooking the bend of the river. There, the men of the 86th OVI turned Morgan back. The 86th OVI had disembarked from the *Dime* and climbed the steep hill to the Barr farm.

Morgan was trapped. His scouts advised against moving south. They had made contact with Colonel Marsh's men south of Rokeby Lock. Colonel Hill had sent Marsh and a small Union force up the river road from McConnelsville.

Unable to move north or south, Morgan decided to split his force. He turned the front of his column east through McElhiney's Hollow at a point about 300 yards south of the Union line at the Eli Barr farm. The raiders skirmished with McFarland's pursuing troops as they moved through the hollow. General Morgan ordered the rear portion of his command lingering at Rokeby Lock to hurry south to the Richard McElhiney house and ride east up the steep hollow directly behind it. The halves of the column would meet on the Zanesville Ridge Road near the point where Stewart Road and Pisgah Ridge Road intersect today.

There are conflicting accounts regarding the body of the young Confederate buried in the hollow behind the house. One account has Morgan's men hastily burying the body and covering it with rocks. Before leaving, they scratched the name, Tommy McGee, on one of the rocks. Richard McElhiney later found and reburied the body. Genealogical research supports the claim that the dead Confederate's name really was Thomas Milton McGee. A second version of events said McElhiney found the body of a young Confederate in the hollow. He buried the body and marked the grave with the name of Tommy McGee. Later, McElhiney claimed that he made up a name for the unknown soldier. A former comrade revisited the site in 1913 and told the McElhineys the soldier's real name was Frederick Rolf.

Tommy McGee grave marker in McElhiney Hollow.

NELSONVILLE TO OLD WASHINGTON

The original stone marker was replaced by the Sons of Confederate Veterans in 1991. The grave site and hollow are on private property and not open to the public.

After crossing McElhiney's Run a mile from the river, the raiders from Barr's farm entered the Zanesville Ridge Road. Emerging from the hollow, they received several well-directed volleys from the persistent men of the 86th OVI, who had moved east on a road that ran parallel to the raiders' path across the deep gulley. To avoid the enemy, Morgan's men turned south on the Zanesville Ridge Road, and then they doubled back toward the northeast along Stewart Road. The rear half of Morgan's troopers followed them. McFarland's bluecoats nipped at Morgan's heels for several miles, engaging in skirmishes with his rear guard. However, the last serious fighting occurred near the schoolhouse that stood at the present-day intersection of White Road and Stewart Road.

One raider was killed and ten were wounded in the fight with the 86th OVI. Two of the raiders were seriously wounded; one was shot in the chest, and the other lost his nose. Both men recovered.

Two hours later, Colonel Hill finally arrived on the scene. He took Zanesville Ridge Road to within a mile of where Morgan had passed earlier. Before returning to the boat, he placed his cannon on a knob and fired on Meloy's barn, thinking that it held rebels. The barn, still standing in 1963, was located less than 0.8 mile south of the intersection of Pisgah Ridge Road and Stewart Road. The structure has since been razed.

Go 0.1 mile on SR 60. There is a **stone marker** on the left to mark the Muskingum River crossing site.

Morgan's Crossing marker

Continue north for another 0.5 mile. There is an **Ohio Historical Marker** in front of the lock house on the left. The Muskingum locks are still used by recreational boaters.

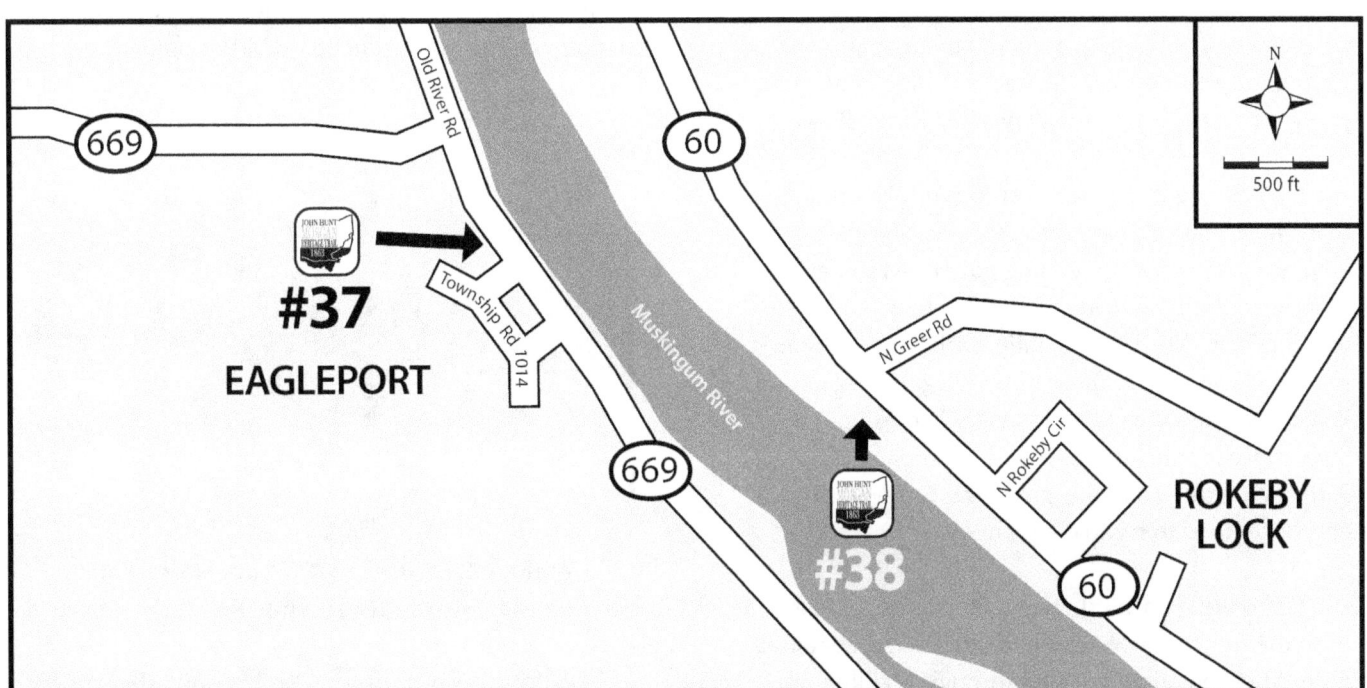
John Hunt Morgan Heritage Trail Interpretive signs #37 and #38 map

JOHN HUNT MORGAN HERITAGE TRAIL INTERPRETIVE SIGN #38

Just beyond the marker at the lock house, turn right onto Greer Road (TR 745). Drive 1.6 miles. Morgan's scouts reported that Union infantry (the 86th OVI) blocked the road 300 yards ahead. To slip out of the trap, Morgan had his column turn off the road near here and head into the wooded ravine of McElhiney's Hollow on the right.

Drive another 0.3 mile. On the left is the Eli Barr farm, where the 86th Ohio Volunteer Infantry gained the ridge and formed in line of battle, forcing Morgan's men to make a detour.

Muskingum River Lock #8 at Rokeby Lock

Continue 0.7 mile to a stop sign; turn right on Pisgah Ridge Road (CR 10). Pisgah Ridge Road is the present name given to the Zanesville Ridge Road.

Go 0.1 mile and turn left onto White Road (CR 64). McFarland's infantry fired on Morgan's advance troopers as they came out of McElhiney's Hollow onto Pisgah Ridge Road less than 0.2 mile south of here. The Union soldiers followed Morgan's rear guard a short distance down Pisgah Ridge Road. When they saw the Confederates ride north on Stewart Road, the infantrymen of Company H, 86th OVI, returned to this point and turned east on White Road to try to cut them off.

Go 0.8 mile on White Road. Stewart Road (TR 273) is on the right; it now dead-ends in less than one-half mile. After the raiders passed through McElhiney's Hollow and crossed the Zanesville Ridge Road, they struck Stewart Road and followed it to this intersection. Here the rear guard received several volleys from Company H, 86th OVI, as Morgan's column turned east on White Road. The Union infantrymen were positioned near a schoolhouse that once stood on the right side of White Road just before its junction with Stewart Road.

Raiders followed Stewart Road from McElhiney's Hollow.

At the "Y" junction of CR 90 (Rex Road) and CR 64, bear right on CR 64. Before crossing the bridge, look across the field on the right. A brick farmhouse owned by James Stewart once stood to the right of the barn in the distance. The owners fired a few shots at Morgan, and the Confederates returned the fire. Bullets were lodged in the bricks and doorway of the house. Before riding on, the raiders helped themselves to pies cooling on the kitchen window sill.

Stewart home, right (now gone), saw action on July 23, 1863.

Continue 1.3 miles to a ""T" intersection and turn left, staying on CR 64 (White Road).

Go 0.1 mile to another "T" and turn left again, onto Trimble Road (TR 278). In 0.6 mile, at the

NELSONVILLE TO OLD WASHINGTON

Morgan-Muskingum County line, the road becomes CR 230 (Trimble Road). It is 1.1 miles to SR 376 (Rockville Road); turn left and go 0.3 mile to the stop sign in Ruraldale. The raiders skirted the town to the east.

Turn right onto Ruraldale Road (CR 31) and drive 2.8 miles to Museville. There, Morgan's men burned the covered bridge across Meigs Creek.

Site of Museville covered bridge

Bear right and continue less than 0.6 mile to a "Y" at Cutler Lake Road (CR 45). Turn left onto CR 31 (Ruraldale Road). Drive 0.8 mile. The Matthew Alexander farmhouse is on the left. Alexander filed a claim for the loss of a horse and bridle.

Matthew Alexander farmhouse

Continue 1.1 miles to another bridge over Meigs Creek. Paisley Road is 0.1 mile beyond the bridge. Morgan sent men left along the road that follows the creek. They moved north toward High Hill, while the main column continued on to Zeno. To the south, flankers followed a parallel road through Meigsville (Lytlesburg).

It is 1.7 miles to SR 284. Morgan passed through Zeno about 2 p.m. Elijah and Judith Stevens lived on the right at the corner. Judith had grown up in Virginia and sympathized with the South. She told Morgan that her daughters, Eliza and Virginia, were at school and had their horse with them. The General promptly sent a detail to escort the girls home. Her pleas not to take the horse were to no avail. It was later recovered but had been harmed by hard use.

Turn left onto SR 284 and drive for 0.2 mile to the junction with SR 340. The Bethel and Frazier Store stood on the left at the curve before the junction. Jesse Frazier filed for the loss of a horse and more than $58 in merchandise from the store. Clement Fuller lived on the left, at the driveway less than 0.1 mile beyond the junction. He lost a valuable horse ($300), a Mexican saddle, and a horse blanket to the raiders.

Turn right on SR 340 (Cumberland Road). You will pass through an area devastated by strip mining.

It is 2.6 miles to the Twin Maple Stock Farm on the left before the junction with International Road (CR 216). In 1863, Theodore Frazee owned this property between the road and Collins Fork. He operated a grocery store and saddlery shop. His store building still stands on the corner.

The adjacent house was the site of Frazee's home. When Morgan arrived, he stopped the looting of the home and shop after exchanging the signal of Freemasonry with Frazee. By then, Frazee had lost two saddles, four bridles, and eight halters. Raiders also pocketed his stock of tobacco and cigars.

Theodore Frazee store and saddlery

The column followed along Collins Fork, crossing the corner of Noble County, while en route to Cumberland, which lies in Guernsey County. Drive 2.6 miles to a stop sign and bear right on SR 340/146.

Go 0.4 mile to the junction with SR 83 (Church Street).

You are in Cumberland (population 362 in 1863). The raiders arrived here between 3 p.m. and 5 p.m. on Thursday. They plundered the stores of Albert G. Squire (total loss: $340) and Albert Holmes (total loss: $227).

Morgan and his staff dined at the Globe House, kept by Doctor J.M. Stone. The 1840s hotel was built into a hillside, and the building's back doors were on the second floor. After dining, Morgan and his staff stretched out on the hotel's many beds for much needed sleep. By 10 p.m., Morgan was on the move again.

The raiders intended to take Stone's horse when they left. Stone offered them $75 not to take the horse. He explained that he needed it to visit a critically ill patient. They took the money and left the horse. Soon after, other raiders came by and took it.

More than 54 horses were taken from the Cumberland area. Six of them belonged to members of the McClelland clan.

Earlier in the afternoon, ten-year-old Mary McClelland made a remarkable Paul Revere-like ride. James C. McCall had ridden north from Zeno, shouting warnings of Morgan's approach. After he gave the alarm at the McClelland house, Mary bridled an unbroken (untrained) three-year-old filly, the only horse in the field, and rode it bareback to warn the men working in the fields that Morgan had arrived.

Along the way, she met a band of raiders. She ignored their commands to halt and rode through the group. She arrived safely but exhausted at the hayfield where the men were working. They lifted her from the horse and quickly led it away to a nearby woods.

Later, a raider was napping on the floor of the home of Mary's grandfather, James McCelland, when scouts warned him of the approach of Union troops. The rebel fled, leaving an army blanket behind. The approaching troops belonged to a small contingent of the 86th Ohio Volunteer Infantry, whose soldiers had been mounted on horses for the purpose of catching Morgan. About 150 mounted infantrymen, parts of Companies A, I, and K, under the command of Major William Kraus, joined General Shackelford's command at Old Washington the next day. Under the leadership of Colonel Wilson Lemert, the 86th OVI would stay with Shackelford for the rest of the campaign in pursuit of Morgan's raiders.

One of the raiders took $25 from Thomas Lindsey and then forced him to listen to a lecture on why he should vote for Clement Vallandigham (a Peace Democrat and leader of the Ohio Democratic Party).

While in the Cumberland area, sixty exhausted raiders deserted and headed back toward the Muskingum River. They were picked up the following day by a detachment of the 86th OVI.

When the raiders left Cumberland between 8 and 10 p.m., a Cumberland man was forced to serve as their guide to Point Pleasant, where he was released.

Morgan's route between Cumberland and Point Pleasant was northeast along the ridge road, portions of which no longer exist.

Drive 0.3 mile on Main Street and turn left onto Cambridge Street (SR 146). Go 0.1 mile. On the left near the old school is **Trail Sign #39**.

JOHN HUNT MORGAN HERITAGE TRAIL INTERPRETIVE SIGN #39

Continue on SR 146. After 2.0 miles, bear right at the junction with SR 672 (Glenwood Road). Go 0.5 mile on SR 672 and turn left onto Garvin School Road (TR 235); you are back on the raiders' route.

NELSONVILLE TO OLD WASHINGTON

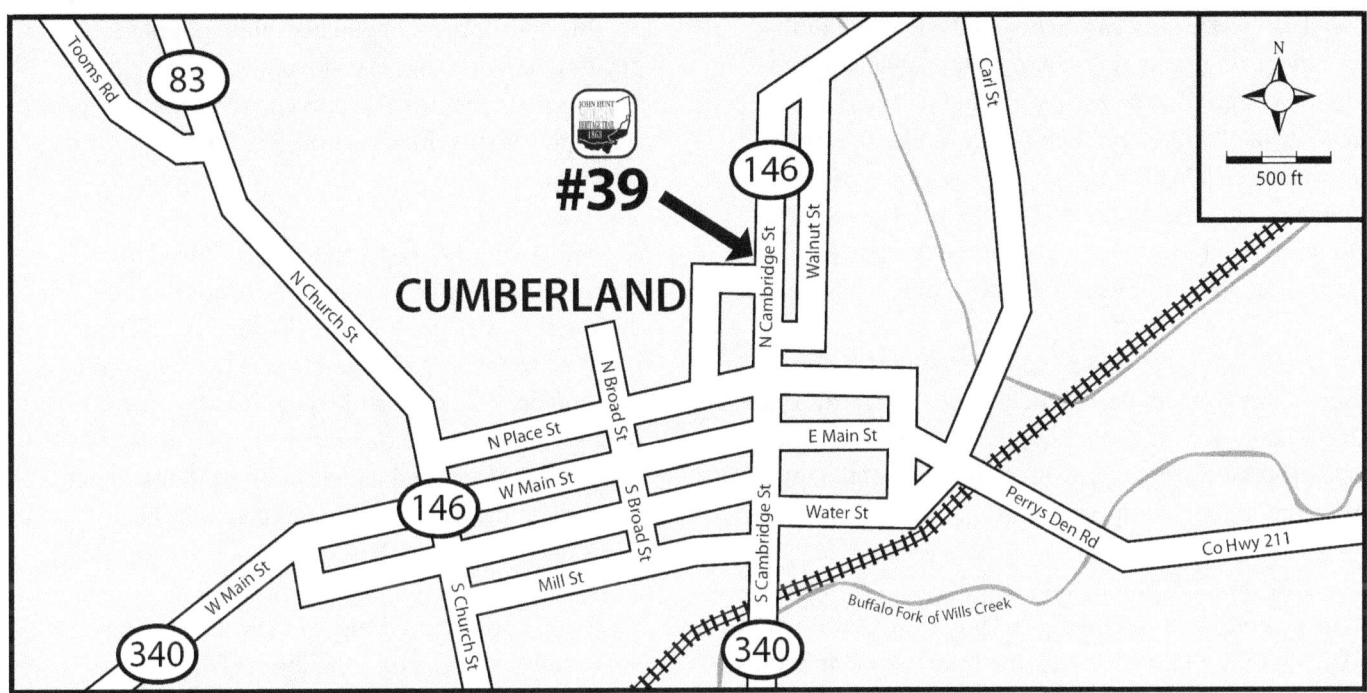

John Hunt Morgan Heritage Trail Interpretive sign #39 map

Go 2.3 miles to a "Y" intersection. Bear right on Cumberland Road (TR 328). The William LaFollette family lived on this road southwest of Point Pleasant. About midnight, the main raider force passed the LaFollette house without stopping. LaFollette breathed a sigh of relief as the tramp of the horses died away in the distance.

Early in the morning, Confederate stragglers arrived and took a prized bay horse from the stable.

A lone rider approached; he was asleep in the saddle. When he failed to respond to the raiders' orders to halt, he was shot. The raiders discovered he was one of their own men, John Happs. Unable to take him with them, they carried him to the LaFollette house and ordered the LaFollettes to fetch a doctor.

The staunch Unionist family protested when the man was left in their care. Doctor William Teeter was summoned from Point Pleasant; he probed for and found the bullet. He told the family the young soldier's condition was critical, but with proper care he might survive. At first, it appeared Happs's wound was fatal; slowly he began to recover. Three months later, a Union officer came for him.

Friday, July 24, 1863

Drive 1.5 miles to a "Y" intersection and bear right on Cumberland Road. Go 0.7 mile to a stop sign. Turn left onto SR 821 and then immediately turn right onto SR 146 (Main Street); you are in Pleasant City.

Until 1887 this town was known as Point Pleasant or Dyson's Post Office. The raiders rode through the town (population 114 at the time) before dawn, doing little damage. They took Harrison Secrest, the owner of the Elk Hotel, as their guide to Campbell's Station. The raiders ignored Secrest's excuse that his wife was ill. At Campbell's Station he was released and allowed to return home on his own horse.

Drive less than 0.2 mile on Main Street; SR 146 turns to the right. Do not turn; continue straight on Main Street. At the "Y" in front of the school, 0.5 mile ahead, reset your odometer and bear left at CR 52 (Pleasant Road).

Drive 0.4 mile. There is a cemetery on the right. Morgan took Kackley Road (TR 2500) (just beyond the cemetery) to Buffalo. The road was abandoned with the construction of Interstate 77.

The local militia had removed the flooring of the covered bridge across Seneca Creek in an attempt to divert Morgan's men. Far from being deterred, the men walked and swam their horses across the stream. Morgan, realizing the locals could quickly replace the flooring, ordered the bridge burned. His men attempted to burn the bridge, but the citizens and pursuing Union troops extinguished the flames.

It is 0.6 mile from the cemetery to SR 313; turn right. You will pass through Buffalo (Hartford in 1863) after driving under I-77; the raiders looted the stores here before moving on. At the time of the raid the population was approximately 103.

Stay on SR 313 (Clay Pike Road) for 3.7 miles. Greenwood Hill is on the right. Union Colonel William Wallace of the 15th Ohio Volunteer Infantry commanded a small force that had been organized at Camp Chase in Columbus. His force consisted of some Ohio militia and two companies of exchanged men from the 3rd Ohio Infantry, under the command of Captain Albert B. Dod (15th U.S. Infantry) and Captain Kinney. Accompanying them was a detachment of Captain Henry M. Neil's 22nd Ohio Battery Light Artillery, composed of two six-pounder, 3.67-inch brass cannons (Lieutenant Amos B. Alger and his single six-pounder brass cannon would reinforce Neil later that day). Wallace's contingent had been sent west from Parkersburg, West Virginia, to Campbell's Station.

Greenwood Hill near Senecaville

Colonel Wallace had placed his 250 men and two cannons in an excellent position on Greenwood Hill. From there, they could have fired on the Confederates as they approached the junction.

Morgan approached Senecaville (population 465 in 1863) just before daybreak. When Morgan and his men appeared, Wallace and his men vanished down the Sarahsville Road (SR 285 South). Not a gun was fired.

Wallace had the opportunity to either force Morgan's surrender, or check his advance until Shackelford arrived. Wallace claimed that he had received conflicting orders. He was first ordered to take the position on the hill; later he was ordered to abandon this position before Morgan arrived. Most accounts of the incident suggest Wallace took one look at the approaching raiders, panicked, and skedaddled.

Wallace regrouped his command and joined Shackelford's force pursuing the raiders.

Continue 0.2 mile to SR 285 in Senecaville. **Trail Sign #40** stands at the far left corner of the intersection.

JOHN HUNT MORGAN HERITAGE TRAIL INTERPRETIVE SIGN #40

Turn left on SR 285 (High Street). At the Senecaville Hotel, Morgan's troops ate the breakfast prepared for Wallace's men.

Truth or legend? One of the most frequently published "Morgan stories" in newspapers after the war came out of Senecaville. A local couple strongly supported the Union. The man enlisted and his wife volunteered to support herself by opening a millinery shop. Before he left, he gave her a loaded pistol with instructions to "shoot the first rebel who comes near the house."

On July 24, she had the opportunity. Peering out through closed blinds, she watched the passing column of Confederates. Morgan, riding near the end of the column, dismounted and approached the house. She reached for the pistol. Aiming through the blinds, she pointed it at the silver star on his chest. She was ready to pull the trigger when she thought, what if some Southern woman shot her husband? She could

NELSONVILLE TO OLD WASHINGTON

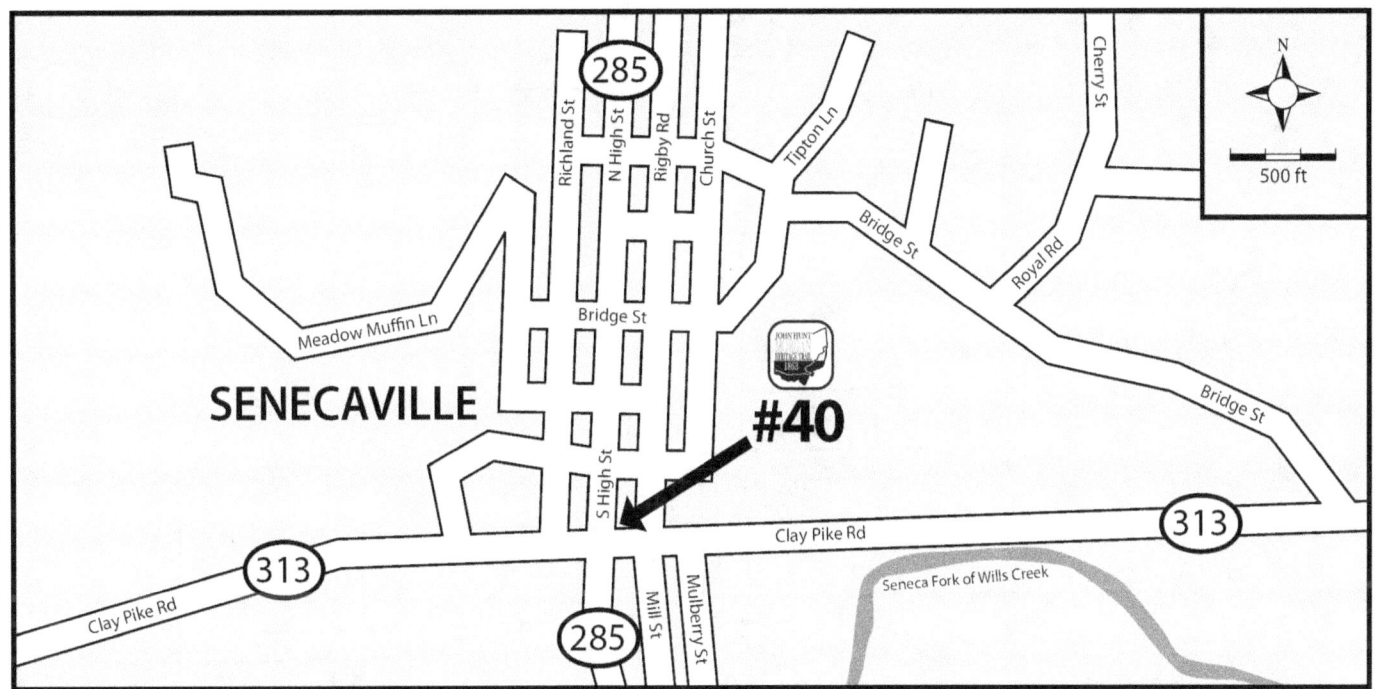

John Hunt Morgan Heritage Trail Interpretive sign #40 map

not cause Mrs. Morgan such suffering; the woman lowered the gun and opened the door.

Morgan politely inquired about the roads to Campbell's Station. After a few minutes' pleasant conversation, she told him what she had considered doing. Deeply moved, he replied, "Do you know why you did not shoot? At that very moment Mrs. Morgan, at our home in Tennessee, was down on her knees praying for my safety. I am sure that she was; several times in the past have I been as near death as I was a few minutes ago, and on my return home afterwards, I would learn that Mrs. Morgan was on her knees praying for me at that very moment."

The James Hartup barn was located several miles north of Senecaville. Several men, including Abraham Depew, were assembled there when a rebel soldier arrived looking for horses. Depew dealt him a blow, knocking him senseless. When he regained consciousness, Depew was standing over him with a club. Under threat of instant death, the raider remained quiet until his comrades had left the area. He was temporarily held in the Cambridge jail and later transported to Columbus.

It is 3.7 miles to the abandoned Baltimore and Ohio Railroad in Lore City (Campbell's Station in 1863). The raiders arrived here about 4 a.m., Friday. **Trail Sign #41** is on the left side of the road next to the bike trail.

Campbell's Station railroad crossing looking west down abandoned railroad. Leatherwood Creek and bridge site on the right. Cars parked on site of Fordyce warehouse and depot.

JOHN HUNT MORGAN HERITAGE TRAIL INTERPRETIVE SIGN #41

Before cutting the telegraph wires in Campbell's Station, one of Morgan's telegraphers, using the name of a Union general, contacted Barnesville. He inquired about the high railroad trestle across Leatherwood Creek at Bailey's Mills between Spencer's Station and Barnesville.

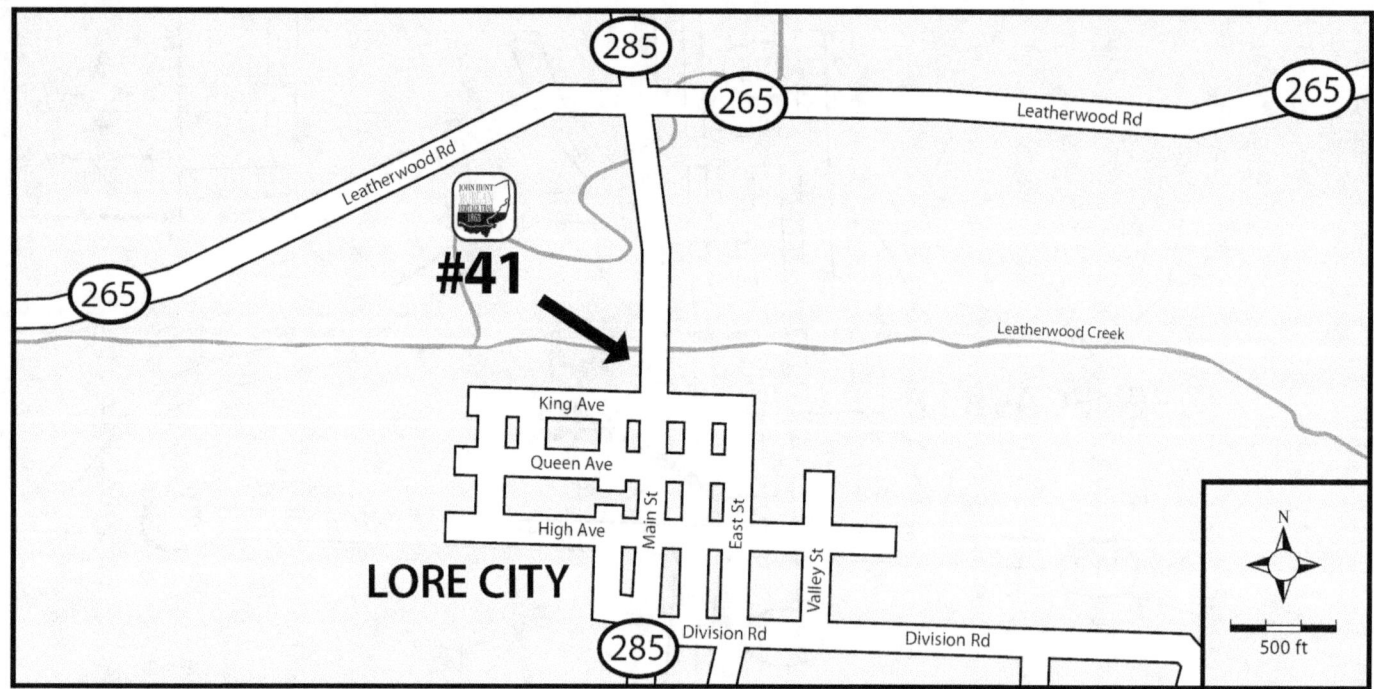

John Hunt Morgan Heritage Trail Interpretive sign #41 map

Provost Marshal David McCartney of the 17th District of Ohio was in the Barnesville office when the message came through. Surmising Morgan intended to burn the span, he sent a message back that there were sufficient men there to defend the bridge.

He then called on the 400-man Millwood Township Militia to guard the trestle, which was considered vital to the war effort. The Central Ohio (Baltimore and Ohio [B & O]) Railroad served as the main route for transporting Union troops and supplies between the eastern and western theatres. The bridge was 75 feet high and more than 1,000 feet long.

A call went out for help in guarding the vital structure; other area militia units soon arrived. Colonel Charlesworth, in charge of the district's militia, established "Camp Trestle" to house and support the men. The men were discharged after four days, when word came of Morgan's capture in Columbiana County. The government later paid each trestle defender for four days' service at soldier's pay of $13 per month.

Prior to Morgan's capture, the panicked citizens of Barnesville voted to surrender their town without a fight, while Morgan was still almost eighteen miles away at Campbell's Station.

After Morgan was captured, papers found on his person suggested he had planned on turning at Campbell's Station to move due east through Barnesville in an attempt to reach the Ohio River at Moundsville, West Virginia, approximately thirty-five miles away. If that had been his intent, he apparently had changed his mind.

Morgan's men were particularly destructive in Campbell's Station. They burned the Fordyce warehouse, which served as the depot, several other railroad buildings, and three freight cars filled with tobacco. Also, Morgan took $4,000 from the Adams Express Company safe. His men cut the telegraph wires.

The John Fordyce residence was also burned. Morgan did not usually burn private property without provocation. The vicious destruction here was unusual; many felt it may have been payback: Captain Samuel W. Fordyce, a son of the town's most prominent businessman, was a daring Union cavalry officer responsible for a number of raids in Kentucky and Tennessee. Morgan or some of his men may have been aware of the relationship.

NELSONVILLE TO OLD WASHINGTON

Thomas Regan, the section foreman of the Central Ohio Railroad, moved westward along the tracks until he found a handcar. After lifting it onto the tracks, he climbed aboard and sped to warn the citizens of Cambridge with the news of Morgan's approach.

James Regan, the son of Thomas Regan, eluded Morgan's pickets and ran eleven miles to Spencer's Station. He arrived in time to warn the train conductor of Morgan's presence in Campbell's Station. By halting the passenger train, he saved approximately $50,000 being shipped by the railroad express company.

Leatherwood Creek is just beyond the abandoned railroad. Morgan ordered the Howe truss bridge burned to check Shackelford's progress.

Continue 3.9 miles north on SR 285. Turn right onto Old Mill Road after passing under Interstate 70 and just before reaching Old Church Road.

JOHN HUNT MORGAN HERITAGE TRAIL INTERPRETIVE SIGN #42

There is an **Ohio Historical Marker** on the left near the top of the hill. It describes Morgan's Raid in Old Washington, referred to as Washington in 1863.

A local man and telegraph operator, Lieutenant Colonel James Laughlin, 1st Ohio Cavalry, was home from the war. He stayed close to the telegraph the previous day, following Morgan's progress. He warned the townsfolk that Morgan was headed their way. In anticipation of the raiders' arrival, the Washington Bank had shipped its money to Wheeling. Valuables were concealed and horses were hidden in the woods away from the roads. Only the children slept that night.

Leatherwood Creek bridge site

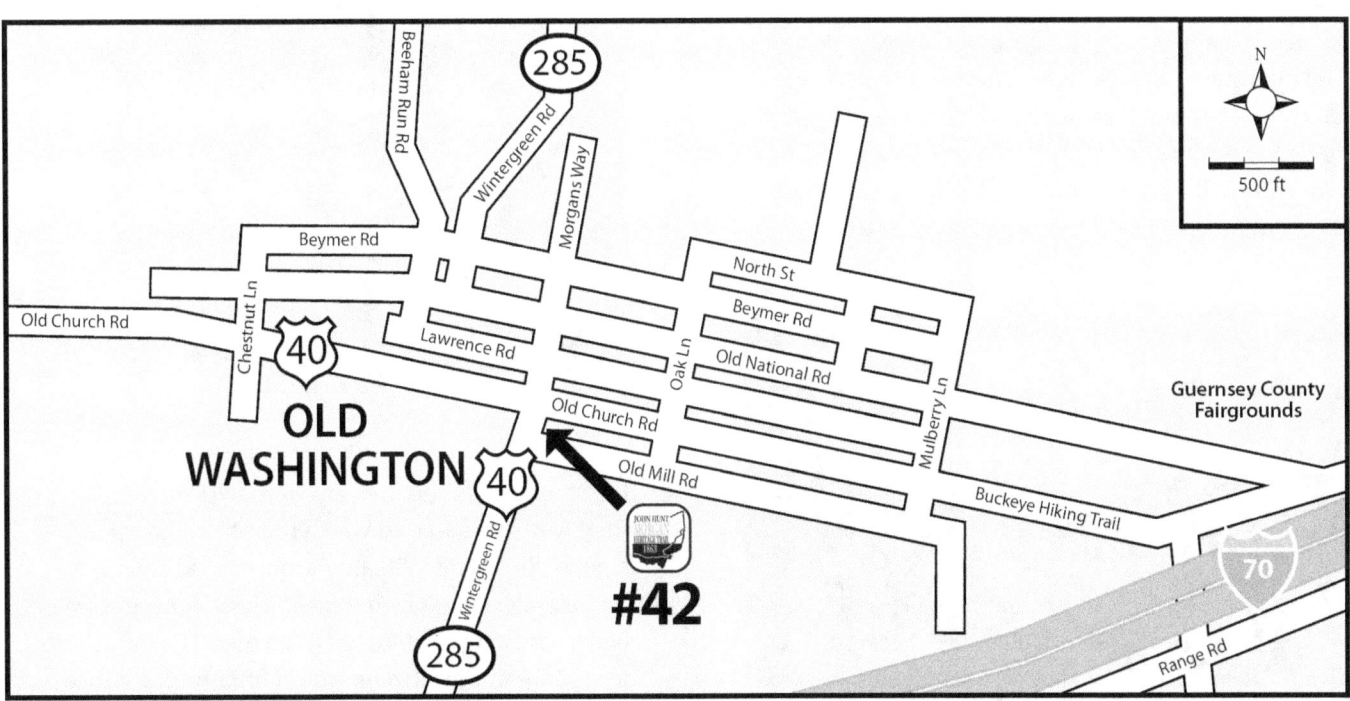

John Hunt Morgan Heritage Trail Interpretive sign #42 map

The following morning, word reached the town that Morgan was only twenty miles away. Laughlin called the Washington Minute Men to arms.

They rode south through Campbell's Station and Senecaville. Laughlin decided to make a stand at a bridge several miles beyond Senecaville. The order was given to destroy the bridge, and soon every plank was removed. His men, positioned near the bridge, did not have long to wait.

When the advance raiders arrived, Laughlin demanded they halt. They responded by veering off both sides of the road, riding through the undergrowth along the bank, and splashing across the shallow stream. The crossing took almost an hour.

The Washington Minute Men fell back to Greenwood Hill where they joined forces with Colonel Wallace's outfit. At the sounds of the approaching rebels, Wallace's force dispersed. It was every man for himself as the defenders raced back to Washington, arriving only minutes before the advance raiders.

The road through the town cemetery is one-way. The entrance to the cemetery is the second road on the right beyond the marker. Follow it through the cemetery; stop when you are about halfway down the hill toward the exit gate. There is a "Baird" grave stone on the right. Park; climb the hill to your left and go over its crest. About halfway down the other side you will find the graves of the three unknown Confederates killed in the skirmish at Washington.

Graves of three Confederates killed at Old Washington.

When Shackelford's Union troops arrived, they positioned the artillery of Captain Neil's 22nd Ohio Battery near here on the cemetery hill. Adjutant Carpenter's detachment of the 1st Kentucky U.S. Cavalry and Captain Ward's Company G of the 3rd Kentucky U.S. Cavalry led the advance. Company G included Twyman's Independent Company of Scouts, an experienced group of trackers from Kentucky.

Leave the cemetery and turn left onto Old Mill Road. Turn right onto Morgans Way (SR 285) and go straight from the stop sign at US 40. The Old Washington city-limit markers proclaim: "Site of Skirmish with John H. Morgan's Confederate Raiders." Go to the next stop sign, which is the Old National Road (old US 40).

Morgan's advance troops reached the town (population 741 at the time) about 8 a.m. on Friday. As they entered town they rode by the Colonial Inn on the southwest corner of the Old National Road and SR 285. In 1863, the house was owned by merchant Albert G. Lawrence, who lost a horse to the raiders. The house became an inn after the war.

The Colonial Inn (c. 1857), home of Albert G. Lawrence.

The anxious citizens of Washington had seen the smoke from the fires in Campbell's Station; they were prepared to watch their town go up in smoke. Reverend William Ferguson was chosen as their spokesman. He met the raiders at the crossroads; he was waving a white handkerchief. The minister told Morgan the citizens would offer no resistance if he would spare their town.

Morgan placed pickets two miles out on all roads leading to the town. The local men were rounded up and held as prisoners at Barton's Grove until they could be paroled.

The raiders were primarily concerned with food and rest. Morgan and fourteen of his staff had breakfast and took naps upstairs at the American Hotel, run by James Smith. The hotel was located on the Old National Road, its site being 206 Old National Road.

Site of the American Hotel (left of post office)

John Lawrence's boot and leather store at 213 Old National Road lost a pair of boots, a bridle, halters, one girth, and two padlocks to the raiders. Upstairs was the Masonic Hall.

Morgan's men ate in private homes; many were lying about the streets resting. Some of them looted William A. Lawrence's store, taking hats, neckties, boots, and socks. William C. Lawrence, who lived at 220 Old National Road, lost merchandise and a barrel of mackerel to the hungry raiders. Living across the street at 225, Francis Rea had owned much of the tobacco burned at Campbell's Station.

Because stage driver Charles Simms had been warned of the raiders' presence in Old Washington, he tossed the mail off the coach before reaching the center of town. Several men hid the mail in a cellar, where it remained until the raiders departed. When Simms stopped the coach, he lost his horses to the raiders, but he had saved the incoming mail. The outgoing mail bag at the post office was ripped open by raiders looking for cash and information regarding movements of the Union army.

The citizens of Cambridge feared Morgan would turn west and attack the county seat. A band of armed Cambridge citizens moved east along the Old National Road, and others joined them along the route. They were prepared to turn Morgan back and save Cambridge.

They halted when they reached Hyde's Hill, 2.2 miles west of Old Washington on the National Road. Two scouts were sent ahead. They panicked when confronted by Morgan's two pickets at Hyde Hill Tavern. Wheeling their horses about, they raced back toward Cambridge. As they passed their comrades, they shouted that Morgan's entire force was behind them. The terrified "army" of volunteers immediately dispersed. Six were captured by Morgan's men but were soon released. Instead of glory, the veterans of the Battle of Hyde's Hill received only ridicule.

View from the Union gun position. From here, Union cavalrymen shot raiders and horses on the Old National Road. As raiders moved up the opposite hill, they came under Union fire. Morgans Way is on the left.

The raiders had been in Washington less than three hours when Shackelford's men arrived.

The following account is from a sixteen-year-old eyewitness, Elizabeth E. McMullen (McMillin):

> Looking to the south we saw Shackleford's army gathering on Cemetery hill. We wondered what would happen and we soon learned. They began firing at the Confederates who, in turn, shot back. Women were screaming and children were crying. The shooting increased. Above the noise of battle we could hear voices coming from the Federal lines,

ordering women and children to run to cellars. I ran into the one that was nearest, where 20 or 30 other persons were gathered.

The firing continued. They were shooting across the town. The Union men were firing from the south; the Confederates from the north. We could hear the bullets whizzing over our heads and the crash of broken windows. It was terrible, as we did not know what would happen to us who were in the direct line of fire."

The Union soldiers continued to fire as the raiders moved from the Old National Road north to the densely wooded area north of town. From there the Confederates continued firing at the approaching Union troops. Then Morgan ordered a withdrawal, and the raiders mounted their horses and fled north toward Winchester. Although only a skirmish, this action was referred to as "The Battle of Washington."

Turn right and drive three blocks on the Old National Road. There is a **stone historical marker** in front of the playground on the left. It was erected by the Sons of Union Veterans in 1927. Although the marker states that Morgan's Raiders were overtaken and defeated at Washington, the raid was not over. It would be two days and many more skirmishes before Morgan surrendered.

Turn around. Reverend Ferguson's Presbyterian church is located beyond the playground at 227 Old National Road.

Old Washington Presbyterian Church

When Ferguson waved his white handkerchief and surrendered Washington to the raiders, he was probably concerned not only about saving the town and its citizens, but also his new church. It had been completed in 1861, at a cost of $12,000. The church is still in use; however, the original tall steeple was replaced in 1936.

When "The Battle of Washington" ended, dead and wounded men and horses were lying in the street. Three raiders were killed, several were wounded, and eight were captured.

The prisoners were held in the old Miller Academy building until the next day, when they were marched to Cambridge. They were imprisoned in the Guernsey County Jail until they could be transferred to Columbus.

Harper's Weekly considered the skirmish in Washington, Ohio, to be of significance. The week following the action, the magazine's editor sent an artist to sketch Morgan's entrance into the town. In the woodcut, Morgans Way is in the foreground and the Presbyterian church is in the background.

1927 marker in Old Washington

NELSONVILLE TO OLD WASHINGTON

Woodcut from *Harper's Weekly*, August 15, 1863

Drive three blocks to Morgans Way/SR 285.

*Side Trip: The Guernsey County Historical Museum has raid-related items. The museum is located in Cambridge. To reach it, turn left on Morgans Way/SR 285 and turn right onto US 40.

Drive 2.2 miles and turn left onto Wardeska Lane (TR 6542). Go 0.1 mile to a driveway on the right.

The private home on the right at 13442 Wardeska Lane is the Hyde Hill Tavern, named after its owner in 1863, Thomas Hyde. General Morgan sent two scouts to the tavern to watch for Union troops coming from Cambridge. It was here that the so-called "Battle of Hyde's Hill" occurred. The house's driveway is a segment of the wartime National Road.

Hyde Hill Tavern

Turn around. About 50 yards down Wardeska Lane from the Hyde Hill Tavern's driveway, on the right, is the original brick-paved remnants of the National Road.

Return to US 40. Turn left onto US 40 and go 6.1 miles west on US 40 to the courthouse square in downtown Cambridge. Turn right onto East 8th Street; at the end of the street, turn left onto Steubenville Avenue, and then make an immediate right turn onto North 8th Street. The museum is located at 218 North 8th Street, one block behind the courthouse. Hours: Tuesdays, Thursdays, and Saturdays, noon–3 p.m. Closed January through March. Phone: (740) 439-5884; Web site: *http://www.visitguernseycounty.com/directory/discover/attractions/guernsey-county-historical-museum.html*

Take US 40 East and return to the junction of SR 285 in Old Washington. Turn left and go one block to Old National Road.*

Chapter Nine
OLD WASHINGTON TO WEST POINT

Friday, July 24, 1863

We will follow Morgan's main column north toward Winterset and Antrim.

A small company rode east to Hendrysburg. There, they turned north, followed a road that no longer exists, and moved up the Stillwater Valley to Moorefield.

Before leaving Washington, General Shackelford's division was reinforced by seven mounted companies of the 86th Ohio Volunteer Infantry (OVI) under Colonel Wilson C. Lemert, which had ridden from Cambridge.

Return to SR 285 (Morgans Way). Go straight and reset your odometer. Leave Old Washington on SR 285 North; the road turns right and goes up the hill. A sharp skirmish occurred just over the top of the hill.

There was a running skirmish for the next three miles to the bridge over Salt Fork. Heavy fighting took place on the William H. Hays farm, which is now occupied by the Buckeye Trail High School at the intersection of SR 285 and Norris Road.

Go 1.1 miles to the intersection with Lake Ridge Road (TR 50). Morgan's rear guard made a brief stand on the farm of Archibald Shipley, located approximately 0.2 mile north of this intersection. Shackelford's advance guard, consisting of Captain Ward's company of the 3rd Kentucky (U.S.) Cavalry and Adjutant Carpenter's detachment of the 1st Kentucky (U.S.) Cavalry, deployed in line of battle here and quickly drove Morgan's men from their position in a dense wood, through which the road to Winchester (Winterset) passed. After the raid, Shipley filed a claim for reimbursement for an ox that was killed by a stray bullet fired during the skirmish.

Continue 1.9 miles on SR 285 to the bridge over Salt Fork creek, before the intersection with Fogle Road (TR 671). Face north toward the bridge.

A second stand occurred here at Salt Fork Bridge, also referred to as the Skirmish at Hanna's Mill. Henry H. Hanna's house once stood on the left

Site of covered bridge over Salt Fork

side of SR 285 at the far end of the present-day bridge. His saw mill operated in the flats behind you on the left. Both buildings are now gone.

After Morgan's column galloped over the bridge, his rear guard removed the wooden planks from the span to prevent the Union cavalrymen from using it. The rear guard then formed a line of battle in the woods on the hill just beyond the bridge.

Ward's and Carpenter's Kentucky cavalrymen deployed in the flat area behind you on the right of the road, which was a meadow in 1863. They dismounted along the creek bank on the Confederates' left flank. Meanwhile, a portion of the 14th Illinois Cavalry forded the creek a few yards to the right of the bridge. Under heavy fire from Morgan's troopers, the Illinois cavalrymen moved steadily up the hill and pushed the Confederates back. Morgan's main force slipped away, gaining a full hour's advantage over the Union troops. Morgan and his rear guard, mounted on fleet horses, were soon able to rejoin the main column.

Three raiders were captured in the skirmish at Hanna's Mill. A Union soldier was wounded and taken to Winterset (Winchester in 1863) for treatment. After this second stand, the raiders were able to outdistance their pursuers.

Samuel Johnson and two other scouts from Winchester were riding toward the Salt Fork Valley when they encountered the raiders. They were impressed to serve as guides to Antrim, where they were released. Morgan kept Johnson's horse, giving him a jaded mount in its place. As the scouts rode back toward Winchester, they met Union soldiers, who confiscated the horse and left Johnson to return home on foot.

It is 2.1 miles from the Salt Fork Bridge to US 22 in Winterset (formally called Winchester). It was reported that as Morgan approached the town, local men serving under Captain Prentiss fled to the oat fields. The women went to the home of the minister for a prayer meeting.

Side Note: Salt Fork State Park is 2.7 miles west on US 22. The lodge, which is located 6.9 miles inside the park, has a mural of Morgan's Raid on the dining room wall. One of the facility's conference rooms is named for Morgan.

Morgan's men left Winchester about 12:30 p.m. A report by Colonel Cyrus P. B. Sarchet of the pursuing militia states that Morgan split his force and sent a small column directly to Antrim, while the main force rode in a feint toward Birmingham. Shackelford followed Morgan. Had Morgan taken the direct route to Antrim, his troops would have been in plain sight of his pursuers along a long stretch of open road.

Cross US 22 and you are on Birmingham Road (CR 71). Drive 2.6 miles and then turn right onto Anderson Road (CR 82). It is 3.7 miles to US 22 in Antrim (population about 237 in 1863).

Madison College was located in Antrim. It closed its doors at the start of the war and never reopened. Citizens rang the college bell to warn of the raiders' approach. Most of the able-bodied men and older boys were away, however, serving with the army or the militia.

Presbyterian minister Alexander L. Knox rode up and down the street, calming the frantic citizens and warning them to hide their horses. He urged them to keep out in the open and not appear frightened.

It was about 2 p.m. when the rebels arrived. The column kept moving; the raiders seemed in a hurry. Some of the men looted Tom Gill's store, taking $30 worth of tobacco, provisions, and clothing. It was reported that Morgan was riding at the rear of the column, in a buggy driven by a black driver. Several of the exhausted raiders rested for a few hours before moving on.

Soon after the raiders departed Antrim, Shackelford's men arrived. As they rode into town, it began to rain. The downpour continued for the remainder of the day. The women of Antrim prepared supper for the hungry pursuers.

Reset your odometer and turn left onto US 22. As you leave Antrim, Madison College was located on the hill on the right, near the intersection with Lodge Road.

Madison College (drawn by Mrs. Paul D. Ewing)

At 3.9 miles, you pass through Londonderry. The town was plotted in 1815 by an Irish immigrant. He named it in honor of his family's hometown. He had grandiose plans for his new town, but they never materialized. By 1860, the population was only sixty-seven.

Colonel Sarchet noted in his report that he was experiencing severe stomach and bowel pain by the time he reached Londonderry. He stopped at the home of his friend Doctor John McCall, who prepared a medicine to relieve his complaints.

Continue 3.8 miles to Smyrna. Reset your odometer at the city limits.

After spending more than twenty-four hours in Guernsey County, the raiders entered Harrison County. The raiders rode through Smyrna about 4:30 p.m. on Friday. Morgan's men stopped briefly to appropriate five horses. They also looted David B. Armstrong's dry goods store and Bartlett Davidson's harness shop.

Stay on US 22 for 0.9 mile. There is a dead-end road on the right (Morrison Road), which led down the hill to the covered bridge across Big Stillwater Creek at Collinsport. The road was closed when Big Stillwater Creek was dammed. Morgan followed Morrison Road.

Morgan crossed and then burned the covered bridge west of Collinsport. The Union artillery and some of the pursuers detoured up the creek to another bridge. Most of the Union troops were forced to ford Big Stillwater Creek. It was not an easy crossing. Sarchet described it: "Crossing by twos, plouting into the mud and water up to the saddle skirts, plunging through, and hallooing back to those in the rear, 'over'; then a steep, slippery bank had to be climbed to reach the road." Once the exhausted men had forded the creek, many laid down on the bank to await the arrival of the men and artillery that had crossed upstream.

Continue 1.3 miles on US 22 and turn right into the rest area parking lot.

JOHN HUNT MORGAN HERITAGE TRAIL INTERPRETIVE SIGN #43

Drive another 0.3 mile on US 22 and turn right onto Belmont Ridge Road (CR 10). It is 0.3 mile to the end of the Piedmont Dam. The lower part of Collinsport, the old mill, and the Stillwater covered bridge sites were to the right, but are now submerged.

Site of Boggs Fork covered bridge

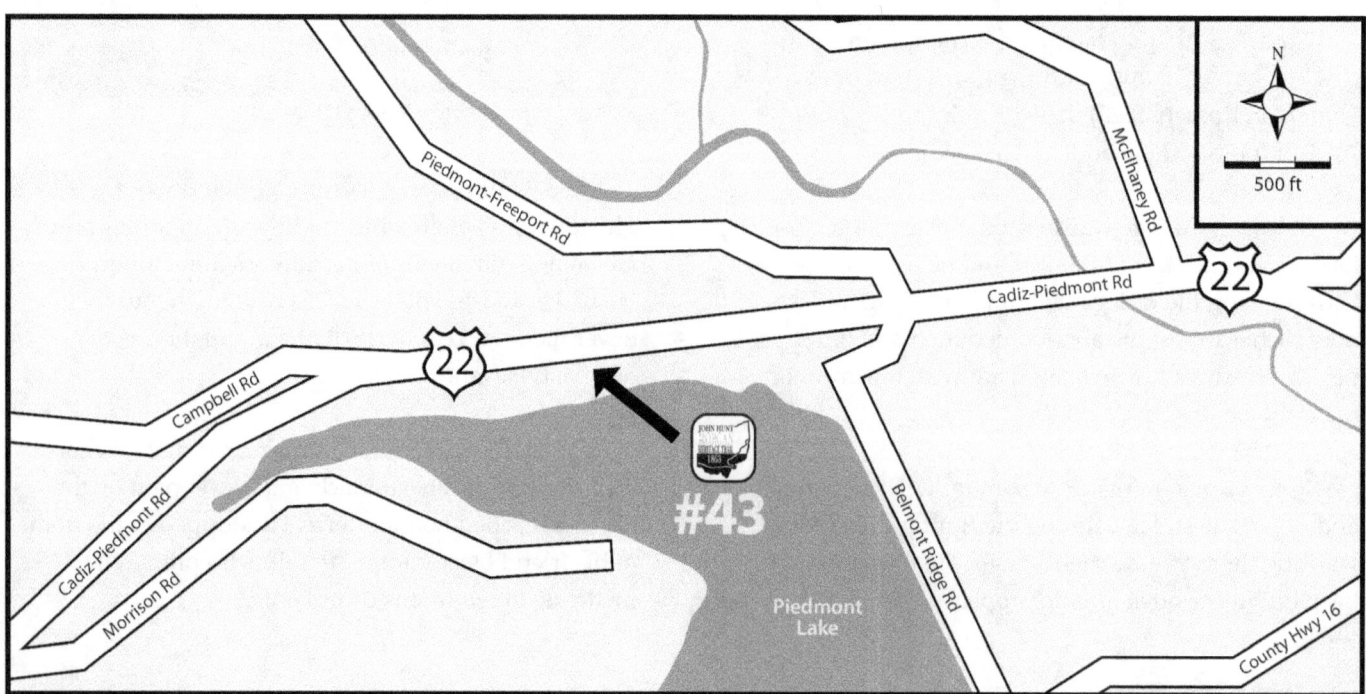
John Hunt Morgan Heritage Trail Interpretive sign #43 map

OLD WASHINGTON TO WEST POINT

Turn left onto CR 16 (Old Piedmont Road) and drive through the upper part of old Collinsport (present-day Piedmont). It is 0.4 mile to the bridge over Boggs Fork. The bridge is in the same location as the Little Stillwater (Boggs Fork) covered bridge burned by the raiders.

Cross the bridge and bear right; it is 0.1 mile to US 22. Turn right and reset your odometer.

Go 1.5 miles to Moorefield. As you enter the town there is an **Ohio Historical Marker** on the right. Pull over at the historical marker.

JOHN HUNT MORGAN HERITAGE TRAIL INTERPRETIVE SIGN #44

Cadiz was the Harrison County seat. The previous evening, July 23, the Cadiz mayor had received a telegraph informing him that Morgan and his men were north of the National Road. A Military Committee was formed and a call went out for men and arms to defend the county.

On Friday afternoon, Cadiz scouts M. J. Brown and John Robinson passed through Moorefield. The men, driving a team of spirited horses, had been sent toward Cambridge to discover the rebels' line of march. Within an hour, the two Cadiz men rushed back through Moorefield, yelling that the rebels were coming. The citizens had also seen the rising columns of smoke from the burning Stillwater Creek bridges.

When Morgan's advance men rode into town, some local men, who had not heeded the warning, took off on their horses. The raiders gave chase. Some of the men were captured and their horses were taken. Other locals won the race and saved their steeds.

Morgan's main force arrived in town about 6 p.m. Pickets were posted east and west of town. The column that had ridden through Hendrysburg rejoined the main force here.

The men were famished and exhausted. They solicited food from every house. Thomas McGee and Samuel West both provided meals for about forty men. One resident commented, "They exhibited abnormal appetites for pound cake and preserves."

After eating, the raiders sought rest and sleep. They took temporary possession of all the houses that had been vacated when the frightened occupants fled

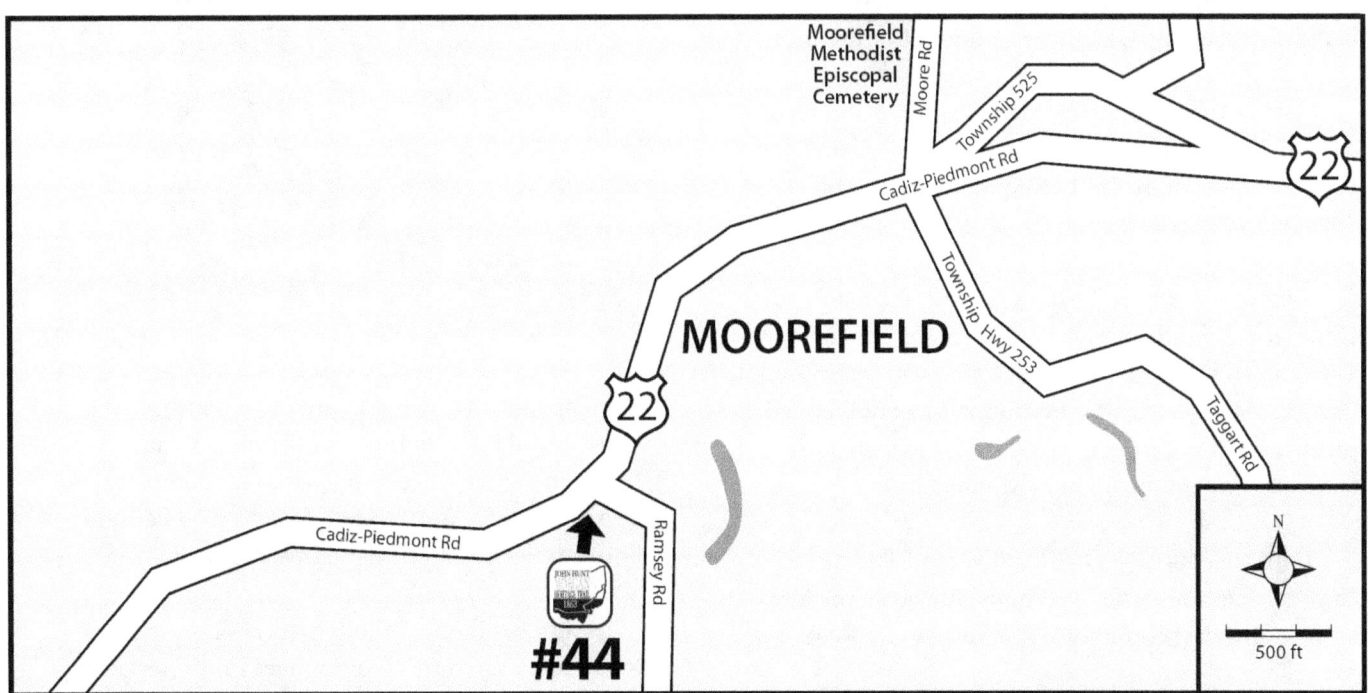

John Hunt Morgan Heritage Trail Interpretive sign #44 map

to the woods. The Confederates did not disturb or forcibly enter any house where families remained at home.

While many of the raiders rested, others visited the town's stores. George L. Wharton's store was later awarded $330 for stolen merchandise.

Drive 0.3 mile on US 22. The Mills Hotel, now a residence, is on the right.

Mills Hotel

Reverend Thomas Crawford 's Moorefield home

Morgan slept in the bed in the parlor while his bodyguards read the news. He did not know he was sleeping on the money, money-orders, and stamps from the post office. The innkeeper, who also served as postmaster, had hidden the valuables between the bed ticks when the Cadiz men sounded the alarm.

After a three-hour nap, Morgan got up and took a stroll down the street. Within an hour he heard the warning shot that indicated the approach of Shackelford's lead troopers.

Delayed by the Stillwater crossing, the main Union force did not arrive in Moorefield until evening. The women were put to work cooking and serving the Union soldiers until after midnight. Most of the men pushed on after Morgan, but some, who were most exhausted, spent the night in Moorefield.

Drive one block on US 22. Reverend Thomas R. Crawford and his wife lived in the house on the left at the northwest corner of US 22 and Moore Road.

Before the raiders arrived, the Crawfords packed their silverware and best clothes in a trunk and sent it along with Lizzie, their adopted ten-year-old niece, to the country home of visiting parishioners. Thomas's wife, Isabel, joined her. Crawford later wrote a detailed account of Morgan's visit to the town.

Reverend T. R. Crawford

The raiders entered Crawford's house. One of them found his sermons. Using one of them, the raider began in a loud voice to preach to his companions. The mock service soon ended when they became bored and started yelling, "Amen! Amen!"

It is 3.0 miles to Nottingham-Holloway Road. Reverend Crawford's Nottingham Presbyterian Church is ahead on the right. The cemetery is located a

OLD WASHINGTON TO WEST POINT

Nottingham Presbyterian Church (c. 1861)

short distance along Nottingham-Holloway Road on the right.

Before leaving Moorefield, Morgan forced Adolphus Julius Schreiber, a local storekeeper, and Jacob Jarvis, the county surveyor, to serve as guides.

On learning that Morgan was conscripting local men to serve as guides, Crawford left his home and hid in a cornfield. He moved through the fields to the church. He was hiding under bushes in the cemetery when the raiders arrived at the nearby church grove.

The minister was terrified, not knowing whether to stay or run. He heard several raiders near the church call out his name; he lay motionless. Then a shout rang out, and the men mounted and rode away.

Reverend Crawford served the church for forty years. He is buried in the front row of the cemetery in which he sought refuge during the raid.

Rev. Crawford's grave

Go 1.4 miles east on US 22. The Rankin Church is on the hill to your left. Raiders rested their horses in the church yard. The present church was built in the 1870s to replace an 1814 log building.

Rankin Methodist Church (c. 1870)

The road ahead (US 22) leads to Cadiz. In 1863, the road ran in front of the church. When scouts warned Morgan that Cadiz was occupied by a strong force of militia, he turned east toward New Athens.

James Kirkpatrick, who lived across the road from the church (where the nearby shed stands), was taken prisoner and forced to serve as the guide to New Athens. He was ordered to ride on the same horse with Schreiber, the 225-pound guide from Moorefield.

At the Thomas A. Gordon farm, about 0.6 mile southeast of Rankin Church on SR 519, the raiders confiscated all the food in the cellar. One saddle-sore Confederate begged Mrs. Mary Gordon for a pillow.

James Clemens lived 0.7 mile down SR 519 from the Gordons on the right side of the road. The raiders pillaged his house, stole two horses, and forced Clemens to ride with them. Morgan noticed a bulge and a rattling noise coming from Clemens's pockets. Clemens said it was only his pipe, but Morgan ordered him to hand it over. Clemens lost the $200 he had pocketed, against his daughter's wishes, when he had heard the Confederates were in the area.

Turn right onto SR 519 and go 3.8 miles to a crossroads. At the time of the raid, this crossroads was known as Stumptown.

Morgan also picked up Clemens's neighbor, Joshua T. Dickerson. Dickerson would direct the raiders through the dense woods north of New Athens. He was first ordered to ride behind the saddle of a cavalryman. Later, he was given a horse, which he was forced to ride without a saddle and bridle.

At Stumptown, the raiders turned left onto Cadiz-Flushing Road (CR 29). Portions of that road no longer exist. Near here, Schreiber was able to escape into a cornfield while the raiders stopped to repair a washed-out culvert.

The raiders traveled over Culbertson's Hill and came out of the woods onto the Cadiz-New Athens Road (SR 9) at the bottom of Webb's Hill, 1.5 miles north of New Athens. From there, they went straight on the Short Creek Valley Road (TR 95) toward Georgetown. After midnight, Morgan's men made camp on the Worley and Dickerson farms.

Unable to follow Morgan, we will follow Shackelford's troops 2.4 miles on SR 519 to the stop sign in New Athens.

Most of the Union troops spent the night in the town. Before leaving the next morning, Shackelford's men ate a hearty breakfast prepared by the grateful townswomen. Because New Athens was an abolitionist stronghold, the citizens were terrified of Morgan and his Southern troops.

*Side Trip: Turn left onto SR 9 and drive 0.2 mile to Franklin College (1825–1921), on the left at 187 North Main Street. The present building was erected in 1900. Moorefield's Reverend Crawford was a graduate. The college was a strong abolitionist institution. The students volunteered to join the Union force; Shackelford politely declined their offer. The museum, which features a Morgan's Raid exhibit, has limited hours: Tuesday, Wednesday, and Thursday, noon–4 p.m., May–September. Phone: (740) 968-1042 or (740) 968-4066; Web site: http://consumer.discoverohio.com/searchdetails.aspx?detail=56010. There is an **Ohio Historical Marker** at the site. Go back to SR 519 and turn left.*

Franklin College as it appeared during the Civil War.

Go 1.0 mile on SR 519 and turn left onto Georgetown Road (CR 41). At 0.7 mile the raiders came in from the left. The raiders had camped along that road at Dan Worley's sugar grove and W. W. Dickerson's farm located 1.0 and 0.8 mile northwest of here. Heavy strip mining has wiped out all vestiges of these farms.

Saturday, July 25, 1863

The raiders broke camp about 4 a.m. Drive 1.6 miles on Georgetown Road. The area of abandoned coal company property on the left was the John N. Hanna farm. Morgan halted here and sent scouts forward. They returned with the news that approximately 1,000 Union men had formed a battle line on the hill at the outskirts of Georgetown.

Knowing that Shackelford was nearby, Morgan chose not to fight. Drive 0.6 mile to the intersection with Jameson Road and look to the right. To avoid a skirmish at Georgetown, Morgan's men turned south here on a road that no longer exists. They rode for approximately 1.3 miles and then turned east to Harrisville. As they moved along that road they were fired on by Shackelford's artillery, the three guns of Captain Henry M. Neil's 22nd Ohio Battery Light Artillery, positioned 0.9 mile away at Hammonds Crossroads. One of Neil's 6-pounder guns, under the guidance of Lieutenant Amos B. Alger, fired thirteen rounds at the fleeing Confederates. Two raiders were wounded, and a number of trees were shattered.

Continue 0.6 mile on Georgetown Road. Here on the outskirts of Georgetown, Morgan's scouts encountered the Harrison County militia. One of Morgan's scouts was captured; the others returned to the Hanna farm.

OLD WASHINGTON TO WEST POINT

The Harrison County Military Committee had requested arms from Governor Tod, but the committee was concerned that the guns would not come in time. The 500 rifles and 40 rounds of ammunition arrived by train about 6 p.m. on Friday. The men of the Cadiz Militia were soon outfitted and fed, after which they marched to Georgetown.

The men were serving under the command of sixty-five-year-old Judge Samuel W. Bostwick. He was an experienced soldier and a major-general of the Ohio militia. Arriving during the night, Bostwick placed his men on the crest of the hill here overlooking the valley road. When several young militiamen wanted to open fire on Morgan's scouts, Bostwick ordered them to hold their fire. He did not want to waste the lives of his young charges.

Go 0.3 mile to the stop sign in Georgetown and turn right onto US 250. **Trail Sign #45** is just beyond the first street on the right.

JOHN HUNT MORGAN HERITAGE TRAIL INTERPRETIVE SIGN #45

At the junction with SR 519, in about 2.2 miles, we rejoin Morgan's men. After turning east at a point 1.4 miles west of here, they came dashing in from the right, under fire from the Union artillery. Shackelford did not pursue Morgan immediately; he delayed leaving Hammonds Crossroads (2.4 miles west of here) for almost two hours. He claimed that his men and horses were exhausted.

Judge Bostwick marched his men from Georgetown to this intersection; he hoped to reach it before Morgan arrived. They were on foot and therefore slower than the mounted rebels. By the time the militiamen arrived here, Morgan's men were already in Harrisville.

Stay on US 250; it is 1.5 miles to Mirics Ridge Road (TR 82) at the Harrisville post office. **Trail Sign #46** is near this intersection.

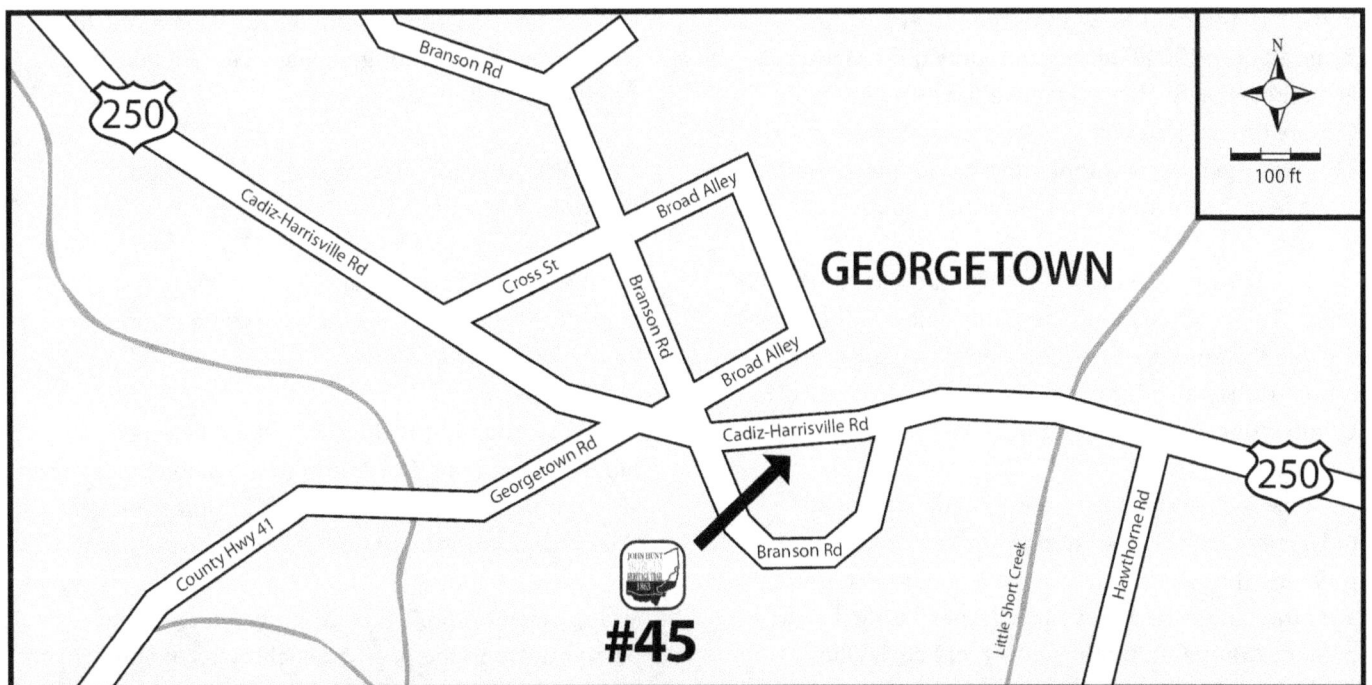

John Hunt Morgan Heritage Trail Interpretive sign #45 map

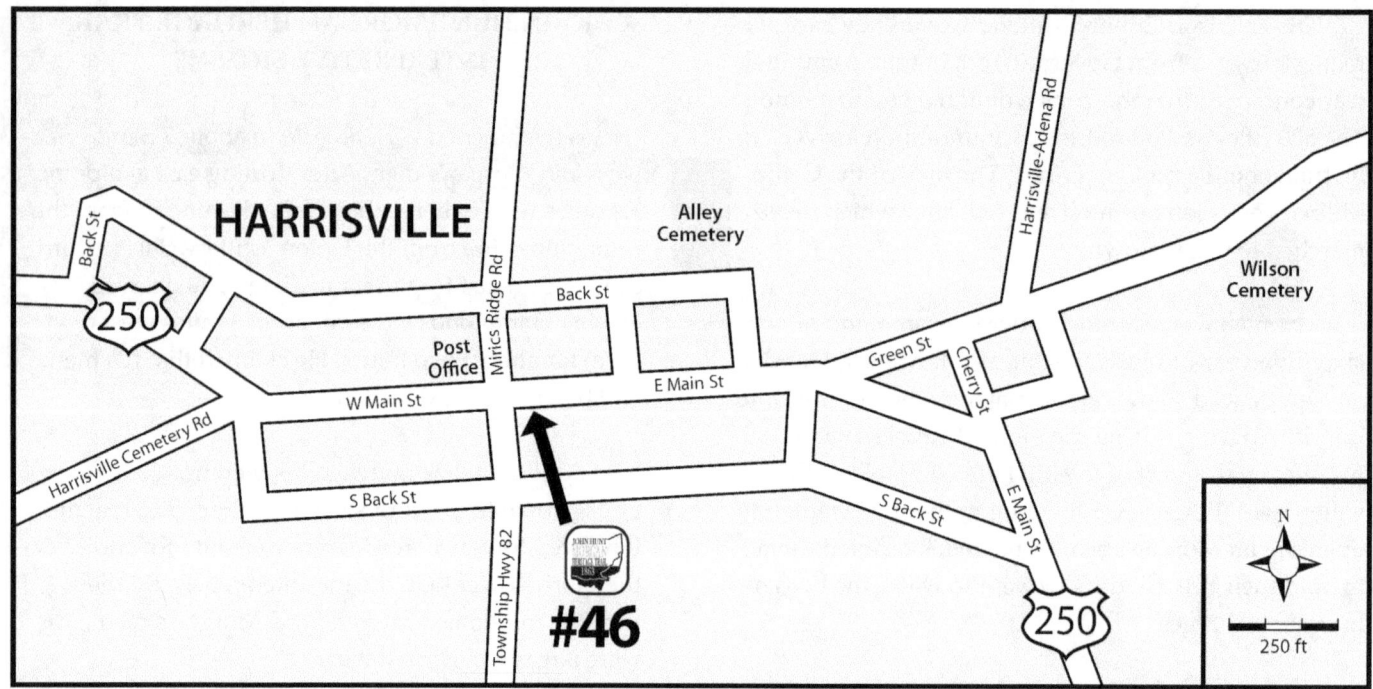

John Hunt Morgan Heritage Trail Interpretive sign #46 map

JOHN HUNT MORGAN HERITAGE TRAIL INTERPRETIVE SIGN #46

Continue on US 250 for approximately 0.1 mile to the "Y" intersection with Green Street (CR 10). Bear left onto CR 10. **Jefferson County (J.C.) Marker #1** is on the left side after you make the turn. Jefferson County erected fourteen Morgan's Raid markers in 1913. This was the most ambitious attempt at interpretative signage by any county along Morgan's route.

The hard-pressed rebels passed through Harrisville about 7 a.m. While there, they stole at least nine horses and ate the food prepared for their pursuers. It was reported they also captured twenty-seven advance Union scouts of the 4th Virginia U.S. Cavalry.

Bostwick and his persistent militia continued to Harrisville; he hoped to prevent the raiders from pillaging the village. They arrived about ten minutes after the raiders had moved out. After eating a hearty breakfast prepared by the women of Harrisville, the Harrison County militia continued its pursuit.

Bostwick's men marched through southwestern Jefferson County all the way to Warrenton, where it was thought the raiders intended to cross the Ohio River. Monday, after Morgan's capture, wagons were dispatched from Cadiz to convey their men home.

Morgan followed Long Run from Harrisville to Ramsey. In 1863, there was a wagon road along the stream; the road no longer exists. We will take the ridge road to Ramsey.

Within a block, stay on CR 10 (Adena Pike, or Harrisville-Adena Road) as it bears to the left. Go 1.5 miles and turn right onto Morning Glow Lane (TR 129). After approximately 1.7 miles, look off to the right. The raiders would have come through that valley following Long Run.

We are again traveling with the rebels as they moved along Long Run through the hamlet of Ramsey. Go 1.2 miles to the stop sign with Mt. Pleasant-Adena Road; continue straight on CR 7 (Dillonvale-Long Run Road). Follow CR 7 for 3.1 miles to a stop sign and turn left onto SR 150. En route, you will have passed through the postwar coal towns of Dunglen, Newtown, and Olszeski.

It is 1.0 mile to an abandoned school on the right in Dillonvale. **J.C. Marker #2** is located in front of the building. At the time of the raid, the town of Dillonvale did not exist. The N. Updegraff Mills were located at the south corner of Rice and Main streets. Updegraff's house still stands on Rice Street near the west corner with Main Street. Stay on SR 150 as it turns left onto Main Street at the stop sign.

By Friday, July 24, it was apparent Morgan was headed toward Steubenville. The Jefferson County Courthouse bell was rung and a temporary militia was organized under command of Captains Prentiss, Walden, Burgess, and Boals.

That same evening Major General William T. H. Brooks, commanding the Department of the Monongahela at Pittsburgh, arrived in Steubenville with three regiments of Pennsylvania militia. He established his headquarters in the passenger depot of the Cleveland & Pittsburgh Railroad at the southwest corner of South and Water streets. He dispatched Colonel James R. Porter's 57th regiment fourteen miles downriver to guard the Warrenton ford near Rayland. Colonel George H. Bemus's 58th regiment was sent seven miles south to guard the ford at LaGrange (Brilliant). Colonel Thomas F. Gallagher's 54th regiment was first posted to guard the ford at Mingo, then at Rush Run between Warrenton and LaGrange. Brooks ordered a locomotive to stand by with steam up to move the forces from one point to another as might be needed.

General Burnside realized Union forces pursuing Morgan across three states had not been able to catch him. Now, by moving fresh troops by rail, Burnside hoped to place them in front of the raiders.

First, on July 23, Major George W. Rue's command was ordered from Covington, Kentucky, to Bellaire, Ohio. Rue's men crossed the Ohio River and boarded a Little Miami Railroad train for Columbus.

Next, Major William B. Way (9th Michigan Cavalry) was sent to Mingo Junction, where he arrived on July 25 with fresh troops and several pieces of artillery. His contingent of approximately 250 men was composed of Companies C, D, E, H, I, and K of his 9th Michigan Cavalry and two rifled guns of Battery L, 1st Michigan Light Artillery (11th Michigan Battery)

under Lieutenant Thomas Gallagher.

Rue's 375 fresh troops included 75 men of his own 9th Kentucky U.S. Cavalry, 120 men of the 11th Kentucky U.S. Cavalry (Maj. Milton Graham), 100 men from Companies C, F, L, and M of the 8th Michigan Cavalry (Lieutenant Nathan S. Boynton), and small detachments of the 1st Kentucky U.S. Cavalry and 12th Kentucky U.S. Cavalry. Rue's force also brought along three 3-inch Ordnance rifles from the 15th Indiana Independent Battery Light Artillery, commanded by Lieutenant William H. Torr. After changing trains in Columbus, they arrived in Bellaire on July 24. As the raiders moved north, Rue's troops, aboard flatcars, also moved to maintain their position between the raiders and the Ohio River.

So there would be no questions as to chain of command, Burnside wired Shackelford, telling him to assume command of the forces under Majors Way and Rue, but to obey any orders given by General Brooks.

It is 0.6 mile to the junction with SR 152. At the junction, stay to the right on SR 150. Reset your odometer.

Go 0.9 mile. Turn left onto CR 8 (Dry Fork Road) before the bridge across Dry Fork Run. As you turn, **J.C. Marker #3** is on your right, near the bridge. **Trail Sign #47** is next to the marker.

JOHN HUNT MORGAN HERITAGE TRAIL INTERPRETIVE SIGN #47

While Morgan was here at Deyarmonville, his scouts returned, and he learned that a Union force was waiting for him six miles away at Rayland (called Portland in 1863). Unable to cross at the Warrenton Ford, located about one mile northeast of Rayland, Morgan again moved north.

Go 1.0 mile on CR 8 and turn right onto TR 118; the name soon changes to CR 20. Near Smithfield, the raiders captured Captain William Collins and some militia. The raiders broke the militiamen's guns against trees and forced Collins to ride a mule back to

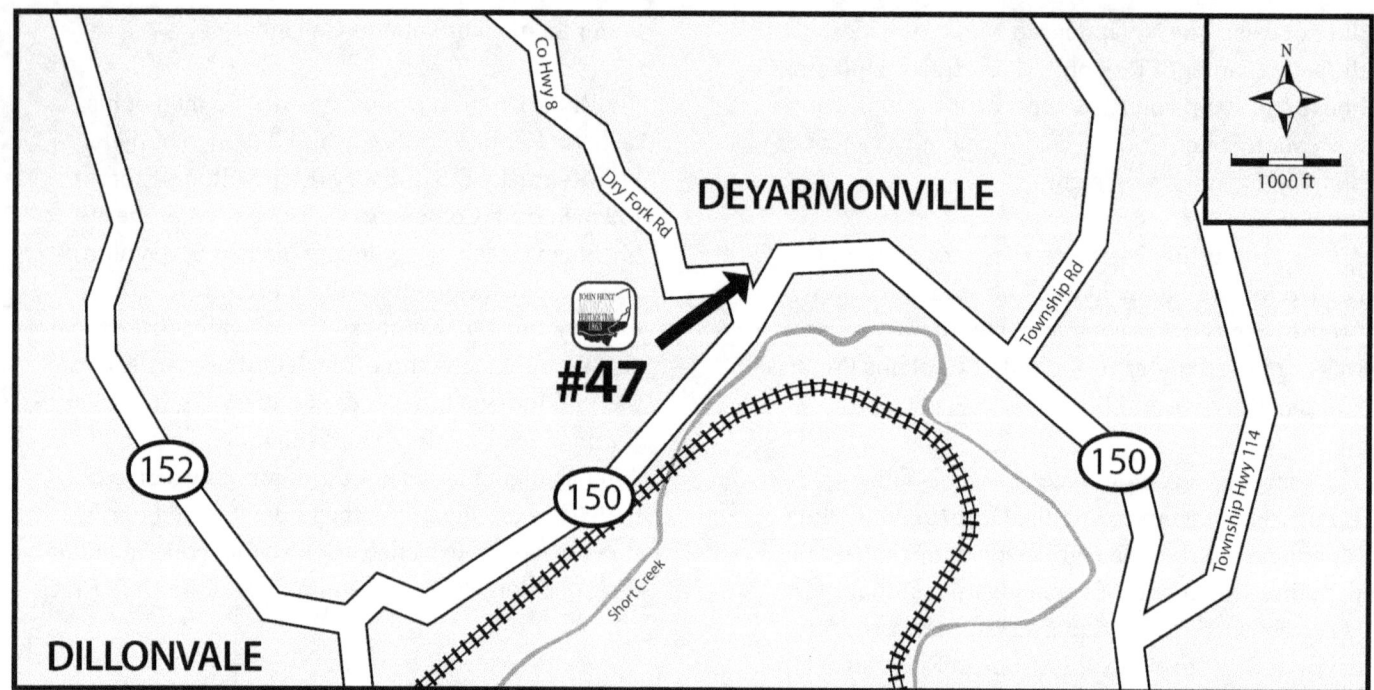

John Hunt Morgan Heritage Trail Interpretive sign #47 map

Smithfield. He was ordered to tell the townsfolk that the raiders were Union men, to be fed and treated well. The citizens responded and the well-fed raiders moved on.

It is 3.5 miles to SR 152; turn right and go 0.3 mile. **J.C. Marker** #4 is located on the left side, in front of the Smithfield Historical Society, next to the post office.

JOHN HUNT MORGAN HERITAGE TRAIL INTERPRETIVE SIGN #48

Before they left Smithfield, raiders unhitched and mounted the four fresh horses hitched to the New Alexandria stage.

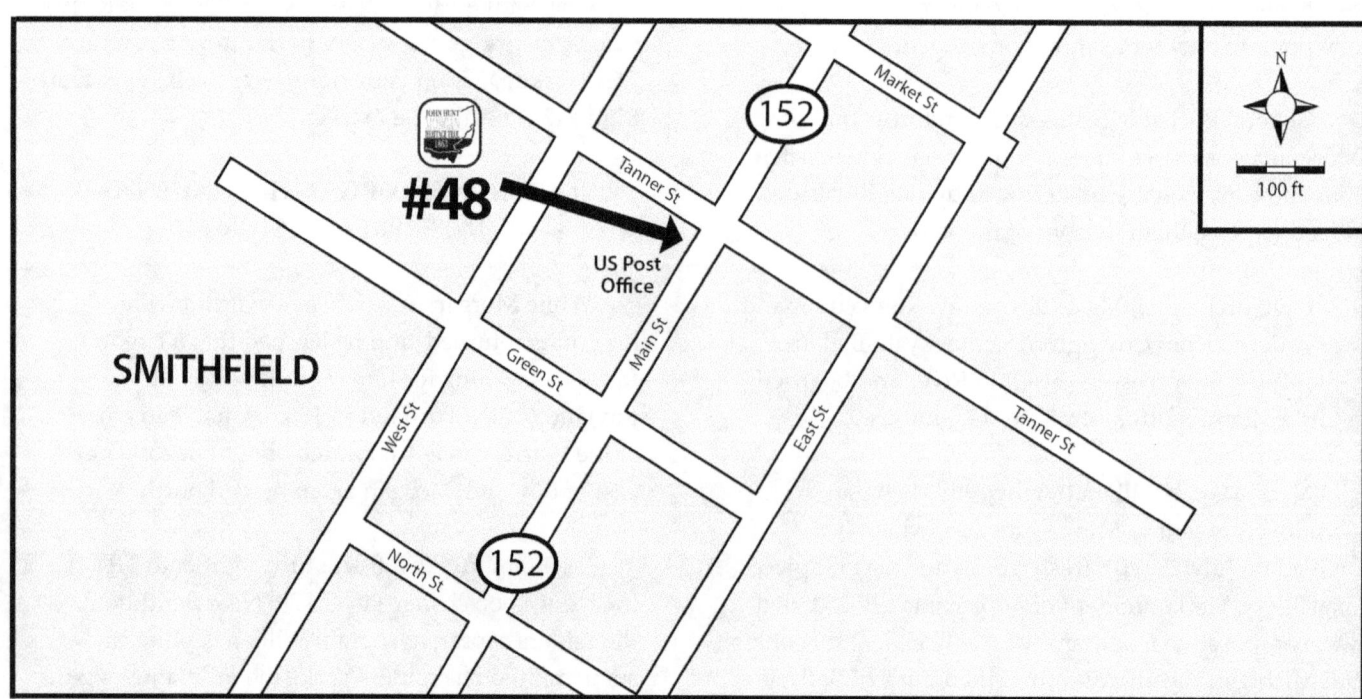

John Hunt Morgan Heritage Trail Interpretive sign #48 map

That afternoon when Shackelford's hungry men arrived in Smithfield, the "cupboards were bare."

Drive 0.2 mile and bear right on SR 151. It is 6.1 miles to New Alexandria. The raiders reached the town about noon. They made brief stops at the stores of James C. Graham and C. A. Wallace, where they appropriated groceries and other articles. When Morgan learned of their looting, he ordered them to desist. Graham received only partial payment for his claim. Wallace was awarded his full claim for $418. The not-so-lucky Robert McIntire received nothing for his loss of eighty-seven gallons of whiskey.

At New Alexandria, Morgan reached his closest point to the Ohio River and a ford since turning away from the river near Addison. The ford at Cox's Ripple was an easy crossing; it was only about four miles away. Eight scouts sent to a hill overlooking the ford returned with a good horse appropriated from W. H. Tarr, and bad news: Union militia guarded the crossing. Morgan again moved north.

Stay on SR 151 when it turns left. Drive 0.1 mile. At the cemetery, bear left onto Chapel Hill Road (TR 184). J.C. Marker #5 is immediately on the right after you turn.

Use caution during the next 0.9 mile, as you descend Chapel Hill and cross the bridge over McIntire Creek.

Turn right onto Ruple Road (CR 74); use extreme caution going through the underpass. Drive 0.4 mile. The road becomes Mingo Junction-Goulds Road halfway there. When Morgan reached this point, he was warned that Colonel Collier's men were waiting for him at Mingo Junction; again he turned north.

Turn left onto Sheep Rock Road (TR 166). J.C. Marker #6 is on the left, as you turn. It is near the junction of McIntire Creek with Cross Creek.

As you approach 0.4 mile, J.C. Marker #7 is on the left. Look to your right and back across Cross Creek. The high spot was the approach to the Steubenville & Indiana (later Pittsburgh, Cincinnati,

S & I railroad bridge approach

& St. Louis) Railroad's "Howe truss" bridge that the raiders burned.

In 1863, the railroad followed Cross Creek around the hill. This section of right-of-way was abandoned after completion of the Gould Tunnel in 1864. The old railroad right-of-way crossed the creek at this point and closely followed the route of the present-day road ahead. Alexander Road Station stood across the creek.

The old road forded the creek in this area. The John Elliott farm was on the opposite bank; Elliott saw Morgan's men cross his land.

After fording the creek, the raiders rode along the creek, and then up the hill to the Ekey Methodist Episcopal Church and School, approximately 1.5 miles from here. From there, the road continued northwest for about two miles before striking present-day CR 26 a quarter-mile west of a crossroads south of Wintersville, now the junction of Fernwood Road (CR 26) and Cross Creek Road. The landscape between the ford and the crossroads has been drastically altered by strip mining; little remains of the old road.

Before riding on, the raiders cut the area's telegraph wires and tore up a section of track. The bridge was still burning when the raiders rode into Wintersville. The state paid the railroad's claim for $3,000 for loss of the bridge and other damages to the railroad.

Because the old road no longer exists, return to CR 74 (Mingo Junction-Goulds Road). Turn left and drive 2.0 miles to Goulds. Where the main road turns right, continue straight onto CR 28 (Goulds Road). Reset your odometer.

Drive 2.1 miles to a "T" intersection and turn right; rely on your odometer reading. Continue 0.4 mile to another "T" intersection and turn left onto CR 26. (This is CR 26, but the name has been changed several times; it may be marked Coal Hill, Fernwood, or Bloomingdale Road.) It is 2.3 miles to Cross Creek Road, where we rejoin the raiders, as they came up from Cross Creek.

Turn right onto Cross Creek Road. Drive 0.1 mile; the Cross Creek Presbyterian Church site and Cemetery are on the left. Pull in the drive beyond the cemetery. **Historical markers** near the front of the cemetery mark the site of the church, which was built in 1837, and the visit by Morgan's men who rested themselves and their exhausted horses in the churchyard and cemetery.

Markers in Cross Creek Church Cemetery, marking site of church built in 1837 and visit of Morgan's Raiders.

When leaving, turn left onto Cross Creek Road. The John Stone farm was in the woods on the left just over 0.1 mile beyond the church. The John Hanna (Hannah) farm was approximately 0.5 mile beyond the Stone farm, on the left near the bend in the road.

Arriving here about 2 p.m., Morgan made another costly error. His men and horses were exhausted. Seeing the Stone and Hanna wheat fields, Morgan decided it was time for a break. The men turned their horses loose in the fields, and then ate their own lunch. A terrified Mrs. Margaret Hanna and her daughter attempted to flee the house, but were called back by Morgan. He promised they would not be molested. He and his staff only wanted something to eat. While Margaret cooked, Morgan napped. Before leaving, Morgan offered to pay Mrs. Hanna for the meal.

Shortly ahead, Cross Creek Road becomes Fernwood Road. Continue straight for 1.3 miles; the Wintersville United Methodist Church is on the left. Turn into the parking lot to view **J.C. Marker #8**, which is located near the corner at SR 43 (Frank P. Layman Boulevard). In 1863, there was no church at this site.

On Saturday morning, General Brooks placed Colonel James Collier in command of the Steubenville militia. While Morgan was lunching at the Hanna farm, Collier's men traveled the "old plank road" (today's Cadiz Road/Frank P. Layman Boulevard) from Steubenville to Wintersville. His force consisted of approximately 500 mounted men with one 6-pounder iron cannon.

Collier sent Captain Frank Prentiss on ahead with a squad of eighteen men. The small squad encountered the raiders here at the junction of Cross Creek Road and the Steubenville Pike. Prentiss ordered his men to scatter and bushwhack the raiders until Collier's regiment came up. One of Prentiss's squad, fifteen-year-old Henry L. Parks, was mortally wounded in the action.

Maxwell's store and tavern stood one block east of here at the southwest corner of Frank P. Layman Boulevard and Welday Street in the village. The women of Wintersville were hiding at the tavern. Margaret Daugherty (Dougherty) was standing at the window when she was severely wounded by a stray bullet. The wound was not fatal. The women then ran under fire to the nearby home of Doctor Abraham Markle, a location more suitable for ladies. Dr. Markle's house stood at the southwest corner of Frank P. Layman Boulevard and S.C. West Lane. After driving off Prentiss's scouts, the raiders looted the stores for supplies and stole four horses in the village.

While the raiders were at Wintersville, they were only five miles from the Ohio River at Steubenville, the home town of President Lincoln's Secretary of War, Edwin M. Stanton. Knowing the town was heavily occupied by Union troops, Morgan again turned north.

A Union friendly-fire incident gave Morgan an hour's reprieve. When Collier's main force arrived, they formed a line of battle on the hill on the east side of Wintersville. Cross Creek Road was clearly visible from the militia's position. When Union Major William Way's advance guard arrived on the Cross Creek Road near here, the militia mistakenly fired on them with their 6-pounder cannon loaded with scrap metal instead of a cannonball. The scrap metal flew in multiple directions, one piece striking Maxwell's Tavern, and the rest harmlessly burrowing into the ground around Way's Michiganders. The cavalrymen dismounted and prepared to defend themselves. Major Way came up and sent an officer forward under a white flag. Collier was advised that he was firing on Union troops.

Leave the parking lot and turn left onto Fernwood Road. Go to the light and turn left onto Frank P. Layman Boulevard (SR 43) for 0.3 mile. Turn right with SR 43 (Canton Road).

Drive 1.8 miles on SR 43 (Canton Road), which was the Richmond Road in 1863. Benjamin Coe's farmhouse is located on the left before the interchange. The 1840s house was remodeled in the 1890s and has a Victorian appearance today.

Benjamin Coe house (c. 1840)

When Morgan arrived, he warned Benjamin's wife, Esther M. Coe, and her family to flee the area before the shooting started. Mrs. Coe, her sister, and the seven Coe children retired to the entrance of a coal bank in the nearby woods. Ross, the thirteen-year-old son, described the raiders' appearance: "They were dressed on all manner of style, dress coats and ragged pants, stove pipe hats and no shoes, others had good citizens' suits. They had all kinds of horses and saddles; some were riding fat farm horses which looked like they were not far from home. One of the rebels rode in a fine carriage pulled by a horse with silver fittings. Another rode one of my father's horses." The Coe House served as a hospital after the Two Ridges Church skirmish.

King's Restaurant, located at the intersection of SR 43 and Sabina Drive, occupies the site of the skirmish. Here Morgan's men were engaged with the men of the 9th Michigan Cavalry, serving under Major William B. Way. Collier's militia was also present; this time they fired at the enemy.

Two of Way's men were wounded. Martin Kane of Company F, 9th Michigan Cavalry, was shot in the chest, with the bullet exiting near his back bone.

After crossing US 22, you will see a church ahead on the left. At the stop light, turn left onto Two Ridge Road; immediately turn right onto Church Drive. Drive a loop around the front of the church.

Two Ridges Church (c. 1887)

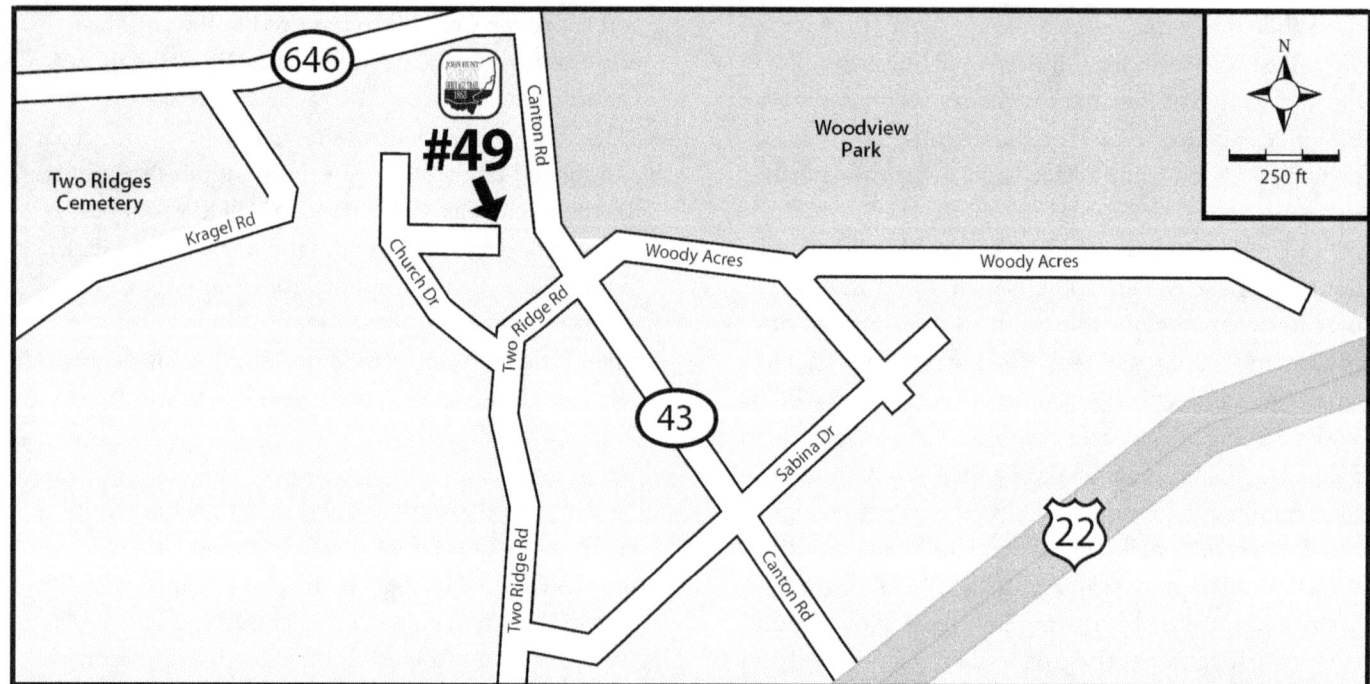

John Hunt Morgan Heritage Trail Interpretive sign #49 map

JOHN HUNT MORGAN HERITAGE TRAIL INTERPRETIVE SIGN #49

The present Two Ridges Church was built after the Civil War on the exact site of the 1853 building. The timbers of the earlier building were used in the construction of the present church. During the Civil War, it was known as Two Ridge Church.

J.C. Marker #9 was moved from its original location, approximately 500 feet south of this spot, when the four-lane highway was constructed in the 1980s. In more recent years, a major highway construction project converted the old two-lane Canton Road into a five-lane highway. At that time the church lost both of its front driveways, and access to the cemetery was altered.

Take Church Drive back to Two Ridge Road and turn left. Turn left again at the stoplight at Canton Road.

To visit the Martin Kane grave, stay in the left lane of SR 43 as you pass the church. Turn left onto the first road, SR 646. Drive 0.1 mile and turn left onto Kragel Road. The cemetery is on the right.

Martin Kane grave

Private Martin Kane's grave is located about halfway back from the gates and slightly to the left. There are two large evergreen trees; Kane's monument is in the fourth row beyond the trees. There is an eagle above the inscription.

OLD WASHINGTON TO WEST POINT

The church or a member of the congregation felt the grave should be marked. However, the name engraved on the monument was misspelled as "Martin Cane." The inscription is badly worn; the August 27, 1863, date is the most legible portion of it.

After the skirmish, Kane was pronounced mortally wounded and carried to the Coe family home. Cared for by Dr. Markle, the Coe family, and neighbors, Kane appeared to be recovering, when he suffered a relapse and died on August 27, 1863, thirty-two days after being wounded.

The other wounded Union soldier, Private James N. Carney, Company D, and a Confederate soldier, W. G. Page, were also taken to Coe's house, where they were treated; both eventually recovered.

Turn around and take Kragel Road back to SR 646; turn right. Turn left onto SR 43 (Canton Road). It is 3.7 miles to the junction with SR 152 (Lisbon Street) in Richmond. **J.C. Marker #10** is located in front of the bank on the right, at the corner.

Morgan passed through Richmond about 5 p.m. The raiders did not stop because Major William Way's cavalry was in close pursuit. Some men near the front fell out for short periods of time and rejoined the end of the column. Morgan was reported to have stopped at the Hout home and demanded food. While he was eating, he realized he and Mr. Hout were about the same build. While his men were stealing the man's horses, Morgan quickly changed into his host's white shirt, dark gray suit, and tie. This fits the description of the outfit Morgan was wearing when he surrendered.

A woman near Richmond upbraided a raider for stealing horses and other property. He replied, "Madam, we have burned better towns than this. Now, just bring on the chicken."

By Saturday evening, General Brooks had moved to the railroad depot at the north end of Riverside Avenue in Wellsville. He repositioned his forces. Porter's regiment was sent from Warrenton to Island Creek, six miles north of Steubenville. Gallagher's and Bemus's regiments were moved another six miles upriver to guard the ford at Shanghai (Empire). They were prepared to move farther upstream to Yellow Creek Ford, east of Hammondsville, or to Babb's Island Ford at East Liverpool. Bemus continued to Hammondsville.

Union Secretary of War Edwin Stanton at one time lived in Richmond. His former home still stands at 110 West Main Street (SR 43).

Continue on SR 43; go 5.2 miles to East Springfield. Turn left onto Unionport Road (CR 39); drive one block and turn right onto Church Street. The East Springfield Methodist Church is on the left; it is the second church structure at the site.

Old Methodist Church bell in East Springfield

The 1846 church was a wooden structure, measuring about 40 x 60 feet. A small steeple over the front door contained the church bell. The building was razed in 1892, but the old bell is displayed in the church yard.

The raiders skirmished with citizens near the town. They arrived at the church at approximately 6 p.m. and broke up the choir rehearsal. Several horses, left standing outside the church, were stolen before their owners came out.

Miss Celia Davidson, a maiden lady of uncertain years living near the church, gallantly resisted the raiders' attempt to take her horse and prevented them from doing so. Bill Huskroff (Huscroft), a local farmer, about to lose his horses, told Morgan that he would pay $360 to keep them. He was told to show his money, which he did. The farmer was "stung": Morgan took the horses and the money.

While in East Springfield, Morgan established temporary headquarters at the hotel kept by Mrs. Deborah McCullough. Morgan was reported to have stayed on his horse with his pistol drawn, while the horse was being shod by Charles Cashell, the village blacksmith. Morgan wanted to insure there would be no "monkey business" to lame his mount.

The raiders stole a total of nine horses in East Springfield. Doctor Thomas Simpson lost his horse, some clothes, three watches, $31 in cash, and his surgical instruments.

The rebels chopped down the "liberty pole" in the village square. Many of the citizens were more upset by the raiders' desecration of the symbol of liberty than they were about the looting and horse stealing.

Sergeant R. Mitchell Crabbs, a member of Company K, 2nd Ohio Volunteer Infantry, was home on disability. He slipped out of the choir rehearsal and hid his horse before the raiders reached the church. He returned and befriended Morgan and his men. He watered their horses and obtained items they needed from the citizens. Crabbs hoped to gather information that would help in the capture of Morgan and his men. He learned that Morgan was trying to reach the ford at Babb's Island, near East Liverpool.

When the raiders were preparing to leave East Springfield, Crabbs declined Morgan's invitation to join the group. He recovered his horse and set out to get in front of Morgan by riding through woods, through fields, and along byways. He passed through Mooretown (now Pravo) and Monroeville (Croxton Post Office) on his way to Salineville. Along the way, he warned the farmers to hide their horses, to prevent the raiders from obtaining fresh mounts.

When Crabbs reached Salineville about 10 p.m., he telegraphed General Brooks to provide him with the information of Morgan's location and intention to cross the river at Babb's Island. Brooks responded by moving Gallagher's 700 men of the 54th Pennsylvania Militia to Salineville. Crabbs's information helped set the trap that resulted in Morgan's capture.

Another East Springfield man, John K. Miller, pretended to be a Southern sympathizer. He intended to volunteer faulty information to mislead Morgan. Instead, he was impressed as a guide. He was released when Morgan's force was later attacked beyond Monroeville.

Turn right onto the alley in front of the church and drive one block to SR 43. There is an old two-story brick house on the left. Local legend has a woman throwing the contents of her "slop jar" from a second-story window onto the raiders below.

East Springfield brick house of local legend

Turn left on SR 43 and drive two blocks. Turn right onto CR 60 (Circle Green Road). **J.C. Marker #11** is located on the right as you turn. Drive 1.1 miles. On the right is the Stewart McClave house. McClave was taken prisoner in East Springfield and served as Morgan's guide.

In 1.3 miles you will pass through Circle Green. Church members returning from a "quarterly meeting" met and described the raiders as some being mounted,

OLD WASHINGTON TO WEST POINT

some not; some being in uniform, but many poorly clad; all being starved looking, dirty, and tired. Morgan was riding near the front of the column in a carriage drawn by two white horses.

Continue 1.3 miles to a stop sign. Turn right onto Wolf Run Road (CR 75). Saturday 11 p.m., Major Way's Union forces camped here, along Wolf Run, and on the hill to the right. Mrs. Wesley Kirk spent the night cooking for the Union soldiers. Only a mile ahead, the raiders slept in the Nebo community.

During the night, Shackelford consulted with Majors Way and Rue. The following plan was adopted: Rue and the 9th Kentucky U.S. Cavalry would be allowed to ride in front and head Morgan off, while Way and the 9th Michigan Cavalry would attack from the rear. Unlike Shackelford's exhausted men and mounts, Way's and Rue's forces were fresh, having just been transported in by rail.

Drive 0.3 mile on Wolf Run Road. On the left is **Trail Sign #50**.

JOHN HUNT MORGAN HERITAGE TRAIL INTERPRETIVE SIGN #50

Go 0.2 mile to the intersection with CR 75A. This place marks the front of Way's camp.

Bear right on CR 75. Go 0.5 mile. Morgan's rear guard camped around Thomas McConnahay's brick house on the left. After 0.2 mile, turn right again, and you are on SR 164. Portions of this road did not exist in 1863; the original road was off to the left.

Drive 0.1 mile. On the left side of SR 164 is the site of the (George) Herdman Taylor house. This was Morgan's headquarters on the night of July 25. Go 0.1 mile; as you cross the bridge, look to the left. The original road crossed Yellow Creek on a covered bridge at the site of the old metal bridge.

Yellow Creek Bridge

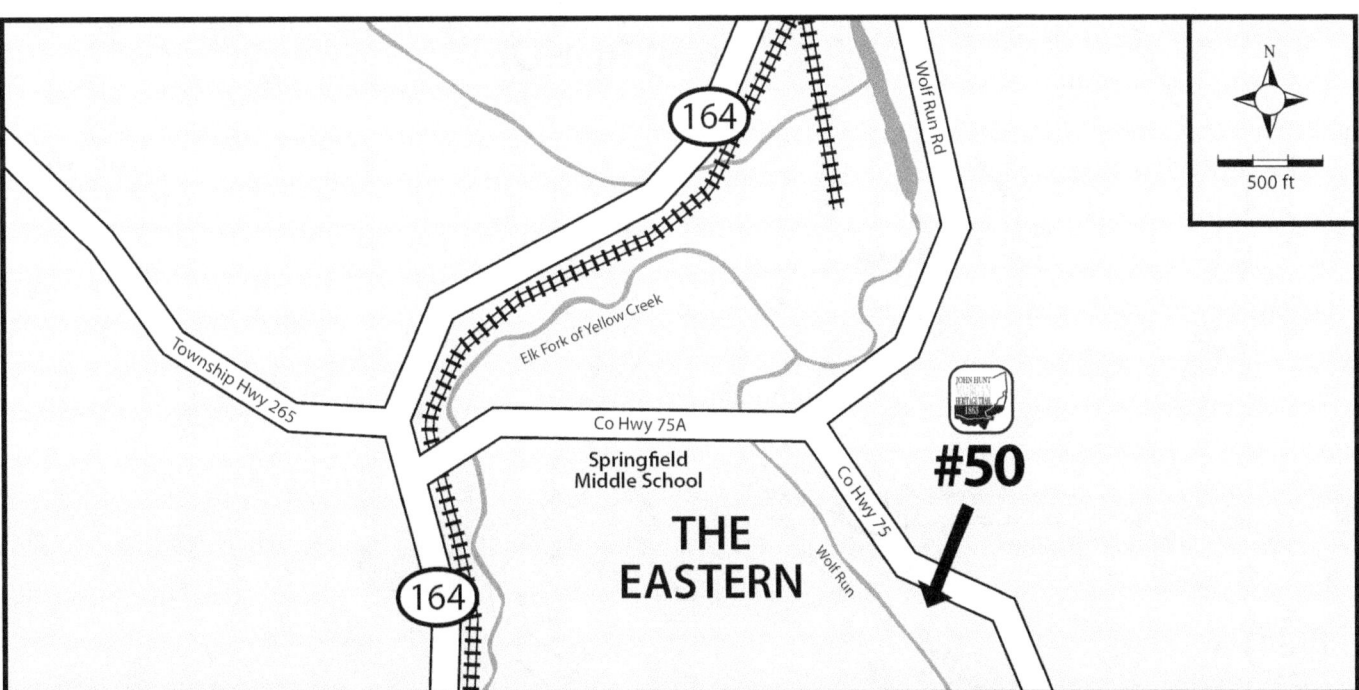

John Hunt Morgan Heritage Trail Interpretive sign #50 map

Continue 0.1 mile to CR 49 (Elkhorn Road) and turn left. Go 0.1 mile and park. There is a path on the left leading to the abandoned bridge known as the "Morgan Burnt Bridge." Jefferson County received $1,000 from the state for the loss of the wooden span.

The raiders burned the covered bridge early on Sunday morning. The stone base (the original site of **J.C. Marker #12**), minus the plaque, is located on the left side of the approach to the bridge. It may be totally overgrown with thorn bushes.

Return to SR 164; turn left. **J.C. Marker #12** is now located on the left in 0.6 mile.

JOHN HUNT MORGAN HERITAGE TRAIL INTERPRETIVE SIGN #51

This was originally the location of **J.C. Marker #13**. Marker #13, which has been lost, contained the following information:

Gen. John H. Morgan
In command of Confederate Troops passed through Nebo Hamlet, located here, July 26, 1863; proceeded northward via Yellow Creek and Nebo-Lisbon roads to Monroeville pursued by Gen. James M. Shackelford commanding 14th Ill. Cav., First Ky. Cav., 9th Mich. Cav., 11th Mich. Bat'y, 86th Ohio Mounted Inf., 2nd Tenn. Mounted Inf. and Steubenville Milita.
Tablet No. 13   *Erected July 1913*

At the far end of the field to the left of where the marker stood are the remains of the last house standing in Nebo. It belonged to David G. Allen, who hosted the raiders in a small cabin that stood at the right front corner of the house. The cabin served as William Hoobler's shoe making shop.

Abandoned house at Nebo is the David G. Allen house, where Confederate captain Ralph Sheldon and his men paid a visit.

Nebo was built around a grist mill located near here on Yellow Creek. The present-day town of Bergholz did not exist during the Civil War.

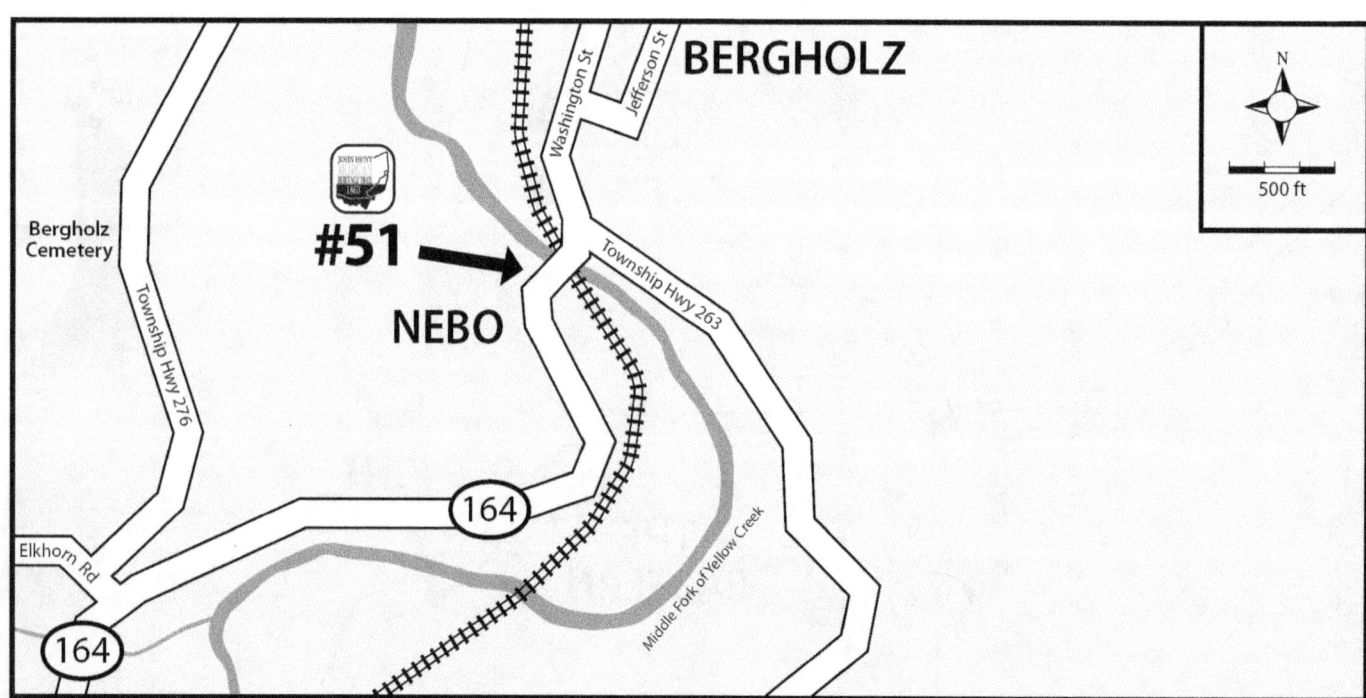
John Hunt Morgan Heritage Trail Interpretive sign #51 map

OLD WASHINGTON TO WEST POINT

The raiders arrived in Nebo about 8 p.m. Their ride to Nebo was another remarkable one. Morgan had traveled more than fifty-five miles that day, having started early that morning from near New Athens.

The (George) Herdman Taylor farm was located near the covered bridge, and Morgan used the farmhouse as his headquarters. Morgan took over half the house. (The building has since been razed. Its site we visited previously.) Mrs. Matilda Taylor and the other Taylor women in the house were forced to prepare a chicken dinner for the general and his staff.

Some of the men spent the night in the old mill, the site of which is located across the highway behind the present-day stables. Several of the officers slept on the floor of John and James Wright's store (it's site is located directly across the highway). They did not bother the money in the cash drawer. They did, however, take clothing, boots, and hosiery. Brevet Lieutenant Colonel Thomas Webber ordered the men to be quiet because Mrs. Elizabeth Wright was sick.

Morgan's advance troops camped in a patch of woods at the David G. Allen farm in Nebo. The hungry raiders ate fourteen loaves of Mrs. Sara Allen's fresh-baked bread, twenty pounds of butter, ten gallons of milk, eight gallons of buttermilk, and several gallons of honey, before lying down to sleep.

Morgan's rear guard camped at the Thomas McConnahay (McConaughey) farm located one-half mile north of the CR 75/CR 75A intersection.

During the night, some of the raiders attempted to burn the home of Reverend Doctor Thomas Simpson, an ardent abolitionist. The fire was put out by other raiders to avoid giving away their location.

During the night, Major Way and the 9th Michigan Cavalry arrived in the area and camped on the hill above The Eastern. Three Union soldiers, Watts, Conley, and Coventry, ran into Morgan's picket line and were captured.

Sunday, July 26, 1863

About 2:30 a.m., the pickets posted approximately 1.5 miles north of town on what is now called Tunnel Hill, were driven in by four scouts sent out from Salineville. Morgan knew Way's men and artillery were at his rear, but the attack from the front was unexpected.

At Morgan's headquarters, Maria Taylor, Herdman's sister, had been instructed to fry more chicken for breakfast. When the alarm came around 3 a.m., the raiders made a hasty departure before the chicken was done. Herdman Taylor, who was forced to serve as their guide, was not allowed time to put on his shoes. After riding several miles, he was released to return home.

Before leaving Nebo, the raiders burned the covered bridge across Yellow Creek south of town on the Springfield Road (the site we visited earlier). The water level was so low that fording it was not a problem for the Union pursuers.

One of the raiders did not respond to the alarm and was left sleeping in the Allens' sheep shed where he was captured later that morning. Three exhausted men, who were unable to ride, were left in the care of John Allmon and others. They were later taken prisoners.

Continue 0.3 mile to Second Street in Bergholz.

*Side Trip: The George Monument was erected by the parents of Thomas George, who was killed at the Battle of Perryville, Kentucky, October 8, 1862. The monument honors not only George, but also all the Ross Township casualties of the Civil War. Nearby, a West Point Foundry 30-pounder 1862 Parrott gun tube rests on a cement mount. The memorial sits on a hill overlooking Lake George.

When the memorial was erected in 1871, it was surrounded by the village of Mooretown (Pravo). The town had some light industry and was the center of a prosperous farming community. All that remains are a few abandoned buildings.

George Memorial

To visit the site, turn right onto Second Street, which becomes CR 53 (Bergholz-New Somerset Road). At 1.1 miles, bear left on the main road. Drive 2.2 miles and turn right into the driveway for the parking lot next to the monument. Park there. The iron stairs to the monument are on the right side of CR 53.

Return to Bergholz and turn right on SR 164.*

Morgan moved from Nebo to Monroeville along what is now SR 164, crossing the corner of Carroll County and passing by Berea (Disciples) Church, which stood at the south corner of SR 164 and TR 293. At the same time, many of Way's men rode through Mooretown, entering Monroeville from the south.

When he left Nebo, Morgan was still hoping to cross the Ohio River. Yellow Creek Ford was more than eighteen miles away at the mouth of Yellow Creek, near Hammondsville. It was almost twenty-six miles to Babb's Island Ford at East Liverpool.

From Second Street, drive 2.2 miles north on SR 164. The ruins of Pott's School are on the right side atop the hill in the bend of the road (just before reaching the intersection at TR 281). On Sunday morning, this was the site of a small skirmish with Way's advance guard where one raider was wounded.

Pott's Schoolhouse stands in ruins.

It is 4.5 miles from Pott's School to Monroeville. Elizabeth McIntosh, living southwest of Monroeville, counted 475 raiders as they rode by her farmhouse.

Stay on SR 164 as it turns left in Monroeville. **J.C. Marker #14** is located immediately on the left. The settlement consisted of a store, a blacksmith shop, and approximately twelve houses. After entering the town around 7 a.m., the raiders plundered Bob Pott's store, once located at the northwest corner of SR 164 and CR 55. Local women were forced to prepare "fast food" for the rebels.

Sixteen-year-old James Cooper Boice was at the home of Robert McMillen when the raiders arrived. Boice had recently received a medical discharge from Company I of the 98th OVI.

When one of the Confederate officers began questioning him, Boice sensed an opportunity to further serve his country. When asked about the number of troops at Hammondsville, Boice, who had no idea about the Union strength there, replied that a man had just ridden in from there and said the town was occupied by about 6,000 soldiers. When asked if there were any Union troops in Salineville, Boice replied, "No, they expect Morgan to go by way of Hammondsville."

OLD WASHINGTON TO WEST POINT

Boice waited until the last of the raiders were a quarter-mile away, and then he followed them. He wanted to see what kind of reception the rebels would get from the large Union force in Salineville.

Monroeville blacksmith James "Paddy" Kerr, an Irish immigrant, refused to replace some horseshoes for the raiders at his shop at the southeast corner of SR 164 and CR 55. He reconsidered after receiving a blow with the flat side of a cavalry sword. Another Monroeville resident, Jimmy Twiss, who lived at the southwest corner, was taken prisoner to serve as a guide for the departing raiders.

Stay on SR 164 for about 0.7 mile. Morgan was headed toward Salineville when his scouts returned and reported the town was full of Union troops. General Brooks had ordered Gallagher's 54th Pennsylvania Militia moved to Salineville by rail. The regiment had arrived in town about 6 a.m.

About the same time the scouts returned, Company H of Major Way's 9th Michigan Cavalry, riding close on Morgan's heels, approached from Monroeville. They engaged Morgan's men near here at about 8 a.m. Morgan abandoned the carriage and mounted his horse. Union soldiers later reported that the carriage contained only a loaf of bread, hard-boiled eggs, and a bottle of whiskey.

Unable to move north or south, Morgan and his men escaped by tearing down a rail fence on the Burson farm, here between Monroeville and Salineville, and riding west down the steep ravine on the left. Some of the horses stumbled and fell. The advancing Union troops fired their carbines at the retreating Confederates. Fifty-five of Morgan's rear guard were captured before they could follow their leader down the ravine. A number of Confederate and Union troopers lay wounded in the road or in the adjacent fields.

Guide Jimmy Twiss's captivity was short-lived. He escaped during the confusion and returned home.

The Union riders did not follow the raiders down the treacherous route. Way understood the futility in chasing Morgan. He would attempt again to get his men in front of Morgan.

We're unable to follow Morgan cross-country, so turn around and retrace your route through Monroeville. Reset your odometer when you pass **J.C. Marker #14** at the intersection of SR 164 and CR 55. Turn right and drive 0.2 mile on SR 164; pull into the cemetery on the right.

JOHN HUNT MORGAN HERITAGE TRAIL INTERPRETIVE SIGN #52

Way's forces approached Monroeville from the south. His horse artillery was set up on the high ground in the Monroeville Cemetery; from here they fired at the raiders as they moved down the ravine. Their shots passed over the raiders' heads. The view is now blocked by trees. Morgan came out of the ravine a half mile west of here and rode across the fields to West Grove Cemetery and John Moore's farm.

Union artillery position in Monroeville cemetery

The prisoners captured in the Monroeville area were taken to Salineville. The wounded were provided food and given medical attention.

Return to SR 164 and turn right. Drive 0.3 mile to TR 294 (Opal Road). The John C. McIntosh house is on the left near the intersection. From McIntosh's orchard, Way's men fired on Morgan's column as it rode westward across the hills and ravines northwest of here. Both Union and Confederate wounded from the Monroeville area were treated on the porch of the house. The McIntosh women provided the wounded soldiers with some old quilted bedcovers to lie on.

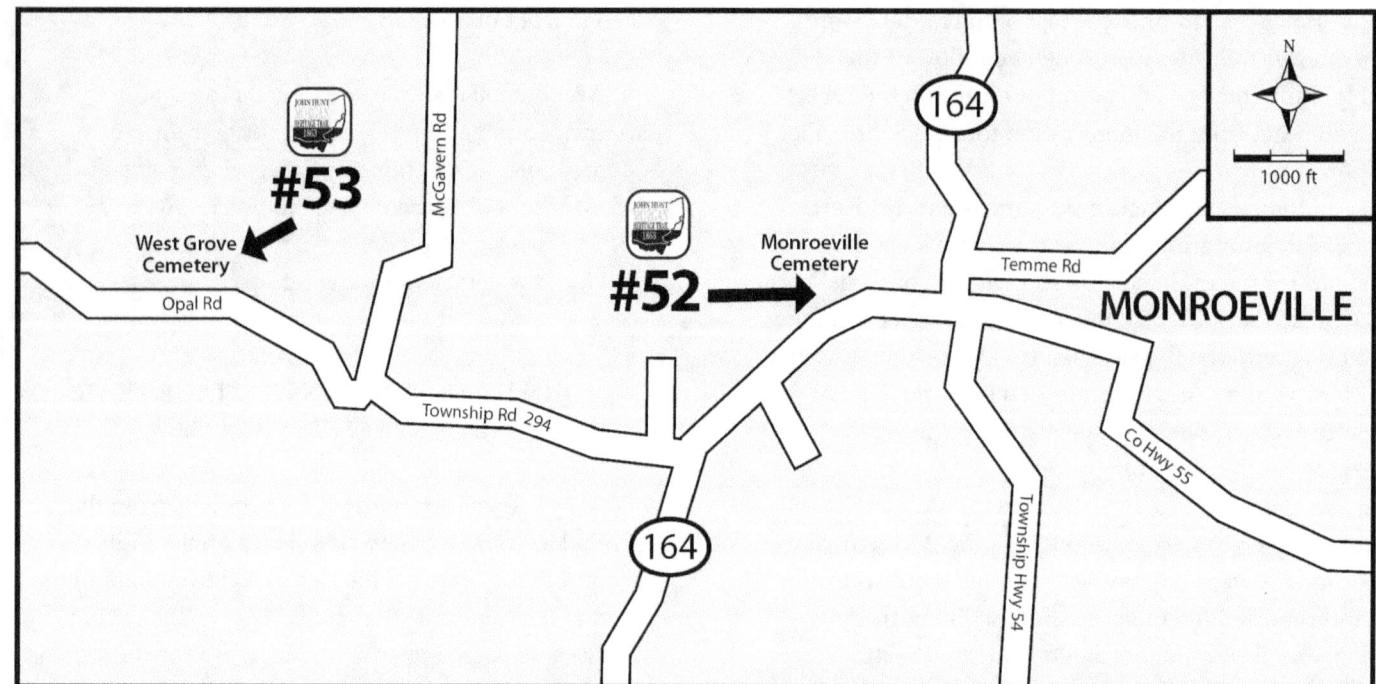

John Hunt Morgan Heritage Trail Interpretive signs #52 and #53 map

The Confederate troopers who had stopped by the house earlier that morning ate from Mrs. McIntosh's crock of cherry butter, drank all the milk, and took all the bread, jams, cold meats, pickles, and pies in the house. Throughout the afternoon and evening the McIntosh women baked up six gallons of pancake batter for the Union soldiers, who had arrived thirty minutes after Morgan's men had hurriedly departed. Young Elizabeth McIntosh later said the Union troops treated her family worse than the rebels had. Morgan's men "acted very gentlemanly," while some Federal soldiers demanded that some of the old men in the neighborhood take the oath of allegiance and pay tribute to prove that they weren't "Copperheads."

Turn right onto TR 294. Reset your odometer. Go 0.5 mile, and make a very sharp left turn onto TR 294 (Opal Road). Drive 0.3 mile to West Grove Cemetery and pull into the drive on the right. The cemetery was the site of another skirmish.

JOHN HUNT MORGAN HERITAGE TRAIL INTERPRETIVE SIGN #53

Union forces chasing Morgan from Monroeville were approaching the cemetery from the east on Opal Road. Riding at a full gallop, they hoped to cut off

Two Confederate graves at West Grove Cemetery

the raiders near McGavern Road, but the raiders' riding skills allowed Morgan and his men to avoid the trap and stay ahead of their pursuers.

Some of Way's men were able to fire a volley, seriously wounding three raiders near the cemetery lane. The wounded men were picked up by the Union soldiers, carried to the John Moore house across the road, and laid on the porch. The family gave them water and tended their wounds as best they could.

WARNING: Current occupants of the Moore house will not tolerate any invasion of their privacy or property. Do not infringe on their land, which is adjacent to the cemetery, and do not stop along the

OLD WASHINGTON TO WEST POINT

John Moore house

township road to take photographs of their house.

John Miller and an unknown boy died that evening and were buried the next day. Their graves are near the right rear of the cemetery. These are the farthest north Confederate graves on a Civil War battlefield in the United States. The third soldier, Frank Bixby, recovered.

Jane Morgan Campbell's grave is in the fourth row from the interpretive sign and near the left rear of the cemetery. The following local legend has been refuted by some of her descendants. Jane Campbell was the mother of William Campbell, one of the Andrews Raiders hanged by the Confederates for his role in seizing the locomotive The General. Jane's stone is next to Keziah Morgan Allison's grave stone.

Graves of Jane Morgan Campbell (left) and Keziah Morgan Allison (right)

Forty to sixty men from the remnants of Johnson's brigade, now serving under Colonel Roy Cluke, made the stand at the cemetery that allowed Morgan to escape west down Opal Road.

Leave the cemetery and turn right. The John Moore house is on the left. You have entered Carroll County.

Go 0.5 mile to Olive Road (TR 310) and turn right. Another 0.6 mile will bring you to Nickel Road (TR 299). Morgan and the main column continued straight before turning right onto a long-abandoned road to reach the James Allison farm.

On Avon Road is the home of General Morgan's second cousin, Keziah Morgan Allison. Her sister, Jane Morgan Campbell, also was there. Both women were staunch Unionists, but Mrs. Allison fed Morgan and gave him a clean shirt. He left some of his wounded men in her care. They were later taken prisoners by the Union soldiers.

Turn right on Nickel Road. Drive 1.3 miles to the junction with Avon Road. After his visit to the Allison farm (0.3 mile to the left), Morgan returned to Nickel Road at this point. Bear right and continue 0.3 mile to SR 39. Riley's Church is near the junction. Salineville is less than three miles to your right.

Riley's Church

Following Morgan's escape, Cluke's rear guard left the West Grove Cemetery and made its way up Nickel Road. Cluke's men crossed the Mechanicstown-Salineville Road here and rode northwest on April Road toward Norristown while Morgan was resting at the Allison farm.

Major Way's forces skirmished with Morgan's main column near Riley's Church. Morgan broke off the engagement and rode west on the Mechanicstown-

Salineville Road.

Turn left on SR 39 toward Mechanicstown; it is 1.2 miles to the **"Northernmost" Raid Monument** on the right.

JOHN HUNT MORGAN HERITAGE TRAIL INTERPRETIVE SIGN #54

The monument is located on what was the Sharp farm during the Civil War. The final skirmish of the raid occurred here, following a fight at the Boring farm just over the hill, about 0.4 mile southeast of the monument. The 9th Michigan Cavalry, serving under Major William B. Way, charged down on the Confederates. After a brief skirmish where Ocean Road meets SR 39, raiders broke and fled across Jonah Queen's cornfield, located 0.6 mile northeast of the monument.

General Morgan assigned Captain Ralph Sheldon and his men from the 2nd Kentucky Cavalry to form the rear guard. Sheldon's men stopped the Michiganders' advance along the road at the location where the monument stands today. The Federals formed behind a fence 30 yards west of here. Sheldon mounted his men and charged the Federals at the fence, scattering them. Way's men would not attack Morgan from that

Northernmost Raid Monument on Sharp's Farm

point forward. The fighting ended around 9:30 a.m.

Lieutenant Smith W. Fisk of the 9th Michigan Cavalry was seriously wounded during the encounter. His wife came from Coldwater, Michigan, to help nurse her husband back to health at the Sharp house. Wesley Taylor and Mr. Kerr, two citizens who had

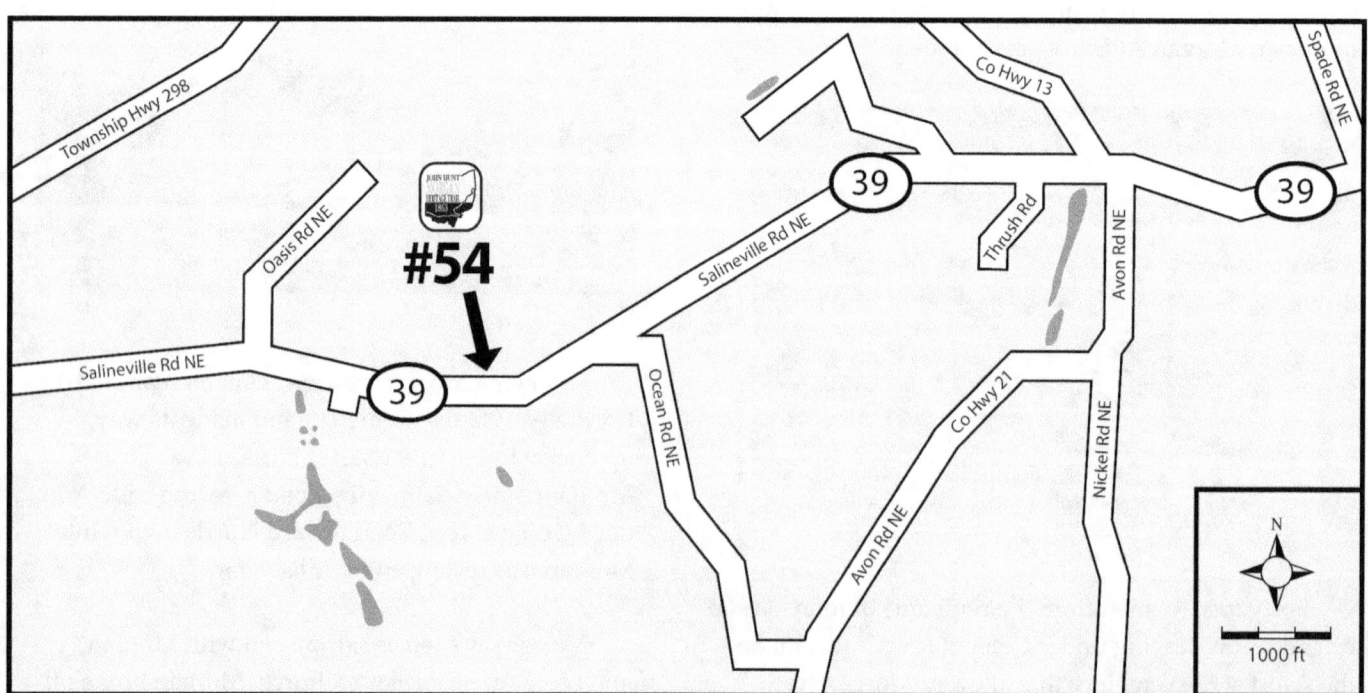

John Hunt Morgan Heritage Trail Interpretive sign #54 map

OLD WASHINGTON TO WEST POINT

joined Way's troopers in the chase, were also wounded. Many Confederates were wounded or captured.

During the morning skirmishes, Union dispatches indicated that about 75 Confederates were killed or wounded and approximately 240 were captured. Historians believe these numbers were inflated by the Union participants. Eyewitness R. Mitchell Crabbs indicated that only about 100 raiders in total were killed, wounded, or captured in the series of skirmishes that have been collectively labeled "The Battle of Salineville." It is the northernmost Civil War battlefield east of the Mississippi River.

Leave the monument and turn right (west) onto SR 39. Morgan traveled north on Oasis Road to April Road, but Oasis Road is now closed. Drive 0.9 mile from the monument to Niblick Road (TR 298); turn right. Go 1.2 miles and turn right onto April Road (CR 13). It is 0.6 mile to Nickel Road (TR 299).

As Cluke's rear guard rode toward Norristown, they used April Road, Nickel Road, Smith Road, Lewis Road, and Aurora Road. While they waited for Morgan in the Norristown area, Cluke's men searched for food and fresh horses.

John Shaw, who lived three miles north of Norristown, lost two horses and some "eatables" — hams, bacon, eggs, cheese, and milk — to the raiders. The claims process for Shaw, like most others, dragged on for years. On June 23, 1879, he received a notice from Joseph Hall, the Claims Attorney in Steubenville, to bring two witnesses and meet him in Salineville on July 9, 1879. We do not know if Shaw ever received payment. Some claims were eventually paid; many were approved but never paid for lack of federal and state funding.

Turn left onto Nickel Road. It is 2.2 miles to Aurora Road (Lewis Road/CR 18/TR 847). Go straight on Smith Road (TR 751); it is 0.8 mile to Saint John's (Summitville) Catholic Church. Morgan's men turned west before reaching the church.

Return to Aurora-Lewis Road (CR 18) and turn right. The raiders regrouped along this road about 10 a.m.

John H. Carey and his sisters were walking from their home in Norristown to the Summitville Catholic Church when they met the raiders. Morgan forced seventeen-year-old John H. Carey to serve as his guide.

Drive 1.6 miles to Apollo Road (CR 12). Morgan rode to the crest of the hill directly ahead and viewed the village of Norristown before turning north.

Turn right onto Apollo Road; go 2.1 miles to Merline Road (TR 268) and turn right. It is 1.3 miles to a five-point crossroads. Continue straight across Nature Road to Fink Road (TR 844). You are now leaving Carroll County and entering Columbiana County. After 0.9 mile turn left on Bethesda Road (CR 731). You will have passed under the old Cleveland & Pittsburgh Railroad. In 1863, the tracks were approximately 0.7 mile farther east. The railroad was relocated in 1917.

It is 0.5 mile to Bethesda United Presbyterian Church. Pull into the parking lot. There is a **historical marker** in the churchyard. The raiders saw many horses at the church. Fearing they might belong to Union cavalry, Morgan turned east to avoid a confrontation. When Union forces arrived, many of the church members, led by their pastor, joined in the pursuit.

Bethesda United Presbyterian Church (c. 1854)

Near the Bethesda Church, Morgan released young Carey. He forced militia Captain William Swaney to serve as a guide to lead him to the Ohio

River crossing.

Turn around; immediately turn left onto Willard Road (TR 843). Go 0.4 mile to the stop sign; cross the Dungannon Road (SR 644) and continue on Willard Road.

This section of the Dungannon Road was built on the old railroad right-of-way. About 11 a.m., the raiders crossed the tracks about a quarter of a mile to our right. Just beyond the tracks was a deep mill race. The raiders followed it north. Here, they found a small wooden bridge near the Willard sisters' house. The raiders turned east on Willard Road.

It is 1.0 mile to the next stop sign at Foundry Hill Road. Cross the road and stay to the left. This section of Willard Road was closed for many years due to strip mining but has been reopened. Drive 1.4 miles to Gavers Road (CR 407). This is the farthest point north reached by Morgan's force and by the Confederacy. Dan McAllister's farm was nearby.

When the raiders were south of Dungannon, with prisoner Dan McAllister guiding them, they heard cannon fire from the direction of Hanoverton (called Hanover in 1863). The home guard was testing its gun; no action took place at Hanoverton.

The raiders turned south toward the valley of the West Fork of Beaver Creek. Morgan was now headed for Babb's Island or Smith's Ferry, located below the mouth of Beaver Creek, near the Pennsylvania state line. Militia defended both crossings.

Turn right on Gavers Road; it is 1.2 miles to a stop sign. About 1.4 miles north of here, on the left side of Trinity Church Road (TR 756), is the Thomas P. Thompson house. This was the northernmost farm raided by Morgan's flankers. The McClellan Covered Bridge still stands across the road from the house.

Go straight onto SR 518. It was about noon when Morgan came out onto Hanoverton-West Point Road.

It is 1.5 miles to Gavers. En route, you will pass the New Lebanon United Presbyterian Church on the

New Lebanon United Presbyterian Church

left. Raiders visited John Fleming's house next door, but found nothing useful except harnesses. Fleming's house stands on the hill just east of the church.

Go straight at the Gavers stop sign. This area was the scene of Burbick's surrender to Morgan. A company of the New Lisbon (present-day Lisbon) horse militia, serving under Captain James Burbick, sent three scouts west to John Fleming's farm, where one scout, Lieutenant Charles D. Maus, was captured by the raiders on the rise in the road in front of the Fleming house.

It is 0.4 mile from the stop sign to a "Y" intersection with Hepner Hollow Road (SR 164). Burbick's small company of militia fell back to the barricade of Captain Cornelius Curry's company of New Lisbon volunteers. Curry's men had loaded an old Mexican War-era smoothbore iron cannon with scraps of iron and had dragged it to the hill above where the Hepner Hollow Road intersects the Hanoverton-West Point Road. With Morgan's approach, all but three of Curry's men disappeared into the woods. The combined militia force now consisted of less than twelve men.

Curry's barricaded position on the hill (left) and SR 164 (out of photo, left).

When Morgan's men reached a point on the West Point Road just opposite the militia position, he sent Maus, the captured scout, under a flag of truce to Curry.

Curry and Burbick accompanied Maus back to Morgan. They worked out an agreement to allow Morgan to pass through the county unmolested. In addition, Burbick would guide Morgan to the river crossing. As they rode along SR 518, 2.0 miles east of here Morgan asked Burbick to accept the surrender of his sick and wounded men.

Stay on SR 518 as it turns right at the "Y." In 1.8 miles, you are at Prosperity Corner. The Steubenville Pike comes in from the south.

When Major George W. Rue's force reached Steubenville, he learned that Morgan was headed toward Salineville. They continued upriver to McCoy's Station (present-day Empire) and detrained at 7 p.m., Saturday. From there, Rue moved his troops to Knoxville, where they spent the night.

Leaving Knoxville at 4 a.m. Sunday, Rue's men followed a road parallel to the one the raiders were traveling. Rue was attempting to stay between Morgan and the Ohio River. By 8 a.m., Rue led his men through Hammondsville and north to Irondale before turning west on the Salineville Road.

Rue reached Salineville after 9 a.m. At this place, after hearing of Morgan's movement toward West Point, General Shackelford ordered Rue to cut off Morgan. Rue's men rode east toward Highlandtown before turning north on the Steubenville Pike. They stopped about three miles south of Prosperity Corner at Bethel United Presbyterian Church; there they acquired a local guide, Doctor David Marquis.

Directly west of Dobson's Mill, the doctor directed them to turn off the pike and follow the West Fork of Beaver Creek. When Rue turned east toward the mill, he ordered a thirty-man detachment to continue to Prosperity Corner and fall in behind the raiders. They were to harass the rear of Morgan's column and prevent him from retreating.

About 0.7 mile south of here, Rue's main force rode east on a private lane to the mill and along the dry creek bottom beyond. After 1.5 miles, the cavalrymen turned left into a narrow gulch that served as a farm lane. It led 0.5 mile toward David Crubaugh's barn and West Point Road. When Rue's cavalrymen reached the road, Rue could see a cloud of dust created by the movement of Morgan's horses about a quarter of a mile to the west. Rue formed his line across the West Point Road; the line extended to the right behind a stretch of woods and to the left into the Crubaugh orchard, behind a high rail fence.

Meanwhile, when Morgan saw Rue's dust cloud on the south side of the creek, he surrendered to Captain Burbick under the condition that his men should retain their side arms, be paroled, and receive safe conduct out of the state. Burbick, under duress, accepted the surrender under those terms.

Continue on SR 518 for 0.8 mile to a private farm lane on the right.

JOHN HUNT MORGAN HERITAGE TRAIL INTERPRETIVE SIGN #55

Approximately 150-200 yards west of here on the north side of SR 518, near a stream, is believed to be the spot where Burbick accepted Morgan's surrender.

Drive for 0.1 mile on SR 518. The house on the right was the home of George C. Adams, built after the Civil War. George's mother, Eliza, lost the last horse stolen by Morgan's men on the raid. In 1863, the Adamses lived 0.1 mile south of here. David Burbick's log house, torn down in the early 1900s, stood between the present house and the highway. The site of the Burbick cherry and apple orchard was a few yards to the right (west) of the present house.

The site of the cherry tree under which Morgan surrendered to Rue and Shackelford is somewhere near the present-day highway, at the location of the former orchard. To your left, directly across the highway from the Adams house, was the John Crawford farm, where Morgan's men stacked their arms. For safety purposes, the Union captors

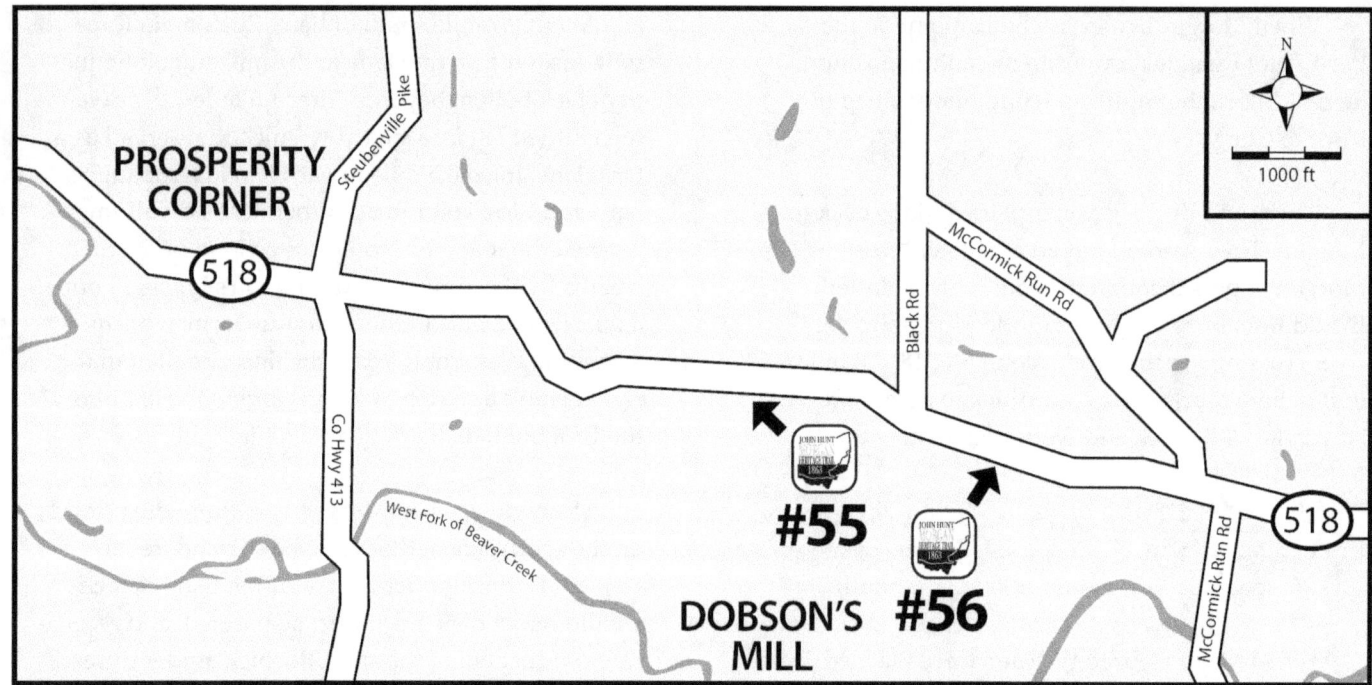

John Hunt Morgan Heritage Trail Interpretive signs #55 and #56 map

afterward discharged the remaining rounds from the surrendered guns, giving the false impression to the surrounding towns that a skirmish was occurring.

Approximately forty yards beyond the Adams house's driveway, on the right side of the highway, is the Burbick Spring, which flows into the creek ahead. A tree stump currently stands above the spring. General Morgan and soldiers of both sides hovered around the spring while the surrender unfolded.

Continue for another 0.1 mile on SR 518 to the top of a rise. There is an abandoned state rest park on the right. Just a few yards ahead, Black Road (TR 784) enters SR 518 from the left. In 1863, this was the eastern boundary of David Burbick's farm. Here, Morgan's lead scouts halted when they saw the Union line across the road to their front. The scouts rode back to Morgan and reported the bad news. Knowing the game was over, Morgan dismounted at the orchard adjacent to the David Burbick house. There he sat down to rest in the grass under the shade of a large cherry tree. He left pickets to guard the Black Road intersection.

When the park was created in the early 1960s, the surrender monument was moved here from the Crubaugh farm. In 2005, when the park closed, the monument was returned to its original site. Continue 0.2 mile. The relocated **Surrender Monument** is on the right. Park in the lot next to it.

JOHN HUNT MORGAN HERITAGE TRAIL INTERPRETIVE SIGN #56

Surrender monument at Crubaugh farm, first dedicated August 11, 1910

OLD WASHINGTON TO WEST POINT

Crubaugh farm on right; West Beaver Church in distance.

This was the David Crubaugh farm. By following Doctor Marquis's directions, Major Rue was able to intercept Morgan by forming his battle line across the road at this location.

Under a flag of truce, Morgan sent Major Theophilus Steele and several raiders toward the Union line. Rue sent three men forward to meet the rebels.

At first, Morgan demanded that Rue surrender. After conferring with Rue, however, the raiders returned with his reply that Morgan must surrender now or fight Major George Washington Rue of the 9th Kentucky U.S. Cavalry. Morgan's men conferred with their leader and reported back to Rue that Morgan had already surrendered — but to whom?

On learning that Morgan was willing to surrender, Rue and an escort rode over to Morgan's position on the David Burbick farm. Many of Morgan's men lay on the grass and drank from the well while the terms of surrender were discussed. Others were sound asleep in the Crawford cherry orchard across the road.

Rue was informed that Morgan had surrendered to Captain James Burbick, a militiaman and Morgan's prisoner at the time the terms were arranged. Rue refused to recognize the surrender to Captain Burbick. Operating an independent command under direct orders from Burnside, Rue accepted Morgan's surrender under Burbick's cherry tree.

Neither Shackelford nor any of his troops took any part in the capture. Yet when Shackelford arrived, as commander in charge, he accepted what became the official surrender.

After twenty-five days of hard riding across nearly 1,000 miles, the sad remnant of General John Hunt Morgan's division of cavalry was brought to bay at this site on Sunday, July 26, 1863, about 2 p.m. When Morgan was captured, he was twelve miles from the Pennsylvania state line.

Morgan surrendered 364 officers and men and more than 400 horses. He gave his fine sorrel mare, Glencoe, to Rue, a fellow Kentuckian and veteran of the Mexican War. Shackelford later confiscated the horse. Morgan gave his silver spurs to his well-respected nemesis, Colonel Frank Wolford.

After the capture, the exhausted men of the North and South rested for several hours, and Eliza Adams fed them before the prisoners were taken to Salineville.

From Salineville, a train carried them to Wellsville, where Shackelford turned the prisoners over to General Brooks. Morgan and the other officers were held at the Whitacre House hotel, where a **monument** stands on the north side of Fourth Street between Main Street and Riverside Avenue. Morgan was given Room #64, the best room in the house. In appreciation, he gave the hotel owner, Thomas Whitacre, his sword. The Missouri House hotel served as a temporary hospital for the sick and wounded raiders.

Morgan and his officers were transferred to Cincinnati the next day. They were tried and found guilty of horse stealing. Treated as common criminals, Morgan and sixty-eight officers were sent to the Ohio State Penitentiary at Columbus. The penitentiary stood on the northwest corner of West Spring Street and West Street, bounded on the north by Neil Avenue and Nationwide Boulevard. A **marker** is at the site.

The enlisted men were sent directly to Columbus and from there to prison camps in Ohio, Indiana, Illinois, and Pennsylvania, including Camp Chase, Johnson's Island, Camp Morton, Camp Douglas, Rock Island, Alton, and Western Penitentiary. Some were also sent to Gratiot Prison in St. Louis, Missouri.

Major Rue and his wife were at the second dedication of the Surrender Monument on September 21, 1910.

It is 0.3 mile to the West Beaver United Presbyterian Church. The parishioners had erected a barricade across the road in front of the church. Although their efforts were for naught, these people were typical of the "Buckeyes" the raiders had encountered since arriving in Harrison.

Morgan and his men met their stiffest resistance of the Great Raid as they traversed Ohio. This unexpected show of defiance from the citizens of Ohio was one of the main factors that led to the raiders' capture. All along the raid route, Morgan's cavalrymen had encountered opposition not only from Union soldiers, but also from ordinary citizens. Many Unionist farmers, storekeepers, businessmen, and housewives performed individual acts of bravery and courage in the face of the enemy.

This concludes the tour. Continue east on SR 518 for 2.8 miles to US 30/SR 45 near West Point.

Other Ohio points of interest related to Morgan's Raid:

McCook House State Memorial. Home of Morgan Raid participant Major Dan McCook. House open Saturday, 10 a.m. – 5 p.m., Sunday, 1 – 5 p.m., Memorial Day – 2nd weekend October; Friday, 10 a.m. – 5 p.m., June – August. Address: 15 South Lisbon Street, **Carrollton, OH**; Phone: (330) 627-3345; Web site: *http://www.ohiohistory.org/*.

"Surrender Tree" at Beaver Creek State Park. Gaston's Mill in the park's Pioneer Village exhibits the trunk of a tree that witnessed General Morgan's negotiations with Major Rue at the Crubaugh farm. Mill is open Saturday – Sunday, 10 a.m. – 4 p.m., May – October. Address: 12021 Echo Dell Road, **East Liverpool, OH**; Phone: (330) 385-3091; Web site: *http://parks.ohiodnr.gov/beavercreek/*.

Wellsville Historical Society River Museum. Museum displays the sword that General Morgan gave to the proprietor of the Whitacre House hotel on July 26, 1863. Museum is open Sunday, 1 – 5 p.m., June – August. Address: 1003 Riverside Avenue, **Wellsville, OH**; Phone: (330) 532-1018 or (330) 532-3941; Web site: *http://www.wellsvilleohio.net/museum.html*.

Spring Grove Cemetery. The final resting place of forty Union generals, one Confederate general (Philip N. Luckett), Salmon P. Chase, and Union and Confederate dead reinterred from Camp Dennison. Morgan's Great Raid participants buried here include: Jacob Ammen (Sec. 51, Lot 84); Jacob D. Cox (Sec. 53, Lot 91); Dan McCook, Sr. (Sec. 10, Lot 1); George W. Neff (Sec. 52, Lot 152); and William B. Way (Sec. 31-A, Lot 293). Cemetery is open daily, 8 a.m. – 6 p.m., year-round. Address: 4521 Spring Grove Avenue, **Cincinnati, OH**; Phone: (513) 681-7526; Web site: *http://www.springgrove.org/*.

Federal headquarters sites in Cincinnati. Gen. Burnside's: 24 East 9th Street; Department of the Ohio: 325 East 4th Street; District of Ohio: SE corner of Broadway and Arch streets.

Greenwood Cemetery. Buried here is General Morgan's captor, Major George Washington Rue (Sec. Milliken, Lot 312). Cemetery is open daily dawn – dusk, year-round. Address: 1602 Greenwood Avenue, **Hamilton, OH**; Phone: (513) 896-9726; Web site: *http://www.greenwoodcemeteryhamilton.com/*.

Major George W. Rue's houses. Two of Rue's houses stand today (both private). One is at 5650 River Road in **Fairfield, OH**. The house he died in is at 236 North 11th Street in **Hamilton, OH**.

Camp Chase Confederate Cemetery. This prisoner-of-war camp held many of Morgan's Men captured on the Great Raid. Some are buried in the cemetery here. Cemetery is open daily dawn – dusk, year-round. Address: 2900 Sullivant Avenue, **Columbus, OH**; Phone: (937) 262-2115; Web site: *http://www.cem.va.gov/cems/lots/campchase.asp*.

Johnson's Island Prison Museum and Confederate Cemetery. The prison confined several officers of Morgan's Division, including Basil Duke and Roy Cluke, who were captured on the Great Raid. Some raiders are buried here. A museum tells the history of the camp and its inmates. Cemetery is open daily dawn – dusk, year-round. Cemetery Address: Johnson Island Causeway & Confederate Drive, **Lakeside Marblehead, OH**. Museum is open Saturday – Sunday, 1 – 4 p.m., Memorial Day – October. Museum Address: Ohio Veterans Home, 3416 Columbus Avenue, **Sandusky, OH**; Phone: (419) 625-2454; Web site: *http://www.johnsonsisland.org/*.

Rutherford B. Hayes Presidential Center. Home and grave of Morgan Raid participant Rutherford B. Hayes. Center is open Tuesday – Saturday, 9 a.m. – 5 p.m., Sunday, noon – 5 p.m. Address: 1337 Hayes Avenue, **Fremont, OH**; Phone: (419) 332-2081; Web site: *http://www.rbhayes.org/*.

Appendix A

ALTERNATE: MIAMITOWN FEINT TOWARD CINCINNATI

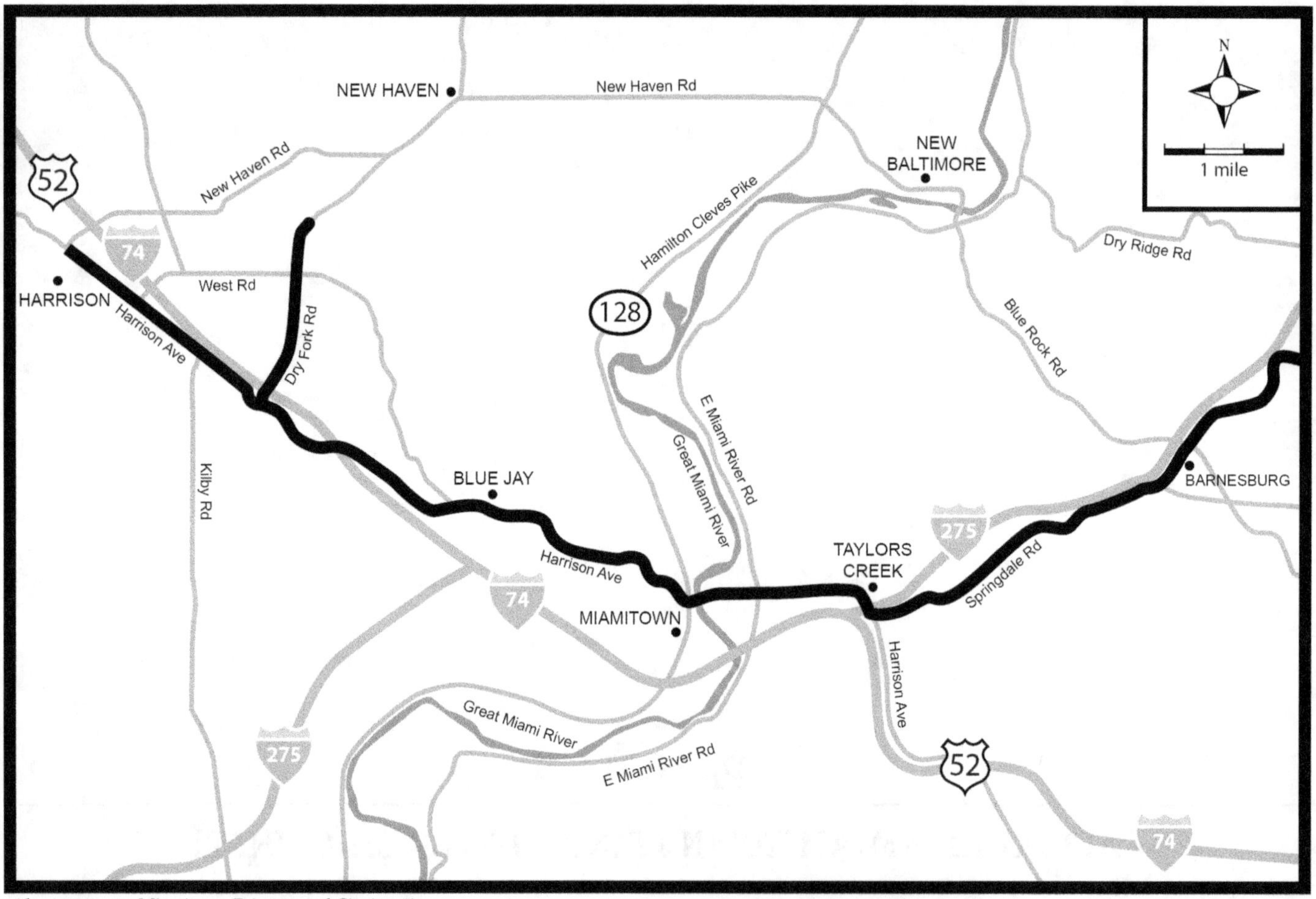

Alternate route; Miamitown Feint toward Cincinnati

Monday, July 13, 1863

At the New Haven Road, the main column turned north. A smaller force of approximately 500 men, detached from Colonel Adam Johnson's brigade, was sent to make a feint toward Cincinnati and burn the Great Miami River Bridge at Miamitown. To follow this group, reset your odometer and continue east on Harrison Avenue.

From New Haven Road, go 1.2 miles on Harrison Avenue. The house on the left, at 10320 Harrison Avenue, was built on the site of the Civil War house of William Jessup. Jessup filed a claim for the loss of a horse taken by the raiders. Later, when the Union forces passed through, he lost another horse, some feed, and meals for twenty-two soldiers. He was never reimbursed for the losses to the Union soldiers.

The house at 10320 Harrison Avenue was built in 1881 on the site of the William Jessup house.

It is 0.7 mile to Dry Fork Road; this section of the road was relocated when the Interstate was built. The original Dry Fork Road was to the east, closer to Dry Fork Creek.

*Side Trip: Turn left on Dry Fork Road to view the homes of two farmers who filed raid claims. Both are on the right side.

ALTERNATE: MIAMITOWN FEINT TOWARD CINCINNATI

Jesse Simonson house (c. 1860)

Go 1.2 miles; the Jesse Simonson house is located at 9700 Dry Fork Road. Simonson lost two horses and a bridle to the Confederates.

Continue 0.5 mile farther; the William G. Oyler house is located at 10210 Dry Fork Road. Four horses were taken from Oyler's pasture. One was later recovered; it had been hurt by hard use while in the hands of the raiders.

William G. Oyler house (c. 1860)

Turn around. Return to Harrison Avenue and turn left.*

Continue 0.2 mile on Harrison Avenue. An old two-story, white-brick inn stands on the left near Dry Fork Creek. The inn, Eighteen-Mile House, was named for the distance from Cincinnati. Raiders stopped here, looking for horses.

Eighteen-Mile House on the banks of Dry Fork Creek (c. 1835)

Drive 2.1 miles to Blue Jay. The white-painted brick house on the right, at 8861 Harrison Avenue, was the home of James D. Rowen. His teenage daughter, Belle, saved the family's horses by hiding them in the woods at the back of the farm. The woods stood in the area that now abuts Interstate 74. The home's present driveway was the original Harrison Pike, before the road was straightened.

James D. Rowen house (c. 1847)

It is 1.8 miles farther to Miamitown (once known as Miami). The old town contains many buildings from the Civil War period.

A small group of Confederates turned north on the New Haven-Miamitown Road (SR 128). They rejoined the main column at Paddy's Run near New Baltimore. *See Appendix B Alternate: Miamitown to New Haven Road.*

The remainder of the detachment continued east in their feint toward Cincinnati, before turning northeast on Springdale Road.

An **Ohio Historical Marker** describes the skirmish that occurred at the bridge here when Morgan's detachment collided with a group of Union scouts.

While Morgan's main column encountered no resistance as it passed through New Haven, Major Bill Raney and his 23 Union scouts and militia ambushed the 500-man detachment that Morgan had sent down the Harrison Turnpike.

Raney, a Cincinnati detective, had positioned his pickets near the eastern end of the turnpike's covered bridge over the Great Miami River. The covered bridge was located on the same site as the present-day Harrison Avenue Bridge. To prevent the Confederates from crossing the river, the Union pickets had pulled up some of the floorboards of the span. Because the water level was low, Morgan's men were able to ford the river and regain the turnpike on the eastern side of the bridge.

Raney's men scrambled for cover behind rail fences and trees lining the turnpike. At 6:15 p.m., the head of the Confederate column appeared on the road. The militia let loose a volley on the unsuspecting cavalrymen, killing two and wounding three. Second Lieutenant Benjamin B. Kirby, Company B, 10th Kentucky Cavalry, was among the wounded. Ike Snow, one of Morgan's best scouts, was captured.

The raiders returned the fire and captured Sergeant Thomas E. King of Company G, 11th Ohio Cavalry. Ironically, King had been captured on September 15, 1862, by CSA General "Stonewall" Jackson's troops at Harper's Ferry, (West) Virginia, where King was serving as a private in Company E of the 60th Ohio Volunteer Infantry (OVI). After being paroled and serving with the infantry for several months, King enlisted with the 11th Ohio Cavalry in June 1863.

Outgunned and outnumbered, Raney's home guards quickly disengaged from the fight, but their gallant attack saved the turnpike bridge from destruction. Because Morgan's men were under orders not to become involved in a prolonged fight, they rode on and did not turn back to burn the bridge.

It is 1.6 miles on Harrison Avenue from Miamitown to Springdale Road. You will pass through Taylors Creek. The area was known as Taylors Creek Post Office in 1863.

Turn left on Springdale Road. Drive 2.9 miles to Schwing's Corner (present-day Barnesburg), where Old Blue Rock Road and Springdale Road meet. At about 7:45 p.m., the detachment rejoined Morgan's main column here as the main column approached the corner from the left and turned onto Springdale Road.

Parmenas Corson house (c. 1860)

It is 0.2 mile to the Parmenas Corson house on the right at 5553 Springdale Road. Corson lost not only a horse, but also a wagon and harness to Morgan's men.

Proceed on Springdale Road to the next intersection, which is Springdale-Blue Rock Connector. Continue straight on Springdale Road to rejoin the main column route.

Appendix B

ALTERNATE: MIAMITOWN TO NEW HAVEN ROAD

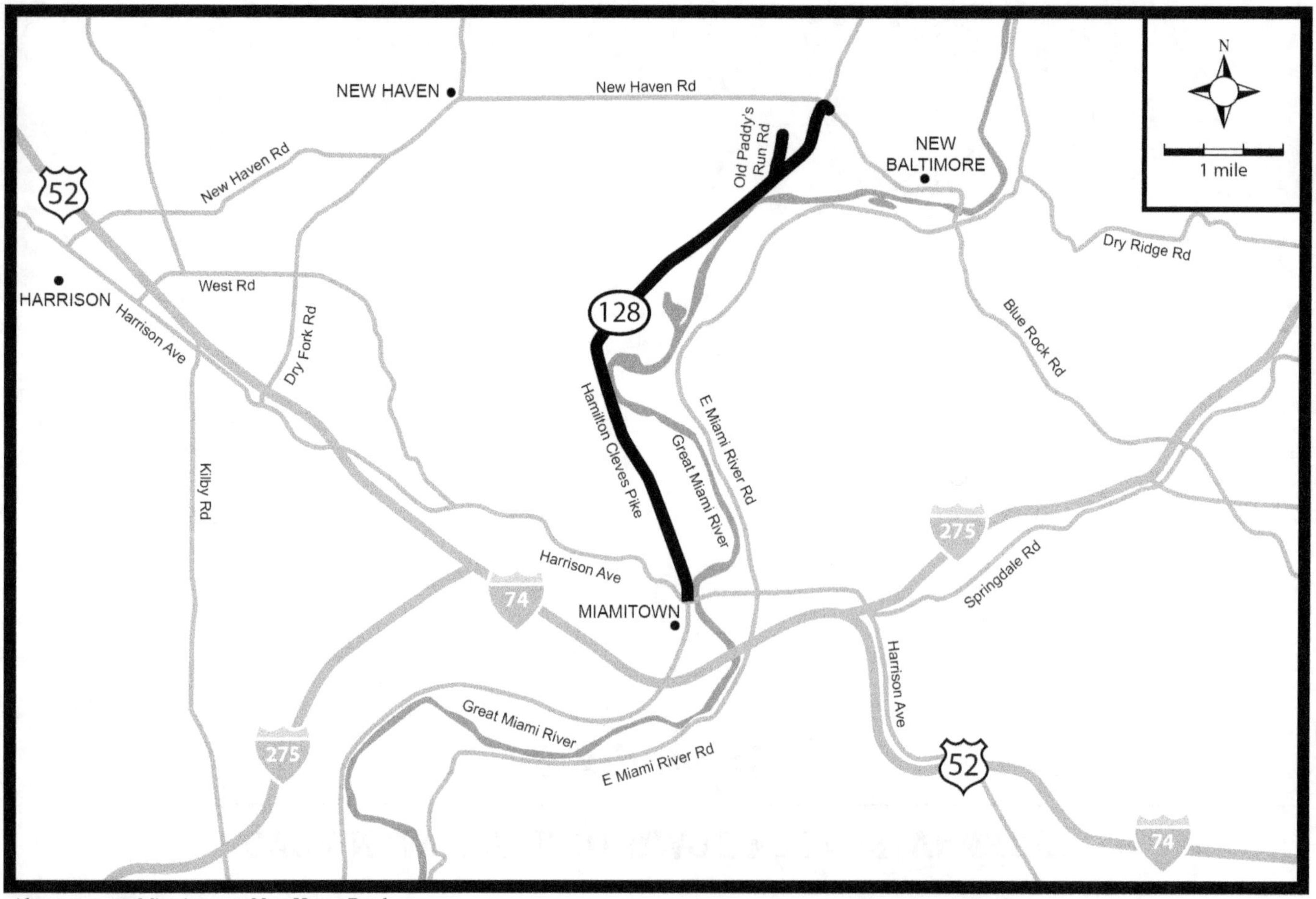

Alternate route; Miamitown to New Haven Road

Monday, July 13, 1863

Before crossing the Great Miami River on Harrison Avenue, turn left (north) on SR 128. There are six houses along this route that belonged to men filing raid claims. All of them lost horses.

Morgan's men were spending twenty-one hours a day in the saddle. Even the best Kentucky bluegrass mounts were breaking down under those conditions. Farm horses picked up in Indiana frequently failed after only several hours on the road.

Go 1.5 miles on SR 128 and park in the driveway on the right, just north of the soccer fields. You can walk to the site of the Martin Werts house, which is adjacent to the soccer fields' maintenance barn. Several of Werts's horses were taken; all were later recovered, except for one valued at $100.

Continue 1.0 mile. The William S. Nugent house sits on the hill on the left at 9461 SR 128. Nugent filed

Martin Werts house (c. 1830) was razed in 2011.

a claim for $127 for a horse and bridle.

Drive 1.4 miles. The Evan Breese house can be seen on the right at 10140 SR 128. Breese lost one horse to the raiders and another to the Union cavalry. He later recovered the animal taken by the raiders. He was awarded $40 for damages to the animal. For the horse "borrowed" by Hobson's troopers, Breese received $120 in compensation.

ALTERNATE: MIAMITOWN TO NEW HAVEN ROAD

In some areas, losses suffered at the hands of Union forces exceeded damages perpetrated by the Confederates. Some citizens felt that the boys in blue were worse than the raiders. Others did not file claims against their losses to the Federals and state militia; they considered it their patriotic duty to support the Northern forces.

Just beyond the Breese house and on the opposite side of the road is a house built by John J. Sater.

After passing the Sater house, turn left on Old Paddy's Run Road. Another house, also built by Sater, is on the left side. John's son, nine-year-old John Elbert Sater, was forced to pump water for the raiders' horses. One of the Confederate officers tied his horse to the wooden structure, which was pulled out of the well when the horse became frightened.

Morgan's Raid claims frequently dragged on for years before being settled, and many never were. After John J. Sater's death, his estate was awarded claims for $670 for loss of four horses, harness, and damages to a fifth horse.

Continue approximately 0.2 mile to the end of Old Paddys Run Road. The original road continued straight to a juncture with the New Haven Road. The farm ahead and to the left was owned by Thomas Pottenger. He filed a $225 claim for the loss of three horses to Morgan's men.

Turn around and return to SR 128. Turn left; it is 0.7 mile to New Haven Road. Turn right and rejoin Morgan's main column before they cross the Great Miami River at New Baltimore.

William S. Nugent house (c. 1845)

Evan Breese house (c. 1830)

John Jones Sater house (c. 1860)

Second John J. Sater house (c. 1850)

Thomas Pottenger farm (c. 1860)

Appendix C

ALTERNATE: NEW HAVEN AREA

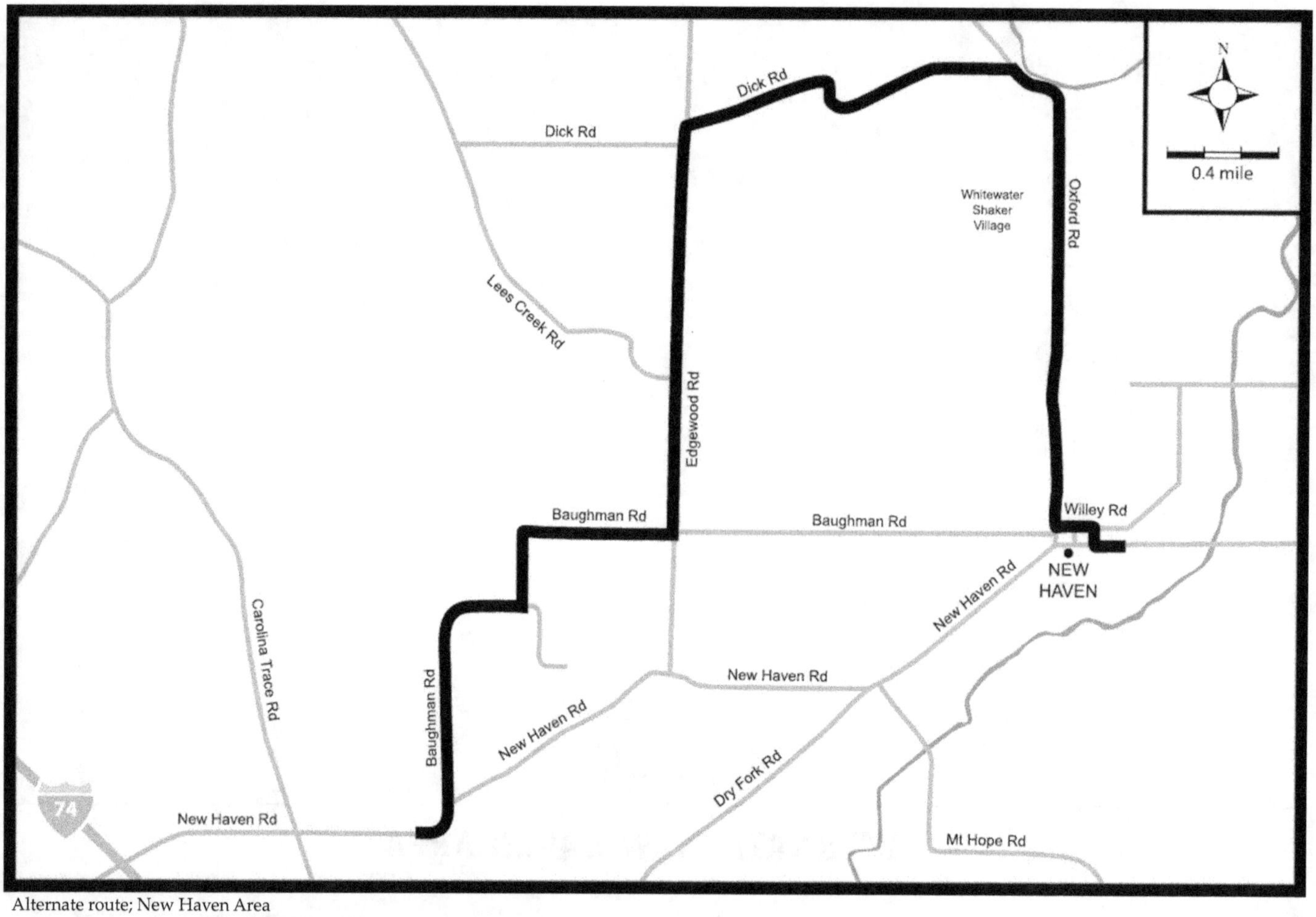

Alternate route; New Haven Area

David L. Mowery

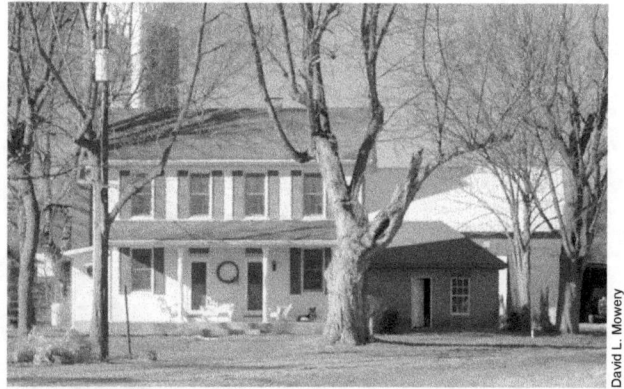

John D. Bowles house (c. 1850)

David L. Mowery

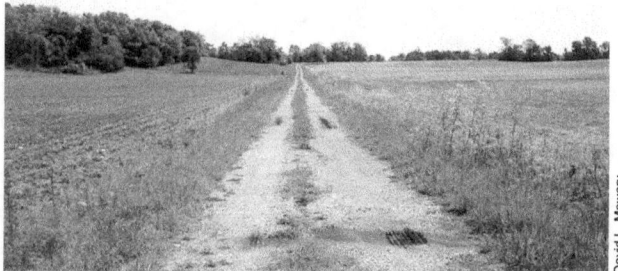

James Williamson farm lane

Monday, July 13, 1863

Turn left from New Haven Road to Baughman Road and drive 0.5 mile. The John D. Bowles house is on the left. Bowles lost a horse valued at $75 to the raiders.

Continue on Baughman Road for 0.9 mile to the junction with Edgewood Road. Turn left and drive 0.8 mile. The farm lane on the right leads to the James Williamson house site. The raiders took a horse and bridle from the farm.

Drive 0.4 mile and turn right onto Dick Road. Go 0.3 mile to the Michael Mann house located on the left. Mann lost two horses to Morgan's men; one was recovered.

ALTERNATE: NEW HAVEN AREA

Michael Mann house (c. 1845)

Shaker South Family Dwelling (c. 1830)

It is 0.8 mile to Oxford Road. Turn right onto Oxford Road and go 0.3 mile. The Trustees' Office Building for the Whitewater Shaker Village Society is on the right. Women of the commune were asked to prepare meals for some of Morgan's men.

Shaker Community Office Building (c. 1855)

The Community was established in 1824 and continued into the early 1900s. It was the fourth and last Shaker community established in Ohio. The Shakers were a religious sect that had fled England prior to the American Revolutionary War to avoid persecution. They gained a reputation for honesty, hard work, and skill in agriculture and hand crafts. The four tenets of their religion were: confession of sin, celibacy, community property, and withdrawal from the world. The Shakers practiced what they preached. They were doomed by their celibate way of life to decline and eventual extinction.

Drive 0.5 mile to the Shaker South Family Dwelling. En route you will pass the Shaker Community Cemetery. Unlike most of the Whitewater Community buildings that were built by Shakers, the South Dwelling was donated by a local woman who joined the society.

A young Shaker boy was at the mill in Harrison when the raiders arrived. He rode home spreading the alarm; he warned neighbors to hide their horses. As a result, most of the community's horses escaped detection. The family at the South Dwelling lost two horses to the Confederates; only one, valued at $75, was listed in the Raid claims.

From an account by MacLean, a member of the Society, "They treated our folks very respectfully and did not enter our buildings." He did not speak as highly of the Union pursuers. Captain John S. Hobart, the leader of Company I, Hendrick Regiment, from Indiana, threatened to burn the buildings and kill "the faithful" if they did not bring in the hidden horses. Elder George Rubush ordered his horses brought to the house, and Hobart selected the two best. The horses were valued at $300.

Drive 0.5 mile to New Haven and turn left onto Willey Road. A store, located at the corner on the right, occupies the site of the Elijah W. Thompson store. The earlier building was destroyed by fire in 1905. The raiders plundered the store, taking almost $500 worth of dry goods, clothing, provisions, and other articles.

The other store in New Haven was owned by Nancy Frost. The raiders purchased dry goods and groceries from Frost, who later filed a $200 claim because payment had been made in worthless Confederate currency.

Elijah W. Thompson store building burned in 1905.

A New Haven news correspondent for the *Cincinnati Gazette* reported that the raiders shouted hurrahs for Clement Vallandigham, a well-known Ohio Peace Democrat, as they rode along. Occasionally, they cheered for Jefferson Davis, the president of the Confederacy. After suffering losses to the raiders, many local Democrats had second thoughts about supporting a man admired by so many horse thieves.

Go two blocks to Fifth Avenue. The second house on the left beyond the intersection was Dr. William H. Bartlett's home, and the next building was his office. The doctor lost one horse, a halter, a bridle, and feed corn to the Confederates. Bartlett filed a claim for $162 but never followed through with it.

Dr. W. H. Bartlett's house (c. 1850) and office (c. 1860)

A small detachment, acting as flankers for Morgan's main force, continued east on Willey Road and turned north on Atherton Road, then they entered Butler County. They went as far north as Shandon (New London, or Paddy's Run Post Office in 1863) before turning east on the Colerain-Brookville Pike to join the rest of the flanking troops in Venice.

The raiders did little damage in Butler County; most of the county's damages came from the Indiana troops marching from Brookville.

Turn right on Fifth Avenue. Go one block and turn left to rejoin Morgan's main column on New Haven Road.

Appendix D

ALTERNATE: GREENHILLS ROUTE

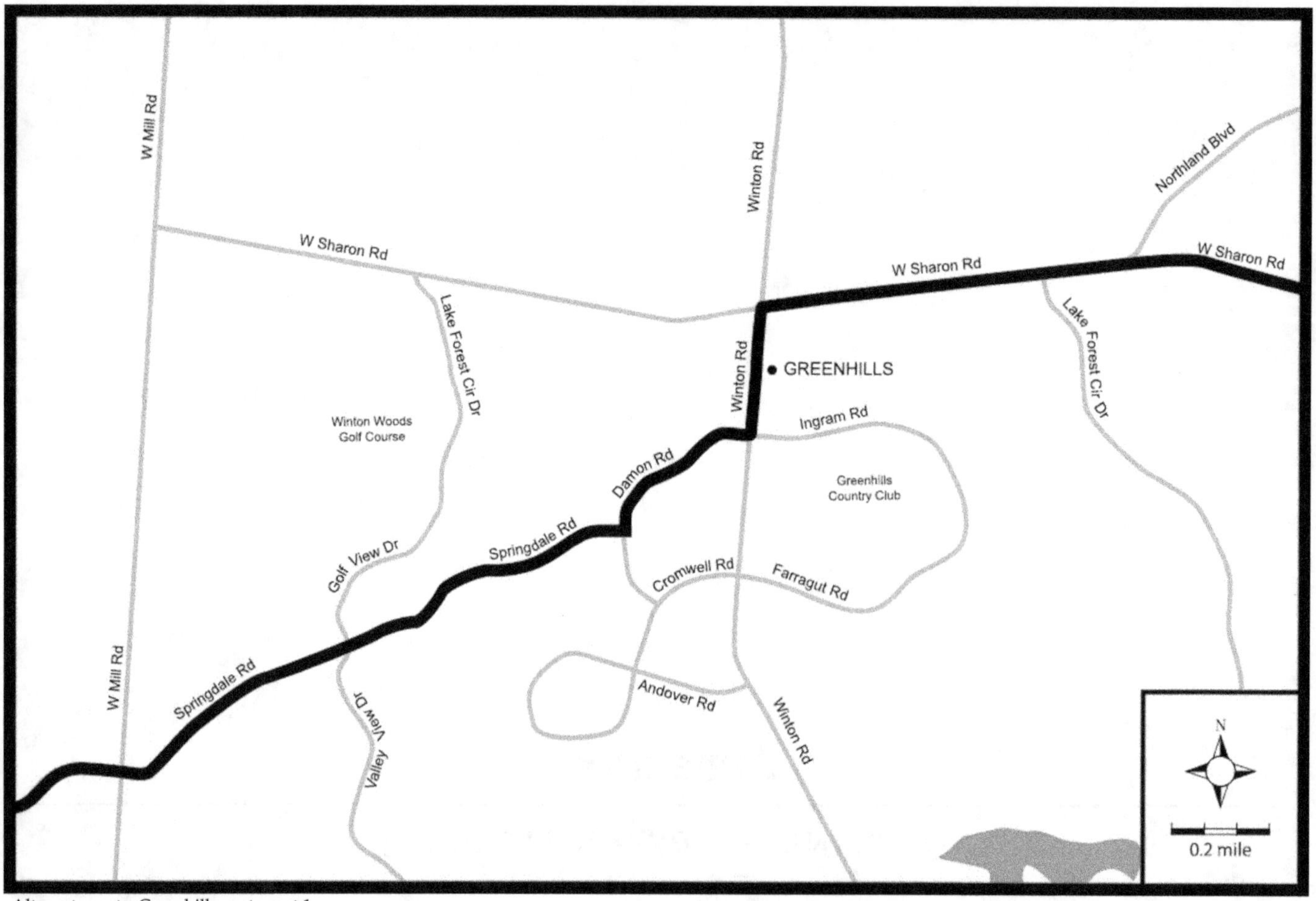

Alternate route; Greenhills route part 1

Tuesday, July 14, 1863

By the time Hobson reached New Burlington at 8 a.m., he was aware that Morgan's forces had passed through Glendale during the early morning hours. There was no reason for all his troops to follow Morgan's path through Springdale. Some did, but many of his men continued east to Glendale, passing through what is now the Greenhills area.

A great many claims were filed for losses to Union forces in what is now the Forest Park and Greenhills area.

Reset your odometer at the stop sign in New Burlington. Go 0.6 mile on Springdale Road to Mill Road. Morgan's men turned north here.

Continue straight on Springdale Road for 1.1 miles to the end of Springdale Road. Turn left onto Damon Road. In 1863, Springdale Road continued straight to Winton Road. The street was closed in the mid-1930s when the federally planned "Greenbelt" community of Greenhills was developed.

Go 0.3 mile on Damon Road and turn left onto Winton Road. It is less than 0.1 mile to the James Whallon house on the right at 11000 Winton Road. Whallon filed a claim for $140 for the loss of one horse appropriated by Union troops.

James Whallon house (c. 1816)

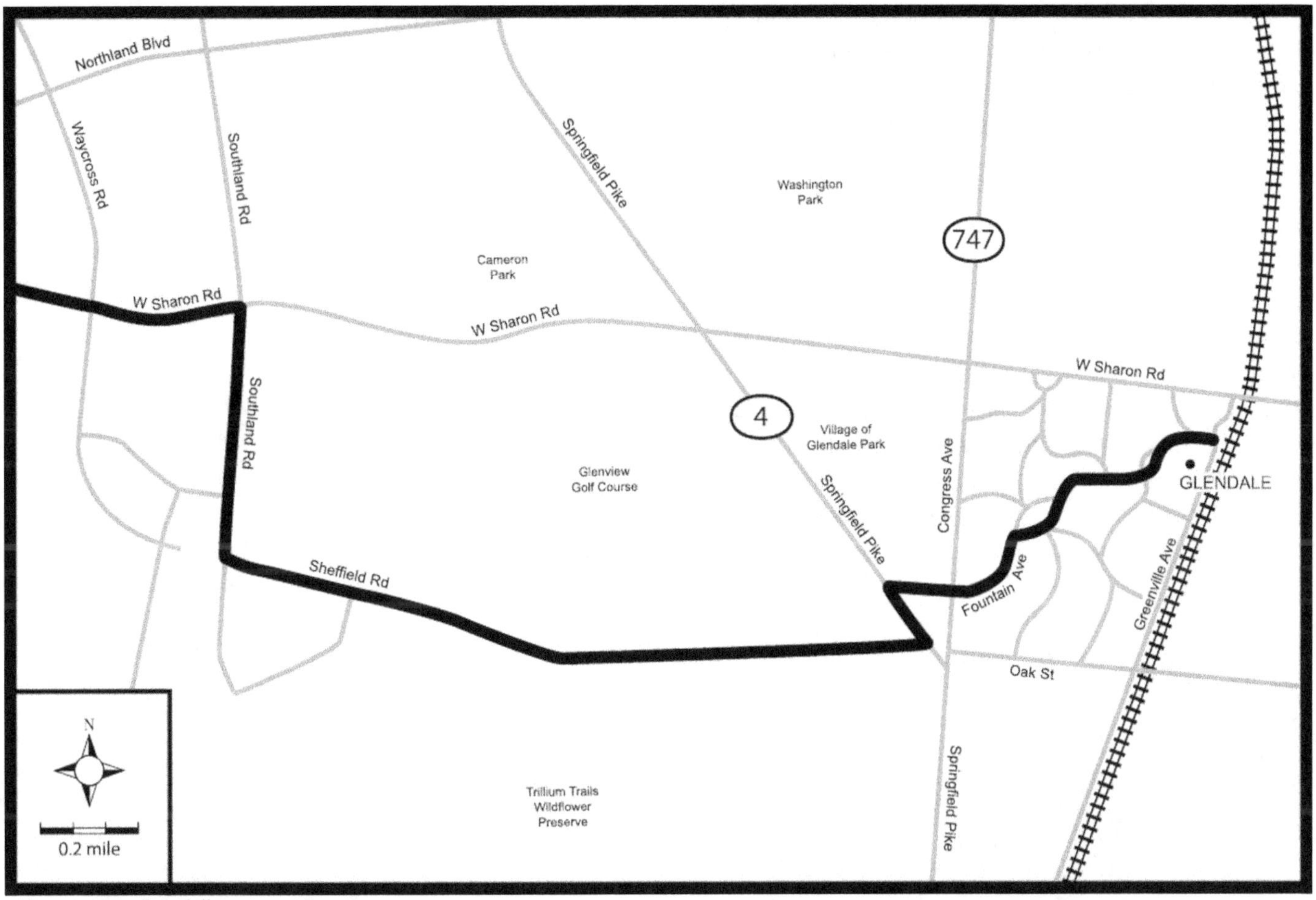

ALTERNATE: GREENHILLS ROUTE

Alternate route; Greenhills route part 2

Continue on Winton Road another 0.1 mile to Sharon Road and turn right. At 1.3 miles, the original road angled to the right through what is now an apartment complex. Continue 0.1 mile on Sharon Road to Southland Road. In 1863, there was no direct road to Glendale. Turn right onto Southland Road for 0.4 mile, and then turn left onto Sheffield Road.

It is 1.3 miles to the Springfield Pike (SR 4). The Century Inn on the southwest corner of Sheffield Road and Springfield Pike was built in 1806. The central two-story portion is the original building. It served as a way station on the pike. The inn was located about halfway between Fort Washington and Fort Hamilton. A toll house stood in the small triangular park across the street from the inn. At the time of the Civil War, the inn was known as the Farmer's Hotel.

Farmer's Hotel (c. 1806)

Turn left onto Springfield Pike and go less than 0.1 mile. Turn right on West Fountain Avenue; the street is not well marked and it is easy to miss. Drive one block and cross Congress Avenue (SR 747).

The large house on the left, at 780 Congress Avenue, is known as "The Pillars." In 1856, Charles Henry Allen built the house around a pre-existing farmhouse. There was an underground passage connecting "The Pillars" to another house across Congress Avenue that belonged to the owner's brother. Other tunnels connected the house to several nearby buildings. These tunnels were used to hide slaves being moved on the Underground Railroad. It was said that horses were hidden in the tunnels before Morgan's men arrived. The tunnels no longer exist.

"The Pillars," the C. H. Allen house (c. 1856)

Continue on West Fountain Avenue. The road splits and comes back together at two different locations, forming several small parks. It is about 0.6 mile to the historic Glendale village square and the old Cincinnati, Hamilton and Dayton Railroad Depot.

At this point, we rejoin Morgan's main column.

Appendix E

ALTERNATE: DUKE'S COLUMN MOVED THROUGH NORTHEASTERN SUBURBS

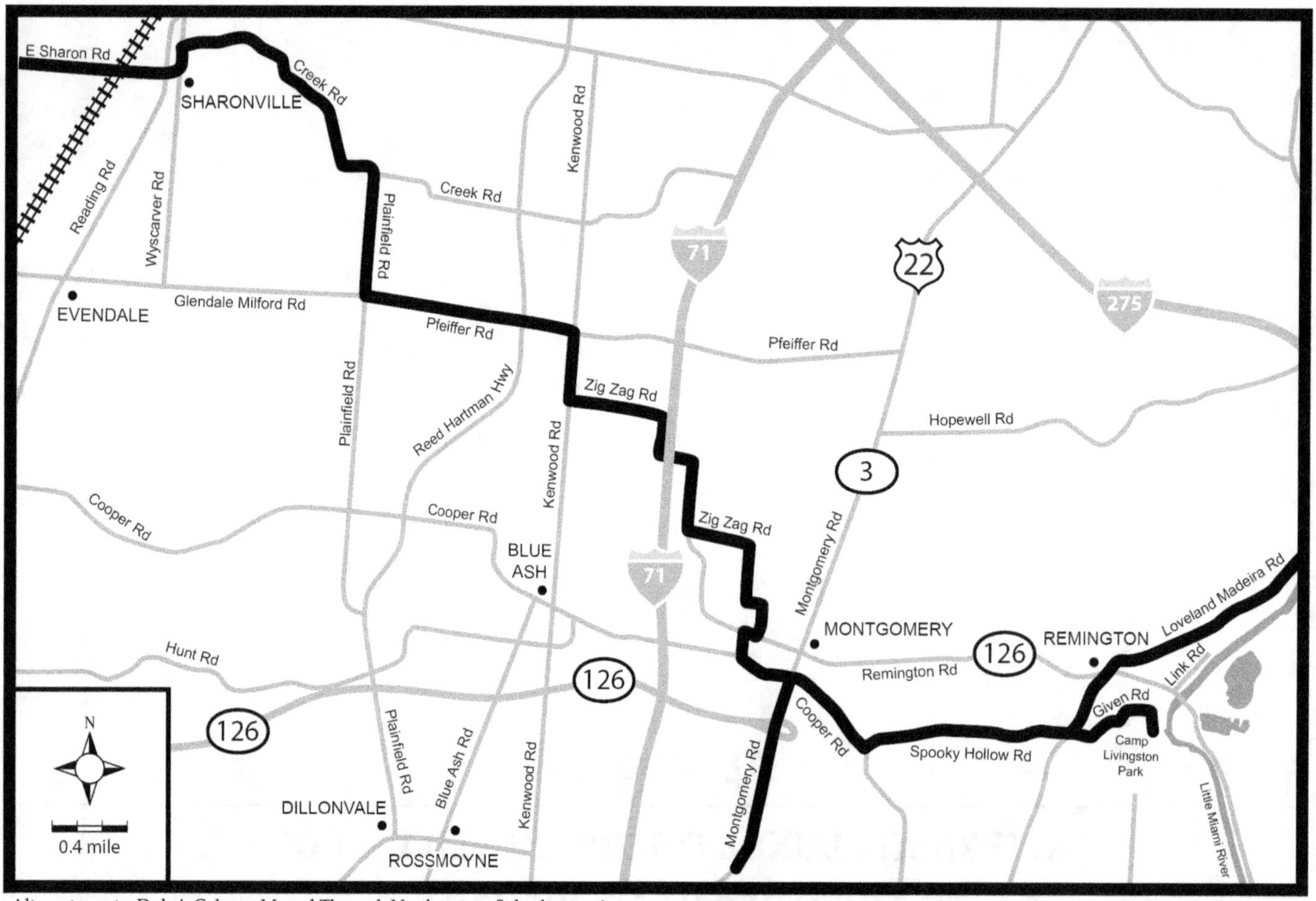

Alternate route; Duke's Column Moved Through Northeastern Suburbs part 1

Tuesday, July 14, 1863

Morgan kept his forces together as they approached Glendale. He feared that a large Union force might have been brought up by rail from Cincinnati. Once safely through Glendale, the raiders would fan out.

Morgan's vanguard entered Sharonville at 3 a.m. Morgan and his officers, including Basil Duke and Adam Johnson, met at the Twelve-Mile House for about half an hour to plan their routes to the Little Miami River. They set Montgomery as their rendezvous point.

Leaving Sharonville, the force divided into two main columns, and these columns then split into many smaller parties. It was about 3:30 a.m. when Morgan, riding with Adam Johnson's force, headed south and then east toward Camp Dennison.

Colonel Basil Duke

ALTERNATE: DUKE'S COLUMN MOVED THROUGH NORTHEASTERN SUBURBS

Colonel Basil Duke left Sharon moving east. A contingent of Duke's men rode north before turning east on Kemper Road. When they reached the Deerfield Road, they turned south toward Montgomery. A small group of these men continued east on Kemper Road, attempting to locate a crossing of the Little Miami River.

To follow Duke's main column from Sharon Road, cross Reading Road and follow Main Street one block to Creek Road.

The building on the left served as the Sharonville Methodist Church until 1981. One of the raiders ordered the minister's wife, Mrs. W. N. Williams, to prepare breakfast. She refused. He then attempted to lead their horse from the barn, but was thwarted by the Reverend. The unarmed man stood his ground and refused to surrender his horse, but the raider prevailed and rode away on the pastor's horse. Williams later filed a claim for $125.

Sharonville Methodist Church (c. 1837)

Turn right on Creek Road. Drive 1.1 miles to the junction with Elljay Drive; turn left on Creek Road.

It is less than 0.2 mile to the junction with Plainfield Road; bear right on Plainfield Road. Go 0.5 mile and turn left on Glendale-Milford/Pfeiffer Road. Drive 1.0 mile and turn right on Kenwood Road.

Go 0.3 mile and turn left on Zig Zag Road. The Archibald Johnston house is located near the corner at 10193 Zig Zag Road. Johnston filed a claim for one horse stolen by the raiders. The horse

Archibald Johnston house (c. 1840)

was valued at $140.

Stay on Zig Zag Road for 1.3 miles. The name is appropriate, so watch the road signs. The house on the left at 9854 Zig Zag Road was the Abraham Crist home. The family saved a bag of jewels by lowering it into a well by the kitchen door. They were lucky; usually the thirsty raiders' first stop was the family well.

Abraham Crist home (c. 1815)

James I. Ross house (c. 1840)

Drive 0.3 mile and turn left on Campus Lane. Go one block and turn right on Todd Drive.

The James I. Ross house is located on the right at

9611 Todd Drive. Ross lost a horse valued at $150 to the raiders. He was also awarded a $130 claim for a horse and saddle appropriated by Union forces.

Continue to the end of the block and turn right on Remington Road. Go one block and turn left on Zig Zag Road. Drive one more block to Cooper Road.

The house on the right at the corner of Cooper and Zig Zag roads was the James Wilder home. Now known as the Wilder-Swaim House, it serves as the home of the Montgomery Historical Society. James Wilder lost two mares to the raiders. One ended up in the possession of the Union 2nd East Tennessee Mounted Infantry, which later reimbursed Wilder for the animal. He filed a claim for $125 for the other horse but was awarded only $86.

James Wilder house (c. 1832)

Turn left on Cooper Road. It is 0.3 mile to Montgomery Road (US 22). At this point you have three options: 1) cross Montgomery Road and follow Duke's column; 2) take the following side trip to enter Montgomery with Morgan's main column; or 3) park and take a walking tour of historic Montgomery and its Morgan Raid sites.

*Side Trip: When Morgan's men were turned back at the rifle pits on the approach to Camp Dennison, they retraced their route back to Montgomery Road where they turned north to the town of Montgomery.

This side trip will take you south on Montgomery Road past several historic homes visited by men riding with the main column. After seeing those houses, you will turn around and re-enter Montgomery on the route used by Morgan.

From Cooper Road, turn right on Montgomery Road (US 22); go 0.1 mile. The Jane Kennedy house is on the right at Number 9257, just before the entrance ramp to the Ronald Reagan Highway. Mrs. Kennedy lost three horses to the raiders. Two were later recovered but had sustained damage. She did not file for the damages, only for the one horse that was never recovered.

Mrs. Jane Kennedy house (c. 1861)

Go 0.4 mile on Montgomery Road. The William Hiatt house is behind the trees on the left. A glimpse of the house may be seen from the driveway. Hiatt lost four horses valued at $500 to the raiders.

William Hiatt house (c. 1860)

Drive about 0.2 mile and turn around near the car dealership on the right. Another big "loser" was Nicholas Todd. His house (c. 1840) stood at 8765 Montgomery Road on the hill now overlooking the car dealership. The house was razed in 2001.

ALTERNATE: DUKE'S COLUMN MOVED THROUGH NORTHEASTERN SUBURBS

The raiders saw a Union flag flying at the Todd house and ordered Mrs. Todd to remove it, or they would shoot it down. The Todd family lost six horses (one was later recovered), a buggy, and harness to the raiders. Two jaded mares were left behind. In the end, Todd profited from the unwelcome swap. The two discarded Kentucky horses became the basis of a very successful postwar trotting stable.

The Nicholas Todd house stood at 8765 Montgomery Road.

After turning around, drive approximately 0.8 mile back to Cooper Road in Montgomery. En route you will pass Moeller High School on the left. Todd's race track was located in the area behind the school.*

The old town of Montgomery was founded in 1795. You may want to stop and visit the historic area. Ask locally for the Walking Tour Map which includes nineteen antebellum structures.

A number of Montgomery buildings have well documented Morgan's Raid histories. With both Johnson's and Duke's columns passing through the area, more than forty homes and farms sustained losses.

*Side Trip: A visit to historic Montgomery. The Universalist Church is located at the corner of Montgomery and Remington roads. It houses many of the original furnishings. The church was used by noted Civil War artist Mort Kunstler for the official Ohio Bicentennial painting of Morgan's Ohio Raid.

Universalist Church (c. 1837)

In the 1840s, the Pioneer Building at 9433 Montgomery Road became the residence of Doctor John Naylor. Naylor served as a surgeon at Camp Dennison during the Civil War.

Pioneer Building (c. 1818)

Raiders visited the Sage Tavern at 9410 Montgomery Road. The tavern was built of logs and later covered with siding. It was once three times as long as it is now. It served as a hotel for teamsters driving wagons between Cincinnati and Columbus. John W. Sage lost his stock of liquor, valued at $10, and his horse, valued at $100, to the raiders. His claim for the horse was eventually honored, although the claim for the liquor was not.*

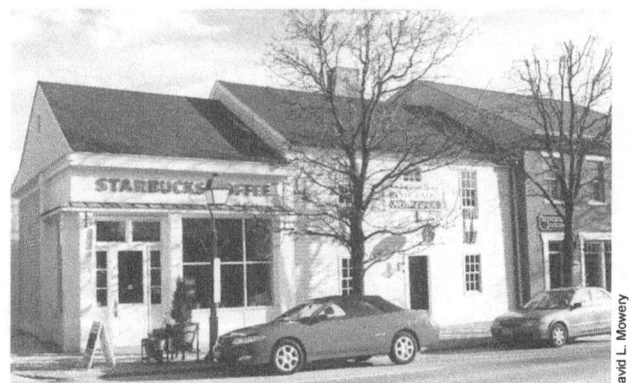

The surviving central portion of the Sage Tavern (c. 1818–1819).

William Hamilton house (c. 1800)

To leave Montgomery, cross Montgomery Road and continue 0.5 mile east on Cooper Road. Turn left on Spooky Hollow Road. It is 0.6 mile to the George Mumert farm. The house is located behind the trees on the left at 8200 Spooky Hollow Road. Mumert lost two horses to the raiders.

George Mumert farmhouse (c. 1825)

Continue 0.3 mile on Spooky Hollow Road and cross Loveland-Madeira Road. Go 0.1 mile and turn left on Given Road. The area is now the Sycamore Creek-Camp Livingston Park. It is 0.3 mile to the William Hamilton house on the left. Hamilton lost a horse to the Confederates.

Porter's Mill was located in the area behind the house. Remains of its stone foundation and the mill race can still be seen at the river bank.

The miller, John Riker, lied to Morgan, telling him Camp Dennison had been reinforced the previous night by 7,000 Union soldiers.

Porter's Mill crossing site

Nearby was a ford across the Little Miami River. This ford was used by most of the men of both Duke's and Johnson's columns. Morgan's artillery and wagons crossed here.

The Livingston Lodge is located next to the Hamilton House. To view the site of the ford, park at the ball fields across the street and walk behind the lodge. As you face the river, the road to the ford was to the right of the lodge in the neighboring yard.

On the opposite side of the river, a remnant of the old road to the ford still exists. John Elliott lived on that road. He filed a claim for $220 for the loss of twenty-five bushels of corn and two horses. He was awarded $150.

Some of the men crossing here were responsible for derailing a train on its way to Camp Dennison. Others moved on to Miamiville and attempted to burn the Little Miami Railroad Bridge. They were thwarted in their attempt and were driven off after a three-hour skirmish.

ALTERNATE: DUKE'S COLUMN MOVED THROUGH NORTHEASTERN SUBURBS

A small contingent crossed at another ford about 300 yards downstream from here. They protected Morgan's right flank.

Turn around. Drive 0.5 mile back to Loveland-Madeira Road and turn right. Drive 0.3 mile; reset your odometer when you cross Remington Road (SR 126).

As you leave Remington, the 1863 road (present-day Link Road) is to your right. It followed the Little Miami River; most of that road no longer exists. Some of Duke's men followed that road north.

It is 1.2 miles on Loveland-Madeira Road to Morgans Trace Drive on the left. During the Civil War, the property was part of the Nathaniel Humphrey farm. The family hid in the root cellar while the raiders took two horses, a saddle, a bridle, a blanket, and two halters from the barn. The Humphreys' home still stands on the corner of Morgans Trace Drive and Farmcourt Lane.

Nathaniel Humphrey house (c. 1849)

Continue 0.2 mile on Loveland-Madeira Road and turn right into Lake Isabella Park, a Hamilton County-owned park and fishing lake. There is a small day-use charge. Follow the road around the lake for approximately 0.6 mile. Before reaching the main parking area at the lodge and docks, turn left at the sign for the Riverside Reservable Lodge.

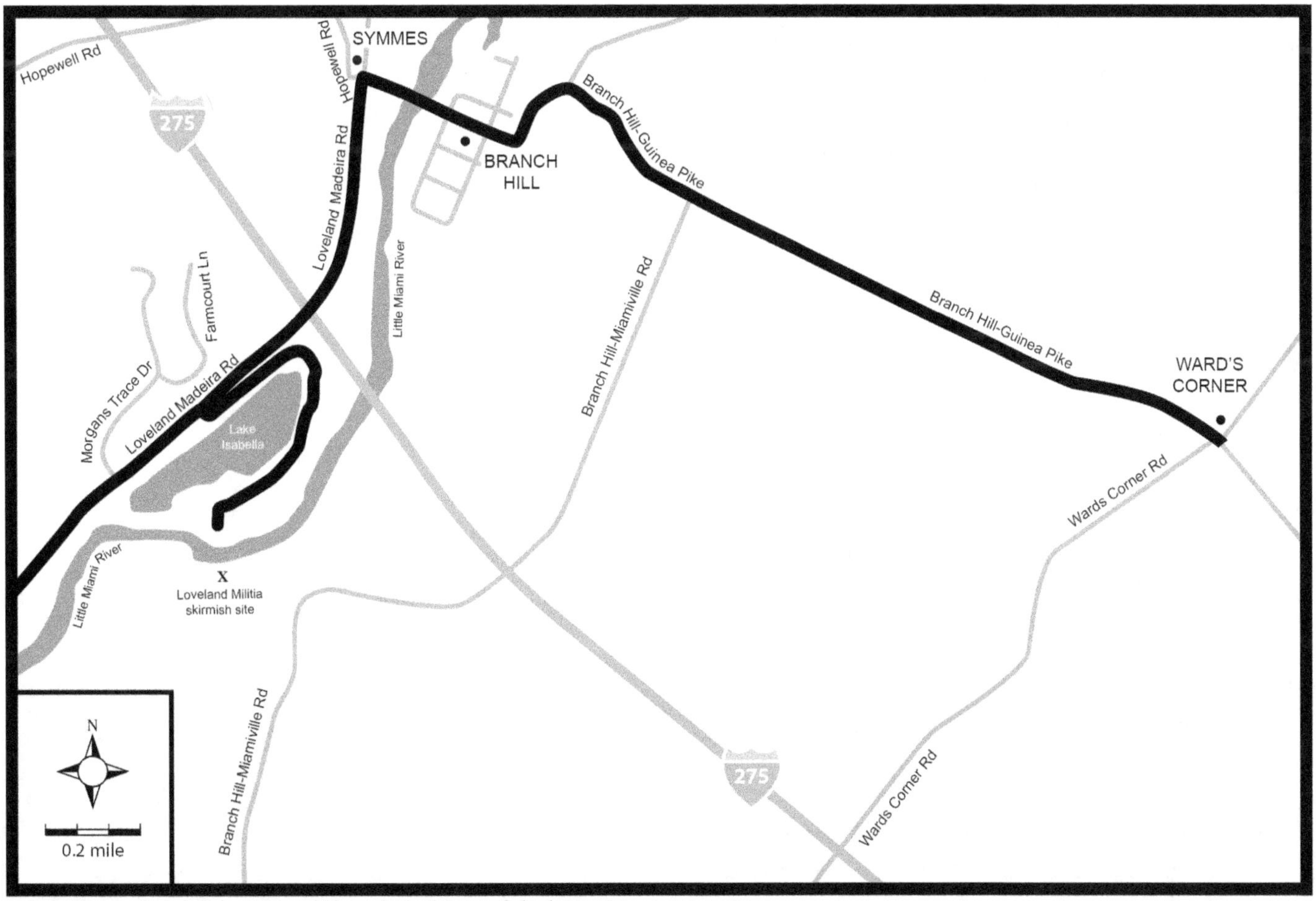

Alternate route; Duke's Column Moved Through Northeastern Suburbs part 2

To view the ford, park and follow the short trail on the left to the wildlife viewing shelter. The ford seen at the end of the trail is about one mile south of Branch Hill. It was used by some of Duke's men. These were probably the same men who had ridden past the Humphrey farm. Their mission was to shield Morgan's left flank.

Little Miami River ford below Branch Hill

While fording the river and crossing the railroad on the opposite bank, the raiders fought a small skirmish with Lieutenant Paxton's scouts from the Loveland militia. After brushing aside the Union scouts, Morgan's troopers stopped at the home of Samuel V. Hill Sr., where they confiscated a horse and a bridle. They continued up the hill to Morgan's headquarters, located at the Jacob H. Thompson House on Branch Hill-Miamiville Road.

Return to your car and drive back to Loveland-Madeira Road; turn right. It is 0.7 mile to Hopewell Road. Turn right and cross the modern bridge over the Little Miami River. The raiders forded downstream to avoid the suspension bridge here. The bridge was guarded by men from Loveland.

You will pass through the village of Branch Hill after Hopewell Road becomes Branch Hill-Guinea Pike; it is 0.7 mile to the junction with Branch Hill-Miamiville Road and Morgan's main column. Paxton's persistent scouts fired on the wagon train and Johnson's men as they turned east at this intersection.

Continue straight on Branch Hill-Guinea Pike to follow Morgan's main column. About 1.1 miles ahead, the scattered Confederate forces came together at Ward's Corner as Morgan prepared to move across Clermont County.

Appendix F

ALTERNATE: FLANKERS THROUGH READING

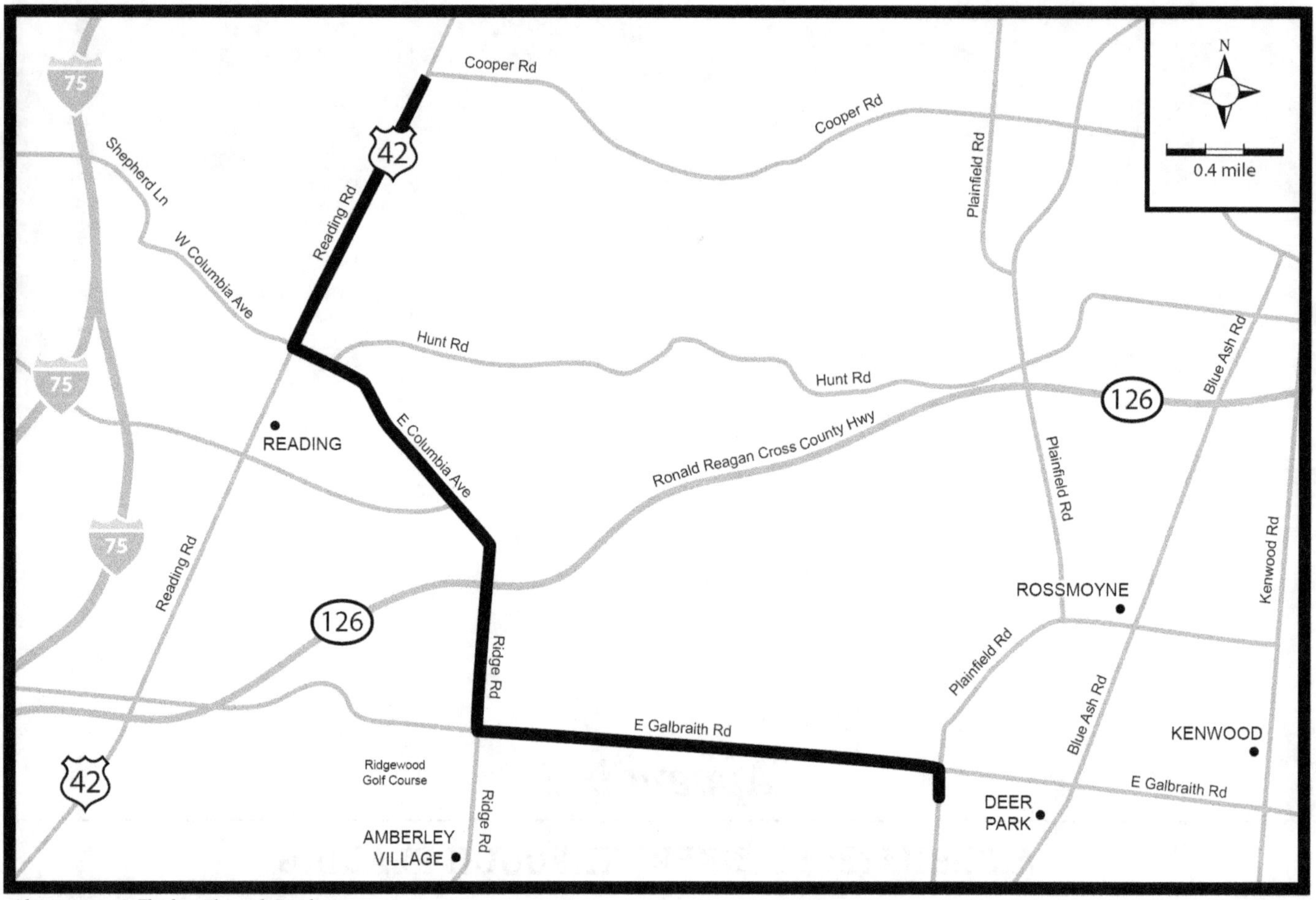

Alternate route; Flankers through Reading

Tuesday, July 14, 1863

When the main column turned east away from Reading, a small company continued south to cover Morgan's right flank. To follow that company, continue 0.9 mile on Reading Road from the Cooper Road intersection. Turn left onto East Columbia Avenue.

It is 0.5 mile to Mount Notre Dame Academy's modern campus. The 1860 building stood nearby at the end of Vine Street. All the original buildings were razed during the 1950s and 1960s.

The Sisters who ran the school heard that a band of Morgan's soldiers was passing through the neighboring woods, seizing all the horses and cattle they encountered. The school's faithful workmen hid the nuns' horses in the basement laundry room, covering the floor with sawdust to prevent the pawing of their hooves from being heard. Morgan's men searched the stable, and on finding it empty, made their way down the hill.

Catholic Telegraph and Advocate, September 8, 1860

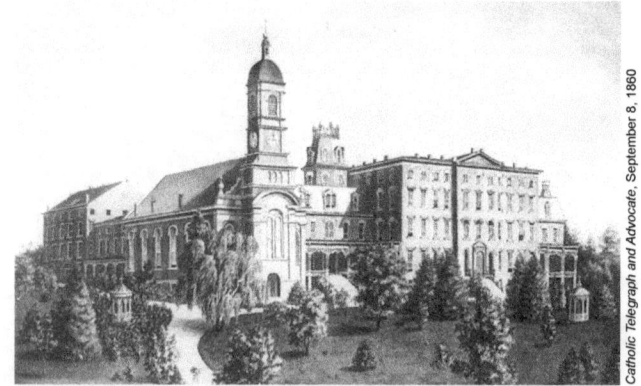

Mount Notre Dame Academy (c. 1890). The 1860 portion of the building is on the far left. The laundry area was in the basement.

Major General William T. Sherman's daughters, Minnie and Eleanor, attended the academy; however, neither was enrolled at the time of Morgan's Raid. In January 1864, Sherman enrolled Minnie in the school on his return trip to Mississippi after a short December furlough with his family in Lancaster, Ohio.

ALTERNATE: FLANKERS THROUGH READING

Continue on East Columbia Avenue, which becomes Ridge Road. It is 0.9 mile to East Galbraith Road. Turn left and drive 0.5 mile; the house on the left, at 3460 East Galbraith Road, belonged to David L. Cosbey. The house is located in present-day Amberley Village; in 1863, the area was known as East Sycamore.

David L. Cosbey house (c. 1860)

Cosbey's horses were in the pasture when the raiders arrived. Brandishing their guns, the rebels ordered one of Cosbey's hired men to catch them. Cosbey lost three horses to the raiders — one brown, one bay, and one sorrel. They were valued at $410.

Continue 0.8 mile to Plainfield Road. Turn right and merge with the main Morgan Trail Route.

Appendix G

ALTERNATE: COMPANY TO GOSHEN

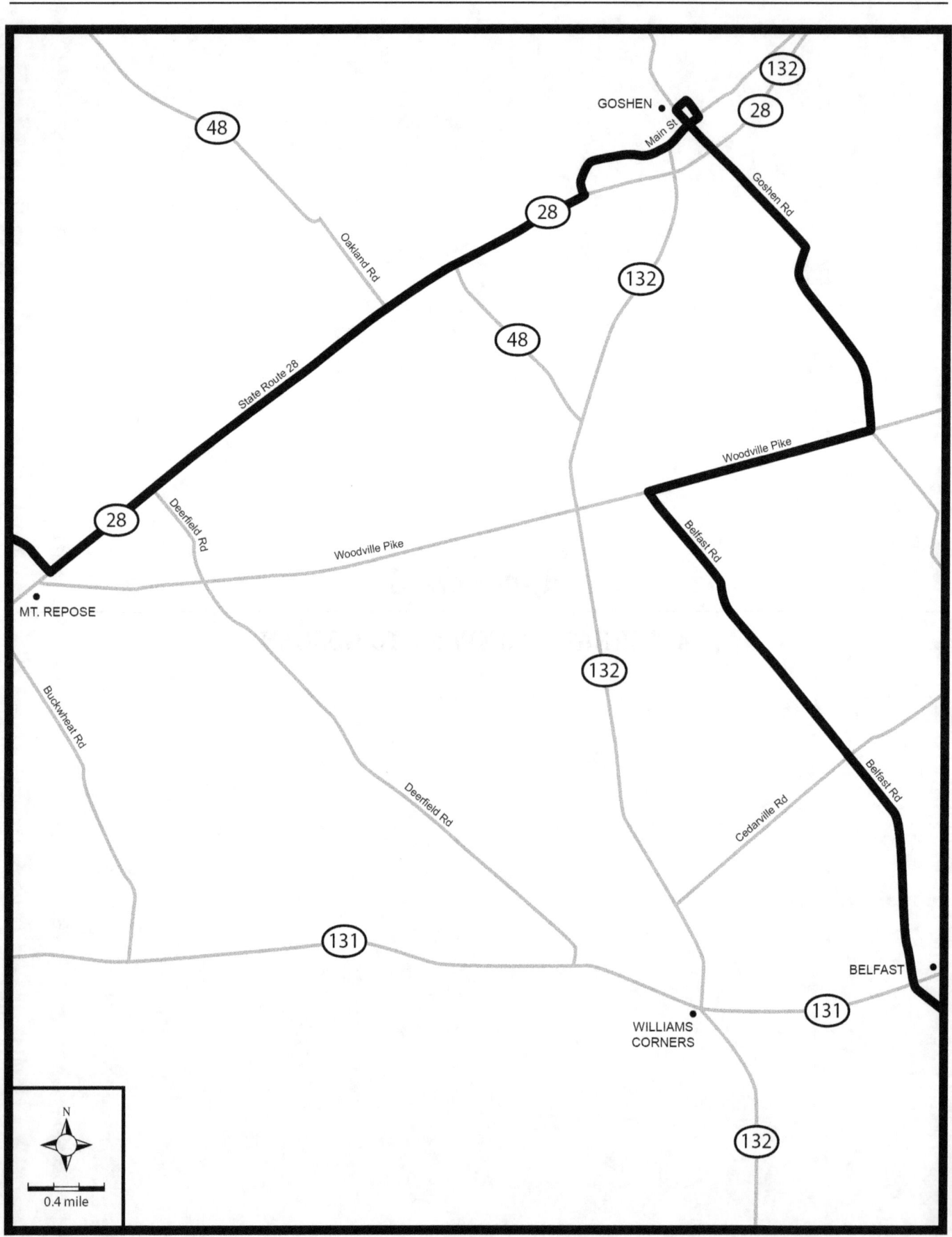

Alternate route; Company to Goshen part 1

ALTERNATE: COMPANY TO GOSHEN

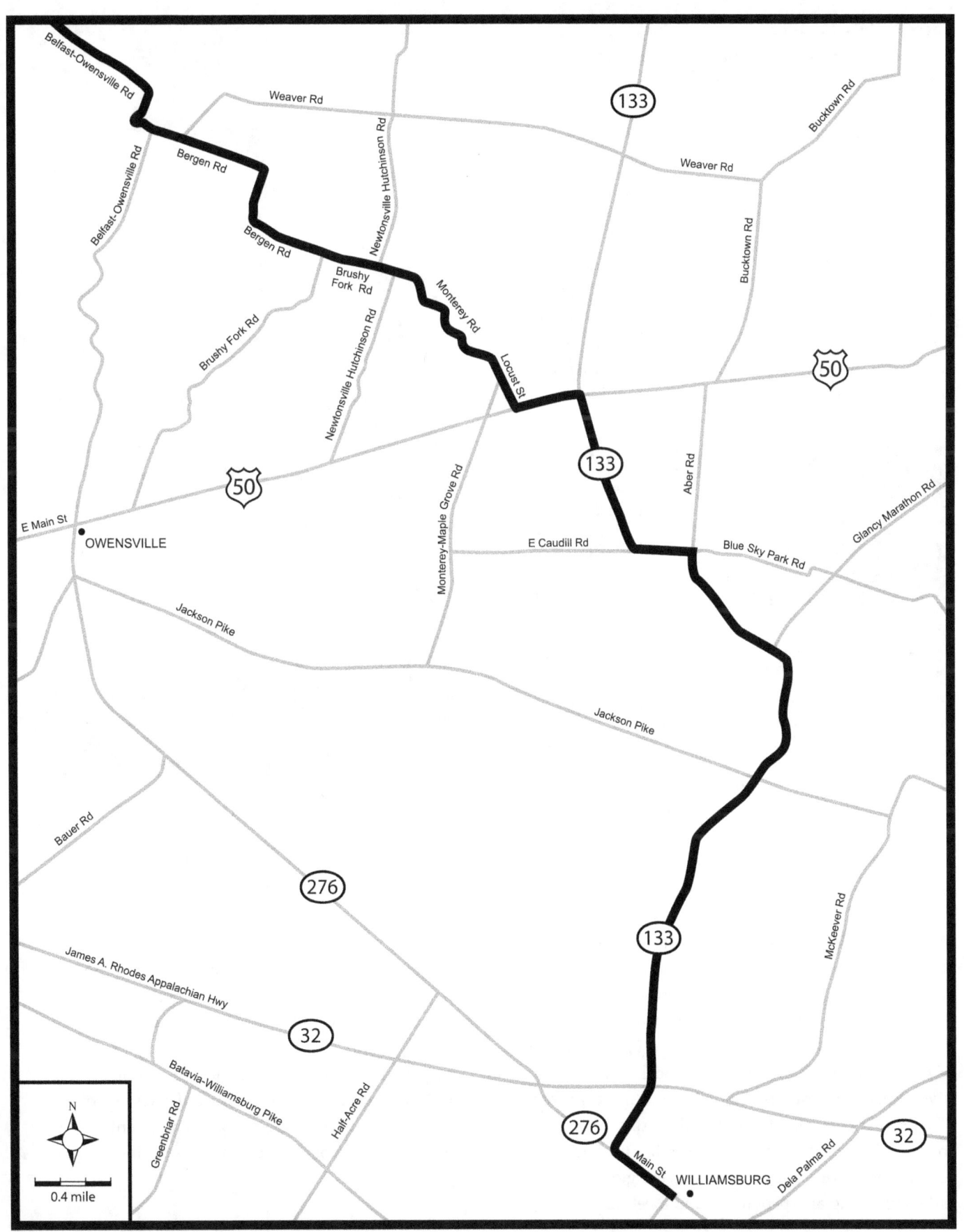

Alternate route; Company to Goshen part 2

Tuesday, July 14, 1863

At Camp Shady (present-day Mount Repose), Morgan sent a company toward Goshen.

From Branch Hill-Guinea Pike, turn left and take SR 28 northeast for 3.1 miles. Turn left onto Old SR 28, which becomes Main Street. Go 0.7 mile and turn left onto Francis Fagin Way. Drive to where Francis Fagin Way ends at George Street. Until 2004, the J. W. Glenn blacksmith shop stood at the end of Francis Fagin Way. The smith protested when the raiders attempted to steal several of his customers' horses. He must have been convincing; the raiders didn't take the horses. Glenn filed a claim for the loss of one horse and blacksmith tools valued at $5.

Site of Tod's Scouts skirmish with Morgan's raiders at Charleston (Manila).

Turn right onto Woodville Pike and drive for 1.1 miles. Turn left onto Belfast Road. Go approximately 0.8 mile. The David Deerwester farm was located on the left at what is now 6276 Belfast Road. The Deerwester house, where several hungry raiders stopped for food, no longer stands.

The J. W. Glenn blacksmith shop, which was razed in 2004.

Turn left on George Street, drive for one block, and then turn left onto Goshen Road. Reset your odometer.

Go 1.7 miles to Woodville Pike. While many of the raiders followed Goshen Road, others fanned out to the east. The small settlement of Charleston (Manila) was located about 0.7 mile to your left at the intersection of Woodville Pike and Manila Road. It was the site of a small skirmish between the raiders and a group of Clermont County men known as Tod's Scouts, serving under Captain Joseph T. Wheeler of the 4th Independent Battalion Ohio Cavalry. Five raiders were reported killed, and thirty captured. The dead are believed to be buried nearby, in unmarked graves. At Shiloh, 1.5 miles beyond Charleston, raiders interrupted a meeting of church elders planning an upcoming camp meeting.

Deerwester house site

One of the young men, Virginia-born John H. Anderson, was smitten by the farmer's twenty-year-old daughter, Katherine. He responded to her pleas to let her father keep his horses. On leaving, he promised to return after the war and marry her. In 1866, he fulfilled that promise. This is one of several instances where Morgan's men returned to marry young women they had met during the raid.

ALTERNATE: COMPANY TO GOSHEN

It is 2.0 miles farther on Belfast Road to its intersection with SR 131. Morgan's men visited the old village of Belfast, which is 0.4 mile off to the left. The town had been founded about 1850.

Cross SR 131 and continue straight on Belfast-Owensville Road. Drive 1.3 miles to the bridge across Stonelick Creek. Pause and enjoy this scenic stream.

Continue 0.1 mile to a "Y" intersection and bear left onto Bergen Road. Reset your odometer. Drive 1.7 miles; Brushy Fork Road comes in from the right. Bergen Road ends at this junction. Continue straight; you are now on Brushy Fork Road.

It is 0.4 mile to a stop sign at Newtonsville-Hutchinson Road. Turn right on Newtonsville-Hutchinson Road and continue driving for 0.1 mile. Bear left on Monterey Road. Drive 1.2 miles and bear left on Locust Street. It is 0.2 mile to US 50; turn left.

Go 0.5 mile to SR 133 and turn right. Follow SR 133 for 6.2 miles to the junction with SR 276 and a merger with Morgan's main column in the area known as "The Big Field." The Big Field, which served as Morgan's first campsite in Ohio, was located just east of the intersection of State Routes 133 and 276. Turn left on SR 133/276 (Main Street) toward downtown Williamsburg; you are back on Morgan's main route.

Appendix H

ALTERNATE: UNION FORCES FROM MULBERRY TO BATAVIA

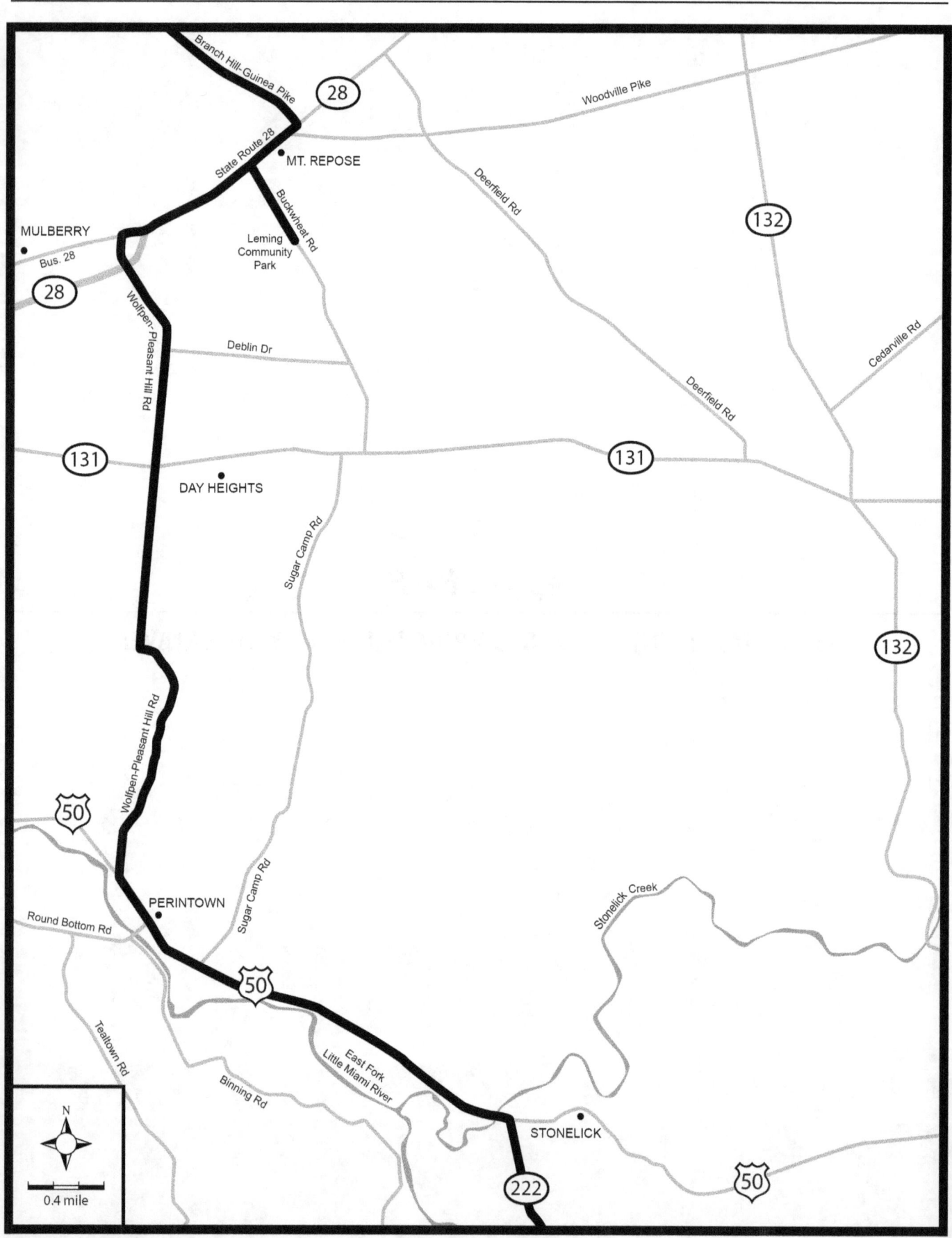

Alternate route; Union Forces from Mulberry to Batavia part 1

ALTERNATE: UNION FORCES FROM MULBERRY TO BATAVIA

After turning right onto SR 28 from Branch Hill-Guinea Pike, reset your odometer. In Mount Repose, Morgan's main column route turned left (east) immediately. To follow Hobson's route from Mulberry to Batavia, continue straight (west) on SR 28.

Wednesday, July 15, 1863

By 2 a.m., Hobson's men were moving out. He ordered the guide to lead them to Batavia.

Before leaving Mount Repose, we will view the home sites of several raid claimants. Drive 0.2 mile on SR 28. The Ezra Simkins house was once located on the left, at 1223 SR 28, immediately beyond the intersection with Jerry Lee Drive. The house was razed in 2005. Simkins's horse was taken by one of Morgan's men.

Ezra Simkins house

Directly across SR 28 from the Simkins house is the site of William Megrue's house and farm. It was here that Union Lieutenant Colonel George Neff's wife, Clara, hid the records and valuables from Camp Dennison. Morgan's men took seven horses from Megrue's barn, but they never found the items from the camp. Clara Neff later commented that the enemy troopers had acted gentlemanly around her and the Megrue family. When Hobson's cavalrymen arrived, they confiscated fifteen bushels of corn and three horses that Megrue had concealed from the Confederates.

Continue to the corner and turn left on Buckwheat Road. It is 0.4 mile to the Leming Community Park on the right. The Leming House is located in the park; the front part of the house dates to 1844. The owner at the time of the Civil War was Randall Henry Leming. His father and three uncles were early settlers of Clermont County, arriving here in 1804. Randall filed a claim for the loss of one horse to the Confederates.

Randall H. Leming house (c. 1844)

Return to SR 28 and turn left. Drive 0.7 mile and turn to the right on Business 28; do not take the bypass. Within 0.1 mile, turn left on Wolfpen-Pleasant Hill Road. Uriah Leming's property was on the right immediately after the SR 28 bypass bridge. Leming was awarded a $125 claim for the loss of a horse to the raiders.

It is 3.8 miles to US 50. Turn left onto US 50 and head into Perintown.

Perintown was known as Perrinville or Perin's Mills in 1863. James Given, a resident of Perintown, wrote the following account in his journal:

> Wednesday, July 15: Foggy but clear morning. Great Morgan excitement at sunrise. General James M. Shackelford's Cavalry Brigade began to pass our house and in the course of two and one-half hours about 4,000 passed in search of Morgan forces and about fifty of them took breakfast and fed their horses with us. They took great numbers of the neighbors' horses and one from us.

Given filed a claim for $100 for the loss of the horse.

It is 2.7 miles on US 50 from Wolfpen-Pleasant Hill Road to SR 222; turn right onto SR 222. Drive 4.1 miles to Batavia. Cross Main Street and drive one block. Turn left onto Spring Street; it is one block to Second Street.

Morgan's men visited the house on the southwest corner at 205 Spring Street. One of the raiders is said to have scratched his initials in the glass pane of a window. In 1863, the house stood next to a livery stable and carriage works.

205 Spring Street (c. 1830)

Turn left onto Second Street and return to Main Street, where you will turn right and drive one block to Market Street. The present-day Clermont County Courthouse is on the left, occupying the same site as the 1863 courthouse.

1863 Clermont County Courthouse

The Union forces arrived in Batavia on Wednesday. The raiders had visited Batavia the previous day.

Tuesday, July 14, 1863

At the "Y" junction just south of Boston (Owensville), a company of 80 to 100 raiders left Morgan's main column. These men turned southeast and followed what is now SR 132 for more than three miles to Batavia.

The citizens at Batavia were expecting the raiders' arrival. Horses had been hidden in nearby woods and ravines. Families had buried their silver. The county treasurer, Elbridge G. Ricker, had taken the county's funds to Cincinnati for safekeeping.

Lieutenant Colonel William Howard was a veteran of the Mexican War and Civil War, having served time as an officer of the 59th Ohio Volunteer Infantry (O.V.I). Howard attempted to form a company of home guards to defend Batavia. A group of men lined up in front of the courthouse, but only two or three were armed. At the approach of the first raiders, the men immediately dispersed.

It was late afternoon when the Confederates arrived; they posted pickets at the outskirts of town. They searched for horses with little success. Several raiders found a pony hidden in the outhouse at William Howard's home. His wife clung to the animal's neck and begged the men not to take it. They agreed; it was too small to be of any use to them.

When "Whig" Holloman's omnibus from Cincinnati arrived in front of the village tavern on Main Street, the raiders took the bus's six horses and mail bags.

The town's stores were locked, and the raiders did not break into them. Residents commented that the men were well-behaved and talked pleasantly with the townsfolk.

The raiders captured a local man dressed in Union blue. The man had served with the 59th O.V.I. and had been discharged and returned to Batavia after the Battle of Perryville, Kentucky. He was forced to

ALTERNATE: UNION FORCES FROM MULBERRY TO BATAVIA

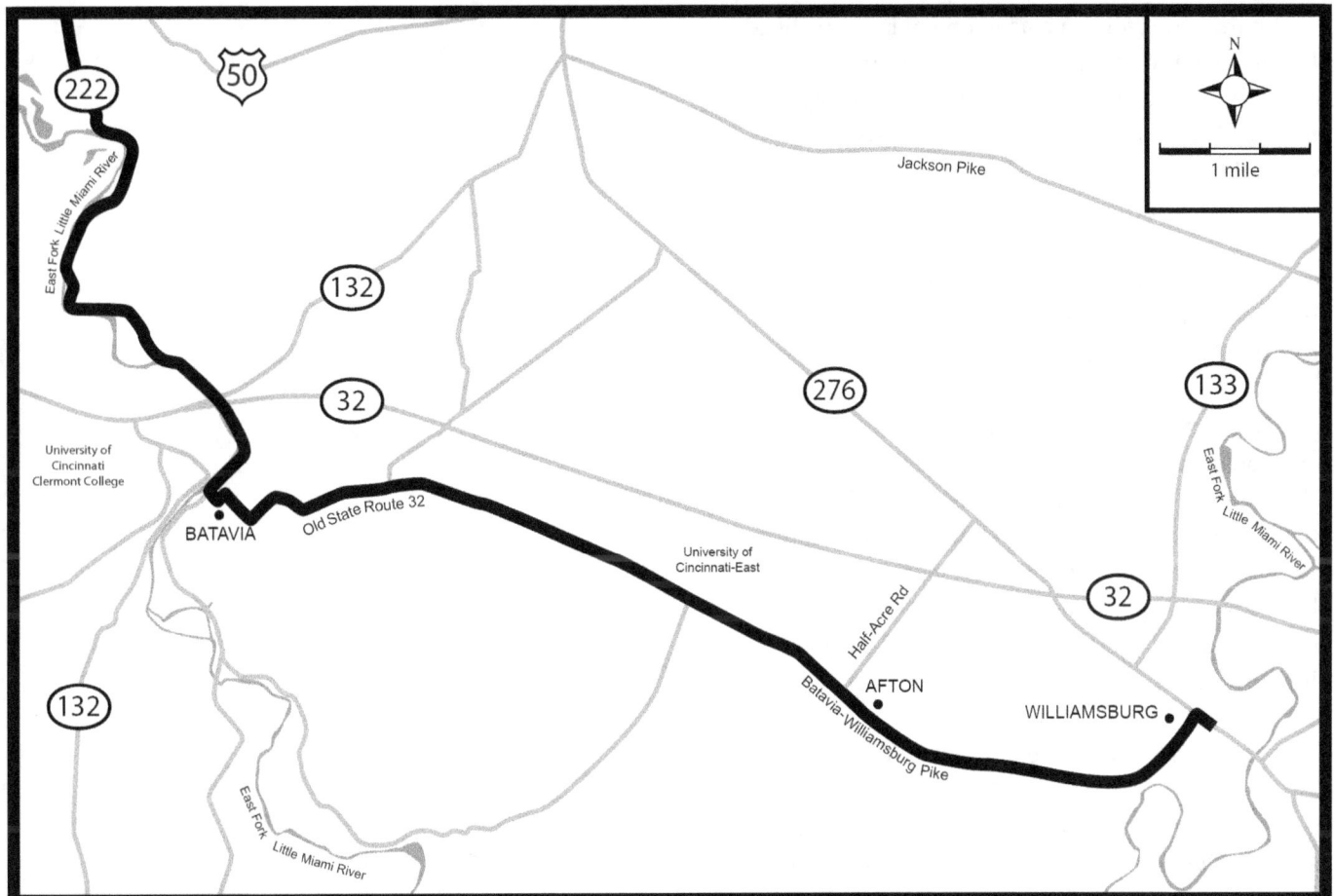

Alternate route; Union Forces from Mulberry to Batavia part 2

ride with the raiders to Williamsburg, where he was released and allowed to return home.

Raider foraging parties moved through the area west and south of Batavia. To visit some of those sites, *See Appendix I: Side Trip to Withamsville, Amelia, and New Richmond.*

After several hours, the raiders left Batavia, riding east on the Williamsburg Pike.

Three or four Batavia men, armed with shotguns, rode out the pike ahead of the raiders. We do not know what they had planned. Regardless of their plans, they were soon captured, and their guns were confiscated. The men were then allowed to return home.

Wednesday, July 15, 1863

By 8 a.m. the following morning, advance Union riders began to arrive in Batavia. Hobson's men had left the Mulberry-Mount Repose area about 2 a.m. Their guide, unfamiliar with the area, was soon lost. It took much longer than it should have to reach Batavia. It was 10 a.m. before Hobson's entire force was in town.

When the men and their mounts arrived, they were exhausted. The soldiers ate, and then they lay down in the yards and on the sidewalks and went to sleep.

Several of the Union soldiers stopped at the corner grocery store of an old German, Adam Kline. They asked him for two plugs of tobacco. He returned with the tobacco and handed it to them. They rode away without paying for it, leaving the furious storekeeper shouting and shaking his fist at them. The previous day, Colonel Dick Morgan had confiscated seventy-five pounds of crackers and eight pounds of cheese from the same store.

By the time Hobson reached Batavia, he realized that his march was being slowed by his artillery and heavy wagons. In an attempt to catch Morgan, he split his command. He sent Colonel August V. Kautz ahead with 400 of his best men mounted on the fastest horses.

Hobson's main force spent most of the day in Batavia. Late in the afternoon, they moved out toward Williamsburg.

Clermont County Judge, James B. Swing, was nine years old at the time of the raid. He later wrote, "They were a fine sight to see as they marched away, real war-worn soldiers of the Union, a long column, riding easily and in perfect order, their flags flying, their carbines slung over their backs, their sabers gleaming in the afternoon sun. The artillery was in the rear and the guns were an interesting sight."

That evening, a regiment of infantry from Camp Dennison arrived in Batavia. They came to support Hobson's men, in case there was to be a battle at Batavia. The troops spent the night near the village and returned to camp the next day.

Long after the raiders left Batavia, panicked militia felled trees across the road in the event the raiders decided to return.

To leave Batavia, follow the route used by the raiders and later by their Union pursuers. Stay on Main Street to Fifth Street. Reset your odometer and turn left. Follow Fifth Street to the edge of town, where it bears right and becomes Williamsburg Pike (Old SR 32).

Drive 4.2 miles on Old SR 32 to Afton. Hiram Sweet lost one horse to the raiders, and the Union confiscated seven from his neighbors.

Continue 2.8 miles to Williamsburg and turn right on Main Street (SR 133/276). Here, the company rejoined Morgan's main column.

Appendix I

SIDE TRIP TO WITHAMSVILLE, AMELIA, AND NEW RICHMOND

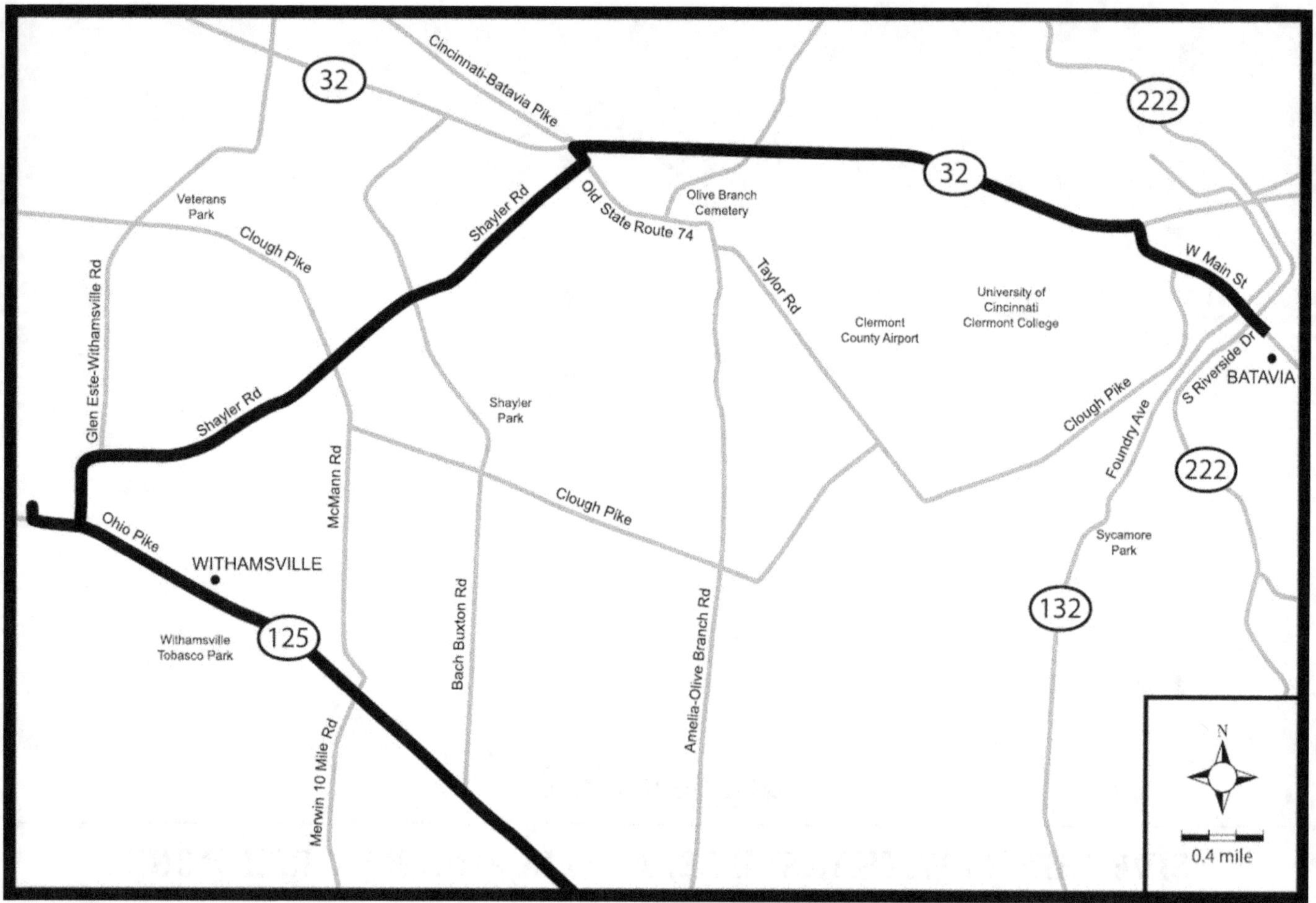

Side Trip to Withamsville, Amelia, and New Richmond part 1

Tuesday, July 14, 1863

As Morgan moved east, foraging parties left the main column. This side trip will take you to three Clermont County communities visited by the raiders. Because these towns were visited by various groups, a few of the roads we follow during this trip were not used by Morgan's men.

Leaving Batavia from the courthouse, follow West Main Street. After passing through the intersection with Riverside Drive (SR 222), reset your odometer as you cross the bridge over the East Fork of the Little Miami River. Continue straight on West Main Street, following the signs to SR 32 West. Drive 3.3 miles on SR 32 to the second junction with Old SR 74 (Batavia Pike) and turn left.

Immediately turn right onto Shayler Road. Continue 2.6 miles to the junction with Glen Este-Withamsville Road. Turn left and drive 0.3 mile to SR 125 (Ohio Pike). Turn right onto SR 125 and go 0.1 mile. Pull into the parking lot of the St. Thomas More Catholic Church on the right.

The foraging party took food from the Bennett House Hotel and horses from the stable. The Bennett House was the village stage-stop. It still stands across the street from the church. Some of the men visited nearby private homes and stables.

Bennett House (c. 1820)

282

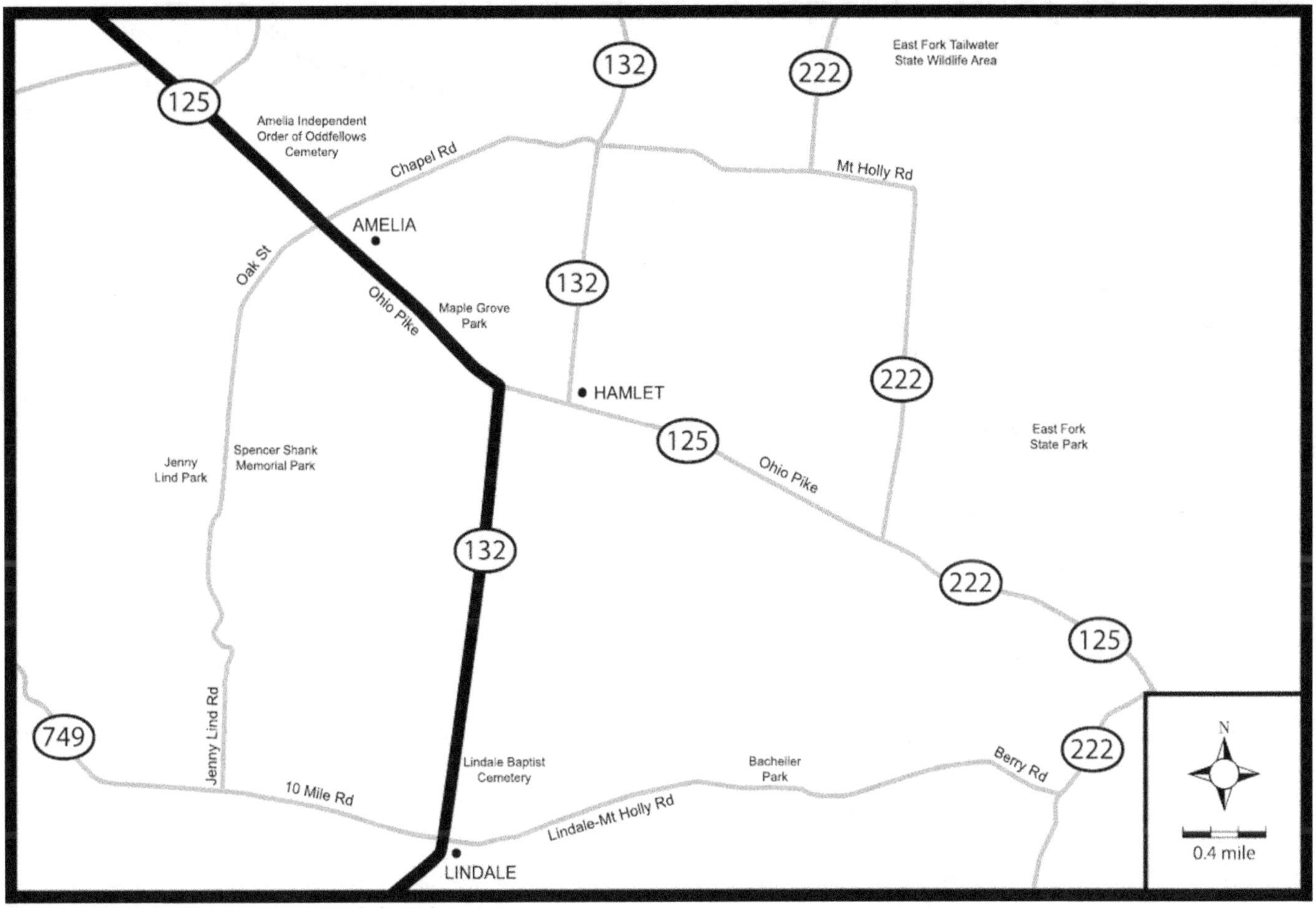

SIDE TRIP TO WITHAMSVILLE, AMELIA, AND NEW RICHMOND

Side Trip to Withamsville, Amelia, and New Richmond part 2

The men spent the night in the Methodist Episcopal Church. The church was built in 1857. About 1930, the building was used as a civic hall until purchased by the Catholic Church in 1944. After the new St. Thomas More Catholic Church was built, the building served as a hall and gym until it was razed in 1999.

The Methodist Episcopal Church was razed in 1999.

The next morning, the raiders left Withamsville, heading east on the Ohio Pike. To follow them, turn left when you leave the church parking lot.

Drive 2.3 miles on SR 125 to Bach-Buxton Road. Near this intersection, Aaron Cleveland made a costly error. Cleveland's Georgetown-to-Cincinnati stagecoach line operated out of Amelia. After stopping at his headquarters to change horses, he continued toward Cincinnati. When his westbound coach topped the rise here, he saw a group of approaching horsemen. He flagged them down to warn them Morgan was in the area. Instead of area militia, the group was a company of raiders, who exchanged their jaded mounts for Cleveland's fresh horses.

Drive 2.6 miles farther on SR 125; the road on the right, Cleveland Lane, led to the stagecoach line operator's home. Continue 0.2 mile; Cleveland's headquarters were located at the far right corner of the junction with present SR 132.

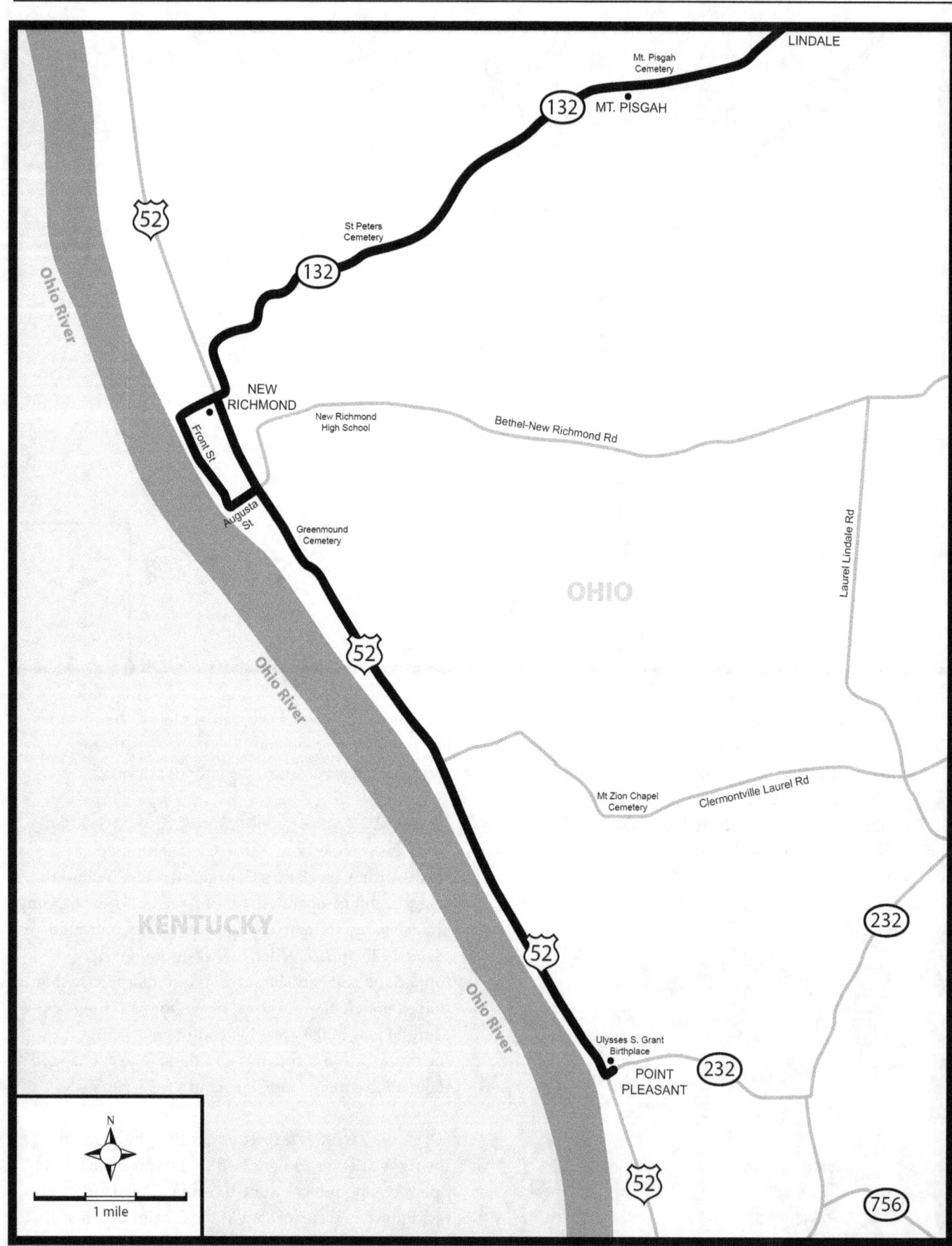

Side Trip to Withamsville, Amelia, and New Richmond part 3

SIDE TRIP TO WITHAMSVILLE, AMELIA, AND NEW RICHMOND

Turn right onto SR 132. It is 7.1 miles to US 52 (Columbia Street) in New Richmond. After crossing the highway, the road becomes Sycamore Street; continue four blocks to Front Street and the Ohio River. Turn left on Front Street; after four blocks the street becomes Susanna Way. Proceed for more than two more blocks on Susanna Way.

Several raiders were reported to have ransacked the Clasgen House at 310 Susanna Way.

The Clasgen Home fronts the Ohio River.

Ohio River at New Richmond

Shortly after leaving the house, the raiders attempted to cross the Ohio River. They were captured midstream by the Union gunboat USS *Moose*.

The gunboat, commanded by Lieutenant Commander Leroy Fitch, was patrolling this section of the river. The USS *Moose* was temporarily stationed at Palestine, less than five miles downriver.

Fitch was damaging or destroying all boats and skiffs along the river to prevent Morgan's men from crossing back into Kentucky. Eri J. Moreton of New Richmond was awarded $150 for damages the U. S. Navy inflicted on two of his flatboats.

At Palestine, eight men filed claims against Fitch and the U.S. Navy. At Moscow, seven miles upstream of New Richmond, Fitch's sailors destroyed several skiffs, and damaged a ferry boat and a wharf boat.

As Morgan moved east, the USS *Moose* continued upstream. On July 19, Fitch's boat prevented Morgan from escaping across the river at Buffington Island and again at Lee Creek.

Continue to the end of Susanna Way. Round the bend to the left as it becomes Augusta Street. Follow Augusta Street for more than four blocks to US 52 (Columbia Street).

*Side Trip: The birthplace of Union Lieutenant General and U.S. President Ulysses S. Grant stands in nearby Point Pleasant, Ohio. The Ohio Historical Society maintains the structure and operates it as a museum open to the public.

To visit Grant's Birthplace State Memorial, turn right onto US 52 and drive 4.4 miles. The house is on the left at the intersection with SR 232.

The house and museum hours are Wednesday–Saturday, 9:30 a.m.–5 p.m., and Sunday 1–5 p.m., April–October. Phone: (800) 283-8932; Web site: *http://www.ohiohistory.org/museums-and-historic-sites/*.

Drive 4.4 miles west on US 52 to Augusta Street in New Richmond.*

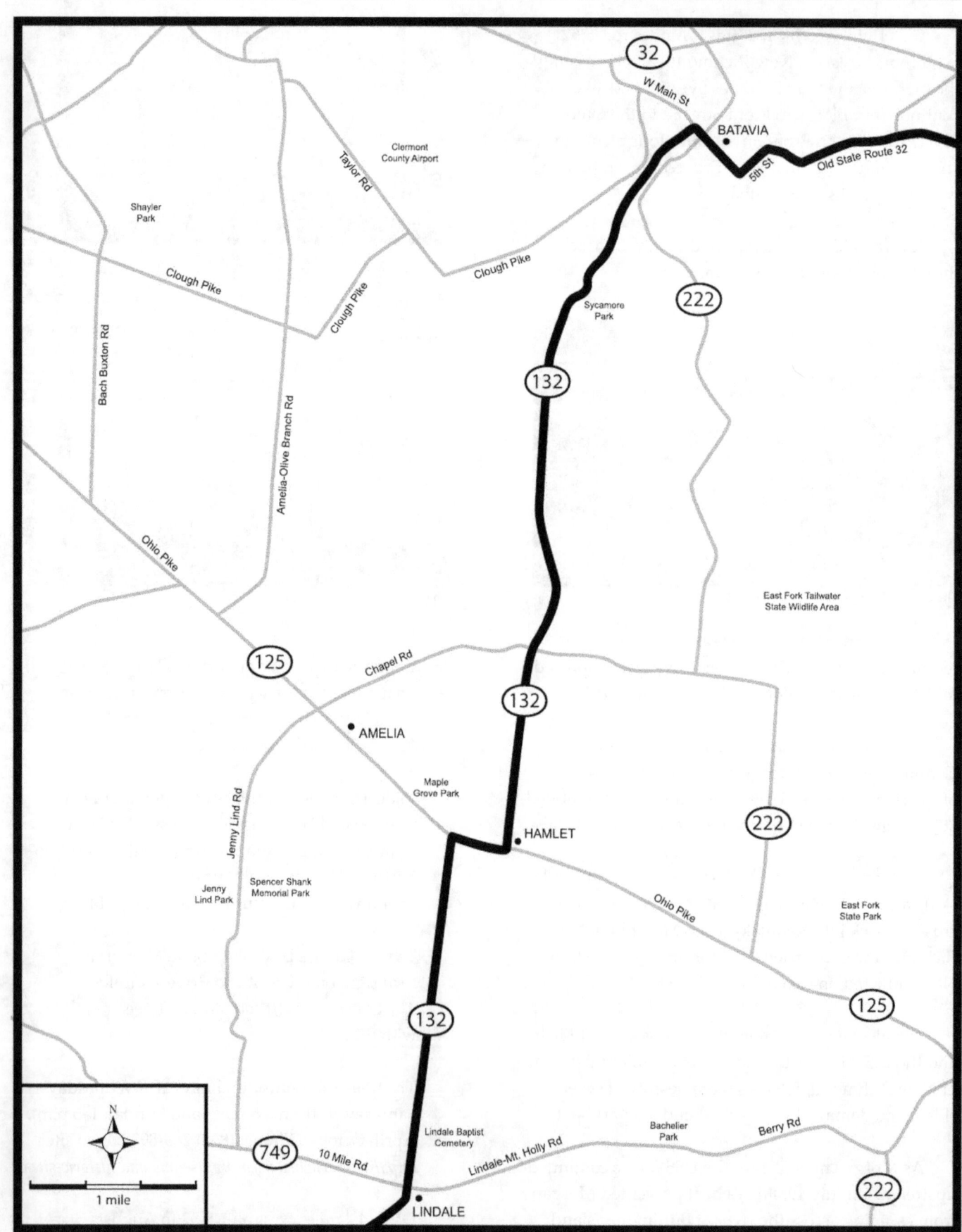

Side Trip to Withamsville, Amelia, and New Richmond part 4

SIDE TRIP TO WITHAMSVILLE, AMELIA, AND NEW RICHMOND

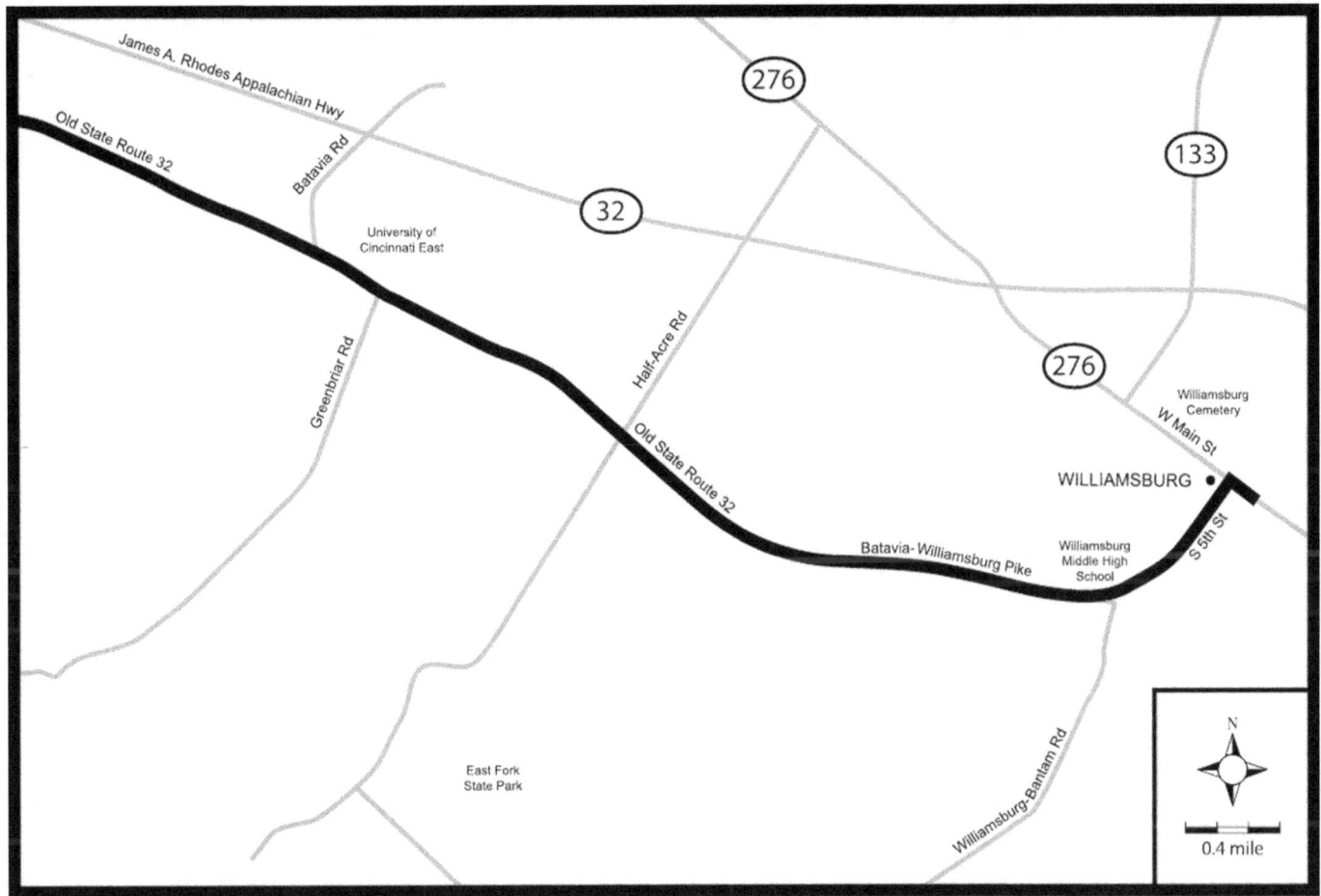

Side Trip to Withamsville, Amelia, and New Richmond part 5

Turn left from Augusta Street to US 52. Go 0.6 mile on US 52 to SR 132 (High Street). Turn right onto SR 132; follow SR 132 north 12.8 miles to West Main Street in Batavia. Turn right onto West Main Street (Old SR 32). Follow Hobson's men 7.4 miles on the Batavia-Williamsburg Pike (Old SR 32), from Batavia to Main Street (SR 133/276) in Williamsburg. Turn right onto Main Street to rejoin Morgan's main column.

Appendix J

ALTERNATE: DICK MORGAN'S COLUMN TO RIPLEY

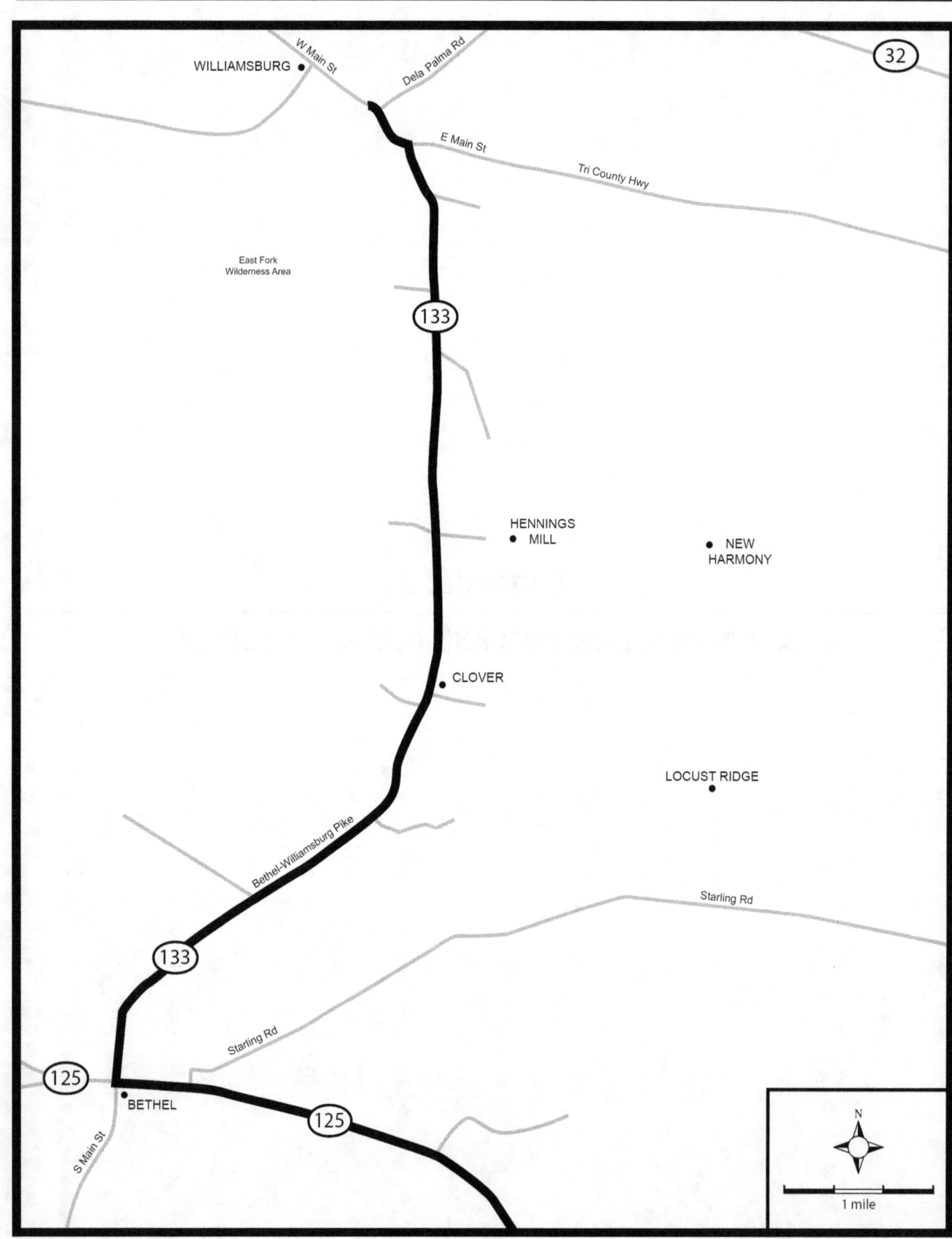

Alternate route; Dick Morgan's Column to Ripley part 1

ALTERNATE: DICK MORGAN'S COLUMN TO RIPLEY

Colonel Richard Morgan

Wednesday, July 15, 1863

To follow Colonel Richard Morgan's 14th Kentucky Cavalry south to Georgetown and Ripley, turn right onto SR 133 where it splits from Tri-County Highway (Old SR 32) on the east side of Williamsburg. Reset your odometer.

We do not fully understand the purpose of Richard Morgan's ride to Ripley with 200-300 men. It is unlikely that the raiders were attempting to cross the river. Arrangements had been made to rejoin the main force at Locust Grove.

Some historians feel that it was a feint devised to fool the pursuing Union forces into thinking that the raiders were planning to cross the Ohio River at Ripley. Others cite earlier threats by the Confederates to wreak havoc on the town, "the hotbed of abolitionism."

After turning on SR 133, there is a dip in the road. Hermon Stone and three friends from the village of Clover rode toward Williamsburg with the intention of ambushing the raiders. As they completed the dip and before they reached the junction, they spotted Morgan's men. Their courage deserted them and they made an abrupt departure.

Drive 2.5 miles on SR 133. The community of Hennings Mill (Coontown) lies one-half mile to the east (left). The town sprang up about 1836. A small company passed through the town and took five horses. Their Union pursuers took three. The men continued east through New Harmony to rejoin the main column at Mt. Orab. The citizens of New Harmony lost six horses to the raiders and two to the Union.

Drive 0.9 mile farther on SR 133. The raiders passed through the village of Clover which had been established about 1849. Little remains of the town. The Clover Cemetery is on the left; in 1863, this was the location of the Clover Methodist Church. Civil War Medal of Honor recipient John H. Wageman is buried here. Wageman served as a private with Company I of the 60th Ohio Volunteer Infantry (OVI). The citation was for his actions at Petersburg, Virginia, on June 17, 1864: "Remained with the command after being severely wounded until he had fired all the cartridges in his possession, when he had to be carried from the field." His grave is near the top of the hill in the middle of the row.

John H. Wageman, Medal of Honor Recipient

Drive 3.3 miles to downtown Bethel.

Side Note: In 1841, U. S. Grant's parents moved to the northwest corner of Water and Charity streets in Bethel. Ulysses visited here often. His wife, Julia, lived here during two of her pregnancies, as she was unable to travel with her military husband. His father, Jesse Grant, was Bethel's first mayor.

Turn left onto SR 125 (East Plane Street) and go 2.1 miles. Here, a small force turned east to New Hope.

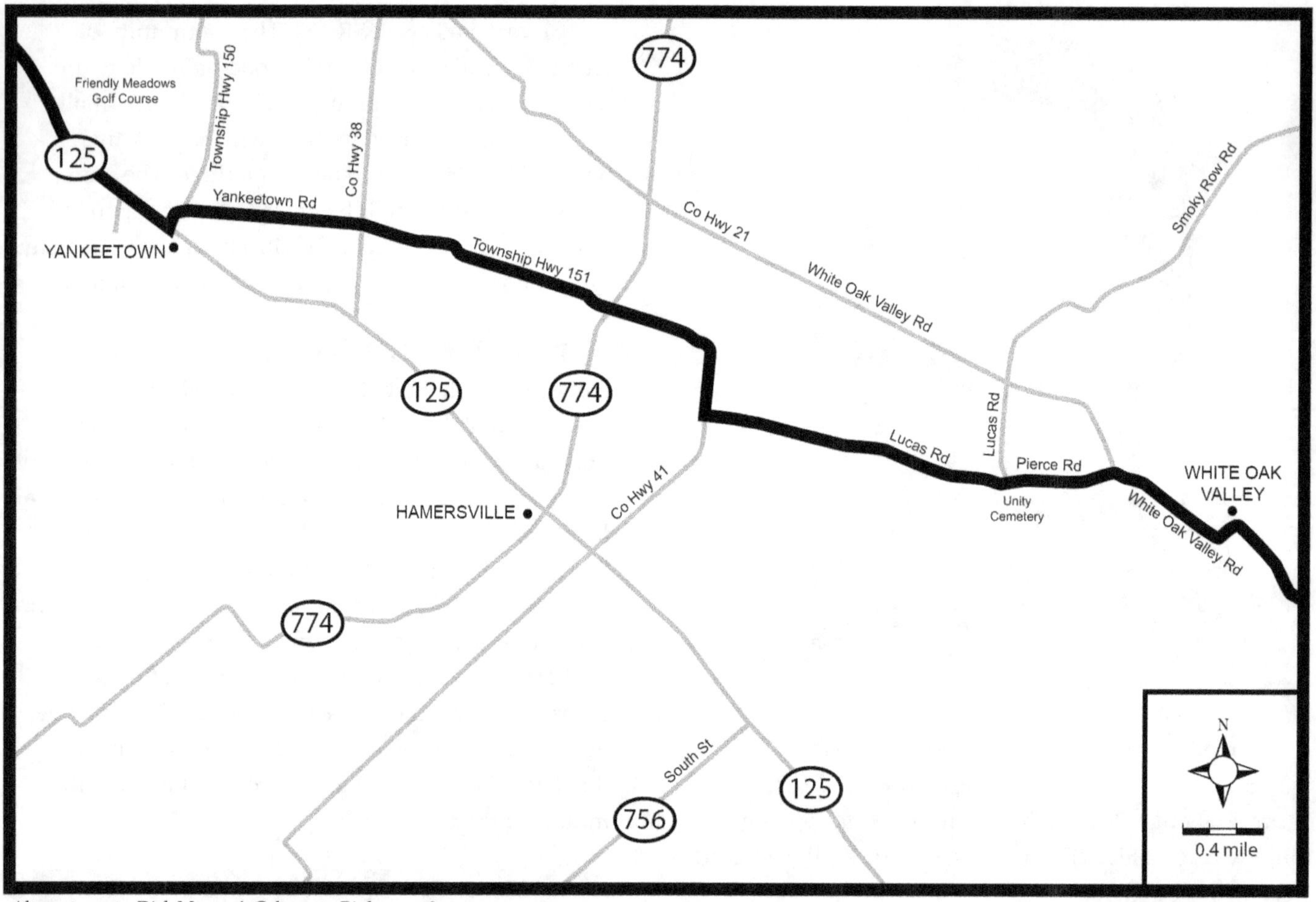

Alternate route; Dick Morgan's Column to Ripley part 2

Continue on SR 125 for 1.7 miles. You will enter Brown County. Turn left at Yankeetown Road (TR 151). (The road is not well marked and is easy to miss.) Stay on Yankeetown Road for 2.9 miles. At the stop sign, turn left onto Lucas Road (CR 41).

Go 1.4 miles to the "Y" intersection and bear to the right on Pierce Road (TR 35). After going 0.5 mile down a hill, you will cross Unity Creek. Turn to the right on White Oak Valley Road (CR 21); it is only 0.6 mile to White Oak Creek. The raiders crossed the covered bridge here but made no attempt to burn it.

Cross the modern bridge and turn right at the "T" intersection to continue on White Oak Valley Road. Reset your odometer. You are passing through the early community of White Oak Valley.

Stay on White Oak Valley Road for 1.4 miles to US 68 and turn right. At 1.1 miles turn right on Mt. Orab Pike (CR 30A), which becomes Main Street; it will take

White Oak Creek Bridge was built in 1857. It no longer stands.

you 2.1 miles to SR 125 in downtown Georgetown.

For your visit to Georgetown, see the driving directions and descriptions included in the Georgetown side trip found in the section titled "Williamsburg to Locust Grove."

After visiting Georgetown, turn left (east) from Main Street onto SR 125 (East State Street). Drive 1.7 miles to US 68. Those wishing to rejoin General John Hunt Morgan's main column at Mt. Orab will turn left

ALTERNATE: DICK MORGAN'S COLUMN TO RIPLEY

Colonel Richard Morgan

Wednesday, July 15, 1863

To follow Colonel Richard Morgan's 14th Kentucky Cavalry south to Georgetown and Ripley, turn right onto SR 133 where it splits from Tri-County Highway (Old SR 32) on the east side of Williamsburg. Reset your odometer.

We do not fully understand the purpose of Richard Morgan's ride to Ripley with 200-300 men. It is unlikely that the raiders were attempting to cross the river. Arrangements had been made to rejoin the main force at Locust Grove.

Some historians feel that it was a feint devised to fool the pursuing Union forces into thinking that the raiders were planning to cross the Ohio River at Ripley. Others cite earlier threats by the Confederates to wreak havoc on the town, "the hotbed of abolitionism."

After turning on SR 133, there is a dip in the road. Hermon Stone and three friends from the village of Clover rode toward Williamsburg with the intention of ambushing the raiders. As they completed the dip and before they reached the junction, they spotted Morgan's men. Their courage deserted them and they made an abrupt departure.

Drive 2.5 miles on SR 133. The community of Hennings Mill (Coontown) lies one-half mile to the east (left). The town sprang up about 1836. A small company passed through the town and took five horses. Their Union pursuers took three. The men continued east through New Harmony to rejoin the main column at Mt. Orab. The citizens of New Harmony lost six horses to the raiders and two to the Union.

Drive 0.9 mile farther on SR 133. The raiders passed through the village of Clover which had been established about 1849. Little remains of the town. The Clover Cemetery is on the left; in 1863, this was the location of the Clover Methodist Church. Civil War Medal of Honor recipient John H. Wageman is buried here. Wageman served as a private with Company I of the 60th Ohio Volunteer Infantry (OVI). The citation was for his actions at Petersburg, Virginia, on June 17, 1864: "Remained with the command after being severely wounded until he had fired all the cartridges in his possession, when he had to be carried from the field." His grave is near the top of the hill in the middle of the row.

John H. Wageman, Medal of Honor Recipient

Drive 3.3 miles to downtown Bethel.

Side Note: In 1841, U. S. Grant's parents moved to the northwest corner of Water and Charity streets in Bethel. Ulysses visited here often. His wife, Julia, lived here during two of her pregnancies, as she was unable to travel with her military husband. His father, Jesse Grant, was Bethel's first mayor.

Turn left onto SR 125 (East Plane Street) and go 2.1 miles. Here, a small force turned east to New Hope.

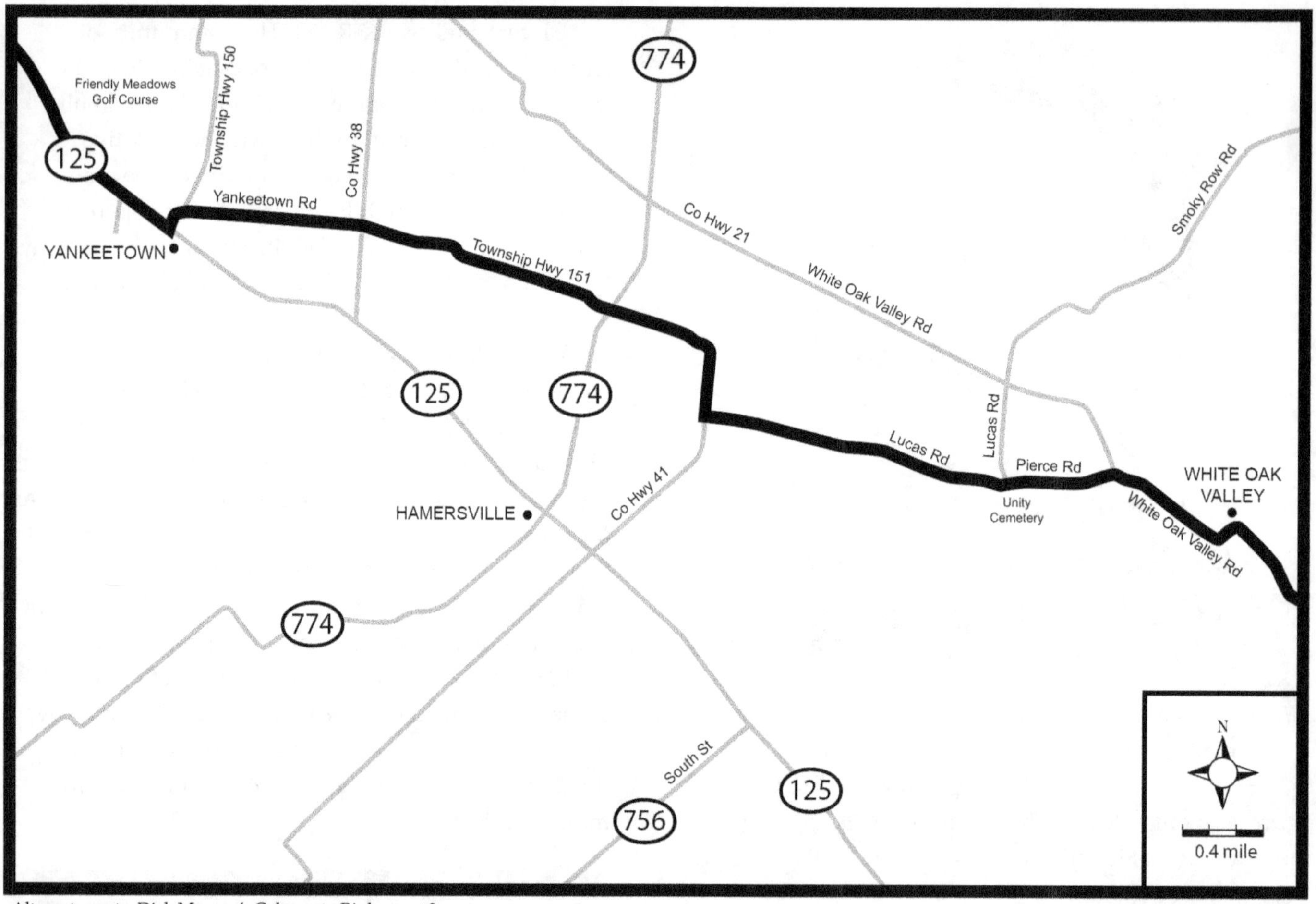

Alternate route; Dick Morgan's Column to Ripley part 2

Continue on SR 125 for 1.7 miles. You will enter Brown County. Turn left at Yankeetown Road (TR 151). (The road is not well marked and is easy to miss.) Stay on Yankeetown Road for 2.9 miles. At the stop sign, turn left onto Lucas Road (CR 41).

Go 1.4 miles to the "Y" intersection and bear to the right on Pierce Road (TR 35). After going 0.5 mile down a hill, you will cross Unity Creek. Turn to the right on White Oak Valley Road (CR 21); it is only 0.6 mile to White Oak Creek. The raiders crossed the covered bridge here but made no attempt to burn it.

Cross the modern bridge and turn right at the "T" intersection to continue on White Oak Valley Road. Reset your odometer. You are passing through the early community of White Oak Valley.

Stay on White Oak Valley Road for 1.4 miles to US 68 and turn right. At 1.1 miles turn right on Mt. Orab Pike (CR 30A), which becomes Main Street; it will take you 2.1 miles to SR 125 in downtown Georgetown.

White Oak Creek Bridge was built in 1857. It no longer stands.

For your visit to Georgetown, see the driving directions and descriptions included in the Georgetown side trip found in the section titled "Williamsburg to Locust Grove."

After visiting Georgetown, turn left (east) from Main Street onto SR 125 (East State Street). Drive 1.7 miles to US 68. Those wishing to rejoin General John Hunt Morgan's main column at Mt. Orab will turn left

ALTERNATE: DICK MORGAN'S COLUMN TO RIPLEY

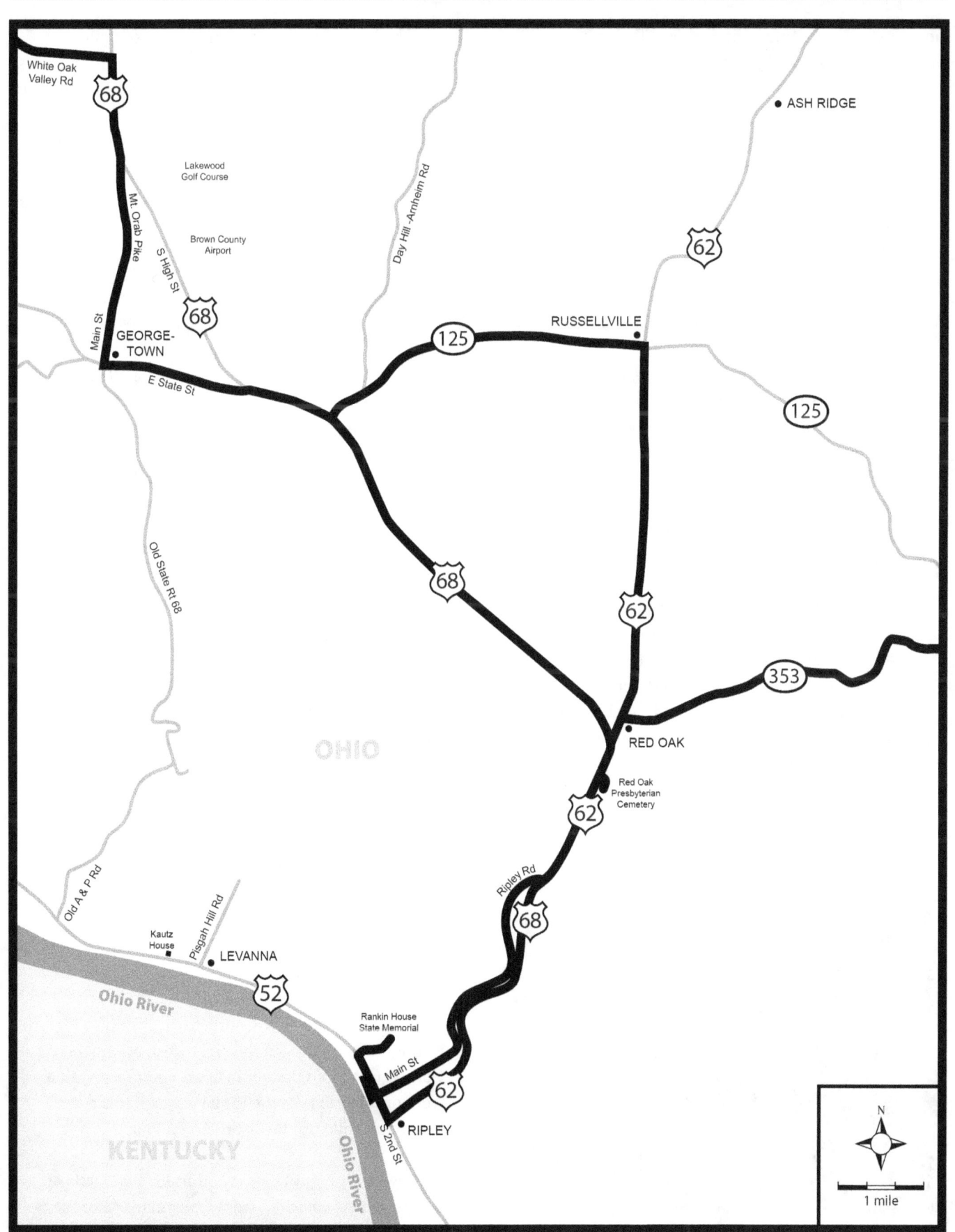

Alternate route; Dick Morgan's Column to Ripley part 3

onto US 68. To continue with Colonel Richard Morgan and the 14th Kentucky Cavalry to Ripley, turn right onto US 68/SR 125.

Drive 0.9 mile to the junction with SR 125; here the column split. One company rode east to Russellville, where they turned south to Red Oak. At Red Oak they rejoined the other column, which had taken a more direct route.

It you choose the direct route, continue on US 68 for 5.1 miles to the junction with US 62 near Red Oak.

*ALTERNATE: To visit Russellville, turn left onto SR 125. It is 4.0 miles to US 62 (Columbus Street) and the village of Russellville. Russellville is an old town with many antebellum buildings.

The raiders arrived in Russellville about noon. Their first stop was at the home of Luther Reed. They were looking for the town well where they could water their horses. Rosa West, a six-year-old neighbor child, was on the Reed porch. Her mother became hysterical when she saw the raiders around her child. One of the soldiers carried the small girl across the street to the distraught mother. He explained that he was a father himself, and Southern soldiers would never harm innocent children.

Some of the raiders rested their exhausted horses in the yard of the Russellville School, which was located on Washington Street at Main Street.

The Russellville School (c. 1855) was razed in 1908.

The Lucas family lived on North Columbus Street, present-day US 62. Martha Ann West Lucas and her teenage daughters were involved with the Underground Railroad. They concealed in the Lucas's attic runaway slaves who traveled from Ripley and Red Oak until they could be moved farther north.

When warned that Morgan's men were approaching, the Lucas daughters hid the family's horses in the woods. The raiders threatened to burn the house if the women did not produce their riding horses. The defiant women swore they owned no horses. The raiders left the Lucas home and turned their attention to looting the general store next door.

While in Russellville, Dick Morgan's men looted the stores of Conn & Mooney, Thomas Mitchell, and Postlewait & Woods. They confiscated food, forage, and ten horses to replace jaded mounts.

Turn right on US 62 and go 4.4 miles to the junction with US 68 near Red Oak.*

It is 1.7 miles to Ripley Road (Russellville Pike in 1863); turn right onto Ripley Road (CR 62). This road enters Ripley from the northeast.

Ripley was prepared to receive Morgan's men. On the previous afternoon (Tuesday, July 14), a company of Germans and a detachment of black Zouaves were posted on this road near the edge of town. ("Zouaves" referred to soldiers who wore the distinctive outfit created by certain light infantry regiments of the French army serving during the 19th century in North Africa.)

Cornick's Run Pike-Georgetown Pike (CR 30) ran through the town from the northwest. Members of Company A, 40th Battalion, Ohio Volunteer Militia, were ordered to take the Ripley cannon to a bend less than a mile up the Georgetown Pike.

Two Union gunboats and thirteen boatloads of troops were dispatched from Cincinnati. After they arrived during the night, the guardsmen on both

ALTERNATE: DICK MORGAN'S COLUMN TO RIPLEY

roads were called back into town.

Go 2.5 miles on Ripley Road and stop. You are approximately where Dick Morgan halted his troops about 1 p.m. Wednesday afternoon. His advance scouts drove in the enemy pickets, but did not enter the town. The scouts had seen two gunboats on the river and the large force of militia in town. Colonel Morgan turned his force around and retraced his route back up the hill.

After the rebels moved on, the Union gunboats and transports stayed on the river, keeping abreast with the raiders and preventing their crossing as they moved upriver. By midsummer, the river was usually low and fordable in many places; even light draft boats could not navigate in the shallow water. The summer of 1863 was an exception. Heavy rains in the upper Ohio valley raised the stage of the river substantially. The weather was Morgan's most effective enemy preventing his escape and creating the conditions necessary for his eventual capture.

Colonel August Kautz lived his childhood west of Ripley. His house stands 0.3 mile west of Pisgah Hill Road at 4853 US 52.

*Side Trip: You may want to visit Ripley, a lovely old river town with a rich history as an abolitionist stronghold. The brochure *Historic Ripley and Underground Railroad Tour* is available from the Brown County Department of Travel and Tourism. Phone: (937) 378-1970; Web site: *http://www.ripleyohio.net/*.

Drive 1.1 miles on Ripley Road (Main Street) to Second Street (US 52). At the far-left corner, the Wiard 3-inch rifled Ripley Cannon is displayed in front of the library. The artillery piece was purchased by the citizens of Ripley for their protection during the war. They paid $1,000 for the cannon and a caisson (a container, often wheeled, for ammunition). Early in the war, Southern raiders had sworn to burn this "damned abolitionist hellhole to the ground ... and show no quarter to its citizens...."

Ripley Cannon

In September 1862, when Basil Duke was threatening northern Kentucky, the home guard took their gun across the river. They attacked Duke at Brooksville and helped drive off the rebels.

The cannon was placed behind a barricade on the Georgetown Pike at Cornick's Run when Morgan threatened in July 1863. After the war, it was fired in salute to Generals Grant and Sherman when they visited Ripley.

There is also a **historical plaque** at the library honoring the "Squirrel Hunters." In August 1862, with General Edmund Kirby Smith's Confederate forces threatening Cincinnati, Governor David Tod issued a proclamation calling Ohio men to defend the city. More than 15,000 answered the call, and Brown County provided 1,300 of them, more than any other Ohio county.

A monument to those who fought for the cause of freedom.

Continue straight on Main Street. It is one block to Front Street and the **monument** to those who fought for the cause of freedom, both abolitionist and military leaders. The monument stands on the bank of the Ohio River, a symbolic gateway to freedom for thousands of runaway slaves who were fortunate enough to cross it.

Turn right at the **monument**; drive 0.2 mile on Front Street. The "**Eliza Sign**" is mounted on a pole on the left, attributed by local tradition as the spot where Eliza crossed the frozen Ohio River in Harriet Beecher Stowe's *Uncle Tom's Cabin*.

Eliza's Sign

Continue 0.1 mile to the Signal House at 234 Front Street. Legend tells us that a light placed in the attic window here indicated it was safe for slaves to be transported to the Rankin House. The house was the home of Colonel Granville Moody, "The Fighting Parson." He raised

Signal House, the home of Colonel Reverend Granville Moody.

1,000 Methodist men to form the 74th OVI. Wounded four times at the Battle of Stone's River, he refused to leave the field. After the war he returned to the ministry.

Moody's daughter, Clifford, married Joseph P. Fyffe in 1865. Clifford often lived in the house while Joseph was at sea with the U.S. Navy. During the Civil War, Joseph commanded the wooden gunboat USS *Hunchback*, with which he attacked two Confederate batteries, causing them to retreat up the James River near Richmond, Virginia. After the war, he rose to the rank of Rear Admiral before retiring in 1894.

The John P. Parker House Museum, the home of John Parker, the famous African-American Underground Railroad conductor, is located on the right in the next block, at 300 North Front Street, between Locust and Sycamore streets. It is open Fridays and Saturdays, 10 a.m.–5 p.m., Sundays, 1–5 p.m., from May through the first weekend in October.
Phone: (937) 392-4188;
Web site at *http://johnparkerhouse.org/*.

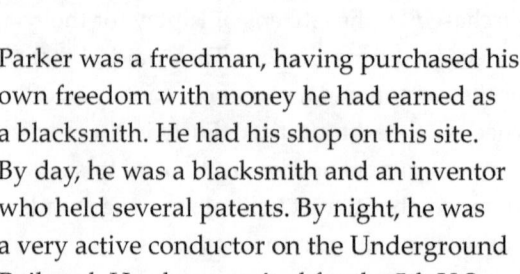

John P. Parker house (c. 1846)

Parker was a freedman, having purchased his own freedom with money he had earned as a blacksmith. He had his shop on this site. By day, he was a blacksmith and an inventor who held several patents. By night, he was a very active conductor on the Underground Railroad. He also recruited for the 5th U.S.

ALTERNATE: DICK MORGAN'S COLUMN TO RIPLEY

Colored Infantry Regiment, which saw heavy action during the Civil War.

Continue on Front Street to Sycamore Street and turn right. It is one block to Second Street (US 52); turn left. Drive 0.1 mile. As US 52 bears left, stay on Second Street to the right. Immediately, turn right onto Rankin Hill Road (TR 556). It is 0.3 mile to the Rankin House Drive on the right. Follow Rankin House Drive to the Rankin House State Memorial parking lot.

Home of Rev. Rankin, immortalized in *Uncle Tom's Cabin*.

The John Rankin House State Memorial is operated by the Ohio Historical Society. Reverend John Rankin's house, on Liberty Hill, is open Wednesday–Saturday, 10 a.m.–5 p.m., Sunday, noon–5 p.m., from the first Tuesday in May through the last Sunday in October. Phone: (937) 392-1627; Web site: *http://www.ohiohistory.org/museums-and-historic-sites/*. This was an important stop on the Underground Railroad. The Rankin family, which included thirteen children, was proud of never having lost a "passenger." It is thought that more than 2,000 escaped slaves stopped here en route from Kentucky to Canada. Reverend Rankin was immortalized in Harriet Beecher Stowe's book *Uncle Tom's Cabin*.

Return to Second Street (US 52) and turn left. The Ripley Museum at 219 North Second Street is open Saturday, 10 a.m.–4 p.m., Sunday, noon–5 p.m., April 1–December 14. Phone: (937) 392-4660; Web site: *http://www.ripleyohio.net/htm/museums.htm*. The house dates back to the 1850s and contains furnishings typical of the Civil War period.

Continue 0.4 mile east on Second Street. Turn left onto US 62/68 North and reset your odometer.

Go 5.0 miles and turn right on Cemetery Road. Follow the gravel road to the Red Oak Presbyterian Church. Built in 1816, the church was used for abolitionists' meetings. Both blacks and whites are buried in the adjoining cemetery.

Red Oak Presbyterian Church

Return to the highway. Turn right onto US 62/68. In approximately 0.1 mile, take US 62 to the right. Go 0.5 mile to SR 353 in Red Oak; turn right.*

If you opted to skip Ripley, turn around and retrace your route on Ripley Road back to US 62/68. Turn left onto US 62/68. Go 1.5 miles and bear right onto US 62. Drive 0.5 mile on US 62 to Red Oak and the junction with SR 353, and then turn right onto SR 353.

The citizens of West Union expected to be visited by the raiders on Wednesday night, but the rebels never arrived. After leaving Ripley, the main force of Colonel Morgan's raiders headed northeast toward Decatur. They planned to rendezvous with General Morgan's column at Locust Grove.

After 4.5 miles, SR 353 merges with SR 125. Go straight on SR 125. It is 0.7 mile to the town square in Decatur. There is a **Civil War monument** in the center of the park. The town of Decatur was established in 1802 as St. Clairsville. The name was later changed to honor Commodore Stephen Decatur,

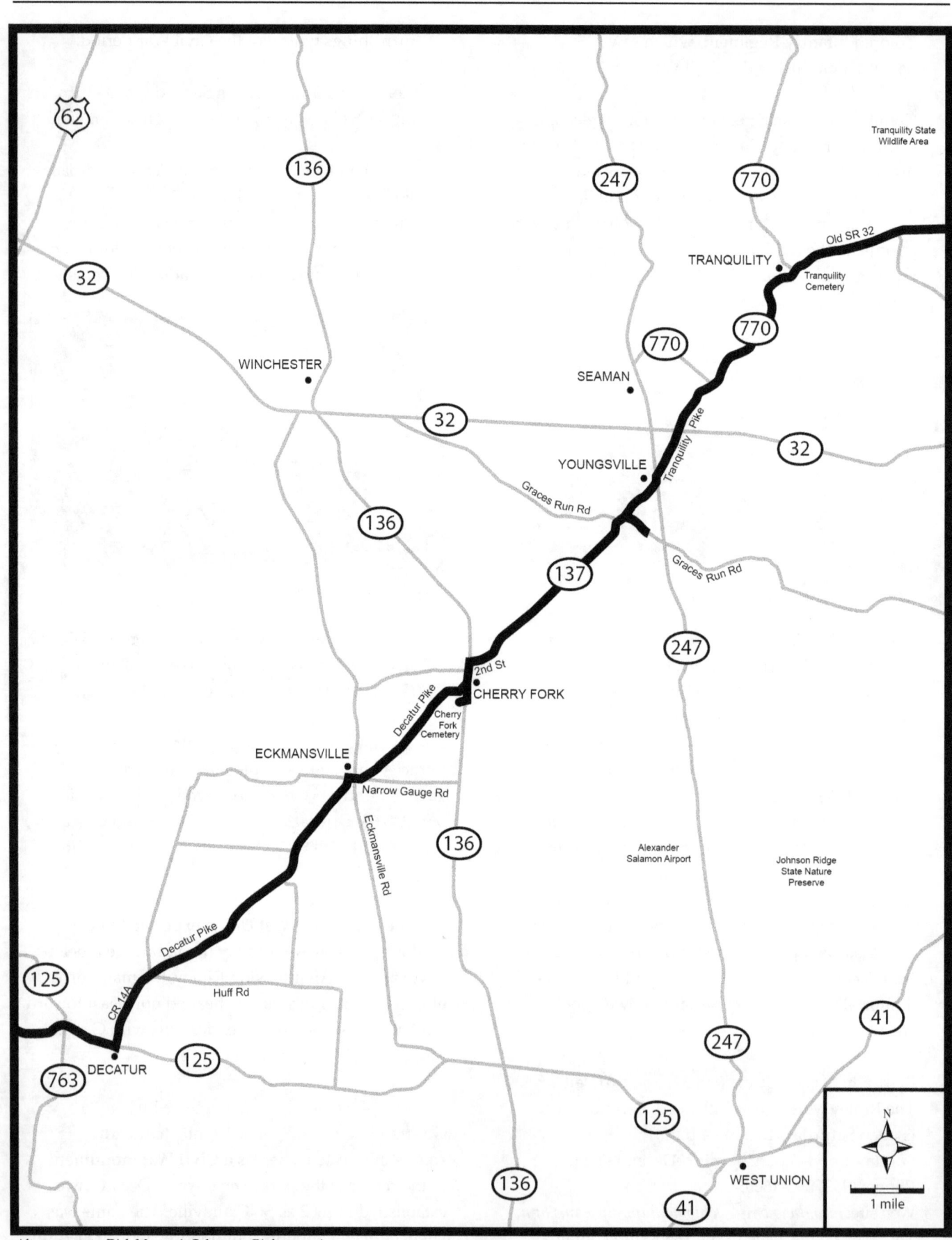

Alternate route; Dick Morgan's Column to Ripley part 4

ALTERNATE: DICK MORGAN'S COLUMN TO RIPLEY

Decatur Civil War Monument

naval hero of the War of 1812.

Turn left on CR 14A, now the Decatur-Eckmansville Road. At the time of the raid, this was known as the Ripley and Tranquility Plank Road.

At 1.0 mile the road splits three ways; take the middle road, which is the Decatur Pike (CR 35). Continue 3.8 miles to Narrow Gauge Road (CR 148) in Eckmansville.

In Eckmansville, the raiders shot and killed William Johnston, an elderly man they thought had fired on them.

They killed the wrong man; Doctor VanMeter had fired the shot and disappeared from sight. When the raiders discovered their mistake, they threatened to burn all the homes in the town.

They asked Reverend David McGill to point out the culprit. He refused and was taken captive.

McGill was forced to ride with the raiders when they left town. They released him at Locust Grove the following morning. The raiders helped themselves to dry goods and clothes at John Morrison's store in Eckmansville.

Turn right on Narrow Gauge Road. It is less than 0.2 mile to a "Y" intersection. Take the main road (Decatur Pike) to the left.

Follow Decatur Pike 1.9 miles to SR 136. Before reaching the highway, the Cherry Fork Cemetery can be seen high on the hill on the right.

Cherry Fork Cemetery on hill

Johnston is buried there. His tombstone reads, "WILLIAM JOHNSTON came to his death by a ball in the head fired by a rebel guerrilla, in the Village of Eckmanville, July 15, 1863. Aged about 60 years."

William Johnston's grave

To visit Johnston's grave, turn right onto SR 136. Turn right into the cemetery and turn right again. Stop and park where the cemetery drive turns left. Walk along the front edge of the cemetery. Johnston's marker is a small stone; a large gray monument sits directly behind it. The engraving on the small stone faces the monument.

When leaving the cemetery, turn left onto SR 136 and drive 0.3 mile. You are crossing Cherry Fork; the rebels burned the covered bridge at this location.

In 1863, the village of Cherry Fork was known as North Liberty.

After crossing the bridge, notice the large green building on the left at the south end of town. This was Jacob N. Brown's general store. The raiders "cleaned out" the store, damaging everything they did not take with them. They also stole Brown's horse valued at $100.

Jacob N. Brown's general store

Drive 0.2 mile and turn right on SR 137. Reset your odometer.

Drive 2.9 miles. Graces Run Road (CR 1) comes in from the left, crosses SR 137, and exits on the right. At this point you may choose to turn right onto Graces Run Road; this was the route taken by Colonel Richard Morgan's column. Grace's Run Road was also used by General John Hunt Morgan's main column as he moved from Winchester to Dunkinsville. For route directions and descriptions, see the section titled "Williamsburg to Locust Grove."

*Alternate: A small company of raiders used the following route through Youngsville and Tranquility to reach Locust Grove. Continue 0.6 mile on SR 137. Turn left onto SR 247 and, immediately, turn right onto Tranquility Pike (CR 14). Reset your odometer. You have just passed through Youngsville. William and James Young's general store suffered a marked inventory reduction after the raiders' visit.

After 1.4 miles on Tranquility Pike, bear right on SR 770. Go another 2.0 miles and you are in the village of Tranquility. When SR 770 turns left, continue straight on Old SR 32 (CR 100).

Go 5.5 miles and turn left onto Marble Furnace Road (CR 101) immediately after passing Ty Drive. Warning: Marble Furnace Road (CR 101) veers to the left and rejoins Old SR 32 in 0.7 mile. The following driving instructions pertain to the first Marble Furnace Road turn off.

It is 0.2 mile to a "Y" intersection where you will bear right on CR 101. Go another 0.2 mile to another "Y" and again bear right on CR 101. You will have crossed Ohio Brush Creek.

Drive 0.2 mile to yet another "Y." Turn left on Cemetery Road (CR 16). Continue 2.4 miles to the junction with SR 41. Turn left on SR 41; it is 0.7 mile to Locust Grove.*

ALTERNATE: DICK MORGAN'S COLUMN TO RIPLEY

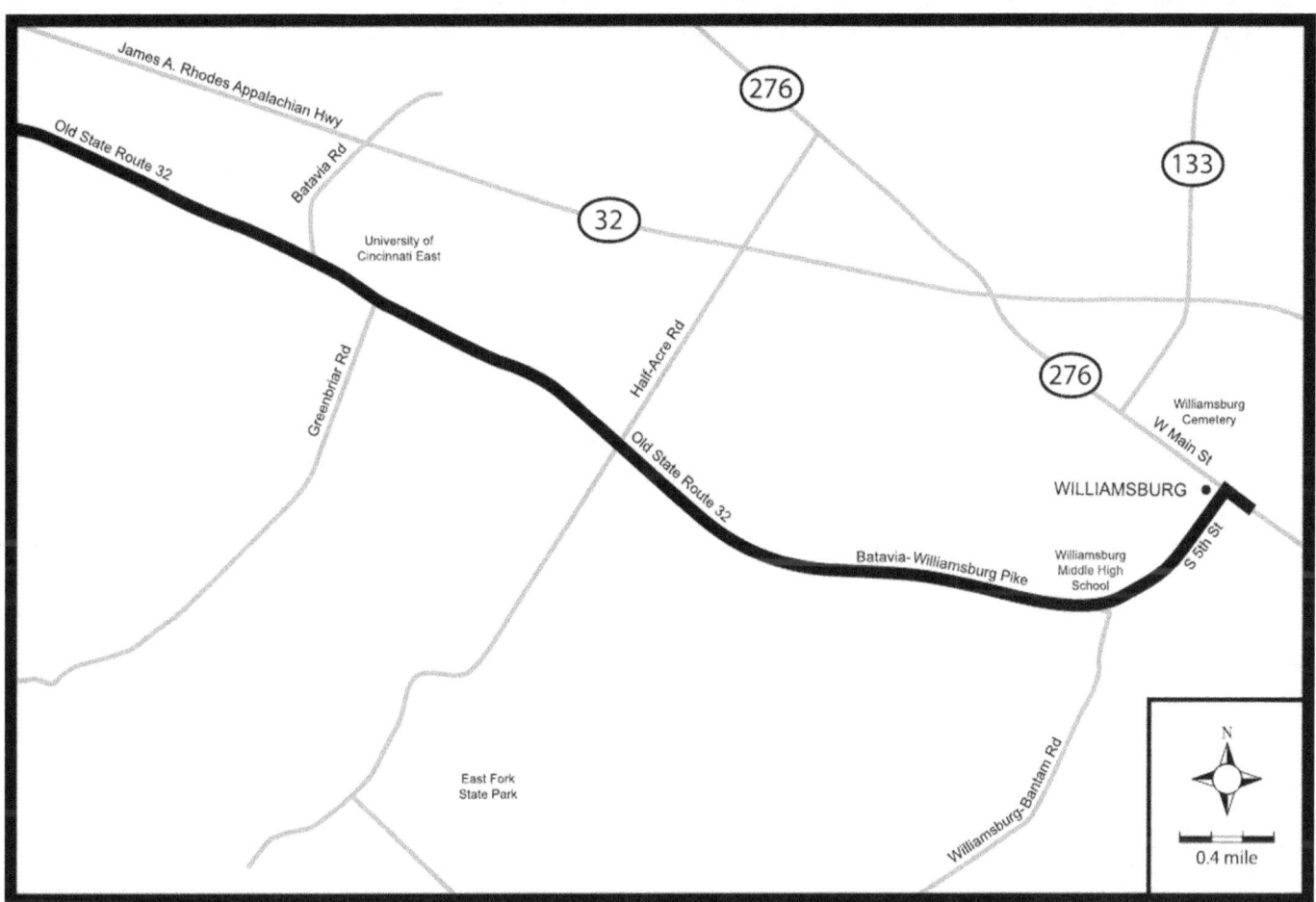

Alternate route; Dick Morgan's Column to Ripley part 5

Appendix K

ALTERNATE: OVER YANKEE HILL TO JASPER

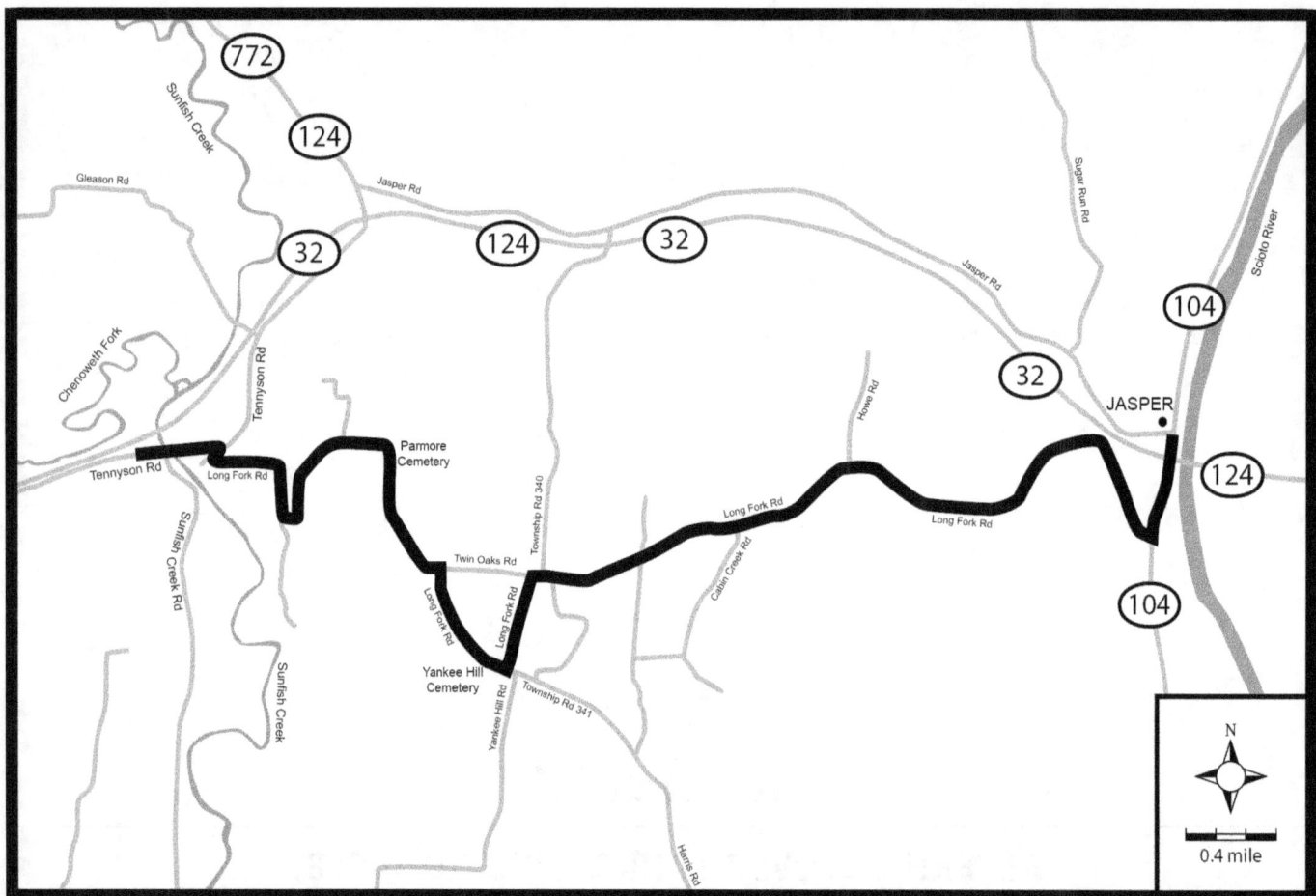

Alternate route; Over Yankee Hill to Jasper

Thursday, July 16, 1863

After crossing Sunfish Creek at noon, Morgan sent a small group of soldiers to the right over Yankee Hill to Long Fork Creek Road. Morgan and the main column moved northeast toward Jasper on the Jasper Road.

After crossing Sunfish Creek, drive 0.2 mile on Tennyson Road and turn right onto Long Fork Road (CR 26). The road makes a number of turns, and the intersections may not be well marked.

Go 1.8 miles to Twin Oaks Road (TR 339); stop before turning right. Yankee Hill is on the right. Straight ahead, the first farm on the left side of Twin Oaks Road belonged to James Bolton. The raiders stopped there and grazed their horses in his meadow. Before leaving, they confiscated his horse, a bridle, a halter, and $6 in cash.

Turn right on Long Fork Road and drive 0.5 mile; you will pass the old Yankee Hill Cemetery. Raiders frequently stopped in country cemeteries to take a break and rest their horses. Having just left Bolton's farm, however, they had no reason to stop here. Immediately turn left on Long Fork Road (CR 26). Go 0.4 mile. Straight ahead at the intersection is the Bolton Farm. Turn right onto Long Fork Road. Reset your odometer.

From here you will follow Long Fork Creek. Go 0.5 mile; the Ellis Dean farm was on the left at the end of this lane. One of the raiders took Dean's horse and pocket watch, and then rode away playing a tune on Dean's accordion.

Drive 2.1 miles farther on Long Fork Road; Long Fork Creek is on the left. In 1863, the road did not continue all the way to the Scioto River. It crossed No Name Creek at a ford near here. On the left side of Long Fork Road, a remnant of the old road leads east

ALTERNATE: OVER YANKEE HILL TO JASPER

to the ford. Morgan's men used the ford and entered Jasper from the southwest.

Continue 0.5 mile; as you approach SR 104, you will cross the Ohio & Erie Canal channel. Turn left onto SR 104 and drive the 0.4 mile into Jasper, where you will rejoin Morgan's main force.

Appendix L

ALTERNATE: JOHNSON'S COLUMN PASSED THROUGH VINTON EN ROUTE TO MIDDLEPORT

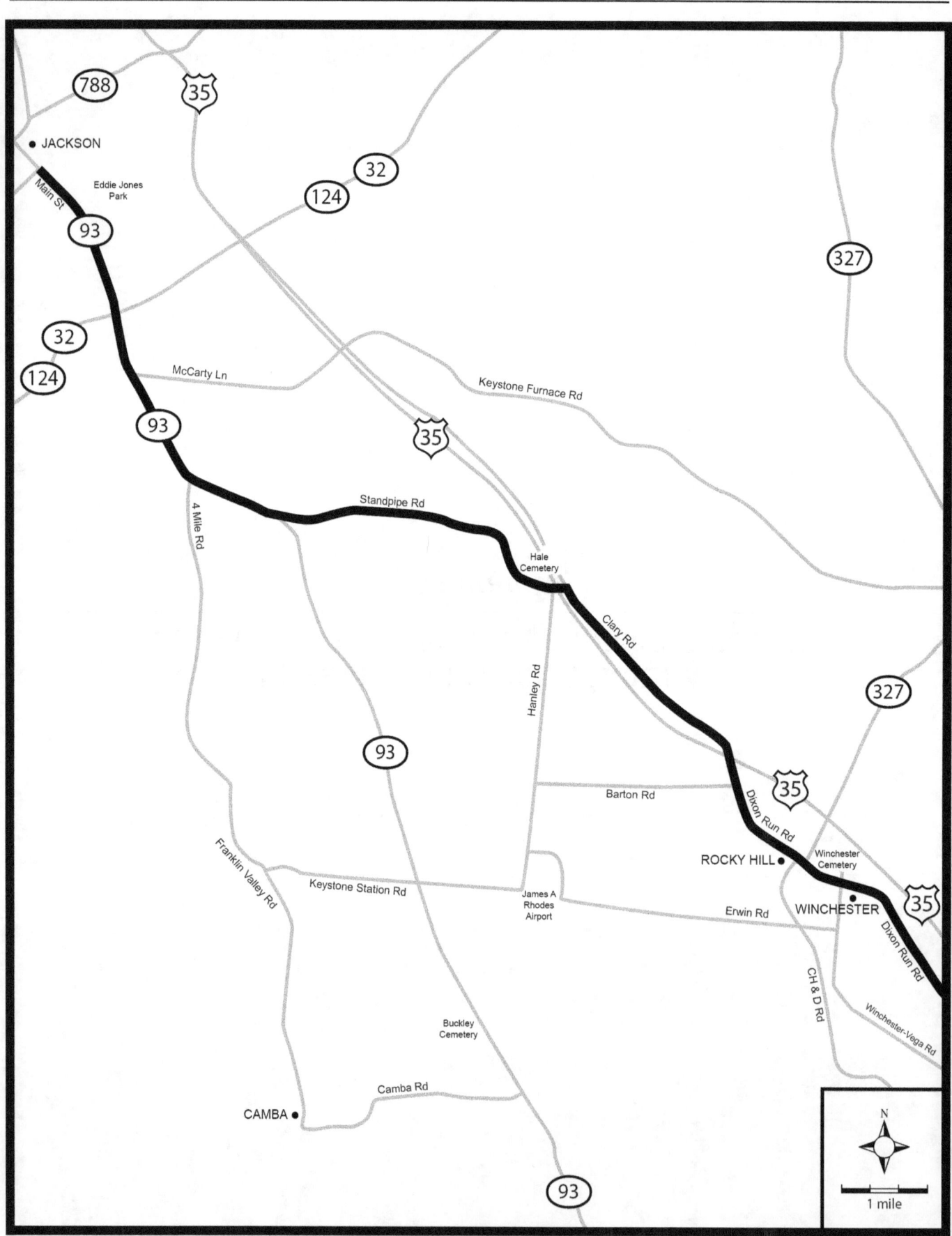

Alternate route; Johnson's Column Passed Through Vinton en Route to Middleport part 1

ALTERNATE: JOHNSON'S COLUMN PASSED THROUGH VINTON EN ROUTE TO MIDDLEPORT

Colonel Adam Johnson

Friday, July 17, 1863

As they left Jackson the raiders split. Morgan and Duke's 1st Brigade moved northeast toward Berlin Crossroads and then east toward Wilkesville.

Colonel Adam Johnson's 2nd Brigade rode southeast toward Vinton, in Gallia County. Both groups headed toward the Middleport-Cheshire area and a possible crossing at Eight Mile Island.

Johnson's men did not ride in a single column; they fanned out, foraging, looting, and stealing horses in many small communities across southeastern Jackson and northern Gallia counties.

A small company of Johnson's men took East Broadway to the old Keystone Furnace Road. The old road closely paralleled present-day US 35 for about 1.6 miles. At that point it angled southeast toward Keystone Furnace and the town of Keystone. Johnson's scattered forces would come together at Keystone before moving into Gallia County.

Reset your odometer at the Jackson courthouse; continue southeast on Main Street (SR 93). We will follow Johnson's main column as it left Jackson. Drive 2.2 miles to a "Y" intersection with Four Mile Road (CR 11). At this point, Johnson sent a small force of approximately sixty men down Four Mile Road to Franklin Valley Road (CR 13), which they followed to Camba.

Jackson County Sheriff John M. Jones was also the commander of the Jackson County militia. It was reported that when he learned Morgan was entering Jackson, he decided it was time to visit his father in Camba. While he was there, four raiders confronted the sheriff in front of the B. B. Evans store and took his jet black horse, Nig. Another report credited local boys with taking the horse, although this was denied by the sheriff. Jones filed a claim for $20 for a saddle and bridle taken from his father's barn.

Andrew Carrick lost one horse, a saddle, and a bridle to the raiders while John Crabill surrendered his horse to a Union rider.

From Camba, the raiders turned southeast to Limestone Furnace, where they sacked the company store, taking $130 worth of boots, shoes, and clothing. After leaving Limestone Furnace, they headed northeast to Vega.

We will follow the route of Johnson's main column to Vega.

About five miles out of Jackson, one of Johnson's men shot and killed "Doc" Harvey Hamilton Burris. It was reported Burris had two guns; after giving up the first gun, he went for the second and was shot. Another account claims Burris was shot without provocation by a drunken rebel soldier.

Continue on Oak Hill Road (SR 93) for 0.6 mile to Standpipe Road (CR 66). A squad of raiders continued another 1.5 miles south on Oak Hill Road to the farm of William and Octavia Johnson.

The previous evening, when Mr. Johnson learned Morgan was approaching Jackson, he took his guns and joined his neighbors in the defense of the county seat; he would spend the night under guard at the fairgrounds. Mrs. Johnson woke nine-year-old William and told him to hide their horses. He joined several men moving their horses to a nearby thicket. Young William hid two of the family's three horses. Once the horses were hidden, they returned to their homes to await the raiders.

The next day, three hungry raiders stopped at the farm. Mrs. Johnson prepared six sandwiches of thickly sliced fresh bread, with butter and honey. After eating, the men tried to take Simon, the unbroken gelding that was still in the Johnson pasture. When a rebel attempted to mount him, Simon threw the man and made off with a rebel saddle and bridle. After chasing him for some time, the men gave up in disgust and left.

Turn left on Standpipe Road and drive 2.1 miles. Cross over US 35 and turn right onto Clary Road (CR 79). After 1.5 miles Clary Road crosses US 35 and becomes Dixon Run Road (CR 41).

Drive 0.8 mile on Dixon Run Road to Rocky Hill. The Rocky Hill Post Office provided service to the surrounding area. From the number of claims filed, Johnson's men must have been busy. The Ross Allison Store lost $78 in dry goods and notions. William Burris lost two horses, three saddles, and two bridles to the raiders. Six other men also filed claims for lost horses. Jesse Clark lost a coat in addition to five bushels of corn and fifty pounds of bacon. Riley Coon filed for damages for burnt fence rails, as well as for confiscated clothing, provisions, and household goods. Williamson Scurlock watched his buggy and harness disappear down the road behind a neighbor's horse. When Union forces arrived in the Rocky Hill area, they appropriated another nine horses.

Continue another 0.3 mile to Winchester on the Gallipolis Pike (present-day Dixon Run Road). Colonel Johnson's men stopped and rested their horses at Winchester.

Go 1.4 miles farther on Dixon Run Road (CR 41). The road again crosses US 35. Immediately after crossing US 35, bear right at the "Y" intersection to Vega Road (TR 130). Drive another 1.4 miles on Vega Road to its intersection with Carmel Bathamia Road (TR 144), where the Vega Road turns directly south. Turn right onto Vega Road (TR 130). It is 0.6 mile to the area that was the town of Vega in 1863.

The sixty raiders who had ransacked the Limestone Furnace company store arrived in front of W. C. Wilmore's store in Vega. Shots were fired, and suddenly the raiders were facing scouts from Colonel James I. David's 9th Michigan Cavalry of Judah's brigade. The action soon moved to the nearby Lackey homestead, where the Confederates took a stand north of the barn. At about that time, two 9th Michigan Cavalry companies arrived and prepared for battle. The raiders wheeled their horses and rode away. So ended "The Battle of Vega," officially known as the skirmish at Centerville, with one man and one horse killed.

With Judah's cavalry units in the area, Johnson turned east. The raiders used several roughly parallel roads in moving from the Winchester-Vega area to Keystone Furnace.

Turn around; drive 0.6 mile north on Vega Road and cross over SR 35. At the next intersection, continue straight on Carmel Bathamia Road (TR 144); in 0.2 mile, follow the road as it turns to the right.

After another 0.6 mile, bear right at the "Y" intersection onto Carmel Bathamia Road (TR 144) and drive 0.6 mile. In Bamzel Lackey's field on the left, Union skirmishers of the 9th Michigan Cavalry engaged the raiders who had been fighting at Vega. The raiders held the high ground on the left, while the Federals formed a battle line along the road from Carmel Church. The Confederates retreated to Keystone Furnace after a few minutes of fighting.

Go 1.1 miles to Carmel Church and turn around; on Carmel Bathamia Road, drive 1.7 miles.

Turn right onto Gomer Davis Road (TR 145). Drive 3.1 miles to Smokey Hollow Road (TR 136) and turn left. Go 0.8 mile and turn right onto Keystone Furnace Road (CR 9). At 1.2 miles you will cross Little Raccoon Creek. The Keystone Furnace remains are on the left, which are typical of the many early furnaces scattered throughout this portion of the state.

ALTERNATE: JOHNSON'S COLUMN PASSED THROUGH VINTON EN ROUTE TO MIDDLEPORT

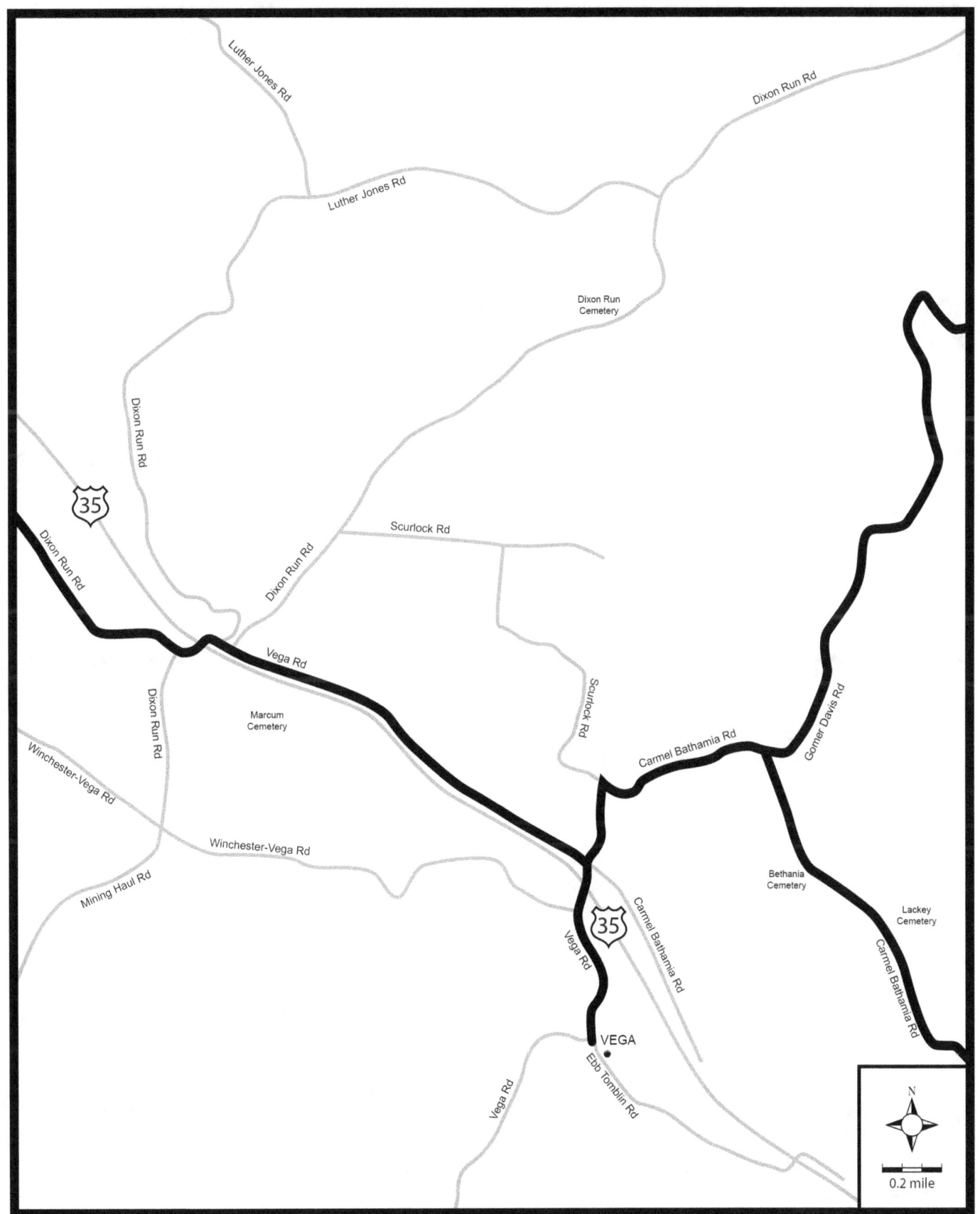

Alternate route; Johnson's Column Passed Through Vinton en Route to Middleport part 2

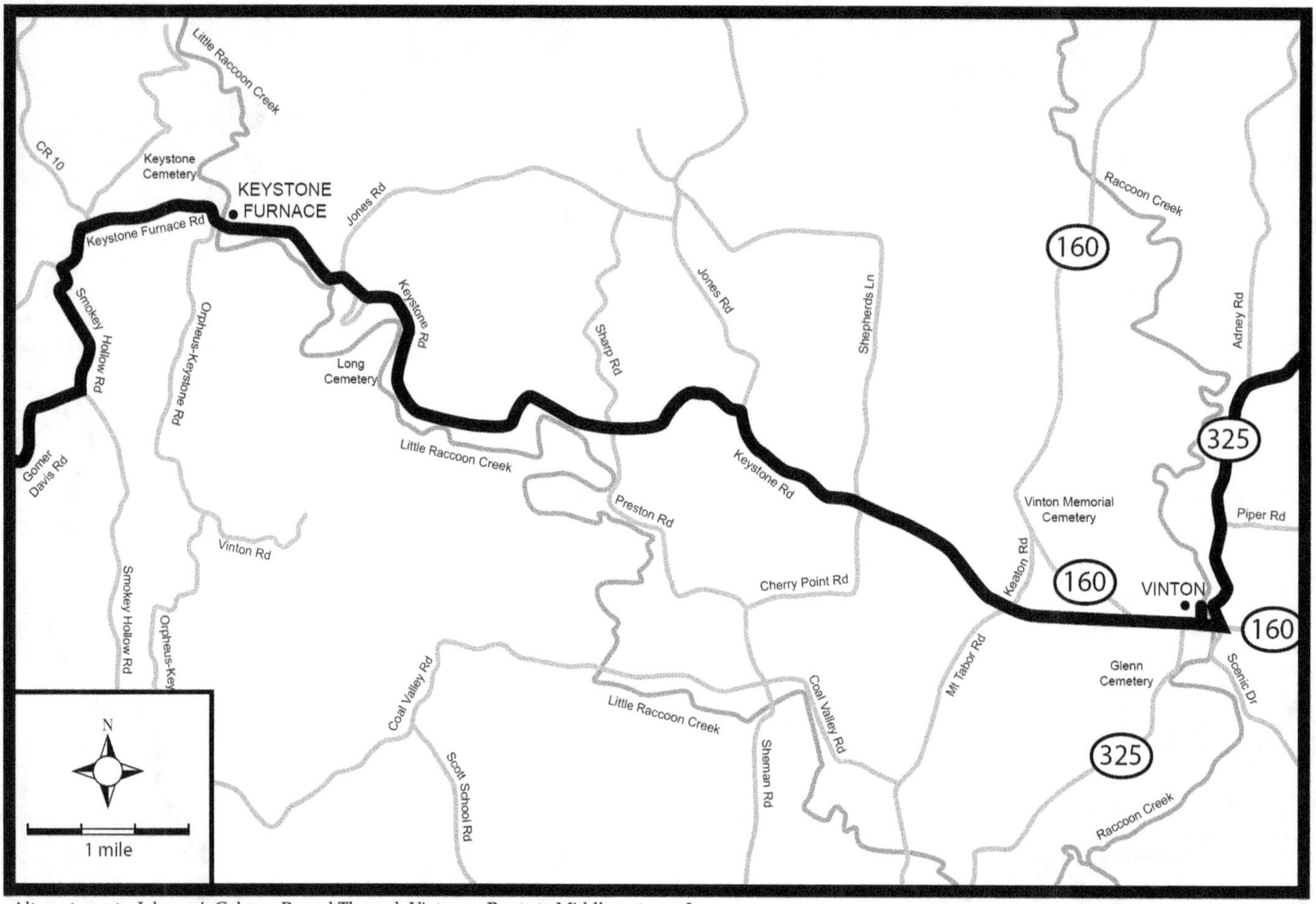

Alternate route; Johnson's Column Passed Through Vinton en Route to Middleport part 3

Remains of Keystone Furnace

At Keystone and in the surrounding region, ten men lost horses to the Confederates; nine others lost horses to Union men. John Kelley filed a claim for appropriated clothing and corn.

The scattered forces rejoined Johnson's main column at Keystone Furnace before moving on to Vinton. They reached Vinton about 6 p.m.

Continue east on Keystone Furnace Road, which becomes Keystone Road (CR 143) when you cross into Gallia County on the way to Vinton. It is 7.2 miles to SR 160 in Vinton. Turn right onto SR 160 (Jackson Street) and go 0.4 mile to Main Street. An **Ohio Historical Marker** is located on the left side of the street in front of the Vinton Post Office.

The raiders took horses, food, and forage in Vinton. One villager noted the soldiers consumed all the patent medicines containing alcohol. They also took all the merchants' tobacco and cigars.

Sixteen-year-old Anselm T. Holcomb was almost shot when he was accused of firing at a Confederate officer. Another raider vouched the young man had been working in his father's post office and store at the time.

The exhausted raiders left Vinton around 8 p.m.

312

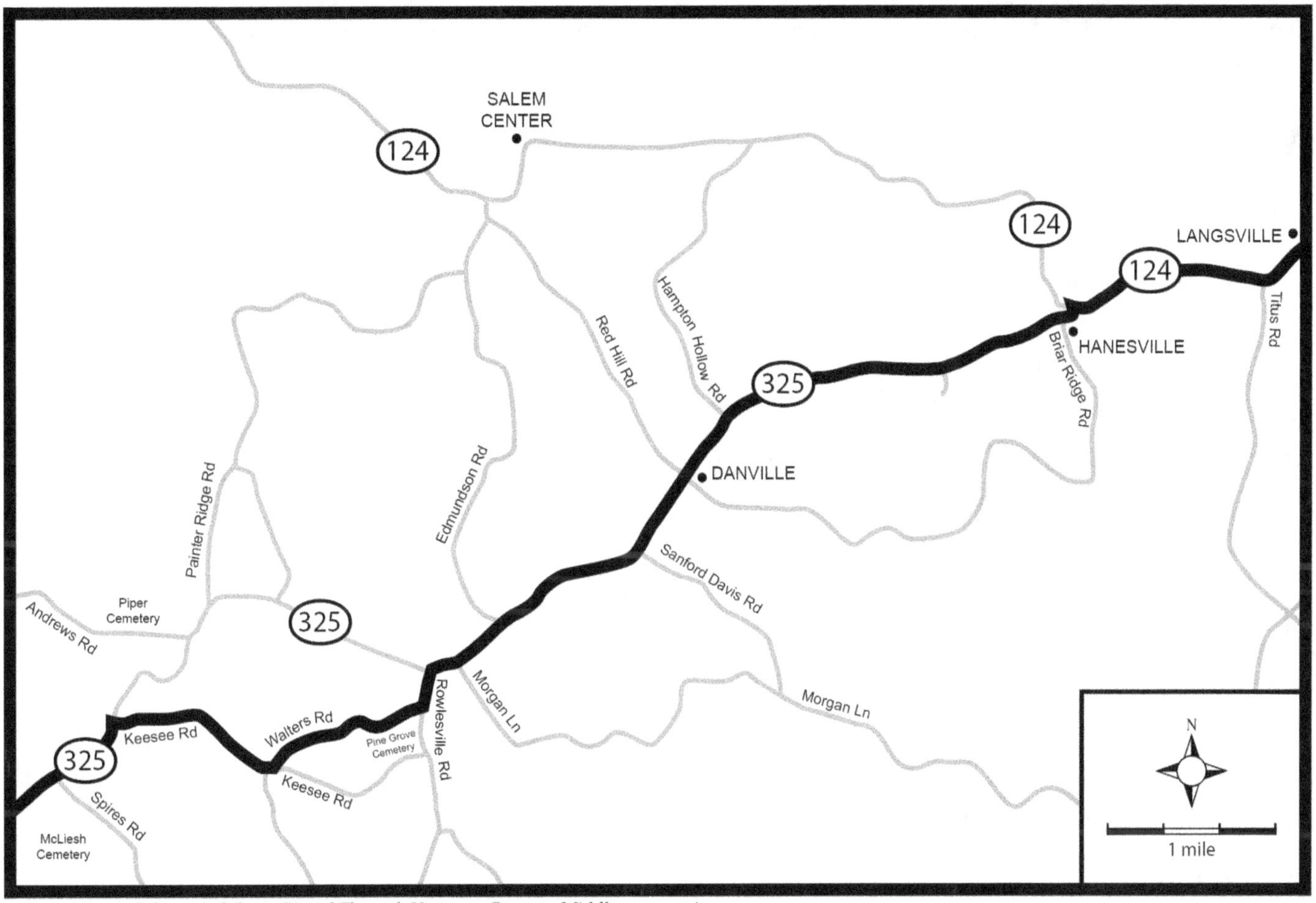

ALTERNATE: JOHNSON'S COLUMN PASSED THROUGH VINTON EN ROUTE TO MIDDLEPORT

Alternate route; Johnson's Column Passed Through Vinton en Route to Middleport part 4

The mill is gone, but the mill-dam remains.

A footbridge built on the covered bridge abutments.

Turn left on Main Street. Go two blocks and turn right on High Street. Park at the bend in the street to view the bridge site. Upstream are the remains of a mill dam. The raiders did not set fire to the mill. A rebel officer told Holcomb that the raiders had received no orders to burn the mill.

Saturday, July 18, 1863

By dawn, Johnson's men were on the road. They crossed the covered bridge over Raccoon Creek and then burned the 120-foot structure. The modern swinging bridge has been built on the original abutments.

Turn around and return to SR 160/325. Turn left onto SR 160/325. Go one block, and after crossing Raccoon Creek, turn left (north) onto SR 325. Reset your odometer.

Go 2.6 miles and turn right onto Keesee Road (TR 709). Reset your odometer here. This road is a rough, narrow, and often steep gravel/dirt path that is not recommended for oversized vehicles. It is the original road that Johnson's men used to reach Morgan's main column. If you want to avoid the rough road, then continue 4.3 miles on SR 325 into Danville. If you want to follow Johnson's actual path, turn onto Keesee Road.

Pay close attention to your odometer, because the road signs may be missing. Drive 1.0 mile on Keesee Road to a fork; turn left at the fork. Go only a few yards to another fork, and bear left to the gravel Walters Road (TR 711). It is another 1.0 mile to a stop sign. Turn left at the paved Rowlesville Road (CR 117). It is 0.2 mile to the intersection with SR 325. Turn right on SR 325.

Go 1.9 miles to Red Hill Road (CR 85). This intersection marks the center of the village of Danville. Morgan's main column, having departed from its camp at Wilkesville earlier that morning, sent its right flankers down the Red Hill Road from Salem Center. The flankers turned here and followed Johnson's column to Hanesville.

The Red Hill Road intersection in Danville.

Continue straight on SR 325. Drive 2.5 miles to the intersection with Briar Ridge Road (CR 2). Here stood the village of Hanesville, which consisted of three houses, a store, a blacksmith shop, a church, and a temperance hall. Before SR 124 was rerouted in the late 1900s, the road from Wilkesville entered here from the left.

Colonel Johnson's men met General Morgan and Colonel Duke's column at this intersection. After foraging the village for food and horses, Johnson's brigade went to the head of Morgan's main column. They rode east from here toward Middleport, where a ferry offered a possible method of crossing the Ohio River. Downstream from Middleport, the Eight Mile Island ford at Cheshire provided another option for Morgan's division to cross the river and return to Confederate territory.

Continue 0.1 mile on SR 325 to its junction with SR 124. Turn right onto SR 124 to get back on Morgan's main route. It is 1.5 miles to Langsville.

Bibliography

Manuscripts

Ohio Historical Society, Columbus, Ohio:

Docket of Claims Presented to the Board of Commissioners of Morgan's Raid Claims, 1864. State Archives Series 2040, MCF #GR3293.

Ford Family Letters Regarding Morgan's Raid, Ohio Memory Digital Collection.

Nelson Banks Sisson Collection, 1840s–1900s, MSS 1299.

Records: 1863 July 14–23, VFM 1210.

Rutherford B. Hayes Presidential Center, Manuscripts Division, Fremont, Ohio:

Katie Huntington and Morgan's Raid, George Buckland Collection.

Newspapers and Newsletters

Belmont Chronicle (St. Clairsville, OH), 1863

Cadiz Republican, 1863

Cincinnati Daily Commercial, 1863

Cincinnati Daily Gazette, 1863, 1873

Cincinnati Daily Times, 1863

Cincinnati Enquirer, 1863, 1949

Cincinnati Times Star, 1933

The Athens Messenger, 1863, 1872, 1930, 1931, 1953

The Dearborn County (IN) *Register*, 1988

The Democrat (Pomeroy, OH), 1927

Gallipolis Daily Tribune, 1863, 1932

The Harrison News, 1872

Highland Weekly News (Hillsborough, OH), 1863

Bibliography

The Hoosier Packet, 2006, 2007

McArthur Democrat, 1863

The Sycamore (Blue Ash, OH) *Messenger*, 1974

Zanesville Daily Courier, 1863

Official Publications

County of Dearborn, Indiana. *Commissioners' Records of Dearborn County, Indiana*. Vols. 6, 7, 11. Lawrenceburg, IN, 1857–1872.

Hewett, Janet B, ed. *The Roster of Confederate Soldiers 1861–1865*. 16 vols. Wilmington, NC, 1995-1996.

———, ed. *The Roster of Union Soldiers 1861–1865*. 33 vols. Wilmington, NC, 1997-2000.

———, ed. *Supplement to the Official Records of the Union and Confederate Armies – Record of Events*. 100 vols. Wilmington, NC, 1994–2001.

Indiana Historic Sites and Structures Inventory. *Dearborn County Interim Report*. Indianapolis, 1983.

Lapham, D. *Report of the Board of Public Works: Whitewater Canal*. Indianapolis, 1837.

Miami Purchase Association. *Historic Inventory of Hamilton County, Ohio*. 12 vols. Cincinnati, 1991.

Moore, Frank, ed. *The Rebellion Record: A Diary of American Events*. Vol. 7. New York, 1862–1867.

Nevins, Richard. *Annual Report of the Adjutant and Inspector General to the Governor of the State of Ohio for the Year Ending December 31, 1863*. Columbus, OH, 1864.

———. *Report of the Commissioners of Morgan Raid Claims to the Governor of the State of Ohio, Dec 15th, 1864*. Columbus, OH, 1865.

Ohio Adjutant General's Department. *Docket of Claims Presented to the Board of Commissioners of Morgan's Raid Claims, 1864*. Columbus, OH, 1864.

Ohio Roster Commission. *Official Roster of the Soldiers of the State of Ohio in the War of the Rebellion, 1861–1866*. 12 vols. Akron, OH, 1886-1895.

Robertson, Jr., James I., ed. *The Medical and Surgical History of the Civil War*. Vol. 6. Wilmington, NC, 1990–92.

Robertson, John. *Michigan in the War*. Lansing, MI, 1882.

State of Ohio. *Clermont County Deed Books*. Vols. 87–105.

———. *Hamilton County By Area Deed Index*. Series 1. Vols. 9–10.

———. *Hamilton County By Area Deed Index*. Series 2. Vol. 24.

———. *Hamilton County Deed Books*. Vols. 93–297.

———. *Hamilton County Mortgage Books*. Vols. 39–256.

———. *Meigs County Deed Index*. Vols. 1–2 (1819–1871).

———. *Meigs County Deed Books*. Vols. 13–58.

United States Census Bureau. *Eighth Census of the United States, 1860, Meigs County, Ohio.*

———. *Eighth Census of the United States, 1860, Hamilton County, Ohio.*

———. *Ninth Census of the United States, 1870, Hamilton County, Ohio.*

———. *Seventh Census of the United States, 1850, Hamilton County, Ohio.*

———. *Tenth Census of the United States, 1880, Hamilton County, Ohio.*

———. *Twelfth Census of the United States, 1900, Columbiana County, Ohio.*

United States Court of Claims. *Kugler's Case: Rebecca E. J. Kugler vs. The United States*. Washington, DC, 1868.

United States War Department. *War of the Rebellion: Official Records of the Union and Confederate Armies*. Vol. 23. Washington, DC, 1880–1901.

Books and Maps

Addington, Larry H. *The Blitzkrieg Era and the German General Staff, 1865–1941*. New Brunswick, NJ, 1971.

Allen, Theodore F. "In Pursuit of John Morgan," *Sketches of War History 1861–1865: Papers Prepared for the Commandery of the State of Ohio, Military Order of the Loyal Legion of the United States*. Vol. V, edited by W. H. Chamberlin, A. M. Van Dyke, and George A. Thayer, 221–242. Cincinnati, 1903.

Ashburn, Joseph Nelson. *History of the Eighty-Sixth Ohio Volunteer Infantry*. Cleveland, OH, 1909.

Austin, L. G. *Illustrated Historical and Business Review of Meigs and Gallia Counties, Ohio*. Springfield, IL, 1891.

Beller, Janet B., and Maxine E. Nason, eds. *Loveland: Passages Through Time*. Loveland, OH, 1992.

Berlin, Jean V., and Brooks D. Simpson, eds. *Sherman's Civil War: Selected Correspondence of William T. Sherman 1860–1865*. Chapel Hill, NC, 1999.

Bibliography

Berry, Thomas F. *Four Years with Morgan and Forrest*. Oklahoma City, 1914.

Brown, Dee Alexander. *Morgan's Raiders*. New York, 1959.

Burkett, Randall K., ed. *Black Biography 1790–1950: A Cumulative Index*. Alexandria, VA, 1991.

Burress, Marjorie Byrnside, ed. *Whitewater, Ohio Village of Shakers, 1824–1916: Its History and Its People*. Cincinnati, 1979.

Burton, Katherine. *Three Generations: Maria Boyle Ewing (1801–1864); Ellen Ewing Sherman (1824-1888); Minnie Sherman Fitch (1851–1913)*. New York, 1947.

Cahill, Lora Schmidt. *The John Hunt Morgan Heritage Trail in Indiana: A Tour Guide to the Indiana Portion of Morgan's Great Raid, July 8--13, 1863*. Attica, OH, 1997.

Canal Society of Indiana. *Whitewater Canal: Cincinnati & Whitewater Canal Hagerstown Extension*. Fort Wayne, IN, 2006.

The Century and Gold Historical Booklet Committee. *Harrison, Ohio: 1850–2000*. Harrrison, OH, 2001.

Colerain Township Bicentennial Committee, Inc. *Our Heritage: Colerain Township*. Cincinnati, 1976.

Corum, James S. *The Roots of Blitzkrieg: Hans von Seeckt and German Military Reform*. Lawrence, KS, 1992.

Crawford, Richard. *Lightning Across the River: The Story of Gen. John Hunt Morgan's Raid on Clermont County, Ohio*. Newport, KY, 1996.

Dabney, Wendell P. *Cincinnati's Colored Citizens: Historical, Sociological, and Biographical*. Cincinnati, 1926.

The Dearborn County Historical Society. *Dearborn County: A Pictorial History*. Vol. 1. Dallas, TX, 1994.

Dearborn County Sesquicentennial Steering Committee. *Remember When: Dearborn County, Indiana, 1966*. Dallas, TX, 1966.

Duke, Basil W. *A History of Morgan''s Cavalry*. Cincinnati, 1867.

———. *Morgan's Cavalry*. New York, 1906.

———. *Reminiscences of General Basil W. Duke, C.S.A.* Garden City, NY, 1911.

Eckley, H.J., and W. T. Perry, eds. *History of Carroll and Harrison Counties, Ohio*. 2 vols. Chicago, 1921.

Ervin, Robert E. *The John Hunt Morgan Raid of 1863*. Jackson, OH, 2003.

Evans, Nelson W., and Emmons B. Stivers. *A History of Adams County, Ohio: From Its Earliest Settlement to the Present Time*. West Union, OH, 1900.

Everts, L. H. *Combination Atlas Map of Butler County, Ohio*. Philadelphia, 1875.

Faran, Angeline L., ed. *Glendale, Ohio: 1855–1955*. Cincinnati, 1955.

Ford, Henry A., and Kate B. Ford. *History of Hamilton County, Ohio*. Cleveland, OH, 1881.

Fout, Frederick W. *The Dark Days of the Civil War, 1861 to 1865: The West Virginia Campaign of 1861, the Antietam and Harper's Ferry Campaign of 1862, the East Tennessee campaign of 1863, the Atlanta campaign of 1864*. St. Louis, MO, 1904.

Fuller, J. F. C. *Armored Warfare: An Annotated Edition*. Harrisburg, PA, 1943.

Gard, Ronald Max. *Morgan's Raid into Ohio*. Lisbon, OH, 1963.

Gates, Henry Louis, Jr. *Clara Ann Thompson, J. Pauline Smith, Mazie Earhart Clark: Voices in the Poetic Tradition*. New York, 1996.

Gause, Isaac. *Four Years with Five Armies: Army of the Frontier, Army of the Potomac, Army of the Missouri, Army of the Ohio, Army of the Shenandoah*. New York, 1908.

Gilbert, Alfred West. *Map of Hamilton County, Ohio*. Cincinnati, 1856.

Glendale Heritage Preservation. *Glendale's Heritage: Glendale, Ohio*. Cincinnati, 1976.

Gorin, Betty J. *"Morgan is Coming!" Confederate Raiders in the Heartland of Kentucky*. Louisville, KY, 2006.

Griffith, William, Jr. *Illustrated Atlas of Gallia County, Ohio (1874)*. Cincinnati, 1874.

Hardesty, H. H. *Illustrated Historical Atlas of Carroll County, Ohio*. Chicago, 1874.

Hart, Basil Henry Liddell. *Strategy*. New York, 1954.

Hayes, Eli L. *Upper Ohio River and Valley – Part XII*. Philadelphia, 1877.

———. *Upper Ohio River and Valley – Part XIII*. Philadelphia, 1877.

Hill, Agnes C. *Tuppers Plains and the Surrounding Area of Olive & Orange Townships: Stories and Pictures of the Yesterdays*. Tuppers Plains, OH, 1985.

Hockersmith, L. D. *Morgan''s Escape: A Thrilling Story of War Times, A True History of the Raid of General Morgan and His Men through Kentucky, Indiana and Ohio*. Madisonville, KY, 1903.

Holland, Cecil Fletcher. *Morgan and His Raiders: A Biography of the Confederate General*. New York, 1942.

Horwitz, Lester V. *The Longest Raid of the Civil War*. Cincinnati, 1999.

John, Don D., ed. *The Great Indiana-Ohio Raid by Brig.-Gen. John Hunt Morgan and His Men, July 1863*. Louisville, KY, 1955.

Bibliography

Johnson, Adam R. *The Partisan Rangers of the Confederate States Army*. Louisville, KY, 1904.

Johnson, E. Polk. *A History of Kentucky and Kentuckians*. Vol. 3. Chicago, 1912.

Kautz, Lawrence G. *August Valentine Kautz, U.S.A.: Biography of a Civil War General*. Jefferson, NC, 2008.

Keller, Alan. *Morgan's Raid*. New York, 1961.

Kjellenberg, Marion S. *Blue Ash 1968 History and Directory: 1793–1968*. Cincinnati, 1968.

———. *History and Directory of Ole' Montgomery: 1795–1967*. Montgomery, OH, 1967.

———. *History and Directory of Ole' Montgomery: The Village of Lovely Homes and Friendly People*. Montgomery, OH, 1960.

Lake, D. J. *Atlas of Athens County, Ohio (1875)*. Philadelphia, 1875.

———. *Atlas of Jackson County, Ohio (1875)*. Philadelphia, 1875.

———. *Atlas of Vinton County, Ohio (1876)*. Philadelphia, 1876.

Lesley, J. P. *The Iron Manufacturer's Guide to the Furnaces, Forges and Rolling Mills of the United States*. New York, 1859.

Logan, India W. P. *Kelion Franklin Peddicord of Quirk's Scouts, Morgan's Kentucky Cavalry, C.S.A.* New York, 1908.

Longacre, Edward G. *Mounted Raids of the Civil War*. New York, 1975.

The Loveland Centennial-Bicentennial Committee, Inc. *Loveland, Ohio: The Story of a Town From Its Beginning*. Loveland, OH, 1976.

Macksey, Kenneth. *Guderian: Panzer General*. London, 1992.

Malczweski, Jerome J., ed. *Village of Evendale: The First Fifty Years*. Evendale, OH, 2001.

Mathews, A. E. *View of Camp Dennison: 16 Miles Northeast of Cincinnati, Ohio*. Cincinnati, 1865.

McAllister, Anna. *Ellen Ewing, Wife of General Sherman*. New York, 1936.

McClure, Stanley W. *The History of Crosby Township, Hamilton County, Ohio*. Harrison, OH, 1999.

———. *The Simonson Family*. Harrison, OH, 1981.

McGavran, S. B. *A Brief History of Harrison County, Ohio*. Cadiz, OH, 1894.

Meigs County Pioneer & Historical Society. *Meigs County, Ohio: From Hardesty's Historical and Geographical Encyclopedia, 1883, and Property Owners as Shown by Map of Meigs County, c. 1867*. Defiance, OH, 1982.

Metzler, William E. *Morgan and His Dixie Cavaliers: An Account of the Confederate Cavalryman's Most Famous Exploits*. Manchester, TN, 1978.

Miami Historical Society of Whitewater Township. *Miamitown: 175 Years 1816–1991*. Miamitown, OH, 1998.

Mount Healthy Sesquicentennial Committee. *Once Upon a Hilltop: Mount Healthy Area Sesquicentennial 1817–1967*. Cincinnati, 1967.

Mowery, David L. *Morgan's Great Raid: The Remarkable Expedition From Kentucky to Ohio*. Charleston, SC, 2013.

New Burlington Civic Association. *New Burlington's Sesqui-Centennial: May 1816–May 1966*. Cincinnati, 1966.

The New York Public Library. *Digital Schomburg African American Women Writers of the 19th Century: A Selection of Public Works*. New York, 1999.

Ogan, Lew. *History of Vinton County, Ohio*. McArthur, OH, 1954.

Park, Clyde W. *Morgan the Unpredictable*. Cincinnati, 1959.

Pattison, Thomas. *Map of Dearborn County, IN, 1860*. Aurora, IN, 1860.

Phillips, R. C. *Map of Hamilton County, OH, 1865*. Cincinnati, 1865.

Poole, Ann. *Deer Park: Past to Present*. Cincinnati, 1987.

Power, Jim. *The "Iron Man" and the "Mississippi Company" of Morgan's Raiders*. Bloomington, IN, 2009.

Price, Gayle H. *Morgan's Raid and the Battle of Buffington Island*. Pomeroy, OH, 1997.

Privett, Audrey R. *Sharonville: Then and Now*. Sharonville, OH, 1988.

Ramage, James A. *Rebel Raider: The Life of John Hunt Morgan*. Lexington, KY, 1986.

Randall, E. O., and Daniel J. Ryan. *History of Ohio: The Rise and Progress of an American State*. Vol. 4. New York, 1912.

Richmond, Robert N., ed. *How General John Hunt Morgan Invaded Morgan County, Ohio, 125 Years Ago – July 23, 1863: A 125th Anniversary Commemoration Booklet*. McConnelsville, OH, 1988.

Robertson, James I., Jr., ed. *The Medical and Surgical History of the Civil War*. Vol. VI. Wilmington, NC, 1991.

Rose, Mary Lou. *History of Blue Ash, Ohio: 1791–1991*. Hamilton, OH, 1991.

———, ed. *History of Montgomery, Ohio 1795–1995*. Montgomery, OH, 1995.

Sanford, Washington L. *History of Fourteenth Illinois Cavalry and the Brigades to Which It Belonged*. Chicago, 1898.

Senour, F., Rev. *Morgan and His Captors*. Cincinnati, 1865.

Bibliography

Simmons, Flora E. *A Complete Account of the John Morgan Raid through Kentucky, Indiana, and Ohio in July 1863*. Cincinnati, 1863.

Simms, Jere H. *Last Day and Last Night of John Morgan's Raid*. East Liverpool, OH, 1913.

Sloan, Mary R. *History of Camp Dennison, Ohio*, 3rd ed. Cincinnati, 2003.

Smith, Sydney K. *Life, Army Record, and Public Services of D. Howard Smith*. Louisville, KY, 1890.

Southworth, Samuel A., ed. *Great Raids in History: From Drake to Desert One*. Edison, NJ, 2002.

Stone, Henry Lane. *"Morgan's Men" – A Narrative of Personal Experiences*. Louisville, KY, 1919.

Surby, Richard W. *Two Great Raids*. Washington, DC, 1897.

Swiggett, Howard. *The Rebel Raider: A Life of John Hunt Morgan*. Indianapolis, 1934.

Taft, Eleanor G. *Hither and Yon on Indian Hill*. Cincinnati, 1962.

Tenney, Luman H. *War Diary of Luman Harris Tenney, 1861-1865*. Cleveland, OH, 1914.

Titus, C. O. *Atlas of Clermont County, Ohio*. Philadelphia, 1870.

———. *Atlas of Columbiana County, Ohio*. Philadelphia, 1870.

———. *Atlas of Hamilton County, Ohio*. Philadelphia, 1869.

Thomas, Edison H. *John Hunt Morgan and His Raiders*. Lexington, KY, 1975.

Tracie, Theodore C. *Annals of the Nineteenth Ohio Battery Volunteer Artillery*. Cleveland, OH, 1878.

Village of Amberley Village. *Amberley Village: Its History and Its People*. Cincinnati, 1990.

Warner, Ezra J. *Generals in Blue: Lives of the Union Commanders*. Baton Rouge, LA, 1992.

Watkins, Dwight G., and Elizabeth Watkins. *Morgan's Light Brigade: Brigadier John H. Morgan's Old Cavalry Division*. Utica, KY, 2001.

Wells, Ruth. *Colerain Township "Revisited": 1794–1994 Bicentennial Year*. Cincinnati, 1994.

White, Virginia S. *Treasured Landmarks of Indian Hill*. Cincinnati, 1993.

Williams, Charles Richard, ed. *The Diary and Letters of Rutherford B. Hayes, Nineteenth President of the United States*. Vol. 2, Chap. 22. Columbus, OH, 1922.

Williams & Company. *Williams' Cincinnati Directory, City Guide, & Business Mirror*. Cincinnati, 1855.

———. *Williams' Cincinnati Directory, City Guide, & Business Mirror*. Cincinnati, 1863.

Wimberg, Robert J. *Cincinnati and the Civil War: Off to Battle*. Cincinnati, 1992.

Woefel, Ann, and Gene Woefel, eds. *Harrison, Ohio: Century and Silver Celebration*. Harrison, OH, 1975.

Wolfe, William G. *Stories of Guernsey County, Ohio: History of an Average Ohio County*. Cambridge, OH, 1975.

Young, Bennett H. *Confederate Wizards of the Saddle*. Boston, 1914.

Wormer, Grover S. "The Morgan Raid," *War Papers Read Before the Michigan Commandery of the Military Order of the Loyal Legion of the United States*. Vol. 2, edited by the Michigan Commandery of the Loyal Legion of the United States, 191–216. Detroit, 1898.

Articles

Bennett, B. Kevin. "The General's Tour – Morgan's Luck Runs Out: The Battle of Buffington Island, July 19, 1863." *Blue and Gray Magazine* XV (Spring 1998): 6–20, 48–65.

Bennett, Pamela J., ed. "Curtis R. Burke's Civil War Journal." *Indiana Magazine of History* 65 (December 1969): 283–327.

———, ed. "Curtis R. Burke's Civil War Journal." *Indiana Magazine of History* 66 (June 1970): 110–172.

———, ed. "Curtis R. Burke's Civil War Journal." *Indiana Magazine of History* 66 (December 1970): 318–361.

———, ed. "Curtis R. Burke's Civil War Journal." *Indiana Magazine of History* 67 (June 1971): 129–170.

Duke, Basil W., Thomas H. Hines and Orlando B. Willcox. "The Romance of Morgan's Rough Riders: The Raid, the Capture, and the Escape." *Century Magazine* (January 1891).

Funk, Arville L., ed. "An Ohio Farmer's Account of Morgan's Raid." *Ohio Historical Quarterly* 70 (July 1961): 244–245.

McCreary, James Bennett. "The Journal of My Soldier Life." *Register of the Kentucky State Historical Society* 33 (July 1935): 191-211.

Miller, William Marion. "Major George W. Rue, the Captor of General John Morgan." *Ohio Historical Quarterly* 50 (April–June 1941): 130–134.

———. "An Unrecorded Incident of Morgan's Raid." *Ohio Historical Quarterly* 54 (April–June 1945): 169–170.

Ohio Historical Society. "John Morgan Raid in Ohio." *Ohio Archaeological and Historical Publications* 17 (January 1908): 48–59.

Rue, George W. "Celebration of the Surrender of General John H. Morgan: An Account by Morgan's Captor, Major George W. Rue." *Ohio Historical Quarterly* 20 (October 1911): 368–377.

Bibliography

Weber, L. J. "Morgan's Raid." *Ohio Archaeological and Historical Publications* 18 (January 1909): 79–104.

Unpublished Manuscripts

Mowery, David L. "A Study of John Hunt Morgan's Ohio Raid Route from Reedsville to Creola, Ohio, July 19–22, 1863," 2nd ed. Unpublished manuscript in possession of the Ohio Historical Society, Columbus, Ohio, 2011.

Pratt, G. Michael. "The Battle of Buffington Island: The End of Morgan's Trail; A Report on the Archaeological Survey, American Battlefield Protection Program Grant No. GA-2255-99-013." Unpublished manuscript in the possession of the Center for Historic and Military Archaeology, Heidelberg College, Tiffin, OH, 2000.

Interviews

Charles Whiting (expert on the Whitewater Canal), in discussion with David Mowery, 2009.

Dale Colburn (Meigs County historian), in discussion with David Mowery, 2011.

Harry Garrison (Cincinnati, Ohio), in discussion with David Mowery about James Poole, March 9, 2003.

Shirley Kaiser (Harrison United Methodist Church), in discussion with David Mowery about Trinity Methodist Church's silver myth, March 12, 2003.

Electronic Sources

Abordo, Mary Beth. *The Riveting Story of James Edward Evans: 1st/3rd KY Cavalry, CSA, Morgan's Raider, Camp Douglas Prisoner of War.* http://evansfamilytreeclimb.blogspot.com.

Bristow, Neil Allen. ed. "Diary of Captain Thomas Monroe Coombs, Co. C, 5th KY Cavalry CSA." *Green Wolf Family History Pages.* http://freepages.genealogy.rootsweb.ancestry.com/~greenwolf/coombs/index.htm.

———, ed. "Letter from Captain Thomas Monroe Coombs, Co. C, 5th KY Cavalry CSA, to his wife Lou, August 14–15, 1863." *Green Wolf Family History Pages.* http://freepages.genealogy.rootsweb.ancestry.com/~greenwolf/coombs/letter.htm.

Hildreth, Darlenea M. *Ancestors of Andrew Tucker.* http://familytreemaker.genealogy.com/users/h/i/l/Darlenea-M-Hildreth-CA/PDFGENE1.pdf.

Historic Map Works. "Historic North America Regional Map: Indiana, Ohio." *Historic Map Works: Residential Genealogy.* http://www.historicmapworks.com.

Masters, Jack, ed. *Wartime Diary of John Weatherred, Bennett's Regiment or 9th Tennessee Cavalry, John Hunt Morgan's Command.* http://www.jackmasters.net/9tncav.html.

MyTopo, a Trimble Company. *Historic USGS Maps Collection (ca. 1900–1920).*
    http://maptech.mytopo.com/onlinemaps/index.cfm.

Pine Brook Antique Maps. *Ohio Antique Maps Collection.*
    http://www.pinebrookmaps.com/servlet/the-North-America-Antique-Maps-cln-United-States-cln-Ohio/Categories.

Seeking Michigan. "1863–07 Letter Fragment from George Ewing – July 1863." *Civil War Manuscripts Collection.*
    http://seekingmichigan.org/wp-content/uploads/2009/08/630700-George-Ewing.pdf.

WMTH Corporation. "The Great Raid, Summer 1863." *Trails-R-Us (Kentucky) – John Hunt Morgan.*
    http://www.trailsrus.com/morgan/map.html.

About the Authors

Lora Schmidt Cahill is a native of Morgan Raid country, having grown up near the Ripley-Dearborn County border at Sunman, Indiana. Fascinated since childhood by the family accounts of the raid and the presence of the Morgan markers, she began collecting the material that eventually led to the publication of her first book, *Thunderbolt: Revisit Southeastern Indiana with John Hunt Morgan* (1995). She also wrote the official guidebook to Indiana's Morgan Raid heritage trail, titled *The John Hunt Morgan Heritage Trail in Indiana: A Tour Guide to the Indiana Portion of Morgan's Great Raid July 8–13, 1863* (1997). Cahill received her B.S. from Capitol University and her master's degree from Ohio State University, both in Columbus, Ohio. She is a founding member of the Ohio Civil War Trail Commission.

David L. Mowery is a native resident of the Cincinnati, Ohio, area and has lived at various points along the path of Morgan's raiders. A graduate of the University of Cincinnati, Mowery has studied American military history, most notably the American Civil War, for nearly thirty-five years. Over that period he has researched and visited more than six hundred battlefields across fifty states and eight countries. Mowery joined the Ohio Civil War Trail Commission in 2001 as its Hamilton County representative, but since then he took on a broader role that included the final design and historical validation of the entire length of the *John Hunt Morgan Heritage Trail of Ohio*. Mowery is the author of *Morgan's Great Raid: The Remarkable Expedition from Kentucky to Ohio* (2013). He also wrote the thesis titled "A Study of John Hunt Morgan's Ohio Raid Route from Reedsville to Creola, Ohio, July 19–22, 1863" (Ohio Historical Society: Columbus, 2011), the first comprehensive study of Morgan's whereabouts during the three controversial days following the Battle of Buffington Island. Mowery has been a member of the Cincinnati Civil War Round Table since 1995, for which group he has written various papers on Civil War subjects. He has also served with the Buffington Island Battlefield Preservation Foundation, the grass-roots organization working to preserve Ohio's only Civil War battlefield.

www.ingramcontent.com/pod-product-compliance
Lightning Source LLC
Chambersburg PA
CBHW080416250426
43670CB00052B/2657